FREE Study Skills DVD Offer

Dear Customer,

Thank you for your purchase from Mometrix! We consider it an honor and privilege that you have purchased our product and want to ensure your satisfaction.

As a way of showing our appreciation and to help us better serve you, we have developed a Study Skills DVD that we would like to give you for <u>FREE</u>. **This DVD covers our "best practices" for studying for your exam, from using our study materials to preparing for the day of the test.**

All that we ask is that you email us your feedback that would describe your experience so far with our product. Good, bad or indifferent, we want to know what you think!

To get your **FREE Study Skills DVD**, email <u>freedvd@mometrix.com</u> with "FREE STUDY SKILLS DVD" in the subject line and the following information in the body of the email:

    a.   The name of the product you purchased.

    b.   Your product rating on a scale of 1-5, with 5 being the highest rating.

    c.   Your feedback. It can be long, short, or anything in-between, just your impressions and experience so far with our product. Good feedback might include how our study material met your needs and will highlight features of the product that you found helpful.

    d.   Your full name and shipping address where you would like us to send your free DVD.

If you have any questions or concerns, please don't hesitate to contact me directly.

Thanks again!

Sincerely,

Jay Willis
Vice President
<u>jay.willis@mometrix.com</u>
1-800-673-8175

MCAT Prep Book

MCAT* SECRETS

Study Guide
Your Key to Exam Success

MCAT Practice and Review for the
Medical College Admission Test

Published by
Mometrix Test Preparation
MCAT Exam Secrets Test Prep Team

Dear Future Exam Success Story:

Congratulations on your purchase of our study guide. Our goal in writing our study guide was to cover the content on the test, as well as provide insight into typical test taking mistakes and how to overcome them.

Standardized tests are a key component of being successful, which only increases the importance of doing well in the high-pressure high-stakes environment of test day. How well you do on this test will have a significant impact on your future- and we have the research and practical advice to help you execute on test day.

The product you're reading now is designed to exploit weaknesses in the test itself, and help you avoid the most common errors test takers frequently make.

How to use this study guide

We don't want to waste your time. Our study guide is fast-paced and fluff-free. We suggest going through it a number of times, as repetition is an important part of learning new information and concepts.

First, read through the study guide completely to get a feel for the content and organization. Read the general success strategies first, and then proceed to the content sections. Each tip has been carefully selected for its effectiveness.

Second, read through the study guide again, and take notes in the margins and highlight those sections where you may have a particular weakness.

Finally, bring the manual with you on test day and study it before the exam begins.

Your success is our success

We would be delighted to hear about your success. Send us an email and tell us your story. Thanks for your business and we wish you continued success-

Sincerely,

Mometrix Test Preparation Team

Need more help? Check out our flashcards at: http://MometrixFlashcards.com/MCAT

TABLE OF CONTENTS

Top 20 Test Taking Tips

1. Carefully follow all the test registration procedures
2. Know the test directions, duration, topics, question types, how many questions
3. Setup a flexible study schedule at least 3-4 weeks before test day
4. Study during the time of day you are most alert, relaxed, and stress free
5. Maximize your learning style; visual learner use visual study aids, auditory learner use auditory study aids
6. Focus on your weakest knowledge base
7. Find a study partner to review with and help clarify questions
8. Practice, practice, practice
9. Get a good night's sleep; don't try to cram the night before the test
10. Eat a well balanced meal
11. Know the exact physical location of the testing site; drive the route to the site prior to test day
12. Bring a set of ear plugs; the testing center could be noisy
13. Wear comfortable, loose fitting, layered clothing to the testing center; prepare for it to be either cold or hot during the test
14. Bring at least 2 current forms of ID to the testing center
15. Arrive to the test early; be prepared to wait and be patient
16. Eliminate the obviously wrong answer choices, then guess the first remaining choice
17. Pace yourself; don't rush, but keep working and move on if you get stuck
18. Maintain a positive attitude even if the test is going poorly
19. Keep your first answer unless you are positive it is wrong
20. Check your work, don't make a careless mistake

Biological and Biochemical Foundations

Structure and Function of Proteins and Their Constituent Amino Acids

Amino acids

Protein molecules are made up of carbon, hydrogen, oxygen, nitrogen, and other atoms. They have many different functions. Proteins are made up of amino acid monomers. Amino acids have basically the same structure. They are made up of an amine group (-NH), a carboxylic acid group (-COOH), and an R group. Every amino acid has a different R group. The R group is also known as the functional group.

The functional groups, because of their unique chemical properties, cause each amino acid to be different. Amino acids, based on their chemical properties, can be divided into twenty naturally-occurring groups. Non-polar, hydrophobic functional groups include: Glycine, alanine, valine, leucine, isoleucine, methionine, phenylalanine, tryptophan, and proline. Polar functional groups include: Serine, threonine, cysteine, tyrosine, asparagine, and glutamine. Charged functional groups that are basic include: Arginine, lysine, and histidine. Charged functional groups that are acidic include: aspartic acid and glutamic acid.

Two amino acids can join through a peptide bond that forms between the carboxylic-acid group of one amino acid and the amine group of another. When amino acids form long chains, they are called polypeptides or proteins. The complexity of proteins is due to the huge number of different amino acids that can be combined in an almost limitless number of ways.

Protein structures are delineated four different ways: Primary, Secondary, Tertiary, and Quaternary. Primary structure is responsible for the proteins overall structure, and determines the interaction as well as the position of the functional groups to each other. Primary structure gives the linear sequence of the amino acids.

Alpha helix and beta sheet are the two primary types of secondary structure. They form the backbone chain of a protein and relate to the interactions of the different atoms in that chain. When the N-H of an amino acid hydrogen bonds with a C=O of another amino acid that is three to four residues earlier, an Alpha helix is formed.

Alpha helices are more likely to form because of the functional groups of the following amino acids: methionine, alanine, uncharged leucine, glutamate, and lysine. Conversely, they are less likely to form in the following amino acids: proline and glycine. This is due to the fact that their functional groups make it more difficult for alpha helices to form. Alpha helices are right-handed and have 3.6 residues per turn. Proteins with alpha helices can span the cell membrane. They are also part of DNA (deoxyribonucleic acid) binding.

When protein strands are stretched so that they hydrogen bond with a neighbor strand, then beta sheets are formed. There are amino acids that make forming beta sheets more likely or less likely, just like alpha helices.

The overall geometric shape of a protein is formed from the interactions of the various functional groups. This is known as the Tertiary structure of a protein. The hydrophobic interactions between non-polar side groups, salt bridges, hydrogen bonds, and disulfide bonds, are all very important for tertiary structure.

When two different polypeptide chains interact, that is when Quaternary structure occurs. It follows the same properties as tertiary structure listed above. Quaternary structure is only possible in proteins that have more than one chain.

Protein structure

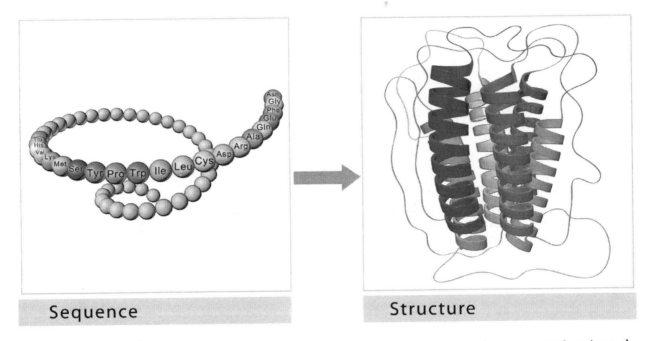

Sequence → Structure

The amino acid chain is what provides the primary structure of a protein. The structure is oriented in a linear chain from left to right in living organisms. The terminal amino acid group is on the left, with the terminal carboxyl group on the right. If the central carbon atom is next to a carboxyl group, then that amino acid is labeled chiral. Chiral amino acids are all designated as L (levorotary). If the amine group is to the right of the central carbon atom then the amino acid is designated achiral. Achiral amino acids are all designated as D (dexter). Looking at the primary structure of a protein can often be used to predict the other structures (secondary and tertiary).

A protein's secondary structure can take three forms depending on the type of hydrogen bonds present: α- helix, β-sheet, or β -turns. An α-helix is a right-handed coiled strand. The amino acid group's side-chain structures extend outside the helix. The oxygen in the C=O peptide bonds form bonds with the hydrogen in the N-H structure, four amino acids below. These side chains are found beside the N-H groups.

When hydrogen bonds are formed between the carbonyl oxygen molecules in one strand with the amino hydrogen molecules in an adjacent strand, then a β-sheet structure is formed. β-sheets are recognized through side by side amino acid structures. Further, β-sheets can be anti-parallel or parallel depending on the orientation of the C-terminus and N-terminus.

When two anti-parallel β strands change direction and form loops instead of a helix or sheet, it is referred to as a β -Turn. The loop ("hairpin" turn) structure is formed from the hydrogen bonds between a carbonyl oxygen and an amine hydrogen. Because loops form most often on the surface of proteins, they interact with other molecules and proteins.

- 3 -

The geometric tertiary structure is formed from bending and folding the protein into the lowest possible energy state and the most stable configuration. The side chain bonds from the amino acids also aid in supporting the structure.

Some proteins are so large that they contain numerous polypeptide chains that interact. These polypeptide chains are considered subunits of the larger protein. These subunits often interact through hydrogen bonding, disulfide-bridges, or salt bridges. These various interactions of the polypeptide subunits of the protein are what form the quaternary structure.

Another means of understanding structure or visualizing the interaction of amino acids in proteins is through a Ramachandran plot or diagram. It is used to theorize possible configurations by recording data points. It can also help validate a theorized structure.

Chemical reactions

Types of chemical reactions
A chemical reaction has occurred when the product(s) differ(s) from the reactants. In other words, if the substance(s) formed differ from the starting substances, then a chemical reaction has taken place. Often this is seen through a change in heat or color, the production of gas (bubbles), or the formation of a precipitate. The table below lists basic chemical reaction types:

Reaction Type	Definition	Example
Decomposition	A compound is broken down into two or more smaller elements or compounds (the opposite of synthesis)	$2H_2O \rightarrow 2H_2 + O_2$
Synthesis	Two or more elements or compounds are joined together to form a new compound (the opposite of decomposition)	$2H_2 + O_2 \rightarrow 2H_2O$
Single Displacement (Substitution Reaction)	A single element or ion takes the place of another in a compound	$Zn + 2HCl \rightarrow ZnCl_2 + H_2$
Double Displacement (Metathesis Reaction)	Two elements or ions each exchange a single atom to form two different compounds, resulting in different combinations of cations and anions in the final compounds	$H_2SO_4 + 2NaOH \rightarrow Na_2So_4 + 2H_2O$
Oxidation-Reduction (Redox Reaction)	Elements undergo a change in oxidation number	$2S_2O_3^{2-}(aq) + I_2(aq) \rightarrow S_4O_6^{2-}(aq) + 2I^-(aq)$
Acid-Base	Involves a reaction between an acid and a base, which usually produces a salt and water	$HBr + NaOH \rightarrow NaBr + H_2O$
Combustion	A hydrocarbon (a compound composed of only hydrogen and carbon) reacts with oxygen to form carbon dioxide and water	$CH_4 + 2O_2 \rightarrow CO_2 + 2H_2O$

Balancing chemical reactions

A chemical equation can be used to show a chemical reaction. Because matter can neither be created nor destroyed, then the same number of atoms on one side of the equation must equal the number of atoms on the other side of the equation when describing a chemical reaction using an equation. Each element must have the same number of atoms on each side of the equation. This is known as "Conservation of Mass" and was described by French chemist, Antoine Lavoisier.

In a chemical equation the starting reactants are to the left side and the products on the right (with an arrow in between pointing to the right). The numbers that are in front of the letters representing the various atomic elements are called "coefficients". The numbers that are below the line and listed after the letters representing the various atomic elements are called subscripts. It is important that the coefficients are multiplied by the subscripts. For example: $2H_2O$ would mean there are 4 hydrogen atoms and 2 oxygen atoms. The coefficient of "2" before the H would be multiplied by the subscript "2" after the H, yielding 4 H (4 hydrogen atoms). The O is deemed to have a subscript of "1", therefore the coefficient of "2" times the subscript of "1" would yield 2 O (2 oxygen atoms). The following chemical equation illustrates a balanced chemical equation (balanced, because there is the same number of hydrogen and oxygen atoms on both sides of the arrow): $2 H_2 + O_2 \rightarrow 2H_2O$. On the left side of the equation there are $2 H_2$ or 4 H's (4 hydrogen atoms) and O_2 or 2 O's (2 oxygen atoms). On the right side of the equation there are still 4 hydrogen atoms and 2 oxygen atoms. They have merely been combined into a new substance. When the number of atoms on both sides of the equation does not match, then the coefficients on one or both sides of the equation have to be changed in order to get them all to equal and thus balance. For example: $Mg + O_2 \rightarrow MgO$ is not balanced. There is 1 Mg on both sides of the equation; however there are 2 Oxygen atoms on the left, but only 1 oxygen atom on the right. One oxygen atom did not simply cease to exist. In order to balance this equation, coefficients must be added. First, 2 oxygen atoms are needed on the right side of the equation, therefore a coefficient of 2 is added in front of the MgO to get the number of oxygen atoms to 2 (2MgO). But now there is a new problem. There are now 2 Mg atoms on the right, but only 1 Magnesium atom on the left. A magnesium atom was not created out of nothing. Therefore a coefficient of 2 is added in front of the Mg symbol on the left side of the equation. The new equation looks like this: $2Mg + O_2 \rightarrow 2MgO$. There are now 2 Mg atoms on the left and 2Mg atoms on the right. There are also 2 Oxygen atoms on the left and 2 Oxygen atoms on the right. This equation is now balanced because the number of atoms is the same on both sides of the arrow. When the final state of the reactant is known, or critical to be known, other letters will be added to the equations to denote the state of the substance whether a solid (s), liquid (l), gas (g), or aqueous (aq).

Catalysts

A catalyst is something that speeds up a chemical reaction without itself undergoing any chemical change. Catalysts help chemical reactions by providing a chemical pathway that requires less energy to start. Activation energy is the amount of energy necessary to start a chemical reaction. If less energy is needed to initiate a chemical reaction, then it can proceed easier and with greater speed. Catalysts only increase the velocity of some chemical reactions. They are very specific in the types of chemical reactions that they assist with. If a catalyst is in the same matter phase (solid, liquid, gas) as the reactants, then it is said to be homogeneous. If it is in a different phase from the reactants, then it is said to be heterogeneous.

Enzymes

Catalysts used in biochemical reactions are called *enzymes*. Enzymes are usually proteins, but not always. The human body uses many different enzymes to catalyze thousands of biochemical reactions. Enzymes interact with particular portions of molecules. The part of the molecule that the enzyme interacts with is called the *substrate*. Different analogies have been used to describe this binding process. One from the late 19th century used a "lock and key" metaphor. The substrate key fits precisely into the active site on the enzyme. This forms what is called the enzyme-substrate complex.

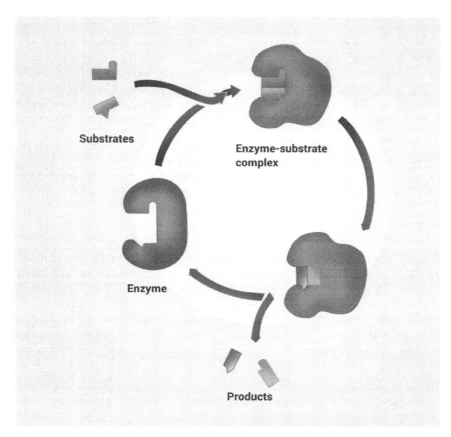

Often *Cofactors* work together with enzymes to catalyze chemical reactions. If the cofactors contain carbon they are said to be organic. And if they do not contain carbon, they are said to be inorganic. Enzymes also work with *coenzymes* in their catalysis. The coenzymes are very closely bonded to an enzyme. Coenzymes are used to move groups of chemicals from one enzyme to another. Cells continuously make coenzymes in order to keep their concentrations as a steady state.

There are many different factors that can impact the catalytic process including: pH, temperature, and the amount of concentration between the substrate and enzyme. Enzymes work best at normal human temperatures of 98.6 F, with an optimal pH close to neutral (7-8). With higher concentrations of enzyme and substrate the rate of catalysis can be increased, but only up to a certain point.

Another form of control of the enzymatic catalytic process involves *feedback inhibition*. In feedback inhibition, the product that the enzyme is designed to produce increases to the point that it begins to interfere directly with the enzyme that helped produce it. It is a safety mechanism for cells to help maintain proper levels without overproduction of certain substances that the enzyme is designed to help produce.

Transmission of Genetic Information from Gene to Protein

DNA and RNA

DNA and RNA are both nucleic acids composed of nucleotides made up of a sugar, a base, and a phosphate molecule. DNA and RNA have three of their four bases in common: guanine, cytosine, and adenine. DNA contains the base thymine, but RNA replaces thymine with uracil. DNA is deoxyribonucleic acid. RNA is ribonucleic acid. DNA is located in the nucleus and mitochondria. RNA is found in the nucleus, ribosomes, and cytoplasm. DNA contains the sugar deoxyribose, and RNA contains the sugar ribose. DNA is double stranded, but RNA is single stranded. DNA has the shape of a double helix, but RNA is complexly folded. DNA contains the genetic blueprint and instructions for the cell. RNA carries out those instructions with its various forms. Messenger RNA, mRNA, is a working copy of DNA, and transfer RNA, tRNA, collects the needed amino acids for the ribosomes during the assembling of proteins. Ribosomal RNA, rRNA, forms the structure of the ribosomes.

DNA and RNA Illustration

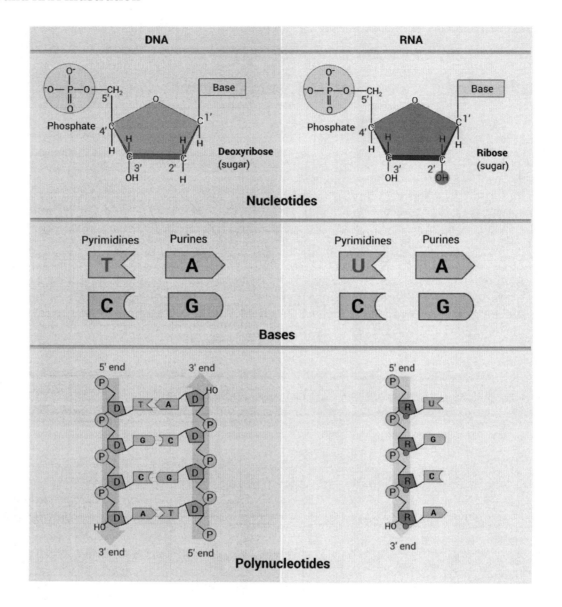

Sugar-phosphate backbone

The DNA molecule consists of two strands in the shape of double helix, which resembles a twisted "ladder." The "rungs" of the ladder consist of complementary base pairs of the nucleotides. The "legs" of the ladder consist of chains of nucleotides joined by the bond between the phosphate and sugar molecules. In DNA, the sugar is deoxyribose. The sugars and phosphates are joined together by covalent bonds. The RNA molecule has one strand instead of two. In RNA, the sugar is ribose. The sugars and phosphates of the nucleotides are joined in the same

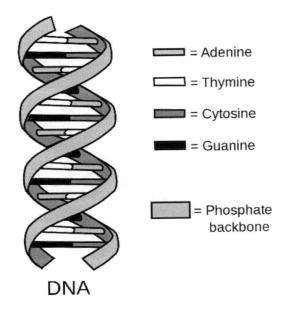

= Adenine

= Thymine

= Cytosine

= Guanine

= Phosphate backbone

DNA

Complementary base pairing

According to Chargaff's rule, DNA always has a 1:1 ratio of purine to pyrimidine. The amount of adenine always equals the amount of thymine, and the amount of guanine always equals the amount of cytosine. DNA contains the bases guanine, cytosine, thymine, and adenine. RNA also contains guanine, cytosine, and adenine, but thymine is replaced with uracil. In DNA, adenine always pairs with thymine, and guanine always pairs with cytosine. In RNA, adenine always pairs with uracil, and guanine always pairs with cytosine. The pairs are bonded together with hydrogen bonds.

Chromosome structure

Prokaryotes contain one DNA molecule. These molecules are usually arranged in a ring that contains all of their genes. Eukaryotes have multiple chromosomes, each containing one DNA molecule. These chromosomes are linear in appearance. Eukaryotic and Archaea bacteria have chromatin that consists of DNA, protein, and RNA. Bacteria do not have histones in their protein. Chromatin is arranged in nucleosomes. A nucleosome is a histone complex with 146 nucleotide pairs wrapped around the histones. The nucleosomes are strung together by a string a DNA. This string of chromosomes coils to form the chromatin. During mitosis, the string is looped and compactly folded to form the chromosome. Eukaryotic chromosomes have telomeres located at their tips. Telomeres are repetitive sequences of DNA that maintain the ends of the linear chromosomes and keep those ends from deteriorating.

DNA replication

DNA replication begins when the double strands of the parent DNA molecule are unwound and unzipped. The enzyme helicase separates the two strands by breaking the hydrogen bonds between the base pairs that make up the rungs of the twisted ladder. These two single strands of DNA are called the replication fork. Each separate DNA strand provides a template for the complementary DNA bases, G with C and A with T. The enzyme DNA polymerase aids in binding the new base pairs together. Short segments of DNA called Okazaki fragments are synthesized with the lagging strand with the aid of RNA primase. At the end of this process, part of the telomere is removed. Then, enzymes check for any errors in the code and make repairs. This results in two daughter DNA molecules each with half of the original DNA molecule that was used as a template.

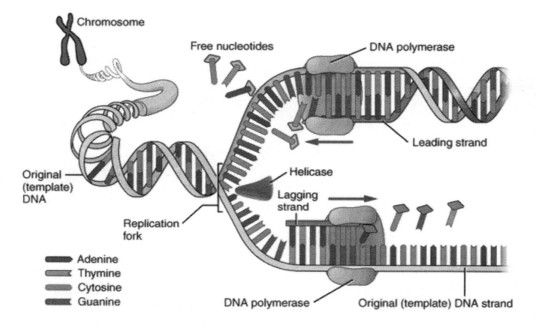

RNA transcription

Transcription is the process by which a segment of DNA is copied onto a working blueprint called RNA. Each gene has a special region called a promoter that guides the beginning of the transcription process. RNA polymerase unwinds the DNA at the promoter of the needed gene. After the DNA is unwound, one strand or template is copied by the RNA polymerase by adding the complementary nucleotides, G with C, C with G, T with A, and A with U. Then, the sugar phosphate backbone forms with the aid of RNA polymerase. Finally, the hydrogen bonds joining the strands of DNA and RNA together are broken. This forms a single strand of messenger RNA or mRNA.

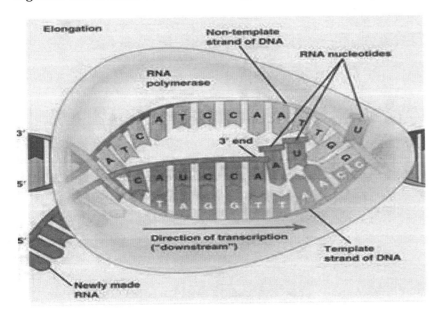

mRNA processing

After mRNA is transcribed, it must be processed. First, during transcription a cap is added. Needed chemicals are readied at the signal sites for cleavage where the polyadenylation will occur. After cleavage, the poly A tail starts to form. The final mRNA strand then with a cap and poly A tail, is ready for splicing. This mRNA strand, which is called the primary transcript, contains one intron and two exons. Once the spliceosome is formed, the intron is cleaved and the two exons are ligated together. After splicing, the working components involved in the splice degrade, and the mRNA strand is ready for translation.

Translation

Ribosomes synthesize proteins from mRNA in a process called translation. Sequences of three amino acids called codons make up the strand of mRNA. Each codon codes for a specific amino acid. The ribosome is composed of two subunits, a larger subunit and a smaller subunit, which are composed of ribosomal RNA (rRNA). The smaller subunit of RNA attaches to the mRNA near the cap. The smaller subunit slides along the mRNA until it reaches the first codon. Then, the larger subunit clamps onto the smaller subunit of the ribosome. Transfer RNA (tRNA) has codons complementary to the mRNA codons. The tRNA molecules attach at the site of translation. Amino acids are joined together by peptide bonds. The ribosome moves along the mRNA strand repeating this process until the protein is complete. Proteins are polymers of amino acids joined by peptide bonds.

Promoters

Promoters are DNA sequences typically 100 to 1,000 base pairs in length that are usually located upstream of the gene needed for transcription. Basically, promoters signal the beginning of transcription. Special proteins called transcription factors, which bind to promoters, subsequently provide binding sites for the RNA polymerase, which is the enzyme that transcribes the RNA. Promoters in the Archaea and Eukaryota domains often contain a nucleotide sequence TATA, which is called a TATA box. The TATA box is usually 25 nucleotides upstream of the transcription start site, and it is the location at which the DNA is unwound.

Enhancers

Enhancers are DNA sequences that regulate gene expression by providing a binding site for proteins that regulate RNA polymerase in transcribing proteins. Enhancers can greatly increase the expression of genes in their range. They can be hundreds or thousands of base pairs upstream or downstream from the genes they control. Some enhancers are located within the gene they control. Enhancers are functional over large distances. Most genes are controlled by two or three enhancers, but some may be controlled by more. Enhancers provide bonding sites for regulatory proteins that either promotes or inhibits RNA polymerase activity. Enhancers are more common in eukaryotes than prokaryotes.

Transcription factors

Transcription factors are proteins that help regulate gene expression in eukaryotes and prokaryotes. Transcription factors bind to the DNA and determine if that sequence of DNA is transcribed into mRNA and then into proteins. In eukaryotes that have promoter or enhancer regions, transcription factors bind near these regions and increase the ability of the RNA polymerase to start transcription. In eukaryotes, because genes are typically turned "off," transcription factors typically work to turn genes "on." The opposite is often true in bacteria, and transcription factors often work to turn genes off.

Operons

Operons control gene regulation. Specifically, operons allow cells to only code for proteins as they are needed by the cell. This allows cells to conserve energy. Operons are segments of DNA or groups of genes that are controlled by one promoter. Operons consist of an operator, a promoter, and structural gene(s). The operator provides a binding side for a repressor that inhibits the binding of RNA polymerase. The promoter provides the binding site for the RNA polymerase. The structural genes provide the sequence that codes for a protein. Operons are transcribed as single units and code for a single mRNA molecule, which produces proteins with related functions. Operons have been found in prokaryotes, eukaryotes, and viruses. For example, the lac (lactose) operon in certain bacteria controls the production of the enzymes needed to digest any lactose in the cell. If lactose is already available in the cell, the lactose binds to the repressor protein to prevent the repressor protein from binding to the operator. The gene is transcribed, and the enzymes necessary for the digestion of the lactose are produced. If there is no lactose that needs to be digested, the repressor protein binds to the operator. The gene is not transcribed, and the enzyme is not produced.

Epigenetics

Epigenetics is the study of modifications in specific gene expression caused by factors that are not genetic. These factors do not cause alternations in the cell's DNA. Epigenetics studies factors or mechanisms that determine if genes are active (switched on) or dormant (switched off). These mechanisms can alter gene functions or gene expressions without altering the sequences of the DNA itself. Modifications to the proteins such as histones that are associated with DNA can switch genes on or off. Some modifications determine the activity level of a gene, which in turn affects a physiological aspect of the health of an individual. The main type of modification is the addition of a methyl group to the histones, known as methylation. Acetylation, the addition of an acetyl group, and phosphorylation, the addition of a phosphoryl group, are also modifications to the proteins associated with DNA that can switch genes on or off or affect their activity level.

Differential gene expression

Because every cell in an organism has an identical genome, the DNA molecules of every cell of that organism are identical. Cells must be specialized for their specific roles. For example, in mammals, there are numerous types of cells such as epithelial cells, nerve cells, blood cells, liver cells, fat cells, and bone cells. The various types of cells differentiate through differential gene expression. Differential gene expression is the expression of different sets of gene by cells with identical DNA molecules. The unused genes in a differentiated cell remain in the cell; they just are not expressed. Actually, only a few genes are expressed in each cell. For example, during mammalian embryonic development, the undifferentiated zygote undergoes cell division through mitosis. As the number of cells increases, selected cells undergo differentiation to become specialized components in the developing tissues of the embryo.

Stem cells

Stem cells are undifferentiated cells that can divide without limit and that can differentiate to produce the specialized cells that each organism needs. Stem cells have varying degrees of potency. Stem cells can be pluripotent or multipotent depending on their source. Embryonic stem cells are harvested from the embryo at the blastocyst stage or from the developing gonads of the embryo. Early embryonic stem cells are pluripotent. This means they have not undergone any differentiation and have the ability to become any special type of cell. After embryonic stem cells begin to differentiate, they may be limited to specializing into a specific tissue type. These stem cells are considered to be multipotent because they can only develop into a few different types of cells. Adult stem cells, also called somatic stem cells, are harvested from organs and tissues and can differentiate into those types of cells in that particular organ or tissue. Umbilical cord blood stem cells can be harvested from the umbilical cord of a newborn baby. Adult stem cells and umbilical cord blood stem cells are multipotent. Induced pluripotent cells (iPS) are somatic cells that have been manipulated to act like pluripotent cells. Experiments have shown that iPS may be useful in treating diseases.

Mutations and mutagens

Mutations are errors in DNA replication. Mutagens are physical and chemical agents that cause these changes or errors in DNA replication. Mutagens are external factors to an organism. The first mutagens discovered were carcinogens or cancer-causing substances. Other mutagens include ionizing radiation such as ultraviolet radiation, x-rays, and gamma radiation. Viruses and microorganisms that integrate into chromosomes and switch genes on or off causing cancer are mutagens. Mutagens include environmental poisons such as asbestos, coal tars, tobacco, and benzene. Alcohol and diets high in fat have been shown to be mutagenic. Not all mutations are caused by mutagens. Spontaneous mutations can occur in DNA due to molecular decay. Spontaneous errors in DNA replication, repair, and recombination can also cause mutations.

Mutations are changes in DNA sequences. Point mutations are changes in a single nucleotide or at one "point" in a DNA sequence. Three types of point mutations include missense, silent, and nonsense. Missense mutations code for the wrong protein. Silent mutations do not change the function of the protein. Nonsense mutations stop protein synthesis early, resulting in no functioning protein. Deletions and insertions remove and add one or more nucleotides to the DNA sequence, which can remove or add amino acids to the protein, changing the function. Deletions and insertions can also cause a frameshift mutation in which the nucleotides are grouped incorrectly in sets of three. Mutations can also occur on the chromosomal level. For example, an inversion is when a piece of the chromosome inverts or flips its orientation.

Mutations can occur in somatic (body) cells and germ cells (egg and sperm) at any time in an organism's life. Somatic mutations develop after conception and occur in an organism's body cells such as bone cells, liver cells, or brain cells. Somatic mutations cannot be passed on from parent to offspring. The mutation is limited to the specific descendent of the cell in which the mutation occurred. The mutation is not in the other body cells unless they are descendants of the originally mutated cell. Somatic mutations may cause cancer or diseases. Some somatic mutations are silent. Germline mutations are present at conception and occur in an organism's germ cells, which are only egg and sperms cells. Germline mutations may be passed on from parent to offspring. Germline mutations will be present in every cell of an offspring that inherits a germline mutation. Germline mutations may cause diseases. Some germline mutations are silent.

Gel electrophoresis

Gel electrophoresis is a technique used to separate macromolecules such as nucleic acids and proteins. Fragments of DNA and RNA are separated according to length. Proteins are separated according to length and charge. The technique is relatively simple. For example, to separate DNA strands, a solution containing the DNA strand is placed in a gel. When an electric current is passed through the gel, the DNA strands migrate from the negative end of the container to the positive end due to their negative charge because of their phosphate ions. Shorter DNA strands migrate faster than the longer DNA strands. This results in a series of bands. Each band contains DNA strands of a specific length. A DNA standard is placed in the gel to provide a reference to determine the strand length. Lengths are measured in base pairs (bps).

Microscopy

Microscopy is used in microbiology. Bacteria, viruses, cell components, and molecules are too small to be seen by the naked eye. Several types of microscopes are available to examine these samples. There are light microscopes, which use visible light to study samples, and electron microscopes, which use beams of electrons. The light microscope (also called the compound microscope) uses two types of lenses (ocular and objective) to magnify objects. These are typically used when studying samples at the cellular level. Basic compound light microscopes are typically used in high school biology classes. Other compound light microscopes such as the dark-field microscope, phase-contrast microscope, and the fluorescent microscope are available for more specific uses. For tiny samples, such as viruses, cell components, or individual molecules, electron microscopes can be used. Electron microscopes use beams of electrons instead of light. Because beams of electrons have shorter wavelengths, electron microscopes have greater resolution than light microscopes. Resolution is the ability of a lens to reveal two points as being distinct. The two types of electron microscopy are transmission electron microscopy (TEM) and scanning electron microscopy (SEM). SEM is a newer technology than TEM and produces three-dimensional images.

PCR

The polymerase chain reaction (PCR) is a laboratory technique used to rapidly copy selected segments of DNA from DNA molecules without cloning. PCR requires only a single cell such as from sperm, hair, or blood to obtain the targeted DNA. PCR is a hot-and-cold cycled reaction that uses a special heat-tolerant polymerase that has been extracted from bacteria. The DNA sample is combined with this special DNA polymerase, primers, and free nucleotides. Primers are synthetic strands of DNA containing just a few bases. Primers attach to the ends of the targeted DNA sequence and act as the substrate for the polymerase. At high temperatures, the DNA molecules separate into two strands, and each strand unwinds. Then the mixture is cooled, and the primers bind to the ends of the targeted DNA segment. The polymerase initiates synthesis between the two primers. When the temperature cycles up again, the DNA separates again into two strands, and the cycle repeats. After 30 cycles, which takes less than three hours, there are more than half a billion of the needed targeted DNA segments.

DNA sequencing

DNA sequencing is a laboratory technique used to determine the order or linear sequence of nucleotides of DNA fragments. A polymerase chain reaction (PCR) is used to isolate the needed DNA segment or DNA template. During PCR, some of each of the nucleotides containing the four bases, G, C, A, and T, is chemically altered and fluorescently tagged with different colors of dye. Also, the chemically altered nucleotides have the dideoxyribose sugar, which contains one less oxygen atom than the usual deoxyribose. When synthesis begins, the polymerase randomly adds either a regular nucleotide or an altered nucleotide. If the polymerase adds an altered nucleotide, synthesis stops. This way, each DNA fragment of the same length is tagged with the same color. Then, electrophoresis is used to separate DNA fragments according to length. The DNA sequence can be read by reading the tags of the shortest fragments to the tags of the longest fragments.

Human Genome Project

In 1990, the Human Genome Project (HGP), which involved scientists from 16 laboratories located in at least 6 different countries, was launched to map the human genome. The project was completed in 2003. The human genome consists of approximately 3.12 billion paired nucleotides. The results were surprising. Prior to the project, scientists thought that the human genome would consist of approximately 100,000 to 140,000 genes, but research showed that the human genome consists of only about 21,000 genes. Prior to the project, scientists thought that each gene coded for one specific protein, but with only 21,000 genes, this could not be correct. Genes must be able to code for more than one protein. Furthermore, scientists discovered that only about 1% of the genes actually code for proteins. Originally, the noncoding DNA was actually called junk DNA, but new research has shown that these genes are involved in gene expressions and in turning genes on and off. Today, more than 21,000 genes have been identified. The genomes of several plants, animal, fungi, protists, bacteria, viruses, and even cell organelles have been studied and mapped. Interesting comparisons can be made between these genomes. For example, the number of genes in an organism's genome does not indicate the complexity of that organism. Humans have approximately 21,000 genes, but the simpler roundworms have approximately 26,000 genes.

Gene therapy

Gene therapy is an experimental but promising technique that introduces new genes into an organism to correct a specific disease caused by a defective gene. In gene therapy, the defective gene is replaced by a properly functioning gene. Gene therapy is most promising for diseases that are caused by a single defective gene. For example, gene therapy was first successfully used to treat severe combined immunodeficiency (SCID). One type of SCID is caused by a single defective gene on the X chromosome. Doctors removed some bone marrow from the test subjects, injected a retrovirus that was carrying the gene, and then reimplanted the bone marrow. The bone marrow cells then have the correct DNA sequence for the production of proteins for much-needed enzymes. Unfortunately, some of the first recipients developed leukemia, and the trials were halted. Later, researchers discovered that the leukemias were related to the location of the insertion of the retroviral vectors.

Cloning

Clones are exact biological copies of genes, cells, or multicellular organisms. There are natural clones and artificial clones. Many clones are produced in nature. Animals that can reproduce asexually by fragmentation or budding produce natural clones. Some plants such as strawberries can reproduce by stolons. Typically, in biology, cloning refers to gene cloning or the cloning of organisms. Gene cloning is the process of splicing genes that are needed to code for a specific protein and introducing them into a new cell with a DNA vector. Gene cloning has been used with bacteria in the production of human insulin and a human growth hormone replacement. Cloning can also occur with an entire organism. This type of cloning is called a somatic cell nuclear transfer. The first mammal clone was Dolly the sheep. In this procedure, a nucleus of a somatic cell from the sheep to be cloned was transferred or injected into a denucleated egg cell of the surrogate mother sheep. The egg was stimulated to divide by electric shock, and then the embryo was implanted into the uterus of the surrogate mother. Dolly was born identical to the egg nucleus donor, not the surrogate mother. Dolly and other cloned mammals typically have serious health problems. Dolly aged prematurely possibly due to the shortened telomeres from the adult somatic cell nucleus.

Genetically engineered cells

Genetic engineering is the manipulation of DNA outside of normal reproduction. This modified DNA is called recombinant DNA. Genetic engineering is prevalent in gene cloning, which is used in the production of genetically modified (GM) organisms and the production of GM food. Gene cloning involves cloning a specific gene that is needed for a specific purpose. Genes can be inserted into cells of an entirely different species. Genetically engineered cells are also called transgenic cells. GM organisms such plants or crops contain recombinant DNA. Many types of organisms such as plants, animals, fungi, and bacteria have been genetically modified. GM crops such as corn and soybeans can be engineered to be herbicide resistant to ensure that herbicides kill the weeds but not the crop plants. Crops can also be modified to be pest resistant in order to kill the insects that might damage the crops. Also, several foods can be genetically modified to increase the nutritional value.

Transmission of Heritable Information from Generation to Generation

Natural selection and adaptation

Charles Darwin popularized the concept of natural selection, and it's one of the primary components of the theory of evolution. Organisms have characteristics, also called traits, some of which are more helpful than others for survival and reproduction. These traits collectively compose an organism's phenotype which is its set of observable characteristics. The phenotype is determined by an organism's genotype which is the term for an organism's set of genes.

Organisms with good traits for survival live long enough to repopulate, often multiple times. Likewise, organisms with favorable reproductive traits repopulate more than their lesser-equipped counterparts. Thus, the more favorable an organism's traits, the more it can create new organisms with those same favorable genes that will in turn produce those favorable traits.

On the contrary, animals with less favorable traits die before repopulating or do not repopulate as much as their better-outfitted counterparts. This stops the continuation of the less favorable traits. Eventually a species as a whole can all have the more favorable traits. Natural selection and adaptation (discussed below) are used as primary building blocks in the theory of evolution.

For example, if a pack of dogs ended up in a particularly cold climate, the longer-haired dogs would likely survive better than the short-haired ones, since they could stay warmer. Over time the dogs with longer hair would reproduce more, meaning that the following generations in the pack would mainly be long-haired varieties. Meanwhile, the shorter-haired dogs would die prematurely, limiting the passing on of their short-haired genes.

Adaptation
Adaption involves a species gaining an alteration in traits that make it more suited for its environment. This increases the ability of the species to survive which raises reproduction rates. This, in turn, increases the commonality of the adaptation within the species. Adaptive radiation is the theory that some species rapidly diversify into different ecological niches.

The most oft-cited example of this is the 13 types of finches that Darwin observed on his trip to the Galapagos Island. The different islands in the chain had unique ecosystems meaning that different traits were needed amongst the finches for optimal survival. Additionally, there were even some variations observed among finches on the same island. Here, it's posited that adaptive radiation occurred among the finches to cause some many variations of traits, particularly among the size and shape of their beaks. Their beak characteristics corresponded with the diets needed in their environment. For example, on islands where seeds were the best food, the finches had short beaks, and on islands where snatching insets was best, they had thin, sharp beaks.

Originally, there was thought to have only been one species of finch in the chain. Finches ill-suited for the island they inhabited either died or moved to another island. Meanwhile, the well-equipped finches thrived until the species each stabilized and became more homogenous.

In order for these adaptations to occur, there has to be some variation in the phenotypes of the species to begin with. This occurs in part by natural variation. For example, there are tall people and short people. If only short people repopulated, then shortness would become more and more common. Additionally, mutations also cause variations in genotypes that would otherwise not occur.

Principles of Bioenergetics and Fuel Molecule Metabolism

Bioenergetics

Bioenergetics involves energy flow within biological systems. The main focus is on the conversion of macronutrients from diet into energy forms that the body uses for work.

Catabolism
Catabolism refers to the process of breaking large molecules down into smaller, usable molecules. For example, when the body converts carbohydrates into energy for a human to live, that is catabolism.

Anabolism
Anabolism, in a way, is the opposite of catabolism. Rather than breaking down the big into the small, anabolism takes materials, post-catabolism, and builds compounds to perform necessary life functions such as constructing structure proteins out of amino acids to create fresh muscle tissue.

Metabolism involves breaking down substances as well as constructing (also known as synthesizing) substances. This is accomplished through metabolic pathways which turn a molecule into one of a number of different substances needed by the body. Each of these involves different reactions and each of which use an enzyme. Catabolic pathways are a type of metabolic pathway. As you would guess based on the information above, these pathways break down large, complex molecules into simple ones and release energy in the process. Anabolic pathways, another type of metabolic pathway, do the reverse and consume energy in order to make simple molecules into complex ones. These pathways work in tandem with each other, as the anabolic pathways run on the energy released from the catabolic ones, a practice called energy coupling.

Reactions within the pathways discussed are either:
1. Exergonic: Reactions that release free energy
2. Endergonic: Reactions that absorb free energy

Free energy (G) is the energy in a system that's available for accomplishing things like chemical reactions. Exergonic reactions, as noted, do not need energy. They are considered to have a negative change in energy ($-\Delta G$) within the reaction since the reactants had more energy that what they produced. Conversely, endergonic reactions need energy and result in a positive change in energy ($+\Delta G$) since the product has more energy than the reactants. Because exergonic reactions do not require energy, they are referred to as spontaneous. When there is no free energy in a system (e.g. a cell) the system is in equilibrium. However, absolute equilibrium only occurs if a cell is dead since cells need free energy to function.

Enzymes, a type of protein, are used to speed up metabolic reactions and pathways by functioning as catalysts. Enzyme don't change the results of the reaction, they just lower the activation energy of such reactions, meaning less energy is required to start them. Enzymes, function in a lock and key format, since their shape only fits into the substrates they are supposed to work on.

ATP
Adenosine Triphosphate (ATP) is a molecule used in many critical metabolic processes like muscle contractions. Its usefulness is derived from its ability to help transfer energy from catabolic to anabolic reactions and from exergonic to endergonic reactions. ATP is created in skeletal muscles.

ATP Hydrolysis

Hydrolysis refers to chemical reactions that break down chemical components using water. ATP hydrolysis, in particular does this in order to split an ATP molecule into adenosine diphosphate (ADP), a hydrogen ion, free energy, and an inorganic phosphate. Note that the "di" in "diphosphate" means it contains two phosphate groups. This straightforward reaction is assisted by the enzyme adenosine triphosphate (ATPase), specifically myosin ATPase. The free energy from this reaction powers cross-bridge recycling.

Below, the ATP hydrolysis reaction can be seen. The equation is split into reactants, enzyme, and the resulting products.

$$ATP + H_2O \longleftarrow ATPase \longrightarrow ADP + P_i + H^+ + Energy$$

The ATP - ADP Cycle

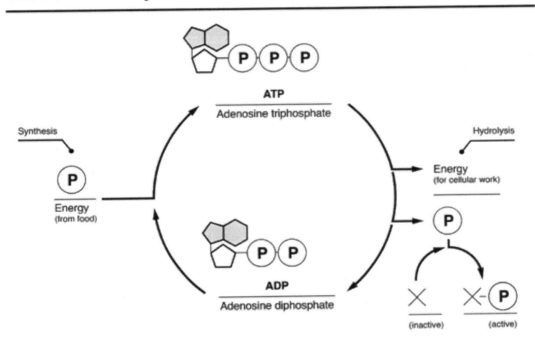

Adenosine Monophosphate (AMP)
This is a product of ADP hydrolysis, which splits off the other phosphate group.

Biological energy systems

Several different biological energy systems operate in muscle cells to produce ATP, and they are discussed below.

Phosphagen System (ATP-phosphocreatine [PC])
The phosphagen system utilizes ATP hydrolysis for high-intensity, explosive exercise which recruits the alactic (not producing lactic acid) anaerobic (not using oxygen) energy system, e.g., a 100-meter sprint or one weightlifting set. Also called the ATP-PCr (adenosine triphosphate-phosphocreatine) or phosphagen energy system, this is the first accessed for exercise. It uses ATP stored in muscles

and then rephosphorylizes the resulting ADP via phosphocreatine. It stops supplying energy when PCr is depleted until muscles have rested and regenerated PCr. High-intensity exercise for up to 90 seconds, e.g., one ice hockey shift or an 800 meter sprint, uses the lactic anaerobic energy system. It functions when the alactic anaerobic system is depleted and the aerobic system cannot handle the exercise intensity's demands. It produces lactic acid as a byproduct in the muscles but does not use oxygen. It directly accesses cellular respiration to convert food energy to supply ATP. Continuous/long-term (beyond 2-5 minutes), lower-intensity aerobic exercise, e.g., running marathons, accesses the aerobic energy system, which depends upon how efficiently oxygen can be sent to and processed by the muscles. It also recruits cellular respiration to get ATP from food energy; however, oxygen is available to the muscles, so no lactic acid is produced.

Creatine Phosphate (CP): Creatine phosphate is found in concentrations within the muscles four to six times larger than the ATP stores found in muscles. The phosphagen system combines a phosphate group from CP with ADP to replenish ATP. CP stores do not last long, which limits the phosphagen system to short bursts of high intensity exercise.
ADP + CP ← Creatine kinase → ATP + Creatine

Creatine Kinase: Creatine kinase is an enzyme used in catalyzation of the combination of ADP and CP to produce ATP and creatine. Too much creatine kinase in blood is correlated with major muscle damage, such as in the heart or kidney, or in the case of overworked muscles, rapid breakdown of muscle tissue. This condition is called rhabdomyolysis, which releases proteins and creatine kinase into the circulatory system which in turn can damage other organs.

Adenylate Kinase: Adenylate kinase (or myokinase) is an enzyme used in catalyzing another reaction which replenishes ATP.
2ADP ← adenylate kinase → ATP + AMP

Law of Mass Action/Mass Action Effect: The law of mass action states that the concentration of reactants, products, or both within a solution will influence the direction of the reactions. The concentration of available reactants directly effects the direction of the reaction and, as a result, these reactions are often called near-equilibrium reactions.

Glycolytic system
Glycolysis: Carbohydrates are broken down in the digestive system and are stored as glycogen in the muscles and liver and as glucose in the blood, which is later used to replenish ATP. This process is referred to as *glycolysis* and is a slower system of ATP replenishment than the single-step phosphagen system. This system is also initially inefficient as it requires some investment in energy prior to utilization. Despite not being a readily available process, this process has some advantages later as it can produce far more ATP due to the larger supplies of glucose and glycogen relative to the small amounts of available CP.

Anaerobic Glycolysis: The body has a limited anaerobic output due to limited ATP replenishment processes. This limit is referred to as the anaerobic threshold or the lactate threshold. The body relies on making lactate out of pyruvate to replace ATP during high-intensity intervals. When the threshold is reached, the body begins pushing pyruvate into the mitochondria to begin the Krebs cycle.

Pyruvate: During anaerobic glycolysis, one molecule of glucose is synthesized into two molecules of pyruvate, which can be either converted into lactate or transported to the mitochondria for the Krebs cycle. Converting pyruvate to lactate in the sarcoplasm takes less time than the Krebs cycle because there are fewer reactions that must take place. The Krebs cycle is dependent on exercise intensity and may work for a longer period of time if the anaerobic threshold is not reached.

When pyruvate is converted to lactate, the enzyme lactate dehydrogenase is responsible for catalysis. Lactate which is left behind through anaerobic glycolysis can be cleared by oxidation and can be cleaned out by blood and moved to the liver for conversion into glucose. This process is called the Cori cycle.

During glycolysis, pyruvate is converted to lactate. The reaction converting pyruvate into lactate is provided below:

Glucose + $2P_i$ + 2ADP → 2Lactate + 2ATP + H_2O

During the Krebs cycle, pyruvate is transported to the mitochondria along with two molecules of nicotinamide adenine dinucleotide (NADH). The Krebs cycle is initiated after the loss of carbon dioxide (CO_2) resulting from pyruvate's conversion to acetyl-coenzyme A (acetyl-CoA) by pyruvate dehydrogenase.

During glycolysis, pyruvate is transported to the mitochondria, producing the following reaction:

Glucose + $2P_i$ + 2ADP + $2NAD^+$ → 2Pyruvate + 2ATP + 2NADH + $2H_2O$

Phosphorylation: During phosphorylation, inorganic phosphate is added to a molecule. Phosphorylation of ADP to ATP takes place when a phosphoryl (PO_3) group is added to ADP.

Substrate-Level Phosphorylation: Substrate-level phosphorylation occurs during anaerobic glycolysis, or fast phosphorylation, and refers to a single enzyme-generated reaction. This process involves using ADP to directly resynthesize ATP and can take place during both anaerobic and aerobic activities to replenish ATP.

Oxidative Phosphorylation: ATP may also be re-synthesized with the actions of the electron transport chain, or ETC during the process of oxidative phosphorylation. In this process, approximately thirty-eight molecules of ATP are produced when a molecule of glucose is subjected to glycolysis, the Krebs cycle, and the ETC. Substrate-level phosphorylation produces about ten percent of the body's ATP production, whereas the oxidative system is responsible for all of the rest.

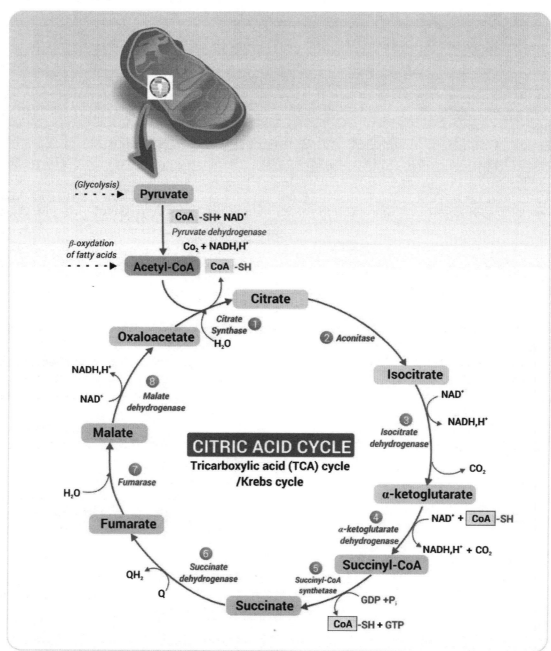

Electron Transport Chain (ETC): The ETC is able to produce and use six molecules of NADH and two molecules of flavin adenine dinucleotide ($FADH_2$) in addition to the two pyruvate molecules produced during glycolysis. Hydrogen atoms are used in this process to produce ATP from ADP by

- 22 -

forming a proton concentration gradient down the ETC, producing the energy necessary in ATP production. NADH and FADH$_2$ molecules re-phosphorylate ADP to ATP through the ETC, making three molecules of ATP per NADH and two ATP molecules per FADH$_2$.

<u>Oxidative system</u>
When the body is at rest and while performing low-intensity exercise, the body is capable of using carbohydrates and fats as substrates to produce ATP. Fats have a higher capacity for producing ATP when compared to carbohydrates and proteins. Proteins are not primary substrates and are only used for energy during long-duration exercise (more than 90 minutes) or during starvation. Approximately 70 percent of ATP production is through the use of fats during times of rest, while carbohydrates take up the remaining 30 percent. Nearly all of the ATP in high-intensity activity changes to coming from carbohydrate metabolism. During longer exercise sessions, carbohydrates are initially used, but metabolism shifts to fat stores as glycogen depletes from the fast metabolism of carbohydrates.

Net ATP Production: The net ATP production from the oxidation of one glucose molecule can be calculated by adding the number of ATP molecules synthesized during each process. During the process of glycolysis, substrate-level phosphorylation produces four ATP molecules and oxidative phosphorylation produces six. Substrate-level phosphorylation during the Krebs cycle produces two ATP molecules and oxidative phosphorylation of eight NADH molecules produces twenty-four molecules of ATP, while two molecules of FADH$_2$ synthesize four molecules of ATP. These processes yield forty total molecules of ATP. Two of these molecules are used by glycolysis, so the production from one molecule of glucose totals up to be thirty eight ATP molecules.

Substrates

<u>Carbohydrates</u>
Carbohydrates are a molecule built from carbon and hydrogen and oxygen, hence the name carbo- for carbon and –hydrates for the hydrogen and oxygen found in water. These molecules take the form of sweet, ring-like sugar molecules. Carbohydrates can exist in single-ring forms, known as monosaccharides, like glucose, fructose, and galactose, or as two-ring disaccharides, like maltose, lactose, and sucrose. Both of these structures are referred to as simple sugars and can easily be broken down to produce quick energy in digestion. Polysaccharides are more complex builds of repeated chains of monosaccharide rings.

Examples of polysaccharides include starches found in plants, glycogen stored in animals, cellulose (a main component of plant cell walls), and chitin (a main component of fungi cell walls and exoskeletons in arthropods).

<u>Lipids</u>
Lipids are hydrophobic molecules that are generally non-polar and are insoluble in water. Lipids such as Triglycerides use glycerol as a backbone which is attached to three long fatty acid chains. Lipids are energy-storage molecules and may take on several forms including:
- Saturated fats – contain no double bonds within their fatty acid tails. Animal foods, including dairy products and meat both contain saturated fat.
- Unsaturated fats – contain double bonds with their fatty acid tails. The double bonds of unsaturated fats cause kinds which makes them remain liquid at room temperature. Most unsaturated fats are plant fats, such as olive oil.

Phospholipids also use a glycerol backbone, but rather than using three fatty acid tails, they only use two. The third tail is traded for a hydrophilic phosphate group. This molecule results in a lipid bilayer where the hydrophilic ends face the extracellular matrix and cytoplasm. The other ends, which "hate" water, face inward towards one another.

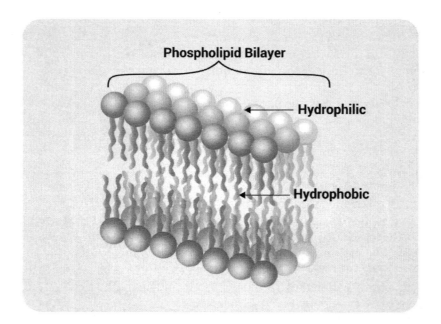

Another type of lipid is steroids, which are all derived from cholesterol which is embedded in cell membranes of animal cells. Steroid hormones, such as testosterone and estrogen work in bodily systems for the regulation of various bodily functions, such as growth and metabolism.

Assemblies of Molecules, Cells, and Groups of Cells within Unicellular and Multicellular Organisms

Cell structure and function

The main functional and structural component of all living organisms is the cell. In 1665, an English scientist named Robert Hooke coined the term *cell*. The encounter that Hooke made in the seventeenth century started the foundation for the concept that we know today as cell theory. There are three principles of cell theory:

1. All organisms are composed of cells.
2. All existing cells are created from other living cells.
3. The cell is the most fundamental unit of life.

The two types of organisms include single-cell and multi-cell organisms. Every cell is confined by a cell membrane, filled with a type of cytoplasm, and coded with a genetic sequence. The cell membrane is a border for the internal and external environments of the cell. This border is a selective permeable membrane that grants access to some molecules by diffusion. Two important pieces of all cell membranes are phospholipids and proteins. The internal environment of the cell is water-based and known as the cytoplasm. The genetic material inside the cell that is passed on to one's offspring is known as the genome.

Prokaryotes and Eukaryotes

The primitive single-celled organisms that have existed on Earth for billions of years are called prokaryotes. The eukaryotes came from prokaryotes through the evolutionary process and have more complexity than the prokaryotes.

Since prokaryotic cells do not have a nucleus, their genome is placed within a nucleoid. These single-celled organisms do not have membrane-bound organelles which perform certain roles within a cell. In contrast, eukaryotic cells have a nucleus that houses the genome, and they have several membrane-bound organelles. Examples include lysosomes, endoplasmic reticula (rough and smooth), Golgi complexes, and mitochondria.

Cell walls are mainly a feature of prokaryotic cells as most eukaryotic cells do not have cell walls. Eukaryotic cells hold DNA in a multiple linear chromosomes while prokaryotic cells hold DNA in a single circular chromosome. The division for prokaryotic cells occurs with binary fission, and eukaryotic cells bring about division with mitosis. Examples of prokaryotes include bacteria and archaea, and examples of eukaryotes include animals and plants.

Nuclear parts of a cell

Nucleus (pl. = nuclei): the main characteristic of eukaryotic cells, and the home of deoxyribonucleic acid (DNA) which is instrumental in making chromosomes. The main task of the nucleus is to control gene expression and guarantee that genetic material is passed on to one's offspring.

Chromosome: the complex thread-like composition of DNA that is located within a cell's nucleus. Inside a human cell are twenty-three pairs of chromosomes which totals to forty-six.

Chromatin: the collection of genetic material that is made of DNA and proteins and forms chromosomes during the cell division process.

Nucleolus (pl. = nucleoli): the largest part of the nucleus in a eukaryotic cell. The main task of the nucleolus is to make ribosomes which are very important to the synthesis of proteins.

Cell membranes
The cell membrane contains the cell's cytoplasm and prevents the intracellular environment from going to its extracellular environment. Their selectively permeable membrane is made of a double layer of phospholipids which is covered with proteins to maintain control of the traffic of items that come into the cell and what leaves the cell. Those proteins in the phospholipid bilayer help with the movement of molecules across the cell membrane.

The term fluid mosaic model is used by scientists to explain the layer of phospholipids and proteins in cell membranes. This model shows phospholipids to have a head region and a tail region. The head area of the phospholipid is hydrophilic which means that is drawn to water. The tails are of the phospholipid is hydrophobic which means that it avoids water. Therefore, the hydrophilic section of phospholipids faces the water that lines the inside of the cell and the water that is on the outside of the cell. For the hydrophobic section, the tails of phospholipids are turned inward between the head regions. Thus, the phospholipid bilayer is constructed.

Since cell membranes are amphiphilic (i.e., they have hydrophilic and hydrophobic areas) adds to the distinct trait of cell membranes' selective permeability. Thus, cell membranes can control the flow of molecules in to and out of the cell.

Size, polarity, and solubility are the factors that decide the possibility of a molecule crossing the cell membrane layer. A small molecule can easily diffuse across cell membranes while a large molecule will have more difficulty. Polarity is the charge of a molecule. Polar molecules are water soluble and have positive and negative charges on their respective poles. Non-polar molecules are fat-soluble and have no charge. Solubility is the ability of a substance (i.e., solute) to break down within a solvent. A soluble substance is able to be broken down in a solvent. An insoluble substance is not able to be broken down in a solvent. Thus, non-polar, fat-soluble substances will move across the cell membrane with greater ease than polar, water-soluble substances.

Passive transport mechanisms
Passive transport is the movement of molecules across a cell-membrane and does not require energy. Simple diffusion, facilitated diffusion, and osmosis are the three types of passive transport.

Simple diffusion needs a concentration gradient which means a differing amount of molecules inside or outside of a cell. In simple diffusion, molecules go from a place of high concentration to a place of low concentration. Facilitated diffusion uses carrier proteins to move molecules through a cell membrane. Osmosis is the movement of water across a selectively-permeable membrane. Water moves from an area of low-solute concentration to an area of high-solute concentration in the process of osmosis.

Active-transport mechanisms
Active transport is the movement of molecules across a cell membrane that demands energy. The process is a good way to move molecules from a place of low concentration to a place of high concentration. Adenosine triphosphate (ATP) is necessary to move against the concentration gradient.

Active transport uses carrier proteins to cross the cell membrane and pump molecules and ions across the membrane such as is performed in facilitated diffusion. The difference between active transport and facilitated diffusion is that active transport uses the energy from ATP to make this transport occur because the ions or molecules are opposing the concentration gradient. An example would be when glucose pumps located in the kidney move all of the glucose into the cells from the lumen of nephron although there is a higher concentration of glucose present in the cell than in the lumen. The reason for this is that glucose is an important food source, and the human body wants to conserve as much as possible. A pump can move one molecule in one direction. The pump can also move multiple molecules in the same direction, which is symports; or the pump can move multiple molecules in different directions, which is antiport.

Active transport also includes the movement the movement of membrane-bound particles into a cell which id endocytosis or out of a cell which is exocytosis. Pinocytosis, phagocytosis, and receptor-mediated endocytosis are the three major forms of endocytosis. Pinocytosis is when the cell intakes only small molecules while drinking. Phagocytosis is when the cell takes in large particles or small organisms while eating. Receptor-mediated endocytosis is when the cell's membrane separates to form an internal vesicle as a response to molecules that are activating receptors on its surface. Exocytosis is the opposite of endocytosis. The membranes of the vesicle bond to the cell's surface while the molecules inside the vesicle are released outside. For nervous and muscle tissue, this is common for the release of neurotransmitters and with endocrine cells for the release of hormones. Excretion and secretion are the two major categories of exocytosis. Excretion is simply the removal of waste from the cell. Secretion is the movement of molecules (e.g., hormones or enzymes) from a cell.

This is an illustration of the cell:

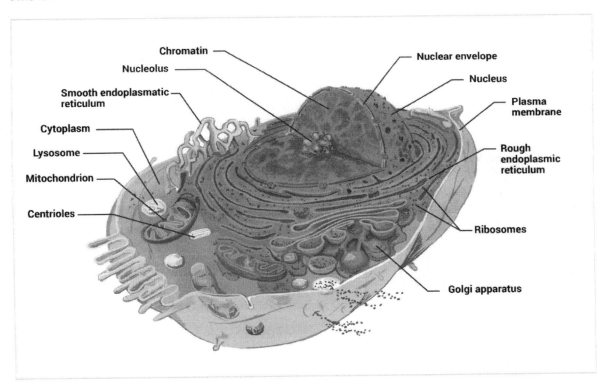

Structure and function of cellular organisms

Organelles, or "little organs," are the specialized pieces within a cell that work on certain tasks. Most organelles are membrane bound and serve as the producer or degrader of chemicals. Eukaryotic cells contain the following organelles:

Nucleus

Surrounded by a nuclear envelope, the nucleus is the home of genetic information in the form of DNA. The nucleus is the most important organelle within the cell. The nucleus is also home to nucleolus which makes ribosomes which are very important for protein synthesis (i.e., gene expression).

Mitochondria

This organelle is the main location for respiration and adenosine triphosphate (ATP) synthesis inside the cell. Mitochondria have two lipid bilayers that make up the intermembrane space and the matrix. The intermembrane space is the space between the two membranes. The matrix is the space inside the inner membrane. The outer membrane of a mitochondrion is smooth, and the inner membrane is folded and forms cristae. Thus, the outer membrane is permeable to small molecules. The cristae hold many proteins that are part of ATP synthesis. During the citric-acid cycle and the electron-transport chain, the results from glycolysis are further oxidized in the mitochondria. The two-layer structure of the mitochondria grants the buildup of H+ ions made during the electron-transport chain in the intermembrane space. This makes a proton gradient and an energy potential. So, this gradient helps with the formation of ATP. It is important to note that mitochondria are a unique organelle in that they have their own DNA and are capable of replication.

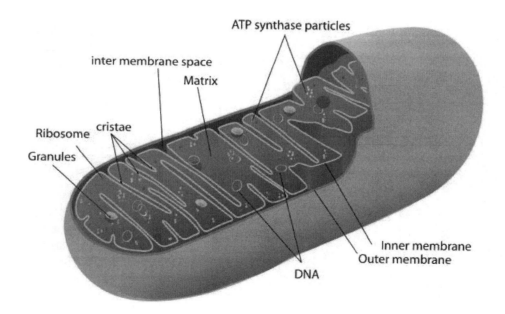

Rough endoplasmic reticulum

The rough endoplasmic reticulum is made of linked membranous sacs known as cisternae with ribosomes along the outside surface. The responsibility of the rough endoplasmic reticulum involves making proteins that will be sent out of the cell.

Smooth endoplasmic reticulum

The smooth endoplasmic reticulum is made of linked membranous sacs which are known as cisternae. The main task of the smooth endoplasmic reticulum is to make carbohydrates and lipids which can be made only for the cell or to change the proteins from the rough endoplasmic reticulum that will be sent out the cell.

Golgi apparatus

The Golgi apparatus is where proteins are changed. The task of the golgi apparatus is in the movement of proteins, lipids, and carbohydrates within the cell. The main composition of the golgi apparatus is its flat layers of membranes known as cisternae. Material is moved in transfer vesicles from the endoplasmic reticulum to the cis region of the golgi apparatus. From the cis region, the material is transported through the medial region, where it is occasionally changed and the leaves through the *trans* region of the endoplasmic reticulum in a secretory vesicle.

Lysosomes

Lysosomes are specialized vesicles which hold enzymes that can digest food, surplus organelles, and foreign matter (e.g., bacteria and viruses) and are only found in animal cells. Often, they break down dead cells in order to recycle cell parts.

Secretory vesicles

Secretory vesicles move and deliver molecules into or out of the cell through the cell membrane. Endocytosis is the movement of molecules into a cell through secretory vesicles. Exocytosis is the movement of molecules out of a cell through secretory vesicles.

Ribosomes

Ribosomes are composed of ribosomal RNA molecules and several kinds of proteins. The main task of ribosomes is to break combine proteins. They have two subunits: small and large. The ribosomes use mRNA as a pattern for the protein, and they use tRNA to bring amino acids to the ribosomes where they are combined into peptide strands with the genetic code from the mRNA. Most ribosomes can be found connected to endoplasmic reticulum membrane.

Cilia and flagella

Cilia are the specialized hair-like projections on some eukaryotic cells that assist with movement. Flagella are the long whip-like projections that are used in the same way as cilia.

Vacuoles

Vacuoles are membrane-bound organelles that are mainly found in plant and fungi cells. However, they can be found in some animal cells. The contents of vacuoles include water and some enzymes. Their main assignment is for intracellular digestion and waste removal while the pressure from the water inside the vacuole aids in the structure of plant cells. The membrane-bound nature of the vacuole grants the storage of harmful material and poisonous substances.

The following organelles are NOT found in animal cells:

Cell walls

Cell walls are found in plants, bacteria, and fungi. They are composed of cellulose, peptidoglycan, and lignin. Each of these materials is sugar recognized as a structural carbohydrate. The carbohydrates have rigid structures that are found outside of the cell membrane. The duty of the cell wall is to defend the cell, maintain the shape of the cell, and help with supporting the structure of the cell.

Chloroplasts

Chloroplasts are organelles that are the site of photosynthesis. They are composed of a double membrane and membrane-bound thylakoids (i.e., discs) that are organized into grana (i.e., stacks). Chlorophyll can be found in the thylakoids, and the light stage of photosynthesis which makes ATP and $NADPH_2$ happens in the thylakoids. Chlorophyll is a green substance that traps the light energy necessary for photosynthesis. In addition, chloroplasts house stroma during which sugar is made, and the stroma is also the place for the dark reaction stage of photosynthesis. The membrane structure of chloroplasts makes it possible for the compartmentalization of the light and dark stages of photosynthesis.

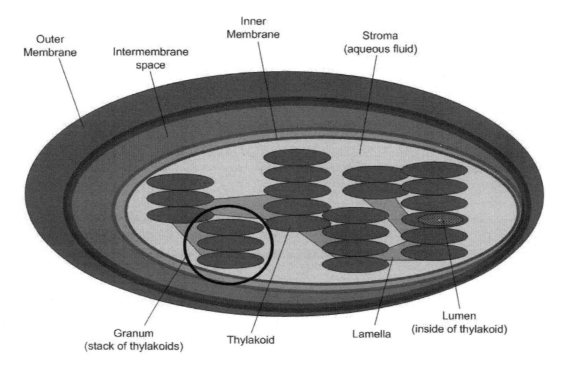

The Structure, Growth, Physiology, and Genetics of Prokaryotes and Viruses

Prokaryotic characteristics and distinctives

In contrast to eukaryotic cells, prokaryotic cells are significantly smaller and simpler. Most notably, prokaryotic cells lack a true nucleus. Prokaryote cells have their DNA arranged in a circular structure that should not be referred to as a chromosome. Most prokaryotes contain one large DNA molecule along with many tiny rings of DNA called plasmids. The DNA material is simply located near the center of the cell in a region called the nucleoid. Prokaryotic cells lack histone proteins, and therefore the DNA is not actually packaged into chromosomes. Instead, the DNA floats freely throughout the nucleoid. Most prokaryotes have cell walls.

The cell walls of organisms from the domain Bacteria differ from the cell walls of the organisms from the domain Archaea. Most bacteria have cell walls outside of the plasma membrane that contains the molecule peptidoglycan. Peptidoglycan is a large polymer of amino acids and sugars. The peptidoglycan helps maintain the strength of the cell wall. Some of the Archaea cells have cell walls containing the molecule pseudopeptidoglycan, which differs in chemical structure from the peptidoglycan but basically provides the same strength to the cell wall.

Bacterial forms

Bacterial cells are most commonly found in one of these three shapes:
- Cocci (spherical)
- Bacilli (rounded cylindrical)
- Spiral (helical)

Cocci cells tend to form groups or chains, though they may be found singly as well. Bacilli cells are more commonly found singly, but may also form pairs or chains. Spiral cells are typically found singly.

Bacterial reproduction

Bacteria have a single circular loop of DNA and cytoplasm with ribosomes enclosed in a plasma membrane. Most bacteria reproduce asexually by binary fission. This is a process in which the cell creates a copy of its DNA and isolates the two copies on opposite sides of the cell. The cell then splits in the middle and becomes two identical daughter produced from one parent cell. Alternatively, some bacteria can transfer genetic material to other bacteria through a process called conjugation, or incorporate DNA from the environment in a process called transformation.

Bacterial growth cycle
Bacteria typically reproduce and then die off in a cycle consisting of four defined phases:
1. Lag phase – initially, the bacteria reproduce slowly as they begin to adapt themselves for a period of rapid growth.
2. Exponential phase – growth begins to take place at an exponential rate. The number of bacteria cells present doubles every set unit of time, and will continue to grow in this manner until some limiting factor is encountered.
3. Stationary phase – eventually, the bacteria come up against a limiting factor. This is most commonly because either the supply of some critical nutrient has been exhausted or some

environmental factor has changed, making reproduction difficult or impossible. At this phase, the bacteria reproduce only enough to maintain their numbers.

4. Death phase – after holding steady for a period of time, the bacteria begin to die off much more quickly than they are able to reproduce.

Bacteria Population Growth

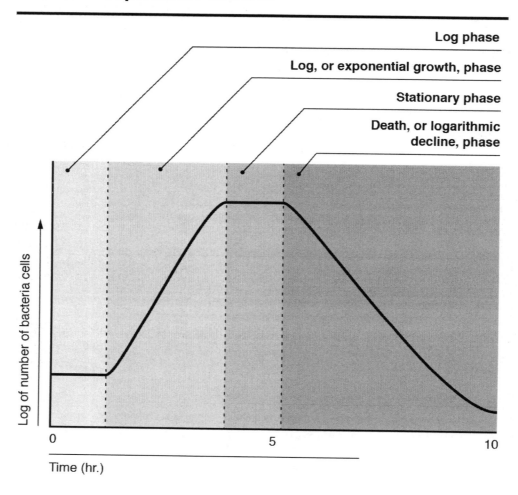

Log phase

Log, or exponential growth, phase

Stationary phase

Death, or logarithmic decline, phase

Log of number of bacteria cells

0   5   10

Time (hr.)

Viruses

Viruses are largely unlike any of the organisms covered thus far. Many people do not even consider viruses to be living organisms for several reasons:

- They lack any sort of cellular structure. Most viruses are simply a strand of DNA or RNA surrounded by a protein coat or capsid. In some viruses, the capsid may also be surrounded by a lipid membrane or envelope.
- They cannot reproduce outside of a living host cell. More specifically, they do not possess the ability to replicate their own DNA. They can reproduce only by hijacking the reproductive capabilities of a host cell and forcing it to reproduce the virus DNA.

- 32 -

- They do not produce, store, and use their own energy. Viruses only use energy once they have infected a host cell, and this energy is itself taken from the host.
- They do not take any action to maintain their internal environment. Living organisms seek to maintain homeostasis, adapting to changes in their surroundings, but viruses do not.

Viruses may be categorized as animal viruses, plant viruses, or bacterial viruses (bacteriophages) based upon the type of organism they are able to infect. In addition to having to be a match for the type of organism, the virus also has to be a match for the type of cell. Cells have receptors that are specifically designed to take in certain substances, so a virus can only infect those cells that have receptors for a substance that the virus is able to mimic. Once a virus binds to the receptor on a suitable host cell, it injects its DNA or RNA through the cell membrane into the host cell. The host cell then begins to replicate this genetic material, producing more viruses and releasing them into the environment.

Depending on the process the cell uses, the cell may continue to reproduce or it may die after releasing the first batch of new viruses.
- In lysis, the cell wall ruptures when the viruses are released. With cellular integrity lost, the cell membrane escapes and the cell is effectively dead.
- In budding, the viruses are released through exocytosis, which allows the cell walls to remain intact longer.

Once viruses are released, they can begin infecting additional host cells. Occasionally, viruses will go dormant within a cell, allowing the cell to continue to survive and function normally. Then at some later time, they will reactivate and force the cell to continue replicating the virus. Since viruses reproduce by forcing a host cell to make an exact genetic copy, viruses can only change by mutation.

Retroviruses are RNA viruses that infect host cells as RNA but then reproduce within the host cell as DNA. This is the opposite of the process by which information is typically transcribed, so the process is called reverse transcription and the enzyme that causes the process to operate in this way is called reverse transcriptase.

Processes of Cell Division, Differentiation, and Specialization

Cell differentiation

The process by which a cell transforms into another type of cell is known as cell differentiation. A less specialized cell becoming a more specialized cell is a common occurrence for this process.

Every human being is made of trillions of cells that go through the stages of dividing and differentiating. The cells that make up the human body start from one cell which is a fertilized egg known as a zygote. From this starting point, the zygote divides and differentiates into cell that will be responsible for certain tasks.

As a human develops in the womb, the process of cell differentiation is the responsibility of genes. The zygote starts dividing through mitosis into a blastula and then a gastrula. Then the endoderm, mesoderm, and ectoderm are made at this point in the process as the three embryonic germ layers. The endoderm is the inner germ layer. The middle germ layer is the mesoderm, and the ectoderm is outer germ layer. From those embryonic germ layers, a majority of the human body systems are made. For example the digestive system is made from the endoderm; the cardiovascular system is made from the mesoderm; the nervous system is made from the ectoderm.

Mitosis and meiosis

Mitosis

Mitosis is an asexual reproduction process that makes two cells that are genetically identical to the parent cell. While there are cells (e.g., red blood cells and neurons) that usually do not divide, the process of mitosis can occur in almost all healthy adult cells. The total number of chromosomes in the cell nucleus of a human is normally forty-six. Every healthy human cell that is known as diploid (2n) has twenty-three pairs of homologous chromosomes because the nucleus contains forty-six chromosomes. Homologous chromosomes are pairs of chromatids with similar pieces that match to similar genes. Examples include the pairs of chromosome-1 or the pairs of chromosome-21.

Mitosis is divided into the following stages:

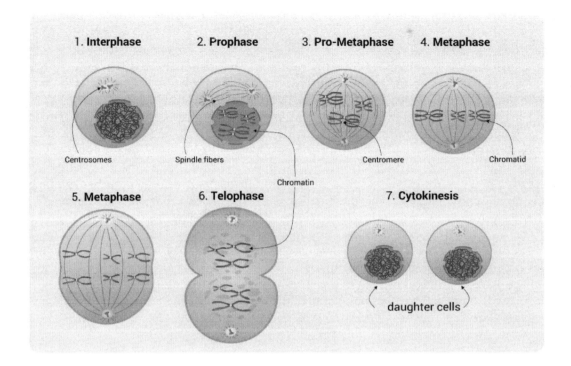

Interphase: The first stage of mitosis is known as which is the point where the cell not dividing; instead, the cell is growing, performing typical maintenance, and synthesizing DNA in the cell nucleus.

Prophase: The already-duplicated chromatin condenses and thus makes chromosomes. Each new chromosome is composed of two identical sister chromatids that are joined by a structure known as a *centromere*. At this point, the nuclear envelope is degraded and spindle fibers form. Then those spindle fibers attach to structures known as *centrioles*. The centrioles separate and move to opposite poles of the cell.

Pro-metaphase: The centrioles build spindle fibers and attach those spindle fibers to the chromosomes.

Metaphase: The chromosomes use tension from the spindle fibers to align in the middle of the cell.

Anaphase: The spindle fibers now contract and separate the chromosomes at their centromere. While being pulled by the spindle fibers, the single chromatids start moving to opposite poles of the cell.

Telophase: The chromatids have finally arrived at opposite poles of the cell. The spindle fibers dissolve, the nuclear envelope reforms, and the chromosomes uncoil back into chromatin.

Cytokinesis: The final stage of mitosis where the separation of the cytoplasm forms two daughter cells that are genetically identical to the parent cell. For animal cells, this occurs through a cleavage furrow. As you can see in the image, the cleavage furrow is a pinching of the cell membrane near the center of the parent cell that continues to deepen until the point where the cell membrane can recombine and split the entity into two cells which are called daughter cells.

Meiosis
Meiosis is a sexual division process that makes four cells called gametes. This process only occurs in specialized cells that are known as sex cells. While the remainder of the human body is made of somatic cells, these sex cells can be found in the ovaries and the testes. The female gamete is known as an egg, and the male gamete is referred to as a sperm. Every gamete is known as haploid (n) instead of diploid (2n) because the gamete has half the number of chromosomes found in a normal, healthy cell. Thus, a gamete totals to twenty-three chromosomes instead of the forty-six which are normally present in somatic cells.

Before the process of meiosis begins, DNA is synthesized, and the chromatin come together to make chromosomes as is done in mitosis. However, the pairs of sister chromatids that are homologous will combine, and they join their centromeres into a single chiasma that makes a tetrad.

At this point begins a process known as crossing over or genetic recombination. This process occurs in prophase I where sections of the different chromatids may separate and rejoin in the same place or possibly a different place. Then, half of a leg of one chromatid may exchange with that of another chromatid. In other words, the chromatids swap some of their genes with each other. An important result of this process is that it increases genetic diversity.

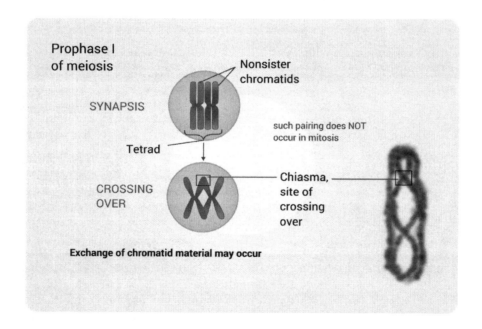

Meiosis is similar to mitosis in that it is divided into the same stages. The steps of prophase, metaphase, anaphase, telophase, and cytokinesis are part of the process. Yet, the end products have half the genetic material of the end products of mitosis. So, another round of division is necessary. This means that meiosis occurs in two parts: meiosis I and meiosis II. Each round is similar to that of mitosis. During meiosis I, homologous chromosome pairs are divided into two daughter cells. Each daughter cell is *haploid* (n). The reason is that while each cell at the end of meiosis I has 46 chromatids half of them are copies of the others. Thus, they are not considered unique genetic material.

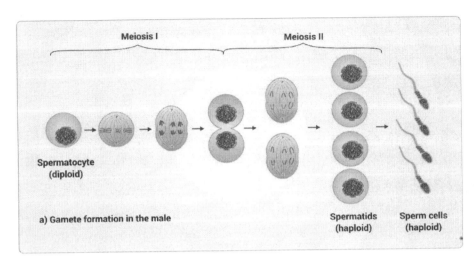

a) Gamete formation in the male

Instead of duplicating DNA or going into Interphase, the daughter cells will move on to prophase II immediately when cytokinesis I is complete. Then, the nucleus breaks down, and the centrioles move to the opposite ends of the cell so the next round of divisions can begin. The process results in four haploid (n) daughter cells. As you may recall, these are the gametes of egg and sperm that were described earlier.

A problem during meiosis and mitosis that can occur in both but is more easily noticed in meiosis is known as nondisjunction. This common problem happens when homologous chromosomes or sister chromatids fail to separate during anaphase. The result of nondisjunction causes the daughter cells to have one more or one less chromosome than would normally occur, and thus we find that genetic conditions stem from this problem. A common example is Down's syndrome where a meiotic egg with nondisjunction is fertilized.

Cell replication

For eukaryotes, cell replication is the duplication of the genetic material (i.e., DNA) and then the division that produces two daughter cells which are identical to the parent cell. The cell cycle is a series of stages that brings about the growth and the division of a cell as well as aiding in the restocking of cells when there are damaged or depleted cells. This cell cycle is completed every twenty-four hours on average for eukaryotic cells.

There are cells like epithelial cells (i.e., skin cells) which are always dividing, and there are cells like mature nerve cells which will never divide. Before mitosis begins, cells are in a non-dividing stage of the cell cycle which you know as Interphase. During Interphase, the cell starts preparation for division by duplicating DNA and the cytoplasmic contents. As you can see in the image, Interphase has three phases: gap 1 (G_1), synthesis (S), and gap 2 (G_2).

The Cell Cycle

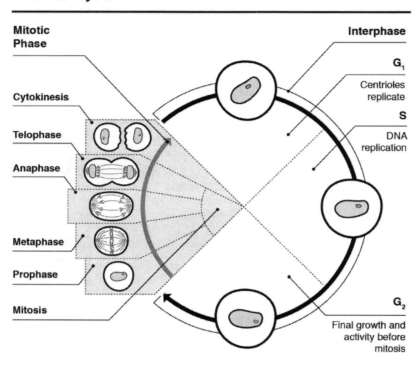

DNA Replication

Replication is the process where DNA makes copies of itself. The governing agent of the major steps of DNA replication is known as enzymes.

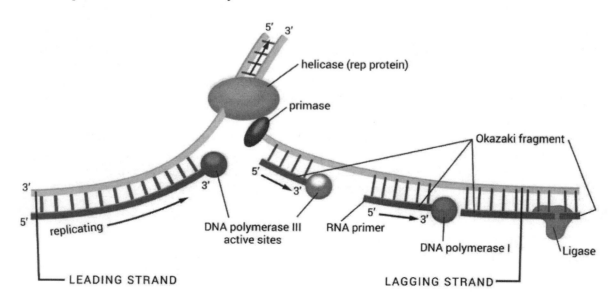

The process of DNA replication starts when *helicase*, an enzyme, uncoils the double helix of DNA. Helicase is able to do this by breaking the weak hydrogen bonds that connect the base pairs. A Y-shape occurs as DNA is uncoiled into a replication fork. The separated strands of DNA will serve as a pattern that will make a new molecule of DNA. The two parts of the replication fork are the leading strand and the lagging strand. As you see in the image, the leading strand is the strand that moves toward the replication fork, and the strand that moves away from the replication fork is known as the lagging strand.

The replication of the leading strand is continuous. DNA polymerase is an enzyme that attaches to the leading strand and adds complementary bases. Replication of the lagging strand of DNA is discontinuous. DNA polymerase produces discontinuous segments that are known as Okazaki fragments which are brought together later by another enzyme known as DNA ligase. When starting the DNA synthesis on the lagging strand, the protein primase lays down a strip of RNA which is referred to as an RNA primer. This primer strip is the piece to which the DNA polymerase can bind. Thus, two copies of the original DNA come from this process. DNA replication is understood as semiconservative. The reason is that half of the new molecule is old, and the remaining is new.

Structure and Functions of the Nervous and Endocrine Systems and Ways in Which These Systems Coordinate the Organ Systems

Endocrine system

The endocrine system is responsible for secreting the hormones and other molecules that help regulate the entire body in both the short and the long term. The endocrine system uses ductless tissues to and glands to secrete hormones into interstitial fluids for bodily regulation. Interstitial fluids surround tissue cells and help to provide a slower process of regulation of physiological needs within the body, whereas the nervous system is responsible for the short term needs. There is a close working relationship between the endocrine system and the nervous system. The hypothalamus and the pituitary gland coordinate to serve as a neuroendocrine control center.

Hormone secretion is triggered by a variety of signals, including hormonal signs, chemical reactions, and environmental cues. Only cells with particular receptors can benefit from hormonal influence. This is the "key in the lock" model for hormonal action. Steroid hormones trigger gene activation and protein synthesis in some target cells. Protein hormones change the activity of existing enzymes in target cells. Hormones such as insulin work quickly when the body signals an urgent need. Slower acting hormones afford longer, gradual, and sometimes permanent changes in the body.

The eight major endocrine glands and their functions are:
- Adrenal cortex – Monitors blood sugar level; helps in lipid and protein metabolism.
- Adrenal medulla – Controls cardiac function; raises blood sugar and controls the size of blood vessels.
- Thyroid gland – Helps regulate metabolism and functions in growth and development.
- Parathyroid – Regulates calcium levels in the blood.
- Pancreas islets – Raises and lowers blood sugar; active in carbohydrate metabolism.

- Thymus gland – Plays a role in immune responses.
- Pineal gland – Has an influence on daily biorhythms and sexual activity.
- Pituitary gland – Plays an important role in growth and development.

Endocrine glands are intimately involved in a myriad of reactions, functions, and secretions that are crucial to the well-being of the body.

Pituitary and Pineal Glands

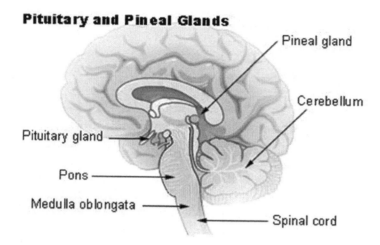

Endocrine functions of the pancreas
Located amongst the groupings of exocrine cells (acini) are groups of endocrine cells (called islets of Langerhans). The islets of Langerhans are primarily made up of insulin-producing beta cells (fifty to eighty percent of the total) and glucagon-releasing alpha cells.

The major hormones produced by the pancreas are insulin and glucagon. The body uses insulin to control carbohydrate metabolism by lowering the amount of sugar (glucose) in the blood. Insulin also affects fat metabolism and can change the liver's ability to release stored fat. The body also uses glucagon to control carbohydrate metabolism. Glucagon has the opposite effect of insulin in that the body uses it to increase blood sugar (glucose) levels. The levels of insulin and glucagon are balanced to maintain the optimum level of blood sugar (glucose) throughout the day.

Thyroid and parathyroid glands
The thyroid and parathyroid glands are located in the neck just below the larynx. The parathyroid glands are four small glands that are embedded on the posterior side of the thyroid gland.

The basic function of the thyroid gland is to regulate metabolism. The thyroid gland secretes the hormones thyroxine, triiodothyronine, and calcitonin. Thyroxine and triiodothyronine increase metabolism, and calcitonin decreases blood calcium by storing calcium in bone tissue.

The hypothalamus directs the pituitary gland to secrete thyroid-stimulating hormone (TSH), which stimulates the thyroid gland to release these hormones as needed via a negative-feedback mechanism. The parathyroid glands secrete parathyroid hormone, which can increase blood calcium by moving calcium from the bone to the blood.

Nervous system

The human nervous system senses, interprets, and issues commands as a response to conditions in the body's environment. This process is made possible by a very complex communication system organized as a grid of neurons.

Messages are sent across the plasma membrane of neurons through a process called action potential. These messages occur when a neuron is stimulated past a necessary threshold. These stimulations occur in a sequence from the stimulation point of one neuron to its contact with another neuron. At the point of contact, called a chemical synapse, a substance is released that stimulates or inhibits the action of the adjoining cell. This network fans out across the body and forms the framework for the nervous system. The direction the information flows depends on the specific organizations of nerve circuits and pathways.

<u>Functional types of neurons</u>
The three general functional types of neurons are the sensory neurons, motor neurons, and interneurons. Sensory neurons transmit signals to the central nervous system (CNS) from the sensory receptors associated with touch, pain, temperature, hearing, sight, smell, and taste. Motor neurons transmit signals from the CNS to the rest of the body such as by signaling muscles or glands to respond. Interneurons transmit signals between neurons; for example, interneurons receive transmitted signals between sensory neurons and motor neurons. In general, a neuron consists of three basic parts: the cell body, the axon, and many dendrites. The dendrites receive impulses from sensory receptors or interneurons and transmit them toward the cell body. The cell body (soma) contains the nucleus of the neuron. The axon transmits the impulses away from the cell body. The axon is insulated by oligodendrocytes and the myelin sheath with gaps known as the nodes of Ranvier. The axon terminates at the synapse.

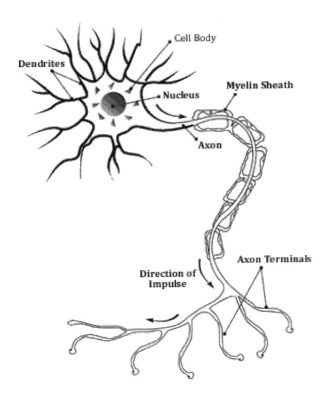

<u>Central nervous system</u>
There are two primary components of the central nervous system:

Spinal Cord: The spinal cord is encased in the bony structure of the vertebrae, which protects and supports it. Its nervous tissue functions mainly with respect to limb movement and internal organ activity. Major nerve tracts ascend and descend from the spinal cord to the brain.

Brain: The brain consists of the hindbrain, midbrain, and forebrain. The hindbrain includes the medulla oblongata, cerebellum, and pons. The midbrain integrates sensory signals and orchestrates responses to these signals. The forebrain includes the cerebrum, thalamus, and hypothalamus. The cerebral cortex is a thin layer of gray matter covering the cerebrum. The brain is divided into two hemispheres, with each responsible for multiple functions. The brain is divided into four main lobes, the frontal lobe, the parietal lobe, the occipital lobe, and the temporal lobes. The frontal lobe located in the front of the brain is responsible for a short term and working memory and information processing as well as decision-making, planning, and judgment. The parietal lobe is located slightly toward the back of the brain and the top of the head and is responsible for sensory input as well as spatial positioning of the body. The occipital lobe is located at the back of the head just above the brain stem. This lobe is responsible for visual input, processing, and output; specifically nerves from the eyes enter directly into this lobe. Finally, the temporal lobes are located at the left and right sides of the brain. These lobes are responsible for all auditory input, processing, and output.

The cerebellum plays a role in the processing and storing of implicit memories. Specifically, for those memories developed during classical conditioning learning techniques. The role of the cerebellum was discovered by exploring the memory of individuals with damaged cerebellums. These individuals were unable to develop stimulus responses when presented via a classical conditioning technique. Researchers found that this was also the case for automatic responses. For example, when these individuals were presented with a puff of air into their eyes, they did not blink, which would have been the naturally occurring and automatic response in an individual with no brain damage.

The posterior area of the brain that is connected to the spinal cord is known as the brain stem. The midbrain, the pons, and the medulla oblongata are the three parts of the brain stem. Information from the body is sent to the brain through the brain stem, and information from the brain is sent to the body through the brain stem. The brain stem is an important part of respiratory, digestive, and circulatory functions.

The midbrain lies above the pons and the medulla oblongata. The parts of the midbrain include the tectum, the tegmentum, and the ventral tegmentum. The midbrain is an important part of vision and hearing. The pons comes between the midbrain and the medulla oblongata. Information is sent across the pons from the cerebrum to the medulla and the cerebellum. The medulla oblongata (or medulla) is beneath the midbrain and the pons. The medulla oblongata is the piece of the brain stem that connects the spinal cord to the brain. So, it has an important role with the autonomous nervous system in the circulatory and respiratory system.

In addition, the peripheral nervous system consists of the nerves and ganglia throughout the body and includes sympathetic nerves that trigger the "fight or flight" response, and the parasympathetic nerves which control basic body function.

Peripheral nervous system

The peripheral nervous system (PNS) refers to all nervous tissue besides the brain and spinal cord. The PNS is divided into the autonomic nervous system and the somatic nervous system and is responsible for all of the functions neglected by the central nervous system.

Autonomic nervous system

The autonomic nervous system (ANS) maintains homeostasis within the body. In general, the ANS controls the functions of the internal organs, blood vessels, smooth muscle tissues, and glands. This is accomplished through the direction of the hypothalamus, which is located above the midbrain. The hypothalamus controls the ANS through the brain stem. With this direction from the hypothalamus, the ANS helps maintain a stable body environment (homeostasis) by regulating numerous factors including heart rate, breathing rate, body temperature, and blood pH.

The ANS consists of two divisions: the sympathetic nervous system and the parasympathetic nervous system. The sympathetic nervous system controls the body's reaction to extreme, stressful, and emergency situations. For example, the sympathetic nervous system increases the heart rate, signals the adrenal glands to secrete adrenaline, triggers the dilation of the pupils, and slows digestion. The parasympathetic nervous system counteracts the effects of the sympathetic nervous system. For example, the parasympathetic nervous system decreases heart rate, signals the adrenal glands to stop secreting adrenaline, constricts the pupils, and returns the digestion process to normal.

Somatic nervous system and reflex arc

The somatic nervous system (SNS) controls the five senses and the voluntary movement of skeletal muscle. So, this system has all of the neurons that are connected to sense organs. Efferent (motor) and afferent (sensory) nerves help the somatic nervous system operate the senses and the movement of skeletal muscle. Efferent nerves bring signals from the central nervous system to the sensory organs and the muscles. Afferent nerves bring signals from the sensory organs and the muscles to the central nervous system. The somatic nervous system also performs involuntary movements which are known as reflex arcs.

A reflex, the simplest act of the nervous system, is an automatic response without any conscious thought to a stimulus via the reflex arc. The reflex arc is the simplest nerve pathway, which bypasses the brain and is controlled by the spinal cord. For example, in the classic knee-jerk response (patellar tendon reflex), the stimulus is the reflex hammer hitting the tendon, and the response is the muscle contracting, which jerks the foot upward. The stimulus is detected by sensory receptors, and a message is sent along a sensory (afferent) neuron to one or more interneurons in the spinal cord. The interneuron(s) transmit this message to a motor (efferent) neuron, which carries the message to the correct effector (muscle).

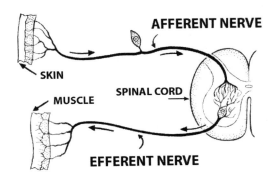

Structure and Integrative Functions of the Main Organ Systems

Anatomy and physiology of various systems of the body

<u>Circulatory system</u>
The circulatory system is a major component of the body which is responsible for transporting fluids and gases, such as blood, hormones, nutrients, and oxygen throughout the body. It is made up of the heart, blood vessels, and blood and is often referred to as the cardiovascular system.

Blood vessels: Blood vessels are the network of tubes that run throughout the body and carry blood. The main types of vessels include arteries, veins, and capillaries, which carry blood in various quantities. Arteries are the largest and carry blood directly from the heart to the rest of the body. Veins act in the opposite way and bring blood from the body back to the heart. Capillaries connect the arteries and veins and help to exchange materials back and forth from blood and cells.

Arteries are less numerous and carry the highest pressure of blood flow, and are therefore stronger and thicker than veins. Arteries are able to also regulate blood-flow through constriction and widening of vessels to ensure that the whole body receives the supply that it needs. These processes are referred to as vasoconstriction (narrowing of blood vessels) and vasodilation (widening of blood vessels). Blood veins have much lower pressure than arteries and contain valves which prevent backflow of blood.

The capillaries are responsible for the most exchange of blood and tissues throughout the body. The three types of capillaries include: continuous, fenestrated, and sinusoidal.
1. Continuous capillaries limit the types of materials that pass into and out of the blood. Their structure includes epithelial cells which are tightly connected together and prevent unwanted matter from being transported into the wrong places. There are more continuous capillaries than the other types of capillaries.
2. Fenestrated capillaries allow the free exchange of material between blood and tissues through openings. Fenestrated capillaries are found in the digestive, endocrine, and urinary systems.
3. Sinusoidal capillaries allow proteins and blood cells through larger openings. Sinusoidal capillaries are found in the liver, bone marrow, and spleen.

Blood: Blood is a liquid tissue used to transport supply cells with nutrients throughout the body and then transport waste away. Adults have between roughly five and six quarts of blood circulating throughout the body. Most of blood is made up of plasma, which is the fluid portion, making up about 55%. The remaining 45% is made up of whole cells and cell parts that contain nutrients and other materials. There are three major types of blood cells:
1. Red blood cells primarily function to carry oxygen out to the rest of the body using a protein called hemoglobin. Iron which is contained in the hemoglobin is what makes blood cells appear red.
2. White blood cells function as part of the immune system by fighting infectious disease. The white blood cells are categorized as one of the following five: neutrophils, lymphocytes, eosinophils, monocytes, and basophils.
3. Platelets play a role in blood-clotting, which helps to heal the body from wounds by stopping the loss of blood. Platelets are cell fragments without nuclei and which are found in large numbers.

The bone marrow is the production hub for all blood cells. Red blood cells are made in the red marrow, whereas white blood cells are made in the yellow marrow.

Heart: The heart is major organ which acts as a powerful blood pump for the whole body. The heart is made up of two parts and four chambers including two atria and two ventricles. The anatomical left and right sides of the heart contain a pair of each and are correspondent to the patient's left and right hand sides.

The heart has four valves that help to keep the chambers separate. The three flaps of the tricuspid valve function to keep blood from backflowing from the ventricle into the atrium where the right atrium and ventricle meets. The two flaps of the mitral valve work similarly between the left atrium and ventricle. The two valves that between the atriums and ventricles and are called atrioventricular valves (AV valves).

The two valves which remain are called semilunar valves (SL valves) and act to regulate blood flow into the two arteries that leave the ventricles. The aortic valve connects the left ventricle to the aorta, while the pulmonary valve connects the right ventricle with the pulmonary artery.

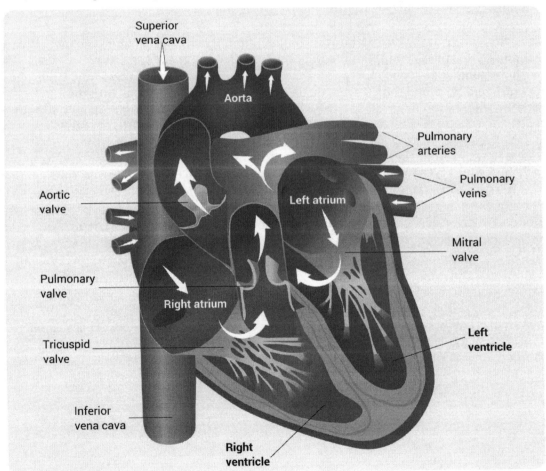

Cardiac cycle: Cardiac activity is quantified by each complete sequence called the cardiac cycle. The cardiac cycle refers to the two phases of the heart (diastole and systole) involving the contraction and relaxation of the heart muscle.

During the diastole phase, the heart relaxes and fills with blood. A corresponding measure is called diastolic blood pressure (DBP), which is the bottom number in a standard blood pressure reading.

During the systole phase, the heart pumps out the blood gathered during the diastolic phase. The corresponding measure of pressure is called systolic blood pressure (SBP), which corresponds to the top number in a standard blood pressure reading. The cardiac cycle is conducted by the heart's electrical conduction system.

Types of circulation

There are five major blood vessels which manage the blood flow to and from the heart. These include the superior and inferior venae cavae, the aorta, the pulmonary artery, and the pulmonary vein.

1. Superior vena cava-a large vein that drains blood from the head and upper body.
2. The inferior vena cava-a large vein that drains blood from the lower body.
3. The aorta-the largest artery in the human body; it carries blood from the heart to body tissues.
4. The pulmonary arteries-these carry blood from the heart to the lungs.
5. The pulmonary veins-these transport blood from the lungs to the heart.

The two types of circulation in the human body include pulmonary circulation and systemic circulation. Pulmonary circulation supplies blood to the lungs so that the blood can be reoxygenated. Deoxygenated blood is routed from the right atrium through the tricuspid valve and into the right ventricle. This blood then travels through the pulmonary valve and into the pulmonary arteries where it then travels to the lungs. The lungs work with the circulatory system to absorb oxygen and release carbon dioxide, which is then transported back into the body. Systemic circulation transports oxygenated blood everywhere in the body except for the lungs. Oxygenated blood flows from the left atrium of the heart through the mitral, or bicuspid, valve into the left ventricle of the heart. The heart routes oxygenated blood from the left ventricle through the aortic valve and into the aorta. This vessel then guides the blood to the systemic arteries and out to the rest of the body. Oxygen and nutrients are exchanged for waste materials and back to the heart via the superior and inferior venae cavae and finally to the right atrium of the heart, which completes the circulatory cycle.

Digestive system

The digestive system is solely responsible for meeting the body's nutritional needs. This system begins with ingestion of foods and drinks, continuing to breaking them down into components which are absorbed for use. After absorption, the nutrients are passed along to the circulatory to transport nutrients to their recipient cells for growth, energy, and repair. The various nutrients are classified as proteins, lipids (or fats), carbohydrates, vitamins, and minerals.

The digestive system is divided into the following:

1. Digestive tract–the pathway for ingestion, digestion, absorption, and excretion. This includes the mouth, pharynx, esophagus, stomach, intestines, rectum, and anus. This subsystem is sometimes called the gastrointestinal tract or alimentary tract. The body uses contractions to push food and products throughout the body. This process is called peristalsis.
2. Accessory digestive organs-including salivary glands, liver, gallbladder, and pancreas. These organs supplement the digestive tract with processing the nutrients throughout digestion.

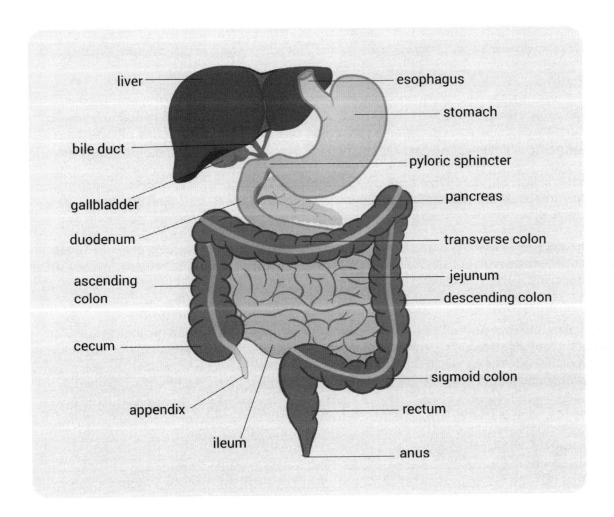

Mouth and stomach

Food and drink are first introduced to the body through the mouth. Mechanical and chemical pre-digestion of the food begin here through saliva and chewing. The teeth and tongue work to soften and shape food into a bolus to be more easily transported by the esophagus. The saliva adds to the pliability of the food. Saliva is produced by the salivary glands and includes amylase, which is a digestive enzyme used for early breaking down of carbohydrates and sugars in food. The largest of the salivary glands are the parotid glands. After swallowing, the food moves through the pharynx and esophagus into the stomach.

As the bolus moves along the digestive tract, it is subjected to more mechanical and chemical digestion in the stomach. The stomach is a large muscular sac-like organ which squeezes and adds more chemical secretions to break the bolus down into a nutrient-filled liquid known as chyme. After the stomach processes the bolus into chyme, it is transported into the small intestine.

The stomach produces many secretions into the lumen of the digestive tract, which is an open space in the digestive tract. Some cells in the stomach produce a hormone called gastrin, which acts to prompt other cells to secrete acid for further digestion. The primary acid involved in this process is hydrochloric acid (HCL), which has a very low pH and can therefore degrade most organic matter and proteins. The stomach secretes a mucous to protect itself from corroding its own cells. If the stomach leaves gaps in the mucosal layer, peptic ulcers can form. The stomach uses enzymes such as proteases and lipases to break down proteins and fats where the gastric acid may have missed.

Small intestine

The small intestine takes over after the stomach. The chyme from the stomach is first passed through the pyloric sphincter, which partly neutralizes the stomach acid with sodium bicarbonate and mucous. Through the pyloric sphincter, the chyme is passed into the duodenum, which is the first section of the small intestine. The chyme then triggers a secretion in the duodenum of secretin and cholecystokinin (CCK), which are hormones used in regulating pH levels and waste management. In specific, the chyme triggers secretion of secretin to release more sodium bicarbonate into the small intestine if the chyme is still too acidic. The CCK then acts to release a substance called bile which further helps to dissolve or emulsify fats and lipids.

The duodenum is the chief site of the fat digestion in the digestive tract because of its use of bile and lipases for breaking down and absorbing lipids. The duodenum also acts as the final primary site of chemical digestion, as the later sections of the small intestine (jejunum and ileum) act more in absorption than in breaking down of chemicals.

The small intestine uses finger-like cell projections, which are known as villi to aid in absorption and can be as long as 40 feet. These projections are used primarily in transferring the nutrients from digested food to the bloodstream for later use. This system is very efficient and uses nearly all of the available nutrients including simple sugars, amino acids, emulsified fats, electrolytes, minerals, and vitamins from a wide variety of sources. Absorption of many nutrients in the intestine is also aided by what is known as intrinsic factor, an agent infused with the chyme in the stomach.

Large intestine

Not all of the food that is ingested is absorbed in the stomach or lumen of the small intestine, but is passed along through the large intestine, also known as the large bowl or colon. Whereas the small intestine is primarily responsible for absorption of nutrients, the large intestine is primarily responsible for absorbing water. The body has now taken nearly all of the useful nutrients out of the chyme and has been categorized as waste, and it is passed through the large intestine until eliminated from the body. The body then removes the liquid from the waste and translates it back into solid stool, or feces.

This final waste first passes from the small intestine into the cecum, which is the first portion of the large intestine. In herbivores, the cecum acts as a place for bacteria to digest cellulose but has little function in human digestion and is known as the appendix. The waste then passes from the cecum into the ascending colon, across the transverse colon, down the descending colon, and finally through the sigmoid colon and into the rectum. The rectum is the final storage location for waste before being eliminated from the body through the anus and outside of the body.

Pancreas

The pancreas is a glandular organ in the digestive tract which serves to release hormones, such as insulin (decreases blood glucose levels) and glucagon (increases blood glucose levels) directly into the bloodstream and through ducts in the body. Both hormones are produced in the islets of Langerhans—insulin in the beta cells and glucagon in the alpha cells. The release of hormones makes the pancreas pertain to the endocrine and exocrine systems as well as the digestive tract.

The major part of the pancreas gland has an exocrine function. This function consists of acinar cells secreting inactive digestive enzymes (zymogens) into the main pancreatic duct. The pancreatic ducts and the common bile ducts join to empty into the small intestine, specifically the duodenum. As these hormones are released, the digestive enzymes activate and help initiate the digestion of carbohydrates, proteins, and fats within chyme.

Immune system

The immunes system functions to prevent and protect the body from infections. This is the body's offense against various harmful microorganisms including bacteria, viruses, fungi, parasites, and other harmful substances.

The body is naturally immune to the permeation of foreign and harmful substances due to physical barriers. This passive immunity is referred to as innate immunity. Forms of innate immunity include skin, mucous membranes, and acids or other chemicals that block or destroy these harmful substances. The skin physically stops unwanted matter from entering the underlying tissue. Mucous membranes both block and remove microorganisms through mucus secretion in the digestive, respiratory, and urinary systems. Other secretions including saliva, tears, and stomach acids use helpful microorganisms and chemicals to block bodily infection. Macrophages and other forms of white blood cells also contribute in eliminating foreign bodies through the processes of direct lysis and phagocytosis (engulfing the foreign body).

The body can also attain acquired immunity by learning information about a type of microorganism. This process takes place through a specific set of events, such as coming into contact with a pathogen and either acquire immunity or by learning how to fight it in a more effective way than with innate immunity alone.

Acquired immunity has two separate phases of response. The first time the body comes into contact with a particular pathogen, macrophages absorb the foreign body and bring it to the lymph nodes. This is often referred to as the primary immune response. The lymph nodes exist throughout the body and work to help the body in the process of adapting this immune response. Within the lymph nodes, the foreign body is presented to cells called helper T lymphocytes, which then activate humoral immunity and cellular immunity. T lymphocytes are often referred to as T cells.

Humoral immunity refers to the protection of the body provided by antibodies. B lymphocytes are cued by the helper T lymphocytes and reproduce themselves into plasma cells and memory cells. These plasma cells are type of B lymphocyte that produce antibodies (also known as immunoglobulins), which are a form of immune proteins. These antibodies bond themselves to identified pathogens and identify them to white blood cells for elimination.

The immune response coordinated by helper T lymphocytes is referred to as cellular immunity. The helper T lymphocytes initially work to identify pathogens and after activation, other T lymphocytes directly attack and destroy identified threats.

Each encounter with known microorganisms is referred to as a secondary immune response. Memory cells previously created during the primary encounter will immediately produce antibodies. Since the various steps in information gathering do not need to take place in a secondary immune response, the response is much swifter and efficient.

Another form of T cells includes Suppressor T lymphocytes, which cat to prevent the immune system from being too active and causing damage to the healthy cells in the body.

<u>Active and passive immunity</u>
Immunization is the process of the body learning to protect the body from infectious microorganisms. Immunization can take place either actively or passively. The immunity that comes through singular or repeated exposure to pathogens is referred to as active immunization. In this process, the body learns how to fight infections on its own either naturally or artificially. Natural immunization happens as a result of encountering an infection naturally through daily life. Artificial immunization may also take place through intentional therapeutic exposure to infectious organisms to preemptively teach the body how to fight a disease. This is very common in today's medical practice.

Most artificial immunization takes place through the use of vaccines. Vaccines are an agent containing weakened, killed, or inactivated pathogens which are administered to a recipient to prevent future infections. These do not always guarantee immunity or may only protect against limited stands of pathogens. Vaccines may be administered through injection, oral ingestion, or through aerosol.

Immunity gained by introducing antibodies into the body is referred to as passive immunity. This process takes place in fetal development and in infants through the temporary passing of immune function from one person to another, typically through the share of antibodies in the womb or through breastfeeding. This type of passive immunity is referred to as naturally acquired, however artificially acquired passive immunity is possible.

Integumentary system

The integumentary system, which consists of the skin including the sebaceous glands, sweat glands, hair, and nails, serves a variety of functions associated with protection, secretion, and communication. In the functions associated with protection, the integumentary system protects the body from pathogens including bacteria, viruses, and various chemicals. In the functions associated with secretion, sebaceous glands secrete sebum (oil) that waterproofs the skin, and sweat glands are associated with the body's homeostatic relationship of thermoregulation. Sweat glands also serve as excretory organs and help rid the body of metabolic wastes. In the functions associated with communication, sensory receptors distributed throughout the skin send information to the brain regarding pain, touch, pressure, and temperature. In addition to protection, secretion, and communication, the skin manufactures vitamin D and can absorb certain chemicals such as specific medications.

Layers of the skin

The layers of the skin from the surface of the skin inward are the epidermis and dermis. The subcutaneous layer lying below the dermis is also part of the integumentary system. The epidermis is the most superficial layer of the skin. The epidermis, which consists entirely of epithelial cells, does not contain any blood vessels. The deepest portion of the epidermis is the stratum basale, which is a single layer of cells that continually undergo division. As more and more cells are produced, older cells are pushed toward the surface. Most epidermal cells are keratinized. Keratin is a waxy protein that helps to waterproof the skin. As the cells die, they are sloughed off. The dermis lies directly beneath the epidermis. The dermis consists mostly of connective tissue. The dermis contains blood vessels, sensory receptors, hair follicles, sebaceous glands, and sweat glands. The dermis also contains elastin and collagen fibers. The subcutaneous layer or hypodermis is actually not a layer of the skin. The subcutaneous layer consists of connective tissue, which binds the skin to the underlying muscles. Fat deposits in the subcutaneous layer help to cushion and insulate the body.

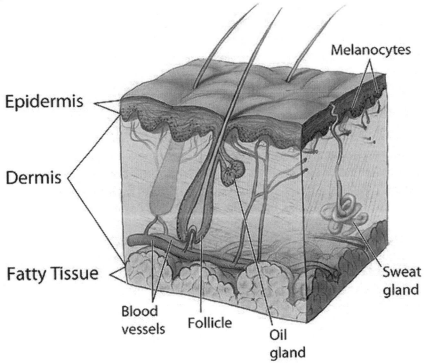

Skin's involvement in temperature homeostasis

The skin is involved in temperature homeostasis or thermoregulation through the activation of the sweat glands. By thermoregulation, the body maintains a stable body temperature as one component of a stable internal environment. The temperature of the body is controlled by a negative feedback system consisting of a receptor, control center, and effector. The receptors are sensory cells located in the dermis of the skin. The control center is the hypothalamus, which is located in the brain. The effectors include the sweat glands, blood vessels, and muscles (shivering). The evaporation of sweat across the surface of the skin cools the body to maintain its tolerance range. Vasodilation of the blood vessels near the surface of the skin also releases heat into the environment to lower body temperature. Shivering is associated with the muscular system.

Sebaceous glands vs. sweat glands

Sebaceous glands and sweat glands are exocrine glands found in the skin. Exocrine glands secrete substances into ducts. In this case, the secretions are through the ducts to the surface of the skin.

Sebaceous glands are holocrine glands, which secrete sebum. Sebum is an oily mixture of lipids and proteins. Sebaceous glands are connected to hair follicles and secrete sebum through the hair pore. Sebum inhibits water loss from the skin and protects against bacterial and fungal infections.

Sweat glands are either eccrine glands or apocrine glands. Eccrine glands are not connected to hair follicles. They are activated by elevated body temperature. Eccrine glands are located throughout the body and can be found on the forehead, neck, and back. Eccrine glands secrete a salty solution of electrolytes and water containing sodium chloride, potassium, bicarbonate, glucose, and antimicrobial peptides.

Eccrine glands are activated as part of the body's thermoregulation. Apocrine glands secrete an oily solution containing fatty acids, triglycerides, and proteins. Apocrine glands are located in the armpits, groin, palms, and soles of the feet. Apocrine glands secrete this oily sweat when a person experiences stress or anxiety. Bacteria feed on apocrine sweat and expel aromatic fatty acids, producing body odor.

Lymphatic system

The lymphatic system is connected to the cardiovascular system through a network of capillaries. The lymphatic system filters out organisms that cause disease, controls the production of disease-fighting antibodies, and produces white blood cells. The lymphatic system also prevents body tissues from swelling by draining fluids from them. Two of the most important areas in this system are the right lymphatic duct and the thoracic duct. The right lymphatic duct moves the immunity-bolstering lymph fluid through the top half of the body, while the thoracic duct moves lymph throughout the lower half. The spleen, thymus, and lymph nodes all generate and store the chemicals which form lymph and which are essential to protecting the body from disease. The lymphatic system works with the immune system and also contains a large number of white blood cells to help identify and attack harmful microorganisms. Organs of the lymphatic system include the spleen, lymph nodes (between 600 and 700 total), tonsils, adenoids, and thymus.

Muscular system

The muscular system is responsible for all of the external motions that the body is able to perform. The muscles correspond and work together with the skeletal system to provide the body with support and protection from the outside world. There are roughly 700 muscles in the body which make up about half of the body's weight.

There are three types of muscle tissue: skeletal, cardiac, and smooth. There are over 600 muscles in the human body. All muscles have these three properties in common:
- Excitability – All muscle tissues have an electric gradient which can reverse when stimulated.
- Contraction – All muscle tissues have the ability to contract, or shorten.
- Elongate – All muscle tissues share the capacity to elongate, or relax.

<u>Types of muscular tissue</u>
The three types of muscular tissue are skeletal muscle, smooth muscle, and cardiac muscle.

Skeletal muscles are voluntary muscles that work in pairs to move various parts of the skeleton. Skeletal muscles are composed of muscle fibers (cells) that are bound together in parallel bundles. Skeletal muscles are also known as striated muscle due to their striped appearance under a microscope.

Smooth muscle tissues are involuntary muscles that are found in the walls of internal organs such as the stomach, intestines, and blood vessels. Smooth muscle tissues or visceral tissue is nonstriated. Smooth muscle cells are shorter and wider than skeletal muscle fibers. Smooth muscle tissue is also found in sphincters or valves that control various openings throughout the body.

Cardiac muscle tissue is involuntary muscle that is found only in the heart. Like skeletal muscle cells, cardiac muscle cells are also striated.

Only skeletal muscle interacts with the skeleton to move the body. When they contract, the muscles transmit force to the attached bones. Working together, the muscles and bones act as a system of levers which move around the joints. A small contraction of a muscle can produce a large movement. A limb can be extended and rotated around a joint due to the way the muscles are arranged. The muscles connect to bones through dense connective tissue called tendons which help provide support and protection in motion.

Movements of muscles all work through contractions working in different directions. Primary movers are called agonists, which provide one specific movement, such as flexion at the knee. Antagonist muscles work in the opposite direction to provide a full range of movements in two directions. The third classification of muscle use is synergist muscles. These muscles may help with motion in one direction, but primarily serve to support the stabilization of a joint or prevent harmful movement.

Reproductive system

The reproductive system of the human body is responsible solely for the production and utilization of reproductive cells, or gametes. The reproductive organs include reproductive organs, the reproductive tract, the perineal structures (external genitalia), and accessory glands and organs responsible for secreting fluids into the reproductive tract.

<u>Male reproductive system</u>
The functions of the male reproductive system are to produce, maintain, and transfer sperm and semen into the female reproductive tract and to produce and secrete male hormones.

The external structure includes the penis, scrotum, and testes. The penis, which contains the urethra, can fill with blood and become erect, enabling the deposition of semen and sperm into the female reproductive tract during sexual intercourse. The scrotum is a sac of skin and smooth muscle that houses the testes and keeps the testes at the proper temperature for spermatogenesis. The testes, or testicles, are the male gonads, which produce sperm and testosterone.

The internal structure includes the epididymis, vas deferens, ejaculatory ducts, urethra, seminal vesicles, prostate gland, and bulbourethral glands. The epididymis stores the sperm as it matures. Mature sperm moves from the epididymis through the vas deferens to the ejaculatory duct. The seminal vesicles secrete alkaline fluids with proteins and mucus into the ejaculatory duct, also. The prostate gland secretes a milky white fluid with proteins and enzymes as part of the semen. The bulbourethral, or Cowper's, glands secrete a fluid into the urethra to neutralize the acidity in the urethra.

Additionally, the hormones associated with the male reproductive system include follicle-stimulating hormone, which stimulates spermatogenesis; luteinizing hormone, which stimulates testosterone production; and testosterone, which is responsible for the male sex characteristics.

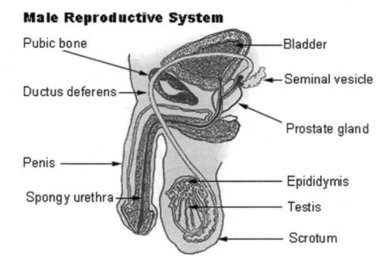

Male Reproductive System

Pubic bone — Bladder

Ductus deferens — Seminal vesicle

Prostate gland

Penis —

Spongy urethra — Epididymis

Testis

Scrotum

Female reproductive system
The functions of the female reproductive system are to produce ova (oocytes, or egg cells), transfer the ova to the fallopian tubes for fertilization, receive the sperm from the male, and to provide a protective, nourishing environment for the developing embryo.

The external portion of the female reproductive system includes the labia majora, labia minora, Bartholin's glands and clitoris. The labia majora and the labia minora enclose and protect the vagina. The Bartholin's glands secrete a lubricating fluid. The clitoris contains erectile tissue and nerve endings for sensual pleasure.

The internal portion of the female reproductive system includes the ovaries, fallopian tubes, uterus, and vagina. The ovaries, which are the female gonads, produce the ova and secrete estrogen and progesterone. The fallopian tubes carry the mature egg toward the uterus. Fertilization typically occurs in the fallopian tubes. If fertilized, the egg travels to the uterus, where it implants in the uterine wall. The uterus protects and nourishes the developing embryo until birth. The vagina is a muscular tube that extends from the cervix of the uterus to the outside of the body. The vagina receives the semen and sperm during sexual intercourse and provides a birth canal when needed.

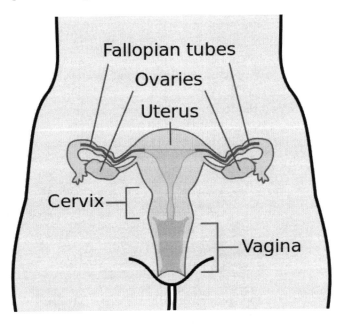

Respiratory system

Structure

The respiratory system can be divided into the upper and lower respiratory system. The upper respiratory system includes the nose, nasal cavity, mouth, pharynx, and larynx. The lower respiratory system includes the trachea, lungs, and bronchial tree. Alternatively, the components of the respiratory system can be categorized as part of the airway, the lungs, or the respiratory muscles. The airway includes the nose, nasal cavity, mouth, pharynx, (throat), larynx (voice box), trachea (windpipe), bronchi, and bronchial network. The airway is lined with cilia that trap microbes and debris and sweep them back toward the mouth. The lungs are structures that house the bronchi and bronchial network, which extend into the lungs and terminate in millions of alveoli (air sacs). The walls of the alveoli are only one cell thick, allowing for the exchange of gases with the blood capillaries that surround them. The right lung has three lobes. The left lung only has two lobes, leaving room for the heart on the left side of the body. The lungs are surrounded by a pleural membrane, which reduces friction between surfaces when breathing. The respiratory muscles include the diaphragm and the intercostal muscles. The diaphragm is a dome-shaped muscle that separates the thoracic and abdominal cavities. The intercostal muscles are located between the ribs.

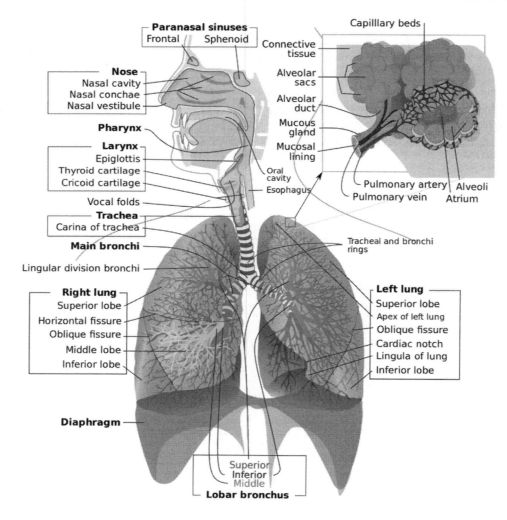

<u>Functions</u>

The main function of the respiratory system is to supply the body with oxygen and rid the body of carbon dioxide. This exchange of gases occurs in millions of tiny alveoli, which are surrounded by blood capillaries.

The respiratory system also filters air. Air is warmed, moistened, and filtered as it passes through the nasal passages before it reaches the lungs.

The respiratory system is responsible for speech. As air passes through the throat, it moves through the larynx (voice box), which vibrates and produces sound, before it enters the trachea (windpipe). The respiratory system is vital in cough production. Foreign particles entering the nasal passages or airways are expelled from the body by the respiratory system.

The respiratory system functions in the sense of smell. Chemoreceptors that are located in the nasal cavity respond to airborne chemicals. The respiratory system also helps the body maintain acid-base homeostasis. Hyperventilation can increase blood pH during acidosis (low pH). Slowing breathing during alkalosis (high pH) helps to lower blood pH.

<u>Breathing process</u>

During the breathing process, the diaphragm and the intercostal muscles contract to expand the lungs.

During inspiration or inhalation, the diaphragm contracts and moves down, increasing the size of the chest cavity. The intercostal muscles contract and the ribs expand, increasing the size of the chest cavity. As the volume of the chest cavity increases, the pressure inside the chest cavity decreases. Because the outside air is under a greater amount of pressure than the air inside the lungs, air rushes into the lungs.

When the diaphragm and intercostal muscles relax, the size of the chest cavity decreases, forcing air out of the lungs (expiration or exhalation). The breathing process is controlled by the portion of the brain stem called the medulla oblongata. The medulla oblongata monitors the level of carbon dioxide in the blood and signals the breathing rate to increase when these levels are too high.

Skeletal system

The skeletal structure in humans contains both bones and cartilage. Over 200 bones in the human body can be divided into two parts:
- Axial skeleton – Includes the skull, sternum, ribs, and vertebral column (the spine).
- Appendicular skeleton – Includes the bones of the arms, feet, hands, legs, hips, and shoulders.

Adult human skeleton

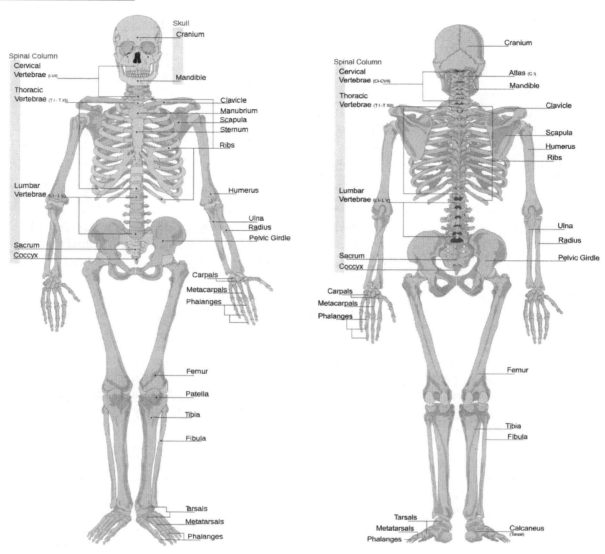

Axial skeleton and the appendicular skeleton

The human skeletal system, which consists of 206 bones along with numerous tendons, ligaments, and cartilage, is divided into the axial skeleton and the appendicular skeleton. The axial skeleton consists of 80 bones and includes the vertebral column, rib cage, sternum, skull, and hyoid bone. The vertebral column consists of 33 vertebrae classified as cervical vertebrae, thoracic vertebrae, lumbar vertebrae, and sacral vertebrae. The rib cage includes 12 paired ribs, 10 pairs of true ribs and 2 pairs of floating ribs, and the sternum, which consists of the manubrium, corpus sterni, and xiphoid process. The skull includes the cranium and facial bones. The ossicles are bones in the middle ear. The hyoid bone provides an attachment point for the tongue muscles. The axial skeleton protects vital organs including the brain, heart, and lungs. The appendicular skeleton consists of 126 bones including the pectoral girdle, pelvic girdle, and appendages. The pectoral girdle consists of the scapulae (shoulders) and clavicles (collarbones). The pelvic girdle consists of two pelvic (hip) bones, which attach to the sacrum. The upper appendages (arms) include the humerus, radius, ulna, carpals, metacarpals, and phalanges. The lower appendages (legs) include the femur, patella, fibula, tibia, tarsals, metatarsals, and phalanges.

Functions of the skeletal system

The skeletal system serves many functions including providing structural support, providing movement, providing protection, producing blood cells, and storing substances such as fat and minerals. The skeletal system provides the body with structure and support for the muscles and organs. The axial skeleton transfers the weight from the upper body to the lower appendages. The skeletal system provides movement with joints and the muscular system. Bones provide attachment points for muscles. Joints including hinge joints, ball-and-socket joints, pivot joints, ellipsoid joints, gliding joints, and saddle joints. Each muscle is attached to two bones: the origin and the insertion. The origin remains immobile, and the insertion is the bone that moves as the muscle contracts and relaxes. The skeletal system serves to protect the body. The cranium protects the brain. The vertebrae protect the spinal cord. The rib cage protects the heart and lungs. The pelvis protects the reproductive organs. The red marrow manufactures red and white blood cells. All bone marrow is red at birth, but adults have approximately one-half red bone marrow and one-half yellow bone marrow. Yellow bone marrow stores fat. Also, the skeletal system provides a reservoir to store the minerals calcium and phosphorus.

The skeletal system has an important role in the following body functions:
- Movement – The action of skeletal muscles on bones moves the body.
- Mineral Storage – Bones serve as storage facilities for essential mineral ions.
- Support – Bones act as a framework and support system for the organs.
- Protection – Bones surround and protect key organs in the body.
- Blood Cell Formation – Red blood cells are produced in the marrow of certain bones.

Bones are classified as long, short, flat, or irregular. They are a connective tissue with a base of pulp containing collagen and living cells. Bone tissue is constantly regenerating itself as the mineral composition changes. This allows for special needs during growth periods and maintains calcium levels for the body. Bone regeneration can deteriorate in old age, particularly among women, leading to osteoporosis.

The flexible and curved backbone is supported by muscles and ligaments. Intervertebral discs are stacked one above another and provide cushioning for the backbone. Trauma or shock may cause these discs to herniate and cause pain. The sensitive spinal cord is enclosed in a cavity which is well protected by the bones of the vertebrae.

Joints are areas of contact adjacent to bones. Synovial joints are the most common, and are freely moveable. These may be found at the shoulders and knees. Cartilaginous joints fill the spaces between some bones and restrict movement. Examples of cartilaginous joints are those between vertebrae. Fibrous joints have fibrous tissue connecting bones and no cavity is present.

<u>Compact and spongy bone</u>

Compact Bone & Spongy (Cancellous) Bone

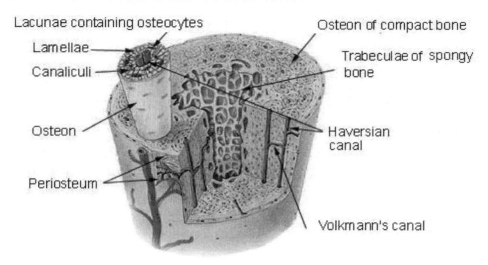

Two types of connective bone tissue include compact bone and spongy bone.

Compact, or cortical, bone, which consists of tightly packed cells, is strong, dense, and rigid. Running vertically throughout compact bone are the Haversian canals, which are surrounded by concentric circles of bone tissue called lamellae. The spaces between the lamellae are called the lacunae. These lamellae and canals along with their associated arteries, veins, lymph vessels, and nerve endings are referred to collectively as the Haversian system.

The Haversian system provides a reservoir for calcium and phosphorus for the blood. Also, bones have a thin outside layer of compact bone, which gives them their characteristic smooth, white appearance.

Spongy, or cancellous, bone consists of trabeculae, which are a network of girders with open spaces filled with red bone marrow.

Compared to compact bone, spongy bone is lightweight and porous, which helps reduce the bone's overall weight. The red marrow manufactures red and white blood cells. In long bones, the diaphysis consists of compact bone surrounding the marrow cavity and spongy bone containing red marrow in the epiphyses. Bones have varying amounts of compact bone and spongy bone depending on their classification.

Special senses

Special senses include vision, hearing and balance, smell, and taste and are differentiated from the general senses due to special somatic afferents and special visceral afferents. These are both types of nerve fibers which communicate with the central nervous system (CNS), as well as their specialized organs devoted to their function. Touch is generally discussed in conjunction with the special senses, however it is not associated with just one particular organ. These special senses help to provide the body with information not directly attributable to a direct stimulus. The skin is the largest organ of the body and contributes the most tactile information including pain, heat, and mechanoreceptors (or pressure sensing).These tactile messages are transported with general somatic afferents and general visceral afferents.

Urinary system

The urinary system is capable of eliminating excess substances while preserving the substances needed by the body to function. The urinary system consists of the kidneys, urinary ducts, and bladder.

Components of the Urinary System

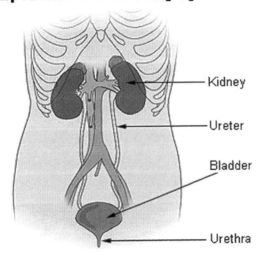

Kidney

Ureter

Bladder

Urethra

<u>Kidneys</u>
The kidneys are bean-shaped structures that are located at the back of the abdominal cavity just under the diaphragm. Each kidney consists of three layers: the renal cortex (outer layer), renal medulla (inner layer), and renal pelvis (innermost portion).

The renal cortex is composed of approximately one million nephrons, which are the tiny, individual filters of the kidneys. Each nephron contains a cluster of capillaries called a glomerulus surrounded by the cup-shaped Bowman's capsule, which leads to a tubule.

The kidneys receive blood from the renal arteries, which branch off the aorta. In general, the kidneys filter the blood, reabsorb needed materials, and secrete wastes and excess water in the urine. More specifically, blood flows from the renal arteries into arterioles into the glomerulus, where it is filtered. The glomerular filtrate enters the proximal convoluted tubule where water, glucose, ions, and other organic molecules are reabsorbed back into the bloodstream.

Additional substances such as urea and drugs are removed from the blood in the distal convoluted tubule. Also, the pH of the blood can be adjusted in the distal convoluted tubule by the secretion of hydrogen ions. Finally, the unabsorbed materials flow out from the collecting tubules located in the renal medulla to the renal pelvis as urine. Urine is drained from the kidneys through the ureters to the urinary bladder, where it is stored until expulsion from the body through the urethra.

Chemical and Physical Foundations

Translational Motion, Forces, Work, Energy, and Equilibrium in Living Systems

Translational motion

There are three key concepts used to describe how matter moves:
- Displacement
- Velocity
- Acceleration

Displacement
Concept: where and how far an object has gone
Calculation: final position – initial position

When something changes its location from one place to another, it is said to have undergone displacement. If a golf ball is hit across a sloped green into the hole, the displacement only takes into account the final and initial locations, not the path of the ball.

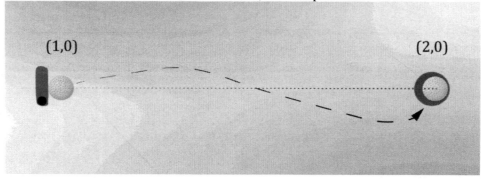

Displacement along a straight line is a very simple example of a vector quantity: that is, it has both a magnitude and a direction. Direction is as important as magnitude in many measurements. If we can determine the original and final position of the object, then we can determine the total displacement with this simple equation:
$$\text{Displacement} = \text{final position} - \text{original position}$$

The hole (final position) is at the Cartesian coordinate location $(2, 0)$ and the ball is hit from the location $(1, 0)$. The displacement is:
$$\text{Displacement} = (2,0) - (1,0)$$
$$\text{Displacement} = (1,0)$$

The displacement has a magnitude of 1 and a direction of the positive x direction.

Velocity
Concept: the rate of moving from one position to another
Calculation: change in position / change in time

Velocity answers the question, "How quickly is an object moving?" For example, if a car and a plane travel east between two cities which are a hundred miles apart, but the car takes two hours and the plane takes one hour, the car has the same displacement as the plane, but a smaller velocity.

In order to solve some of the problems on the exam, you may need to assess the velocity of an object. If we want to calculate the average velocity of an object, we must know two things. First, we must know its displacement. Second, we must know the time it took to cover this distance. The formula for average velocity is quite simple:

$$\text{average velocity} = \frac{\text{displacement}}{\text{change in time}}$$

Or

$$\text{average velocity} = \frac{\text{final position} - \text{original position}}{\text{final time} - \text{original time}}$$

To complete the example, the velocity of the plane is calculated to be:

$$\text{plane average velocity} = \frac{100 \text{ miles east}}{1 \text{ hour}} = 100 \text{ miles per hour east}$$

The velocity of the car is less:

$$\text{car average velocity} = \frac{100 \text{ miles east}}{2 \text{ hours}} = 50 \text{ miles per hour east}$$

Often, people confuse the words *speed* and *velocity*. There is a significant difference. The average velocity is based on the amount of displacement, a vector. Alternately, the average speed is based on the distance covered or the path length. The equation for speed is:

$$\text{average speed} = \frac{\text{total distance traveled}}{\text{change in time}}$$

Notice that we used total distance and *not* change in position, because speed is path-dependent.

If the plane traveling between cities had needed to fly around a storm on its way, making the distance traveled 50 miles greater than the distance the car traveled, the plane would still have the same total displacement as the car.

The calculation for the speed: For this reason, average speed can be calculated:

$$\text{plane average speed} = \frac{150 \text{ miles}}{1 \text{ hour}} = 150 \text{ miles per hour}$$

$$\text{car average speed} = \frac{100 \text{ miles}}{2 \text{ hours}} = 50 \text{ miles per hour}$$

Acceleration

Concept: how quickly something changes from one velocity to another

Calculation: change in velocity / change in time

Acceleration is the rate of change of the velocity of an object. If a car accelerates from zero velocity to 60 miles per hour (88 feet per second) in two seconds, the car has an impressive acceleration. But if a car performs the same change in velocity in eight seconds, the acceleration is much lower and not as impressive.

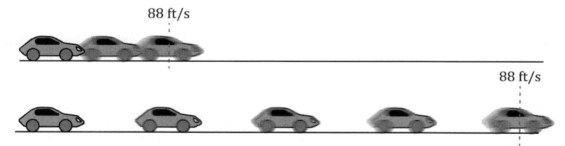

To calculate average acceleration, we may use the equation:

$$\text{average acceleration} = \frac{\text{change in velocity}}{\text{change in time}}$$

The acceleration of the cars is found to be:

$$\text{Car \#1 average acceleration} = \frac{88 \text{ feet per second}}{2 \text{ seconds}} = 44 \frac{\text{feet}}{\text{second}^2}$$

$$\text{Car \#2 average acceleration} = \frac{88 \text{ feet per second}}{8 \text{ seconds}} = 11 \frac{\text{feet}}{\text{second}^2}$$

- 64 -

Acceleration will be expressed in units of distance divided by time squared; for instance, meters per second squared or feet per second squared.

Force

Concept: a push or pull on an object
Calculation: $Force = mass \times acceleration$

A force is a vector which causes acceleration of a body. Force has both magnitude and direction. Furthermore, multiple forces acting on one object combine in vector addition. This can be demonstrated by considering an object placed at the origin of the coordinate plane. If it is pushed along the positive direction of the x-axis, it will move in this direction; if the force acting on it is in the positive direction of the y-axis, it will move in that direction.

However, if both forces are applied at the same time, then the object will move at an angle to both the x and y axes, an angle determined by the relative amount of force exerted in each direction. In this way, we may see that the resulting force is a vector sum; that is, a net force that has both magnitude and direction.

Resultant vectors from applied forces:

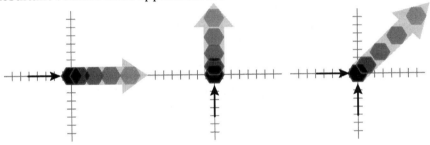

Newton's three laws of mechanics

The questions on the exam may require you to demonstrate familiarity with the concepts expressed in Newton's three laws of motion which relate to the concept of force.

Newton's first law – A body at rest will tend to remain at rest, while a body in motion will tend to remain in motion, unless acted upon by an external force.

Newton's second law – The acceleration of an object is directly proportional to the force being exerted on it and inversely proportional to its mass.

Newton's third law – For every force, there is an equal and opposite force.

First Law: Concept: Unless something interferes, an object won't start or stop moving

Although intuition supports the idea that objects do not start moving until a force acts on them, the idea of an object continuing forever without any forces can seem odd. Before Newton formulated his laws of mechanics, general thought held that some force had to act on an object continuously in order for it to move at a constant velocity. This seems to make sense: when an object is briefly pushed, it will eventually come to a stop. Newton, however, determined that unless some other force acted on the object (most notably friction or air resistance), it would continue in the direction it was pushed at the same velocity forever.

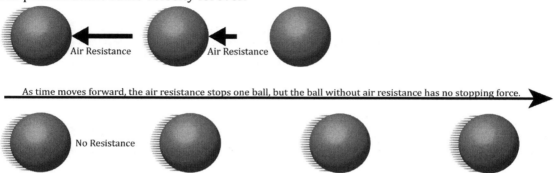

Second Law: Concept: Acceleration increases linearly with force.

Although Newton's second law can be conceptually understood as a series of relationships describing how an increase in one factor will decrease another factor, the law can be understood best in equation format:

$$Force = mass \times acceleration$$

Or

$$Acceleration = \frac{force}{mass}$$

Or

$$Mass = \frac{force}{acceleration}$$

Each of the forms of the equation allows for a different look at the same relationships. To examine the relationships, change one factor and observe the result. If a steel ball, with a diameter of 6.3 cm, has a mass of 1 kg and an acceleration of 1 m/s², then the net force on the ball will be 1 Newton.

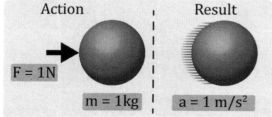

Third Law: Concept: Nothing can push or pull without being pushed or pulled in return.

When any object exerts a force on another object, the other object exerts the opposite force back on the original object. To observe this, consider two spring-based fruit scales, both tipped on their sides as shown with the weighing surfaces facing each other. If fruit scale #1 is pressing fruit scale #2 into the wall, it exerts a force on fruit scale #2, measurable by the reading on scale #2. However, because fruit scale #1 is exerting a force on scale #2, scale #2 is exerting a force on scale #1 with an opposite direction, but the same magnitude.

Mass
Concept: the amount of matter

Mass can be defined as the quantity of matter in an object. If we apply the same force to two objects of different mass, we will find that the resulting acceleration is different. Newton's Second Law of Motion describes the relationship between mass, force, and acceleration in the equation: *Force = mass x acceleration*. In other words, the acceleration of an object is directly proportional to the force being exerted on it and inversely proportional to its mass.

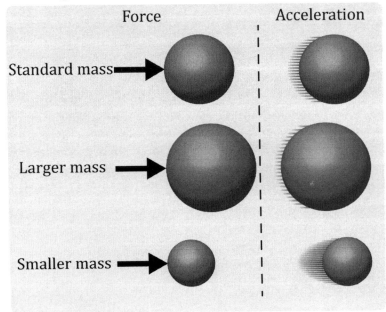

- 67 -

Normal force
Concept: the force perpendicular to a contact surface

The word "normal" is used in mathematics to mean perpendicular, and so the force known as normal force should be remembered as the perpendicular force exerted on an object that is resting on some other surface. For instance, if a box is resting on a horizontal surface, we may say that the normal force is directed upwards through the box (the opposite, downward force is the weight of the box). If the box is resting on a wedge, the normal force from the wedge is not vertical but is perpendicular to the wedge edge.

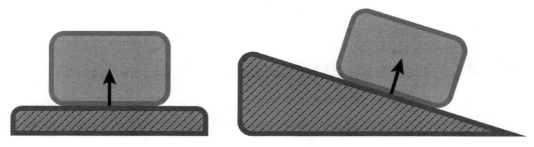

Friction
Concept: Friction is a resistance to motion between contacting surfaces

In order to illustrate the concept of friction, let us imagine a book resting on a table. As it sits, the force of its weight is equal to and opposite of the normal force. If, however, we were to exert a force on the book, attempting to push it to one side, a frictional force would arise, equal and opposite to our force. This kind of frictional force is known as static frictional force.

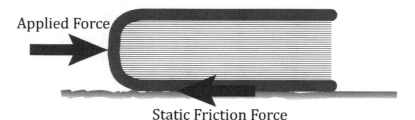

Static Friction Force

As we increase our force on the book, however, we will eventually cause it to accelerate in the direction of our force. At this point, the frictional force opposing us will be known as kinetic friction. For many combinations of surfaces, the magnitude of the kinetic frictional force is lower than that of the static frictional force, and consequently, the amount of force needed to maintain the movement of the book will be less than that needed to initiate the movement.

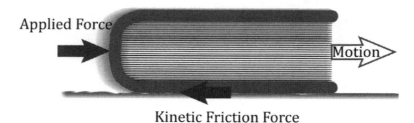

Kinetic Friction Force

Equilibrium

An object is in equilibrium when the sum of all forces acting on the object is zero. When the forces on an object sum to zero, the object does not accelerate. Equilibrium can be obtained when forces in the y-direction sum to zero, forces in the x-direction sum to zero, or forces in both directions sum to zero.

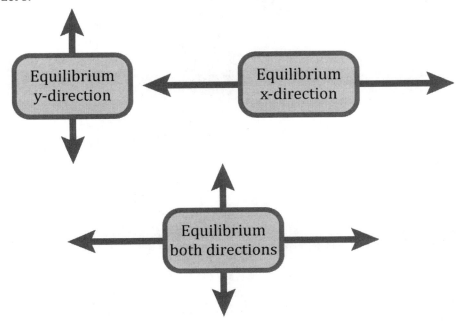

In most cases, a problem will provide one or more forces acting on object and ask for a force to balance the system. The force will be the opposite of the current force or sum of current forces.

Balance the forces

Given: Answer:

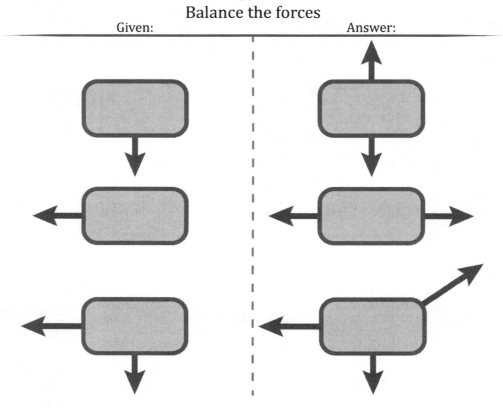

Torques and lever arms

Many equations and concepts in linear kinematics and kinetics transfer to rotation. For example, angular position is an angle. Angular velocity, like linear velocity, is the change in the position (angle) divided by the time. Angular acceleration is the change in angular velocity divided by time. Although most tests will not require you to perform angular calculations, they will expect you to understand the angular version of force: torque.

Concept: Torque is a twisting force on an object
Calculation: $Torque = radius \times force$

Torque, like force, is a vector and has magnitude and direction. As with force, the sum of torques on an object will affect the angular acceleration of that object. The key to solving problems with torque is understanding the lever arm. A better description of the torque equation is:

Torque = force × the distance perpedicular to the force to the center of rotation

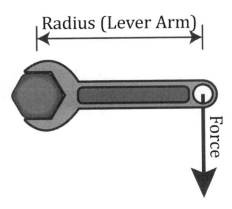

Because torque is directly proportional to the radius, or lever arm, a greater lever arm will result in a greater torque with the same amount of force. The wrench on the right has twice the radius and, as a result, twice the torque.

Alternatively, a greater force also increases torque. The wrench on the right has twice the force and twice the torque.

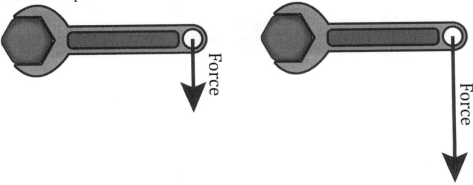

Work

Concept: Work is the transfer of energy from one object to another
Calculation: Work = force × displacement

The equation for work in one dimension is fairly simple:
$$Work = Force \times displacement$$
$$W = F \times d$$

In the equation, the force and the displacement are the magnitude of the force exerted and the total change in position of the object on which the force is exerted, respectively. If force and displacement have the same direction, then the work is positive. If they are in opposite directions, however, the work is negative.

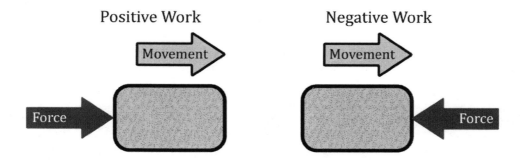

Mechanical advantage

Concept: the amount of change a simple machine provides to the magnitude of a force
Calculation: output force/input force

Mechanical advantage is the measure of the output force divided by the input force. Thus, mechanical advantage measures the change performed by a machine. Machines cannot create energy, only transform it. Thus, in frictionless, ideal machines, the input work equals the output work.

$$Work_{input} = Work_{output}$$
$$force_{input} \times distance_{input} = force_{output} \times distance_{output}$$

This means that a simple machine can increase the force of the output by decreasing the distance which the output travels or it can increase the distance of the output by decreasing the force at the output.

By moving parts of the equation for work, we can arrive at the equation for mechanical advantage.
$$\text{Mechanical Advantage} = \frac{force_{output}}{force_{input}} = \frac{distance_{input}}{distance_{output}}$$

If the mechanical advantage is greater than one, the output force is greater than the input force and the input distance is greater than the output distance. Conversely, if the mechanical advantage is less than one, the input force is greater than the output force and the output distance is greater than the input distance. In equation form this is:

If Mechanical Advantage > 1:

$$force_{input} < force_{output} \text{ and } distance_{output} < distance_{input}$$

If Mechanical Advantage < 1:
$$force_{input} > force_{output} \text{ and } distance_{output} > distance_{input}$$

Conservative and non-conservative forces

Forces that change the state of a system by changing kinetic energy into potential energy, or vice versa, are called conservative forces. This name arises because these forces conserve the total amount of kinetic and potential energy. Every other kind of force is considered non-conservative. One example of a conservative force is gravity. Consider the path of a ball thrown straight up into the air. Since the ball has the same amount of kinetic energy when it is thrown as it does when it returns to its original location (known as completing a closed path), gravity can be said to be a conservative force. More generally, a force can be said to be conservative if the work it does on an object through a closed path is zero. Frictional force would not meet this standard, of course, because it is only capable of performing negative work.

Energy

Concept: the ability of a body to do work on another object

Energy is a word that has found a million different uses in the English language, but in physics it refers to the measure of a body's ability to do work. In physics, energy may not have a million meanings, but it does have many forms. Each of these forms, such as chemical, electric, and nuclear, is the capability of an object to perform work. However, for the purpose of most tests, mechanical energy and mechanical work are the only forms of energy worth understanding in depth. Mechanical energy is the sum of an object's kinetic and potential energies. Although they will be introduced in greater detail, these are the forms of mechanical energy:
- Kinetic Energy – energy an object has by virtue of its motion
- Gravitational Potential Energy – energy by virtue of an object's height
- Elastic Potential Energy – energy stored in compression or tension

Neglecting frictional forces, mechanical energy is conserved.

As an example, imagine a ball moving perpendicular to the surface of the earth, with its weight the only force acting on it. As the ball rises, the weight will be doing work on the ball, decreasing its speed and its kinetic energy, and slowing it down until it momentarily stops. During this ascent, the potential energy of the ball will be rising. Once the ball begins to fall back down, it will lose potential energy as it gains kinetic energy. Mechanical energy is conserved throughout; the potential energy of the ball at its highest point is equal to the kinetic energy of the ball at its lowest point prior to impact.

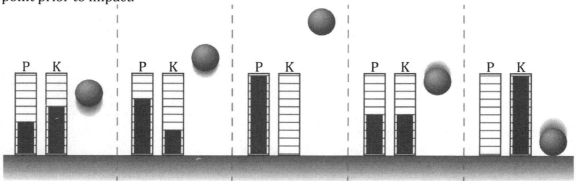

In systems where friction and air resistance are not negligible, we observe a different sort of result. For example, imagine a block sliding across the floor until it comes to a stop due to friction. Unlike a compressed spring or a ball flung into the air, there is no way for this block to regain its energy with a return trip. Therefore, we cannot say that the lost kinetic energy is being stored as potential energy. Instead, it has been dissipated and cannot be recovered. The total mechanical energy of the block-floor system has been not conserved in this case but rather reduced. The total energy of the system has not decreased, since the kinetic energy has been converted into thermal energy, but that energy is no longer useful for work.

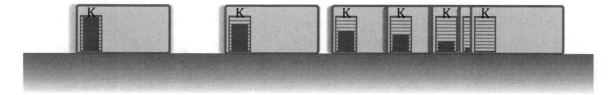

Energy, though it may change form, will be neither created nor destroyed during physical processes. However, if we construct a system and some external force performs work on it, the result may be slightly different. If the work is positive, then the overall store of energy is increased; if it is negative, however, we can say that the overall energy of the system has decreased.

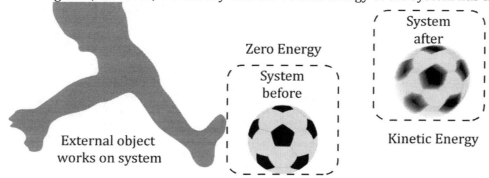

- 74 -

Kinetic energy

The kinetic energy of an object is the amount of energy it possesses by reason of being in motion. Kinetic energy cannot be negative. Changes in kinetic energy will occur when a force does work on an object, such that the motion of the object is altered. This change in kinetic energy is equal to the amount of work that is done. This relationship is commonly referred to as the work-energy theorem.

One interesting application of the work-energy theorem is that of objects in a free fall. To begin with, let us assert that the force acting on such an object is its weight, equal to its mass times g (the force of gravity). The work done by this force will be positive, as the force is exerted in the direction in which the object is traveling. Kinetic energy will, therefore, increase, according to the work-kinetic energy theorem.

If the object is dropped from a great enough height, it eventually reaches its terminal velocity, where the drag force is equal to the weight, so the object is no longer accelerating and its kinetic energy remains constant.

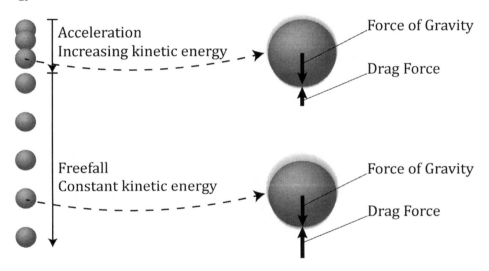

Gravitational potential energy

Gravitational potential energy is simply the potential for a certain amount of work to be done by one object on another using gravity. For objects on earth, the gravitational potential energy is equal to the amount of work which the earth can act on the object. The work which gravity performs on objects moving entirely or partially in the vertical direction is equal to the force exerted by the earth (weight) times the distance traveled in the direction of the force (height above the ground or reference point):

$$\text{Work from gravity} = \text{weight} \times \text{height above the ground}$$

Thus, the gravitational potential energy is the same as the potential work.

$$\text{Gravitational Potential Energy} = \text{weight} \times \text{height}$$

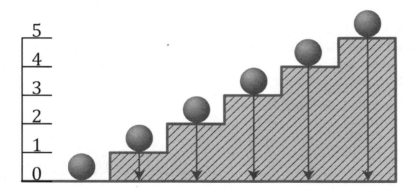

Elastic potential energy

Elastic potential energy is the potential for a certain amount of work to be done by one object on another using elastic compression or tension. The most common example is the spring. A spring will resist any compression or tension away from its equilibrium position (natural position). A small buggy is pressed into a large spring. The spring contains a large amount of elastic potential energy. If the buggy and spring are released, the spring will push exert a force on the buggy for a distance. This work will put kinetic energy into the buggy. The energy can be imagined as a liquid poured from one container into another. The spring pours its elastic energy into the buggy, which receives the energy as kinetic energy.

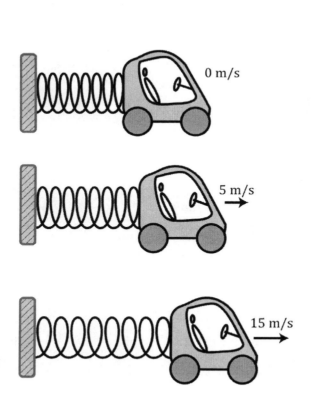

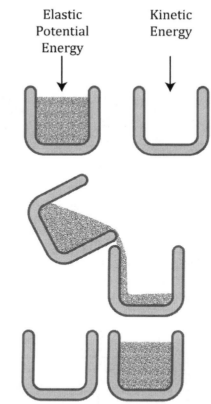

Power
Concept: the rate of work
Calculation: work/time

On occasion, you may need to demonstrate an understanding of power, as it is defined in applied physics. Power is the rate at which work is done. Power, like work and energy, is a scalar quantity. Power can be calculated by dividing the amount of work performed by the amount of time in which the work was performed.

$$\text{Power} = \frac{\text{work}}{\text{time}}$$

If more work is performed in a shorter amount of time, more power has been exerted. Power can be expressed in a variety of units. The preferred metric expression is one of watts or joules per seconds. For engine power, it is often expressed in horsepower.

Periodic motion

Velocity, amplitude, wavelength, and frequency
The velocity of a wave is the rate at which it travels in a given medium. It is defined in the same way that velocity of physical objects is defined, a change in position divided by a change in time. A single wave may have a different velocity for every medium in which it travels. Some types of waves, such as light waves, do not require a medium.

Amplitude is one measure of a wave's strength. It is half the verticle distance between the highest and lowest points on the wave, the crest and trough, respectively. The vertical midpoint, halfway between the crest and trough, is sometimes called an equilibrium point, or a node. Amplitude is often denoted with an A.

The wavelength is the horizontal distance between successive crests or troughs, or the distance between the first and third of three successive nodes. Wavelength is generally denoted as λ.

Frequency is the number of crests or troughs that pass a particular point in a given period of time. It is the inverse of the period, the time required for the wave to cycle from one crest or trough to the next. Frequency, f, is generally measured in hertz, or cycles per second.

Velocity, wavelength, and frequency are not independent quantities. They are related by the expression:

$$v = \lambda \times f$$

Transverse and longitudinal waves
Transverse waves are waves whose oscillations are perpendicular to the direction of motion. A light wave is an example of a transverse wave. A group of light waves traveling in the same direction will be oscillating in several different planes. Light waves are said to be polarized when they are filtered such that only waves oscillating in a particular plane are allowed to pass, with the remainder being absorbed by the filter. If two such polarizing filters are employed successively and aligned to allow different planes of oscillation, they will block all light waves.

Longitudinal waves are waves that oscillate in the same direction as their primary motion. Their motion is restricted to a single axis, so they may not be polarized. A sound wave is an example of a longitudinal wave.

Importance of Fluids for the Circulation of Blood, Gas Movement, and Gas Exchange

Fluids

Now that we've covered how solid objects react to forces, we will move on to fluids. A fluid is either a liquid or a gas. As we begin our coverage of fluid behavior, we will relate it to what we've just covered about solids.

If a block of ice is set inside a pot, its mass will exert a downward force on the bottom of the pan, and the pan will exert an upward force on the bottom of the block of ice. The force in each case is spread over the area of contact between the two objects, such that there is pressure between the two objects. Pressure is calculated as force over area, or in this particular case:

$$Pressure = \frac{weight\ of\ ice}{area\ of\ contact}$$

When the ice melts, it will still have the same mass, and will still exert the same amount of force on the bottom of the pan, but the force will now be spread equally across the entire bottom surface of the pan, which means the pressure will actually be less since the area is larger.

The Behavior of Solids and Liquids Compared

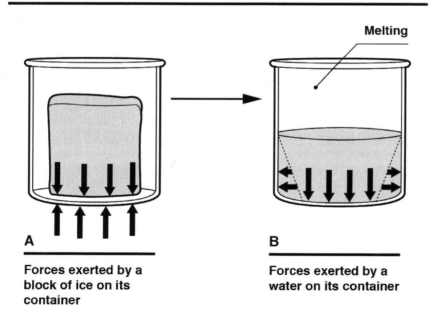

A

Forces exerted by a
block of ice on its
container

B

Forces exerted by a
water on its container

In addition to the pressure exerted on the bottom of the pan, there will be a pressure exerted on the sides of the pan. The pressure on the bottom of the pan will be uniform (i.e., the same at every point), but the pressure on the sides of the pan will increase with depth (i.e., it will be greater near the bottom than near the water line).

To expand on this concept, water will exert a pressure on any solid surface submerged in the water, and the magnitude of the pressure will depend entirely on the depth of the water at every point. If a block of wood is submerged in water, the water will exert pressure on all sides, but the highest pressure will be on the bottom surface of the block since it is at the greatest depth. This upward pressure on a submerged object is called the buoyant force and is the reason that many objects are able to float in water.

Floatation of a Block of Wood

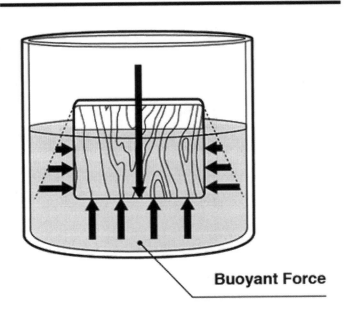

Buoyant Force

If an object is placed slowly into water, it will stop sinking at the point at which the buoyant force is equal to the object's weight. The magnitude of the buoyant force on an object is equal to the weight of water displaced. This means that only an object with a lower density than water will float in water. If a block of solid steel were placed into water, it would simply sink to the bottom because each cubic inch of steel weighs more than the cubic inch of water it is displacing, so the buoyant force is never able to match the weight of the block.

Sailing ships that are made of metals such as steel are able to float because they are partially hollow. Even though the hull of the boat is denser than water, the total mass of the boat divided by the volume of the part of the boat that is designed to be submerged comes out to be less than the density of water.

Although this principle of buoyancy is most easily understood when applied to solids floating in liquids, it also holds for liquids floating in liquids or gases floating on gases. The lower density liquid or gas will rise to the surface. If three or more fluids in a contained space are left to settle, they will organize themselves into distinct layers based on density. However, because these density differences are relatively small in magnitude, minor perturbations of the fluids will cause them to intersperse once again. If the difference is too small (as when heavily water-based fluids are mixed), there will be no discernible layering.

Pascal's Law

Pascal's law states that when a fluid is enclosed (i.e., it doesn't have anywhere to go), any pressure that is exerted on one part of a fluid will be transmitted to all parts of the fluid. This means that fluids can be used to magnify the effect of a force by applying a small force over a small area and seeing a large force result over a large area. This principle is most easily illustrated in the design of the hydraulic jack.

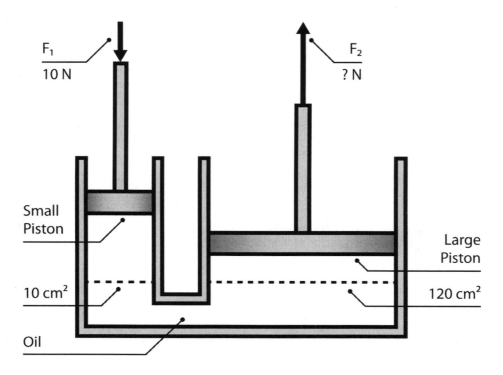

Suppose the small piston has an area of 10 cm² is being depressed with a force of 10 N, while the large piston has an area of 120 cm². To calculate the upward force on the large piston, consider that the pressure in each cylinder is the same:

$$P_1 = P_2$$

$$P_1 = \frac{F_1}{A_1} = \frac{10\ N}{10\ cm^2} = 1\frac{N}{cm^2}; \quad P_2 = \frac{F_2}{A_2} = \frac{F_2}{120\ cm^2}$$

$$F_2 = 1\frac{N}{cm^2} \times 120\ cm^2 = 120\ N$$

The force is 120 N or 12 times the force applied to the smaller piston. You may note that the ratio of the two forces is the same as the ratio of the two areas, so you can often use the shortcut of dividing one area by the other and then multiplying the known force by that same ratio. It is important to remember that in hydraulic systems, the larger piston will always have the larger force. Note, however, that this increased force comes with the side effect of reduced movement distance. If the hydraulic jack is being used to lift a heavy object, the small piston in our example would have to be lowered by 12 inches in order to raise the larger piston by only 1 inch.

As an additional example, consider the hydraulic brake systems of motor vehicles. The force that is exerted on the brake pedal is applied over a small area to the fluid system. This pressure is then transmitted through the fluid to the larger surface area of the brake pistons (same pressure over larger area means greater force), to apply friction to the brake pads and rotors, which slows the vehicle down.

Flow rate

Fluids are often transported in pipes from place to place. The rate at which the fluid is moving is called its volumetric flow rate, or simply its flow rate (usually denoted as Q). It is measured in units of volume per second (m³/s or ft³/s). This is most easily calculated by taking the cross sectional area of the pipe and multiplying it by the velocity of the fluid in the pipe:

$$Q = A \times v$$

By examining this equation, you can see that for a given pipe, a higher velocity will yield a higher flow rate. Similarly to achieve a given flow rate, the velocity in a large pipe would not need to be as high as the velocity in a smaller pipe.

As an example, consider a water pipe with a cross sectional area of 1000 cm². Water is flowing through the pipe at a velocity of 3 meters per second. The volumetric flow rate can be found with the equation shown above:

$$Q = A \times v = 1000 \; cm^2 \times \left(\frac{1 \; m}{100 \; cm}\right)^2 \times 3 \frac{m}{s} = 0.3 \frac{m^3}{s}$$

If volumetric flow rate is known, it can be used to calculate quantities like fill times. Suppose the water pipe above is draining into a 6000 m³ tank. How long will it take to fill the tank with water? To go from volumetric flow rate to volume, you would multiply the flow rate by time, so to get the time required to fill, you would divide the volume by the flow rate:

$$Q = 0.3 \frac{m^3}{s}; \quad V = 6000 \; m^3$$

$$t = \frac{V}{Q} = \frac{6000 \; m^3}{0.3 \frac{m^3}{s}} = 20,000 \; s = 5 \; hr, 33 \; min, 20 \; sec$$

Bernoulli's equation

The energy of a system of flowing fluid has three major components: the kinetic energy, the potential energy, and the fluid pressure. Bernoulli's equation relates the three in this way:

$$\frac{v^2}{2} + Zg + \frac{P}{\rho} = C$$

All terms in this equation are given in units of energy per unit mass of the fluid (J/kg). The first term in this equation is the kinetic energy term. It is the fluid velocity (v) squared over 2. The second term is the potential energy term. It is the height above ground or some other reference point (Z) times the acceleration due to gravity (g). The third term is the pressure term. It is the internal pressure of the fluid (P) divided by the fluid density (ρ). The sum of these three terms is equal to a constant (C) for a given flowing fluid and height reference point. In general, g and ρ will be constant, and Z will be constant for a level pipe.

Much can be gleaned from looking at this equation, but the most important thing to see is that the pressure and the velocity are inversely related. When one goes up, the other goes down. However, it is an additive relationship, not a multiplicative one; the two are inversely related, but not inversely proportional. This trade off is most easily seen when the pipe size changes. As the pipe gets smaller, the fluid has to travel faster to maintain the flow rate, but with this increase in velocity comes a decrease in pressure.

Ideal gas law

The ideal gas law is a combination of several relationships of gas properties discovered across multiple centuries. It is most commonly stated in this way:

$$PV = nRT$$

In this equation, P is the pressure of the gas, V is its volume, n is the number of moles of gas present, R is the gas constant, and T is the temperature. This equation relates the properties of an ideal gas in a defined contained space.

The gas law is often applied by holding all but two of the quantities constant, so it is reduced to a directly or inversely proportional relationship between those two. For example, if there is a fixed quantity of gas present, and the temperature is held constant, the product of volume and pressure will be a constant value such that:

$$P_1 V_1 = P_2 V_2$$

Similarly, if the quantity and volume of a gas are fixed, the ratio of pressure to temperature will be constant as seen here:

$$\frac{P_1}{T_1} = \frac{P_2}{T_2}$$

Other important information related to gas behavior and gas law calculations are given below:
- The temperature of a gas is a measure of the kinetic energy of the molecules. Molecules in a gas are in a constant state of motion and the temperature of the gas reflects the average speed at which they are moving.
- Related to n, the number of moles of gas present, a mole is defined as 6.022×10^{23} molecules of the gas. The molar mass of a substance, which is one of the values commonly shown for each element on the periodic table, is the mass of 6.022×10^{23} molecules of the substance, listed in units of grams per mole.

Real gases

The ideal gas law does not account for confounding factors related to molecular size or molecular attraction, so it is most accurate when applied to gases with small molecules at high temperature and low pressure. For cases where the ideal gas law is not sufficiently accurate, there are other equations that may be used to better reflect the real situations. The foremost of these is the Van der Waals equation, which is commonly written in this way:

$$\left(P + \frac{an^2}{V^2}\right)(V - nb) = nRT$$

Here the constants a and b are based on the physical properties of the gas in question. They can be looked up in tables or, more likely, will be given if they are needed.

Electrochemistry and Electrical Circuits and Their Elements

Electric charge

Atoms are usually neutrally charged because there are an equal number of positively charged protons and negatively charged electrons. Electrons, however, can move from one atom to another when the conditions are right. This changes the balance of charges on both atoms, making the one it left more positively charged, and the one it moved to more negatively charged. Think of the example of someone rubbing a balloon on the carpet. The balloon transfers some of its electrons to the carpet, becoming positively charged. When it is held near something else that has no net charge, such as hair, the balloon is attracted to the hair. Most things in nature try to obtain and maintain a neutral charge, so when two objects of dissimilar charges are brought together, electrons will move from the more negatively charged object to the more positively charged object.

Dissimilar charges are attracted to each other, but equal charges repel each other. Positives are attracted to negatives, but repel other positives. When any charge gets near any other charge, a force is created. This force is calculated by using the Coulomb's Law equation;

$$F = k\frac{q_1 q_2}{r^2}$$

where
   F is the force generated between the charges (in Newtons),
   k is a constant always equal to 8.99×10^9,
   q_1 is the magnitude of the first charge (in coulombs),
   q_2 is the magnitude of the second charge (in coulombs), and
   r is the distance between the two charges (in meters).

Basic electrical concepts

Electrical current is a flow of charge, a transfer of electrons in a material. Materials that can easily transfer electrons are the best choice for use in electrical applications; these materials have high *conductivity*. For example, metals usually have much higher conductivity than wood or plastics. The best conductors have very few electrons in their outermost (valence) shells. The fewer the number of valence electrons, the easier it is for one electron to transfer to another atom. That's why electrical wires are made of metal (usually copper, because it has just two valence electrons) rather than other materials. Materials that are bad at transferring electrons impede the flow of charge and are called *insulators*.

Electrical current is defined as a quantity of charge over an amount of time. It can be calculated using the formula;

$$I = \frac{q}{t}$$

where
   I is the electric current (in amps),
   q is the electric charge (in coulombs), and
   t is the time (in seconds).

One amp of current is equal to a coulomb of charge moved in one second. Direct current (DC) is a unidirectional, constant flow of charge. Alternating current (AC) is a flow of charge that changes direction or magnitude regularly.

Electric voltage is the difference in electric potential energy between two points per unit electric charge. It is measured in Volts (V), which are equal to a joule of energy per coulomb of charge.

Electrical resistance is the measure of how difficult it is to pass an electric current through a conductor. It is measured in Ohms (Ω), which are equal to a volt per amp.

The relationship between current, voltage, and resistance is known as Ohm's law. The law states that current is directly proportional to voltage:

$$V = I \times R$$

where V is voltage, I is current, and R is resistance. Rearranging this equation allows the calculation of any of the three variables: $R = \frac{V}{I}$ or $I = \frac{V}{R}$.

Elements of an electric circuit can be connected one after the other, in *series*, or they can all be connected to the same point, in *parallel*. More complex circuits may have some elements in series and some in parallel. When resistors in a simple circuit are arranged in series, their equivalent resistance is the sum of all the resistance values. In the circuit below, three resistors are in series, and their equivalent resistance is:

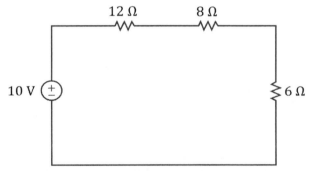

$$R_{eq} = R_1 + R_2 + \cdots + R_n = 12 + 8 + 6 = 26\Omega.$$

For resistors in parallel, the equivalent resistance is the reciprocal of the sum of the reciprocals of the resistors. For the circuit below, the equivalent resistance is:

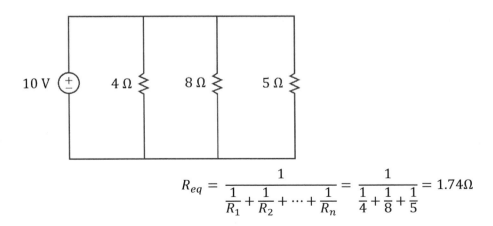

$$R_{eq} = \frac{1}{\frac{1}{R_1} + \frac{1}{R_2} + \cdots + \frac{1}{R_n}} = \frac{1}{\frac{1}{4} + \frac{1}{8} + \frac{1}{5}} = 1.74\Omega$$

To cause a flow of current, a voltage (a difference in levels of charge) must be present. Current will always want to flow from a higher level of charge to a lower level of charge. You can think of this principle like water responding to the force of gravity; it will always flow downhill. In battery-operated circuits, current flows from the positive terminal of the battery to the negative terminal, passing through the other elements in the circuit.

Some materials in nature, like magnetite, generate magnetic fields. When shaped into a rod, magnetite will naturally have one magnetically positive and one magnetically negative end; these are called *poles*. By a similar principle to electric charge, opposite poles attract each other and like poles repel each other.

In many cases, magnetic fields can be generated or amplified by passing an electric current through a material. In fact, all current-carrying wire produces a magnetic field, albeit usually a small one. Just as electrically charged objects create forces on other charged objects, so magnetized objects create forces on other magnetic objects.

Batteries

Simple battery cell

A galvanic (or voltaic) cell consists of a container with electrolyte solution and two dissimilar electrodes to and from which the current flows. Chemical reaction of the electrolyte on the electrodes develops positive and negative charges at the electrodes. When the electrodes are connected through an external circuit, electrons are transferred through the circuit which results in electric current.

In lead-acid batteries used in cars, a solution of sulphuric acid is the electrolyte. It combines with lead and lead oxide at the electrodes to form lead sulphate and gives up and absorbs electrons at the two electrodes. These electrons flow from the cathode to the anode in the external circuit through the electrical loads.

The voltage produced per cell is constant for any specific set of materials, so batteries with higher voltage outputs have multiple cells connected in series. The physical size of the battery determines its current capability and energy capacity. The surface area of the electrodes determines the maximum current, and the electrode size and quantity of electrolyte determine the overall energy capacity of the battery.

Types of batteries

The two classes of batteries are primary and secondary. Primary batteries require no charging, while secondary batteries are designed for many cycles of charging and discharging. Flashlights use primary batteries while the storage battery in a car is a secondary battery.

There are also two classifications of batteries based on the form of their electrolyte. Dry cells contain electrolyte that is a semi-solid gel while wet cell electrolyte is liquid.
Battery capacity is measured in ampere-hours which is simply the length of time that a specific current can be sustained multiplied by this current.

In secondary batteries, the specific gravity of the electrolyte is affected by how fully battery is charged. This can be measured with a hydrometer.

Gases can form at the electrodes of a secondary battery if it is overcharged. In a lead-acid car battery these gases are hydrogen and oxygen, and an explosion can result if a spark is introduced.

How Light and Sound Interact with Matter

Optics and waves

Electromagnetic spectrum
The way light moves is often described as being like the movement of waves. Light contains characteristics of waves such as having amplitude (peak height from the midpoint), a wave front, a wavelength or cycle, a period, and energy. Light moves faster than anything that humans have attained at roughly Light travels at 3.00×10^8 m/s.

Light that operates on different wavelengths, or the distance between two crests (or wavefronts) has different effects on the physical world. The faster moving light or types of light with longer wavelengths are invisible to the naked eye and include infrared, television, radio, and microwaves. The next set of light is called the visible spectrum, roughly having wavelengths of 10^{-7} m. The human eye can interpret these wavelengths as being red, which has the longest wavelength, orange, yellow, green, blue, indigo, and violet.

There are also wavelengths that are too short for the human eyes to recognize as belonging to the visible spectrum. These wavelengths are called the electromagnetic spectrum and contain ultraviolet light, x-rays, and gamma rays. The wavelengths outside of the visible spectrum can be harmful to humans with direct exposure. The most common example of harmful exposure includes exposure to ultraviolet light from being in the sun or from x-rays, which are commonly used in the medical field. Ultraviolet light is mostly filtered out by the Earth's atmosphere, but the fraction that is able to penetrate is often trapped by pollutants. Since the ultraviolet light is able to enter but cannot escape, this is referred to as the greenhouse effect. This effect not only harmful to humans, but directly adds to global warming, or the Earth increasing in temperature over time.

Basic characteristics and types of waves
Mechanical waves are a type of wave that is translated either longitudinally or transversely through a medium, which includes solids, liquids, and gases.

Longitudinal waves have motion parallel motion to the direction in which the wave is travelling. A good visual example of this is compressing and releasing a spring with one side that is tied down. The spring (or wave) travels in a way that springs up and down along the length of the spring.

Transverse waves have motion perpendicular to the direction in which the wave is travelling. These waves act differently from longitudinal waves by bouncing up and down across the width, rather than the length of the wave. This is easily visualized by a loose cord, such as jump-rope, which has been tied off at one end and shaken up and down. The waves will move up and down across the length of the cord.

Waves may also contain a combination of both longitudinal and transverse motion. A good example of this type of wave is that of the ocean, which has peaks and troughs occurring across its amplitude and also has particles that oscillate up and down.

Mechanical waves happen across a medium (solids, liquids, or gas), and can transport energy, sound, and light. These kinds of waves cannot operate without matter. Electromagnetic waves, however, are able to transmit energy without a medium.

Relatively recently, gravitational waves have been proved and verified, however, the effects of such are still much unknown. Gravitational waves are thought to have impact of the curvature of space and time, and carry energy called gravitational radiation. These waves act like ripples that spread outward from their source in the form of radiant waves.

<u>Basic wave phenomena</u>
Waves can experience a variety of effects when crossing from one medium to another or through a boundary. Refraction takes place when a wave travels through one medium into another medium of a different type. The wave then bends from the change of density in its traveling medium. Since the density across which the wave is traveling changes, so changes the speed of the wave. This is noticeable with a straw in a glass of water, as from a side view, the straw will appear to sharply bend where the water and air in the glass meet. Since the density of water is higher than that of air, the wave speed is slowed and changes make the straw appear to be bent.

Waves are not always able to penetrate a medium and may bounce back. This is called reflection. This happens when a light wave comes into contact with a mirror, which then bounces the light in a new direction. This is how people see their reflection in mirrors and also can be useful for making a room look brighter than it is, by spreading the light through reflection.

Waves encounter diffraction when passing through a slit or around an obstacle. Light generally travels in straight lines, but as it passes through these narrow points, it will diffract. Light can bend around obstacles or pass through small openings, but the light will then spread out on the other end of the obstacle in what is called a diffraction pattern.

Light can also enter mediums of specific shapes that cause dispersion. Dispersion causes the various wavelengths in a light source refract at different rates and separate out. This causes white light that passes through a prism to separate out into rainbow-colored components, since each color travels at a different wavelength.

These interactions with various mediums can have different effects due to the characteristics of the matter. Some objects may be able to reflect some wavelengths and absorb others, depending on the characteristics of the boundaries. Colors of objects are not actually contained by that object, but are the wavelengths of light which are being transmitted by that object, either by refraction, reflection, diffraction, or production of a wavelength. For example, a table may appear to be red, but it is only positive that the table is transmitting a wavelength associated with the color red.

Waves are also subject to interference from objects or other waves as they interact. Depending on the direction and type of waves involved, this could be either constructive interference or destructive interference. In constructive interference, the waves actually work together and add to one another due to working in the same direction as the other. Deconstructive interference works in an opposing way and waves are moving in different directions from one another and detract from each others' strength. When a wave encounters a boundary, the direction or energy in a wave can be impacted and alter the whole wave. This is often referred to as scattering. Polarization works in a way that changes the oscillations of a wave, which can alter the appearance of that light as a result. This is often used in car windows or sunglasses to remove "glare" and improve visibility of light passing through the glass.

Internal reflection is an effect that happens when waves hit a boundary and are either completely reflected or cannot escape. As a result of this effect, objects such as a brilliant cut diamond appear to be brighter and more colorful than diamonds cut into different angles. Waves become trapped inside the diamond due to the internal reflection and bounce around until released in angles dictated by the shape.

Both light and sound waves are subject to an effect called the Doppler Effect. This effect is predicated by the relative motion of the observer either toward or away from the source of the wave. As an ambulance moves closer to a person, the waves are seemingly shorter and this makes the pitch seem to be higher as a result. As the source moves away from the observer, the effect is reversed and waves appear lengthened. Both the apparent shortening and lengthening of light and sound waves are attributed to the Doppler Effect. The true wavelength never changes, but the relative motion causes adverse effects in the observation of the waves.

In light, the Doppler Effect would cause approaching light to appear bluer and light would appear redder when moving away from the light source. This is commonly referred to as the red-blue shift. This effect is much harder to observe than in sound waves.

Basic optics
Mirrors cause virtual images to appear as a result of reflecting light. The image is not an exact copy of the real image, as light is warped due to the optic principles involved. A piece of glass with a coating in the background will become a reflective surface called a plane mirror. A reflection then causes an image to appear in the mirror resulting from the light bouncing across the plane. What the human eye interprets is an unmagnified reflection so long as the mirror is un-curved. Curved mirrors can also be used for reflection, but the image will not be truly representative of the image it is reflecting. Depending on the shape of the curve, an image can be enlarged, shrunken, or warped in odd ways. This is evidenced by funhouse mirrors, which dramatically change the reflected image of people who use them. Curved mirrors also effect the apparent distance of the objects reflected, making the objects appear closer or farther away.

Images can be made in other ways than simple reflection. Lenses use refraction of light to translate an image through a medium (commonly made of glass) to a human eye. Microscopes allow for the magnification of small objects to make them more visible to the human eye. In many cases, this may include objects which are normally invisible to the human eye. Telescopes work similarly, but rather than magnifying small objects, they allow the observer to view objects that are far away. Prisms are glasses that are able to split the wavelengths of light into their base components, spreading a white light into each of the colors within the visible spectrum.

Sound
Sound travels in waves in a similar way to light, but always requires a medium. Sound waves act as vibrations across a solid,liquid, or gas and experiences many of the wave phenomena including Doppler effect and refraction. As sound waves travel across air, the human ear translates the different frequencies, directions, and intensities to help with comprehension of sounds.

Resonant objects have a natural frequency due to density and shape of its matter. As a result, objects such as a tuning fork have a predetermined pitch. When used, the vibrations move at a specific rate and create an audible sound. The tuning fork is consistent enough that it acts as a reliable measure for matching frequencies of a specific tone or note. Sound waves are categorized by frequency which is measured in a unit called Hertz (cycles per second).

Whereas the pitch of a sound is measured in hertz, the level (or volume) of a sound wave is measured with what is called the *decibel* (dB) scale. Decibels measure the sound intensity based on a change in air pressure resulting from the sound waves in question. The name decibel is named for its inventor, Alexander Graham Bell, and is specifically measured as 1/10th of a *bel*. The decibel scale is logarithmic in scope, and is measured in factors of 10. For example, a 10 dB increase is ten times the sound intensity.

Atoms, Nuclear Decay, Electronic Structure, and Atomic Chemical Behavior

Atomic number and mass number

The atomic number of an element is the number of protons in the nucleus of an atom of that element. This is the number that identifies the type of an atom. For example, all oxygen atoms have eight protons, and all carbon atoms have six protons. Each element is identified by its specific atomic number. The mass number is the number of protons and neutrons in the nucleus of an atom. Although the atomic number is the same for all atoms of a specific element, the mass number can vary due to the varying numbers of neutrons in various isotopes of the atom.

Subatomic particles

The three major subatomic particles are the proton, neutron, and electron. The proton, which is located in the nucleus, has a relative charge of +1. The neutron, which is located in the nucleus, has a relative charge of 0. The electron, which is located outside the nucleus, has a relative charge of –1. The proton and neutron, which are essentially the same mass, are much more massive than the electron and make up the mass of the atom. The electron's mass is insignificant compared to the mass of the proton and neutron.

Isotope

Isotopes are atoms of the same element that vary in their number of neutrons. Isotopes of the same element have the same number of protons and thus the same atomic number. But, because isotopes vary in the number of neutrons, they can be identified by their mass numbers. For example, two naturally occurring carbon isotopes are carbon-12 and carbon-13, which have mass numbers 12 and 13, respectively. The symbols $^{12}_{6}C$ and $^{13}_{6}C$ also represent the carbon isotopes. The general form of the symbol is $^{M}_{A}X$, where X represents the element symbol, M represents the mass number, and A represents the atomic number.

Radioactive decay and half-life

Radioactivity or radioactive decay occurs when an unstable atom splits to form a more stable atom and emits some type of radiation. An atom's nucleus contains protons and neutrons. The protons have positive charges and repel each other, but the repulsive force between protons is only relevant over very small distances. The neutrons help separate the protons, enabling the strong nuclear force to hold the atom together. As the atomic number increases, this becomes more and more difficult. All atoms with atomic numbers greater than 83 are unstable. The three basic types of radioactive decay are alpha decay, beta decay, and gamma decay. The *half-life* is the length of time it takes for one-half of the atoms of a radioactive substance to decay into a new type of atom.

Beta decay

Beta decay is radioactive decay in which there is an emission of a beta particle, a high-energy electron or positron. For an electron emission, it is known as beta minus (β-) decay. For a positron emission, it is known as beta plus (β+) decay. In β- decay, a neutron is converted into a proton, an electron, and an antineutrino, ν_e:

$$n \rightarrow p^+ + e^- + \overline{\nu}_e$$

This is because a down quark is converted to an up quark, emitting an electron and an antineutrino.

In β+ decay, a proton is converted into a neutron by means of an up quark becoming a down quark, emitting a positron and a neutrino:

$$energy + p^+ \rightarrow n + e^+ + \nu_e$$

Unlike β- decay, β+ decay cannot occur spontaneously. It requires an input of energy.

In both types of beta decay, the atomic number changes, but the mass number remains constant.

Alpha decay

Alpha decay is a type of radioactive decay in which an alpha particle is ejected from the nucleus. An alpha particle is the nucleus of a helium atom, consisting of 2 protons and 2 neutrons. Ejection of an alpha particle reduces the parent nuclide's atomic number by 2 and its mass number by 4. An example of alpha decay is given by:

$$^{238}U \rightarrow ^{234}Th + \alpha$$

Alpha decay can be looked at as nuclear fission, in which the parent nucleus splits into a pair of daughter nuclei. Alpha decay is governed by the strong nuclear force, or the force between two or more nucleons. Alpha particles are ejected from the nucleus at speeds around 15,000 km/s with a typical kinetic energy of 5 MeV.

Mass spectrometers

Mass spectrometers are used to find the charge-to-mass ratio of ionized materials. An ionized particle of known mass, but unknown charge, is sent at a known velocity into a perpendicular magnetic field of known magnitude. Since the magnetic field is perpendicular, the tangential speed of the particle is constant. The force on a particle with constant tangential speed is equal to mv^2/r, where r is the radius of curvature of the particle's path. The force exerted by the magnetic field can be calculated as qvB, since it is perpendicular to the particle's direction of motion. Equating these two expressions gives us $q/m = v/rB$, allowing us to find the charge-to-mass ratio if we measure the radius of curvature.

Electronic energy transition (emission/absorption of energy) in atoms

An electron must gain or absorb energy to transition to a higher or excited state, and the electron will emit that energy when it transitions back to the ground state. The ground state of an electron is the electron's lowest state of energy or when the electron is in the energy level that it normally occupies. An electron can gain energy if it absorbs a photon or collides with another particle. When an electron occupies an energy level higher that its normal level or ground state, it is in an excited state. The excited state is an unstable state, and the electron will return to the ground state as quickly as possible.

Electronic absorption/emission spectral lines

The emission spectrum of a substance is a specific pattern of bright lines, bands, or continuous radiation that is determined by the frequencies of the electromagnetic spectrum that are emitted due to an electron's transition from a higher state to a lower state. The absorption spectrum is the electromagnetic spectrum interrupted by a specific pattern of dark bands that is determined by the frequencies of the electromagnetic spectrum that are absorbed by a particular substance. The number of lines in the emission spectrum equals the number of lines in the absorption spectrum for a particular substance. In the emission spectrum and the absorption spectrum, the frequencies correspond to the orbitals of the atoms that are involved. A substance can be identified by its emission spectrum or its absorption spectrum.

Pauli exclusion principle

The Pauli exclusion principle describes the unique address or location of each electron in an atom. Each electron has a unique or exclusive set of four quantum numbers indicating the electron's energy level, subshell, orbital orientation, and magnetic moment. Every orbital can hold a maximum of two electrons, but even if two electrons occupy the same orbital resulting in identical energy levels, subshells, and orbital orientations, they must have opposite spins, which means that their magnetic moment quantum numbers will differ.

Groups and periods in the periodic table

A group is a vertical column of the periodic table. Elements in the same group have the same number of valence electrons. For the representative elements, the number of valence electrons is equal to the group number. Because of their equal valence electrons, elements in the same groups have similar physical and chemical properties. A period is a horizontal row of the periodic table. Atomic number increases from left to right across a row. The period of an element corresponds to the highest energy level of the electrons in the atoms of that element. The energy level increases from top to bottom down a group.

Atomic number and atomic mass in the periodic table

The elements in the periodic table are arranged in order of increasing atomic number first left to right and then top to bottom across the periodic table. The atomic number represents the number of protons in the atoms of that element. Because of the increasing numbers of protons, the atomic mass typically also increases from left to right across a period and from top to bottom down a row. The atomic mass is a weighted average of all the naturally occurring isotopes of an element.

Assigning atomic symbols to elements

The atomic symbol for many elements is simply the first letter of the element name. For example, the atomic symbol for hydrogen is H, and the atomic symbol for carbon is C. The atomic symbol of other elements is the first two letters of the element name. For example, the atomic symbol for helium is He, and the atomic symbol for cobalt is Co. The atomic symbols of several elements are derived from Latin. For example, the atomic symbol for copper (Cu) is derived from *cuprum,* and the atomic symbol for iron (Fe) is derived from *ferrum.* The atomic symbol for tungsten (W) is derived from the German word *wolfram.*

Arrangement of metals, nonmetals, and metalloids in the periodic table

The metals are located on the left side and center of the periodic table, and the nonmetals are located on the right side of the periodic table. The metalloids or semimetals form a zigzag line between the metals and nonmetals as shown below. Metals include the alkali metals such as lithium, sodium, and potassium and the alkaline earth metals such as beryllium, magnesium, and calcium. Metals also include the transition metals such as iron, copper, and nickel and the inner transition metals such as thorium, uranium, and plutonium. Nonmetals include the chalcogens such as oxygen and sulfur, the halogens such as fluorine and chlorine, and the noble gases such as helium and argon. Carbon, nitrogen, and phosphorus are also nonmetals.

Metalloids or semimetals include boron, silicon, germanium, antimony, and polonium.

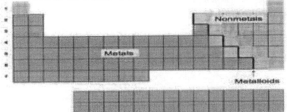

Arrangement of the transition elements

The transition elements belong to one of two categories consisting of the transition metals and the inner transition metals. The transition metals are located in the middle of the periodic table, and the inner transition metals are typically set off as two rows by themselves at the bottom of the periodic table. The transition metals correspond to the "*d* block" for orbital filling, and the inner transition metals correspond to the "*f* block" for orbital filling. Examples of transition metals include iron, copper, nickel, and zinc. The inner transition metals consist of the lanthanide or rare-earth series, which corresponds to the first row, and the actinide series, which corresponds to the second row of the inner transition metals. The lanthanide series includes lanthanum, cerium, and praseodymium. The actinide series includes actinium, uranium, and plutonium.

Electron configuration and the periodic table

Electron configurations show a direct correlation to the periodic table. The periodic table can be divided into blocks representing *s, p, d,* and *f* subshells. The energy level corresponds to the row or period of the periodic table. The subshells, *s, p, d,* or *f* are related to the block's group numbers. The *s* block corresponds to groups 1A and 2A. The *p* block corresponds to groups 3A–8A. The *d* block corresponds to the 10 groups of transition metals, and the *f* block corresponds to the two rows of inner transition metals (14 groups) located at the bottom of the table.

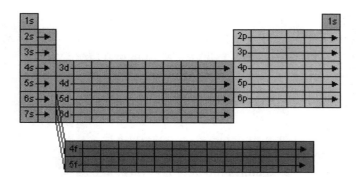

Electron configuration and chemical and physical properties

The chemical and physical properties of atoms are related to the number of valence electrons the atom possesses. Atoms (except hydrogen and helium) seek to have eight electrons in their outer shell as stated in the octet rule. A full octet corresponds to full *s* and *p* orbitals. Noble gases all have full *s* and *p* orbitals and are inert. To fulfill the octet rule, elements in groups 1A (alkali metals) and 2A (alkaline earth metals) tend to lose one or two electrons, respectively, forming cations. Elements in group 6A (chalcogens) and group 7A (halogens) tend to gain one or two electrons, respectively, forming anions. Other elements such as carbon (group 4A) tend to form covalent bonds to satisfy the octet rule.

Chemical reactivity

Atoms of elements in the same group or family of the periodic table tend to have similar chemical properties and similar chemical reactions. For example, the alkali metals, which form cations with a charge of 1+, tend to react with water to form hydrogen gas and metal hydroxides. The alkaline earth metals, which form cations with a charge of 2+, react with oxygen gas to form metal oxides. The halogens, which form anions with a charge of 1−, are highly reactive and toxic. The noble gases are unreactive and never form compounds naturally.

Ionization energy

Ionization energy is the amount of energy needed to remove an electron from an isolated atom. Ionization energy decreases down a group of the periodic table because the electrons get farther and farther from the nucleus making it easier for the electron to be removed. Ionization energy increases across a period of the periodic table due to the decreasing atomic size, which is due to the increasing number of protons attracting the electrons towards the nucleus. These trends of ionization energy are the opposite of the trends for atomic radius.

Electron affinity

Electron affinity is the energy required to add an electron to a neutral atom in the gaseous phase of an element. Electron affinity values typically range from less negative to more negative. If electrons are added to a halogen such as fluorine or chlorine, energy is released and the electron affinity is negative. If electrons are added to an alkaline earth metal, energy is absorbed and the electron affinity is positive. In general, electron affinity becomes more negative from left to right across a period in the periodic table. Electron affinity becomes less negative from the top to the bottom of a group of the periodic table.

Electronegativity

Electronegativity is a measure of the ability of an atom that is chemically combined to at least one other atom in a molecule to attract electrons to it. The Pauling scale is commonly used to assign values to the elements, with fluorine, which is the most electronegative element, being assigned a value of 4.0. Electronegativity increases from left to right across a period of the periodic table and decreases from top to bottom down a group of the periodic table.

Metric units and symbols

Quantity	Name	Symbol
Mass	Kilogram	kg
Volume	Liter	L
Length	Meter	m
Time	Second	s
Absolute temperature	Kelvin	K
Amount of a substance	Mole	mole
Energy	Joule	J
Pressure	Pascal	Pa
Force	Newton	N
Frequency	Hertz	Hz
Electric current	Ampere	A
Luminous intensity	Candela	cd

Conversion problems
Perform each of the following conversions:
  1. *250.0 mL to L*
  2. *0.050 mg to kg*
  3. *113 °F to K*

1. 250.0 mL to L

Because 1 L contains 1,000 mL, the conversion factor is $\left(\frac{1\,L}{1,000\,mL}\right)$. Using dimensional analysis and multiplying, $(250.0\,mL)\left(\frac{1\,L}{1,000\,mL}\right) = 0.2500$ L.

2. 0.050 mg to kg

Because 1kg contains 1,000 g, and 1 g contains 1,000 mg, the conversion factors are $\left(\frac{1\,kg}{1,000\,g}\right)$ and $\left(\frac{1\,g}{1000\,mg}\right)$. Using dimensional analysis and multiplying, $(0.0500\,mg)\left(\frac{1\,g}{1,000\,mg}\right)\left(\frac{1\,kg}{1,000\,g}\right) = 5.00 \times 10^{-8}$ kg.

3. 113 °F to K

Substituting 113 °F into the formula $°C = \frac{5}{9}(°F - 32)$ yields $°C = \frac{5}{9}(113 - 32) = 45.0\ °C$. Then, substituting 45.0 °C into the formula $K = °C + 273.15$ yields $K = 45.0 + 273.15 = 318\ K$.

Avogadro's number, molar mass, and the mole

Avogadro's number is equivalent to the number of atoms in 12 g of the carbon-12 isotope or the number of atoms in 1 mole of carbon-12. Avogadro's number is numerically equal to approximately 6.022×10^{23}. Just like a dozen eggs represents 12 eggs and a pair of shoes represents 2 shoes, Avogadro's number of atoms represents 6.022×10^{23} atoms. *Molar mass* is the mass of one mole of a substance in grams. The *mole* is Avogadro's number of anything. For example, 1 mole of carbon atoms is 6.022×10^{23} carbon atoms, and 1 mole of CCl_4 contains 6.022×10^{23} molecules of CCl_4.

Problem #1
Determine the mass of 2.50 moles of O_2. (The atomic mass of oxygen is 16.0 u.)

To convert from moles of O_2 to mass in grams of O_2, use the dimensional analysis method with the molar mass of O_2. The molar mass of O_2 is 2(16.0 g) or 32.0 g. This molar mass can be written as the conversion factor $\left(\frac{32.0\ g\ O_2}{mol\ O_2}\right)$. Then, using dimensional analysis, multiply $(2.50\ mol\ O_2)\left(\frac{32.0\ g\ O_2}{mol\ O_2}\right)$. The "mol O_2" cancels from the numerator of the first factor and the denominator of the second factor resulting in 80.0 g O_2.

Problem #2
Determine the number of moles of 100.0 g of $C_{12}H_{22}O_{11}$. (The atomic masses of C, H, and O are 12.0 u, 1.0 u, and 16.0 u, respectively.)

To find the number of moles of a sample of $C_{12}H_{22}O_{11}$, first, calculate the molar mass to be used in dimensional analysis. The molar mass of $C_{12}H_{22}O_{11}$ = 12(12.0 g) + 22(1.0 g) + 11(16.0 g) = 144.0 g + 22.0 g + 176.0 g = 342 g. This means that every mole of $C_{12}H_{22}O_{11}$ has a molar mass of 342 g. To convert from grams to moles, use dimensional analysis as follows:
$(100.0\ g\ C_{12}H_{22}O_{11})\left(\frac{1\ mol\ C_{12}H_{22}O_{11}}{342\ g}\right) = 0.292\ mol.$

Problem #3
Given the reaction $3H_2\ (g) + N_2\ (g) \rightarrow 2NH_3\ (g)$, explain how to determine how many grams of nitrogen gas are needed to produce 100.0 g of ammonia. (The molar mass of N_2 = 28.0 g; the molar mass of NH_3 = 17.0 g.)

One approach to working out this problem is to use the dimensional analysis method all the way through the work of the problem. Conversion factors using the molar masses of NH_3 and N_2 are used as well as a mole ratio from the balanced chemical equation. The approach is to convert from grams of NH_3 to moles of NH_3, then to convert moles of NH_3 to moles of N_2, and finally to convert the moles of N_2 to grams of N_2.

$\left(\frac{100.0\ g\ NH_3}{1}\right)\left(\frac{1\ mol\ NH_3}{17.0\ g}\right)\left(\frac{1\ mol\ N_2}{2\ mol\ NH_3}\right)\left(\frac{28.0\ g\ N_2}{1\ mol\ N_2}\right) = 82.4\ g\ N_2.$

Calculating an empirical formula and a molecular formula of a compound

To find the empirical formula of a compound, first, calculate the masses of each element in the compound based on the percent composition that is given. Then, convert these masses to moles by dividing by the molar masses of those elements. Next, divide these amounts in moles by the smallest calculated value in moles and round to the nearest tenth. These calculations provide the subscripts for each element in the empirical formula. To find the molecular formula, divide the actual molar mass of the compound by the molar mass of the empirical formula.

<u>Example</u>
Find the empirical formula and the molecular formula for hydrogen peroxide given that it has a composition of 5.94 % hydrogen and 94.1 % oxygen. (The atomic mass for hydrogen = 1.008 u; the atomic mass of oxygen = 16.00 u.)

To find the empirical formula, calculate the masses of each element in hydrogen peroxide for a sample size of 100.0 g. Calculating 5.94 % of 100.0 g yields 5.94 g of hydrogen. Calculating 94.1 % of 100.0 g yields 94.1 g of oxygen. Next, convert the masses of these elements to moles. Multiplying $(5.94 \text{ g hydrogen}) \left(\frac{\text{mol hydrogen}}{1.008 \text{ g}} \right) = 5.89$ mol hydrogen. Multiplying $(94.1 \text{ g oxygen}) \left(\frac{\text{mol oxygen}}{16.00 \text{ g}} \right) =$ 5.88 mol oxygen. Now, divide these amounts by the smallest value of moles that was calculated and round to the nearest tenth. For hydrogen, $\left(\frac{5.89}{5.88} \right) = 1.0$, and for oxygen, $\left(\frac{5.88}{5.88} \right) = 1.0$. These calculations are the subscripts for the empirical formula. Therefore, the empirical formula of hydrogen peroxide is HO. To find the molecular formula, find the molar mass of the empirical formula (HO) by adding 1.008 g + 16.00 g = 17.008 g. To perform the calculation, the molar mass of hydrogen peroxide would need to be given. If the problem states that the actual molar mass of hydrogen peroxide is 34.016 g, divide this molar mass by the molar mass of the empirical formula: $\frac{34.016}{17.008} = 2$. Multiply each subscript of the empirical formula by 2. The molecular formula for hydrogen peroxide is H_2O_2.

Calculating percent composition when given the molecular formula

To find the percent composition when given the molecular formula, first find the molar mass of the compound. Next, find the percent contributed by each element of the compound by dividing the molar mass of the element (remembering to multiply through by the subscripts of the molecular formula) by the molar mass of the compound. Finally, check the calculations by totaling these individual percents of the elements to ensure their combined total is 100 %. This may be slightly off if any of the numbers used were rounded.

<u>Example</u>
Find the percent composition of methane (CH_4). (The atomic mass of carbon = 12.01 u; the atomic mass of hydrogen = 1.008 u.)

To find the percent composition of methane, first find the molar mass of methane. The molar mass of methane is given by 12.01 g + 4(1.008 g) = 16.042 g. Next, find the percent contributed by the carbon and the percent contributed by the hydrogen. For the carbon, $\% \text{ C} = \frac{12.01 \text{ g/mol}}{16.042 \text{ g/mol}} \times 100 \% =$ 74.87 %. For the hydrogen, $\% \text{ H} = \frac{4(1.008) \text{ g/mol}}{16.042 \text{ g/mol}} \times 100 \% = 25.13 \%$. Finally, check to see that the total of the calculated percents is 100 %. There may be a slight difference due to rounding. For methane, 74.87% + 25.13 % = 100%.

Physical and chemical properties

Chemical properties cannot be seen or measured without chemical reactions. Physical properties can be seen or measured without chemical reactions. These properties are color, elasticity, mass, volume, and temperature.

Mass measures how much of a substance is in an object.

Weight measures the gravitational pull of the Earth on an object.

Density is a measure of the amount of mass per unit volume.
The formula to find density is mass divided by volume (D=m/V). It is expressed in terms of mass per cubic unit (e.g., grams per cubic centimeter (g/cm^3)).

Volume measures the amount of space taken up.
The volume of an irregular shape can be known by finding out how much water it displaces.

Specific gravity measures the ratio of a substance's density to the density of water.

Physical changes and chemical reactions are everyday events. Physical changes do not bring about different substances. An example is when water becomes ice. It has gone through a physical change, not a chemical change. It has changed its state, not what it is made of. In other words, it is still H_2O.

Chemical properties deal with the particles that make up the structure of a substance. Chemical properties can be seen when chemical changes happen. The chemical properties of a substance are influenced by its electron configuration. This is decided somewhat by the number of protons in the nucleus (i.e., the atomic number). An example is carbon that has 6 protons and 6 electrons. The outermost valence electrons of an element mainly decide its chemical properties. Chemical reactions may give or take energy.

Oxidation-reduction reactions

An oxidation-reduction reaction is a reaction in which one of the reactants loses one or more electrons and the other reactant gains one or more electrons. The reactant that loses the electron(s) undergoes oxidation. The reactant that gains the electron(s) undergoes reduction. A common phrase to help remember this is *LEO the lion says GER*, where *LEO* represents *loss of electrons is oxidation* and *GER* represents *gain of electrons is reduction.* Oxidation cannot take place without reduction, and reduction cannot take place without oxidation.

Oxidation, reduction, oxidizing agent, reducing agent, oxidation states

Oxidation can be defined as any process involving a loss of one or more electrons.

Reduction can be defined as any process involving a gain of one or more electrons.

Oxidizing agent can be defined as the reactant in an oxidation-reduction reaction that causes oxidation. The oxidizing agent is reduced.

Reducing agent can be defined as the reactant in an oxidation-reduction reaction that causes reduction. The reducing agent is oxidized.

Oxidation states, also known as oxidation numbers, represent the charge that an atom has in a molecule or ion.

Balancing a chemical equation

According to the law of conservation of mass, the mass of the products must always equal the mass of the reactants in a chemical reaction. Because mass is conserved, the number of each type of atom in the products must equal the number of each type of atom in the reactants. The key to balancing a chemical reaction is in balancing the number of each type of atom on both sides of the equation. Only the coefficients in front of the reactants and products may be changed to accomplish this, not the subscripts in the molecules themselves. Try balancing the largest number of a type of atom first. Also, check if any odd numbers need to be changed to even. Always leave the uncombined elements to balance until the end.

Example #1
Balance the equation KNO_3 (s) → KNO_2 (s) + O_2 (g).

First, determine the types and numbers of each type of atom on each side of the equation:

Reactants		Products	
K	1	K	1
N	1	N	1
O	3	O	4

"Oxygen" needs to be balanced. Add a coefficient of "2" to the left side to force "oxygen" to be even and update the counts:

Reactants		Products	
K	2	K	1
N	2	N	1
O	6	O	4

Now, balance the potassium and nitrogen by placing a coefficient of "2" in front of the KNO_2 and update the counts:

Reactants		Products	
K	2	K	2
N	2	N	2
O	6	O	6

The equation is now balanced: $2KNO_3(s)$ → $2KNO_2(s) + O_2(g)$.

Example #2
Balance the equation $C_2H_2(g) + O_2(g) \rightarrow CO_2(g) + H_2O(g)$.

First, determine the types and numbers of each type of atom on each side of the equation:

Reactants		Products	
C	2	C	1
H	2	H	2
O	2	O	3

"Oxygen" needs to be balanced, but remember to leave the uncombined oxygen reactant until the end. "Carbon" also needs to be balanced. Add a coefficient of "4" to the CO_2 on the right side and a coefficient of "2" in front of the C_2H_2 and update the counts:

Reactants		Products	
C	4	C	4
H	4	H	2
O	2	O	9

Balance the "hydrogen" by adding a "2" in front of the H_2O and update the counts:

Reactants		Products	
C	4	C	4
H	4	H	4
O	2	O	10

Finally, balance the "oxygen" by adding a "5" in front of the O_2 on the left.

The equation is now balanced: $2C_2H_2 (g) + 5O_2 (g) \rightarrow 4CO_2 (g) + 2H_2O (g)$.

Balancing a chemical equation involving a simple oxidation-reduction reaction

One method to balance simple oxidation-reduction reactions is to split the reaction into half-reactions. First, write the oxidation half-reaction and the reduction half-reaction. Remember the phrase *"LEO the lion says GER,"* which is a reminder that the loss of electrons is oxidation, and the gain of electrons is reduction. Next, balance the electrons by multiply the equation(s) by the necessary factor(s). Finally, cancel the electron(s) and combine the balanced oxidation and reduction half-reactions into a balanced net chemical equation.

Example #1
Balance the following chemical equation involving an oxidation-reduction reaction: $Na + O_2 \rightarrow Na^+ + O^{2-}$.

In order to balance the equation $Na + O_2 \rightarrow Na^+ + O^{2-}$, first, write the individual half-reactions:

oxidation: $Na \rightarrow Na^+ + e^-$
reduction: $O_2 + 4e^- \rightarrow 2O^{2-}$.

Next, balance the number of electrons by multiplying the oxidation half-reaction by 4:

oxidation: $4Na \rightarrow 4Na^+ + 4e^-$
reduction: $O_2 + 4e^- \rightarrow 2O^{2-}$.

Finally, cancel the electrons and combine the half-reactions into the net reaction:

$4Na + O_2 \rightarrow 4Na^+ + 2O^{2-}$.

Example #2
Given the following equation at standard temperature and pressure (STP),

$4Fe\ (s) + 3O_2\ (g) \rightarrow 2Fe_2O_3\ (s)$, explain how to determine the volume of $O_2\ (g)$ needed to produce 10.0 moles of $Fe_2O_3\ (s)$.

One method to determine the volume of $O_2\ (g)$ needed to produce 10.0 moles of $Fe_2O_3\ (s)$ is to use dimensional analysis with the mole ratio for the balanced chemical equation. Because 3 moles of O_2 (g) produce 2 moles of $Fe_2O_3\ (s)$, the needed mole ratio is $\left(\frac{3\ \text{moles}\ O_2}{2\ \text{moles}\ Fe_2O_3}\right)$. Also, at STP, one mole of a gas has a volume of 22.4 L. This can be written as a conversion factor of $\left(\frac{22.4\ L}{1\ \text{mole}\ O_2}\right)$. Using dimensional analysis, $(10.0\ \text{mol}\ Fe_2O_3)\left(\frac{3\ \text{moles}\ O_2}{2\ \text{moles}\ Fe_2O_3}\right)\left(\frac{22.4\ L}{1\ \text{mole}\ O_2}\right) = 336\ L$.

Example #3
Given the following equation at STP,

$C_3H_8\ (l) + 5O_2\ (g) \rightarrow 3CO_2\ (g) + 4H_2O\ (g)$, explain how to determine the volume of $O_2\ (g)$ needed to burn 1.00 kg of $C_3H_8\ (l)$.

One method to determine the volume of $O_2\ (g)$ needed to burn 1.0 kg of $C_3H_8\ (l)$ is to use dimensional analysis with conversion factors for the molar mass, number of moles, and liters of gas at STP. The conversion factor for the molar mass of C_3H_8 can be written as $\left(\frac{1\ \text{mol}\ C_3H_8}{44.1\ \text{grams}\ C_3H_8}\right)$. Because 1 mole of $C_3H_8\ (l)$ requires 5 moles of $O_2\ (g)$, the needed mole ratio is $\left(\frac{5\ \text{moles}\ O_2}{1\ \text{mole}\ C_3H_8}\right)$. Also, at STP, one mole of a gas has a volume of 22.4 L. This can be written as the conversion factor $\left(\frac{22.4\ L}{1\ \text{mole}\ O_2}\right)$. Using dimensional analysis, $(1.0\ \text{kg of}\ C_3H_8)\left(\frac{1000\ g}{1\ kg}\right)\left(\frac{1\ \text{mole}\ C_3H_8}{44.1\ g\ C_3H_8}\right)\left(\frac{5\ \text{moles}\ O_2}{1\ \text{mole}\ C_3H_8}\right)\left(\frac{22.4\ L\ O_2}{1\ \text{mole}\ O_2}\right) = 2.54 \times 10^3\ L\ O_2$.

Example #4
Given the following equation,

$2Na\ (s) + Cl_2\ (g) \rightarrow 2NaCl\ (s)$, explain how to determine the amount in grams of Na (s) needed to produce 500.0 g of NaCl (s).

One method to determine the amount in grams of Na (s) needed to produce 500.0 g of NaCl (s) is to use dimensional analysis with conversion factors for the molar mass and number of moles. The conversion factor for the molar mass of NaCl (s) can be written as $\left(\frac{1\ \text{mol}\ NaCl}{58.44\ g\ NaCl}\right)$. Because 2 moles of Na (s) produce 2 moles of NaCl (s), the needed mole ratio is $\left(\frac{2\ \text{moles}\ Na}{2\ \text{moles}\ NaCl}\right)$. The conversion factor for the molar mass of Na can be written as $\left(\frac{22.99\ g\ Na}{1\ \text{mole}\ Na}\right)$. Using dimensional analysis, $(500.0\ g\ NaCl)\left(\frac{1\ \text{mol}\ NaCl}{58.44\ g\ NaCl}\right)\left(\frac{2\ \text{moles}\ Na}{2\ \text{moles}\ NaCl}\right)\left(\frac{22.99\ g\ Na}{1\ \text{mole}\ Na}\right) = 196.7\ g\ Na$.

Example #5
Given the following equation at STP,

2Na (s) + Cl_2 (g) → 2NaCl (s), explain how to determine the volume of Cl_2 (g) needed to produce 1.00 kg of NaCl(s).

One method to determine the volume of Cl_2 (g) needed to produce 1.00 kg of NaCl (s) is to use dimensional analysis with conversion factors for the molar mass, number of moles, and liters of gas at STP. The conversion factor for the molar mass of NaCl can be written as $\left(\frac{1\ mol\ NaCl}{58.44\ g\ NaCl}\right)$. Because 1 mole of Cl_2 (g) produces 2 moles of NaCl (s), the needed mole ratio is $\left(\frac{1\ mole\ Cl_2}{2\ mole\ NaCl}\right)$. Also, at STP, one mole of a gas has a volume of 22.4 L. This can be written as a conversion factor $\left(\frac{22.4\ L}{1\ mole\ Cl_2}\right)$. Using dimensional analysis, (1.00 kg NaCl)$\left(\frac{1000\ g}{1\ kg}\right)\left(\frac{1\ mol\ NaCl}{58.44\ g\ NaCl}\right)\left(\frac{1\ mole\ Cl_2}{2\ mole\ NaCl}\right)\left(\frac{22.4\ L\ O_2}{1\ mole\ O_2}\right)$ = 191.65 L Cl_2, which rounds up to 192 L because 191 L will not be enough.

Limiting reagent in a reaction

The limiting reagent, or limiting reactant, is the reactant that determines or "limits" the amount of product formed. The limiting reagent is totally consumed in the chemical reaction. The other reactants in the chemical reaction must be present in excess amounts than what is needed. The excess reactants will be left over after the limiting reactant is consumed. To determine the limiting reagent from the balanced chemical equation, select one of the products and calculate how much of that product can be produced from each reactant. The reactant that produces the least amount of that product is the limiting reactant or limiting reagent.

Calculating the percent yield for a chemical reaction

To calculate the percent yield for a chemical reaction, use the formula

$$\text{percent yield} = \frac{\text{actual yield}}{\text{theoretical yield}} \times 100\ \%.$$

The actual yield should be stated in the problem or determined experimentally. The theoretical yield can be calculated from the balanced chemical equation with dimensional analysis using conversion factors for molar mass and number of moles. Divide the actual yield by the theoretical yield. This is a decimal that can be converted to a percent by multiplying by 100 and adding the percent sign.

Example #1
Given that 100.0 g of H_2 (g) react with 350.0 g of O_2 (g), explain how to determine the limiting reactant and the amount of excess reactant that remains.

2H_2 (g) + O_2 (g) → 2H_2O (g).

To determine the limiting reactant, first determine the amount of H_2O that can be produced from each of the reactants:

(100.0 g H_2) $\left(\frac{1\ mole\ H_2}{2.016\ g\ H_2}\right)\left(\frac{2\ moles\ H_2O}{2\ moles\ H_2}\right)\left(\frac{18.016\ g\ H_2O}{1\ mole\ H_2O}\right)$ = 893.7 g H_2O.

$$(350.0 \text{ g O}_2) \left(\frac{1 \text{ mole O}_2}{32.00 \text{ g O}_2}\right) \left(\frac{2 \text{ moles H}_2\text{O}}{1 \text{ mole O}_2}\right) \left(\frac{18.016 \text{ g H}_2\text{O}}{1 \text{ mole H}_2\text{O}}\right) = 394.1 \text{ g H}_2\text{O}.$$

Because O_2 produces the least amount of H_2O, O_2 is the limiting reagent. Therefore, H_2 is the reactant that is in excess. Calculating the amount of H_2 consumed in this reaction:
$$(350.0 \text{ g O}_2) \left(\frac{1 \text{ mole O}_2}{32.00 \text{ g O}_2}\right) \left(\frac{2 \text{ moles H}_2}{1 \text{ mole O}_2}\right) \left(\frac{2.016 \text{ g H}_2}{1 \text{ mole H}_2}\right) = 44.10 \text{ g H}_2 \text{ (consumed)}.$$

Subtracting this amount from the original amount yields the excess amount: $100.0 \text{ g H}_2 - 44.10 \text{ g H}_2 = 55.91 \text{ g H}_2$ (excess).

Example #2
Find the percent yield in the following reaction if 200.0 g of solid $KClO_3$ produced 100.0 g of solid KCl.

$2KClO_3 \text{ (s)} \rightarrow 2KCl \text{ (s)} + 3O_2 \text{ (g)}.$

To calculate the percent yield if 200.0 g of solid $KClO_3$ produced 100.0 g of solid KCl, first calculate the theoretical yield of KCl or the maximum amount of KCl that can be produced.

Theoretical yield:
$$(200.0 \text{ g KClO}_3) \left(\frac{1 \text{ mole KClO}_3}{122.6 \text{ g KClO}_3}\right) \left(\frac{2 \text{ moles KCl}}{2 \text{ moles KClO}_3}\right) \left(\frac{74.55 \text{ g KCl}}{1 \text{ mole KCl}}\right) = 121.6 \text{ g KCl}.$$

The formula to calculate percent yield is percent yield $= \frac{\text{actual yield}}{\text{theoretical yield}} \times 100 \%$. Substituting in the 100.0 g of KCl for the actual yield and the 121.6 g of KCl for the theoretical yield,
percent yield $= \frac{100.0 \text{ g}}{121.6 \text{ g}} \times 100 \% = 82.24 \%$.

Example #3
Balanced equation for the combustion of methane

The molecular formula for methane is CH_4. For a combustion equation, the reactants are methane (CH_4) and oxygen gas (O_2). The products of this combustion reaction are water vapor (H_2O) and carbon dioxide (CO_2). Setting up the equation yields the following reaction:
$CH_4 \text{ (g)} + O_2 \text{ (g)} \rightarrow CO_2 \text{ (g)} + H_2O \text{ (g)}.$

This equation must still be balanced. Finally, the combustion of methane is given by the following reaction:
$CH_4 \text{ (g)} + 2O_2 \text{ (g)} \rightarrow CO_2 \text{ (g)} + 2H_2O \text{ (g)}.$

Example #4
Balanced equation for the neutralization of hydrochloric acid, HCl (aq), with sodium hydroxide, NaOH (aq)

In a neutralization reaction, an acid reacts with a base to form a salt and water. The salt forms from the cation of the base and the anion of the acid. The salt formed from these reactants is NaCl with the Na^+ from the base and the Cl^- from the acid. Water forms from the remaining H^+ and OH^- ions:
acid + base → salt + water

$HCl \text{ (aq)} + NaOH \text{ (aq)} \rightarrow NaCl \text{ (aq)} + H_2O \text{ (l)}.$

<u>Example #5</u>
Balanced equation for the decomposition reaction of solid lithium carbonate (Li_2CO_3)

The general form for a decomposition reaction is AB → A + B. However, this metal oxide has three elements and may at first not seem to fit the general form. When many metal carbonates are heated, they form the metal oxide and carbon dioxide gas. In this case, the products will also be compounds. In this decomposition reaction, when heated, solid lithium oxide decomposes to form solid lithium oxide and gaseous carbon dioxide:
$$Li_2CO_3(s) \xrightarrow{\Delta} LiO(s) + CO_2(g).$$

<u>Example #6</u>
Balanced equation for the dehydration of ethanol

Ethanol (C_2H_5OH) can be dehydrated to produce ethane (C_2H_4). The gaseous ethanol is passed over a hot aluminum oxide catalyst to produce ethane and water.

$$\text{ethanol} \xrightarrow{\text{aluminum oxide}} \text{ethane + water}$$

$$C_2H_5OH\ (g) \xrightarrow{Al_2O_3} C_2H_4\ (g) + H_2O\ (l).$$

This can also be shown in the form of condensed structural formulas:
$$CH_3CH_2OH \xrightarrow{Al_2O_3} CH_2 = CH_2 + H_2O.$$

Single- and double-replacement reactions

Single-replacement reactions, which are also known as single-displacement reactions or substitution reactions, have the general form of A + BC → AC + B. An example of a single-replacement reaction is the displacement of hydrogen from hydrochloric acid by zinc metal as given in the following equation:
$$Zn\ (s) + 2HCl\ (aq) → ZnCl_2\ (aq) + H_2\ (aq)$$

Double-replacement reactions, which are also known as double-displacement reactions, have the general form of AB + CD → AD + CB. An example of a double-replacement reaction is when aqueous solutions of lead(II) nitrate and potassium iodide react to form solid lead(II) iodide and aqueous potassium nitrate as given by the following equation:
$$Pb(NO_3)_2\ (aq) + 2KI\ (aq) → PbI_2\ (s) + 2KNO_3\ (aq)$$

<u>Example #7</u>
Identify each reaction type as a single- or double-replacement reaction, and predict the products of the following equations:

1. $Mg\ (s) + 2\ H_2O\ (l) →.$
2. $Pb(NO_3)_2\ (aq) + 2\ KI\ (aq) →.$

1. This reaction must be a single-replacement reaction because the left side corresponds to the left side of the general equation A + BC → AB + C. In this case, the magnesium replaces some of the hydrogen, and the products are hydrogen gas and magnesium hydroxide.
$$Mg\ (s) + 2H_2O\ (l) → Mg(OH)_2\ (aq) + H_2\ (g).$$

2. This reaction must be a double-replacement reaction because the left side corresponds to the left side of the general equation AB + CD → AD + CB. In this case, the Pb^+ cation from the $Pb(NO_3)_2$ bonds with the I^- anion from the KI to form solid PbI_2. The NO_3^- anion from the $Pb(NO_3)_2$ bonds with the K^+ cation from the KI to form aqueous KNO_3. $Pb(NO_3)_2$ (aq) + 2KI (aq) → PbI_2 (s) + 2KNO_3 (aq).

<u>Example #8</u>
Balanced equation for the oxidation-reduction reaction of metallic zinc powder and aqueous copper(II) sulfate

According to the activity series, zinc is more reactive than copper. Therefore, the zinc is oxidized, and the copper is reduced. Write the half-reactions:
oxidation: $Zn → Zn^{2+} + 2e^-$.

reduction: $Cu^{2+} + 2e^- → Cu$.

Cancel the electrons and combine the two half-reactions into the net equation:
$Zn + Cu^{2+} → Zn^{2+} + Cu$.

Finally, add the symbols to indicate the state of each reactant and product:
Zn (s) + Cu^{2+} (aq) → Zn^{2+} (aq) + Cu (s).

Interestingly, this equation can also be written as the following single-displacement reaction:
Zn (s) + $CuSO_4$ (aq) → $ZnSO_4$ (aq) + Cu (s).

This single-displacement reaction has the same net ionic equation after canceling out the spectator ions.

<u>Example #9</u>
Balanced equation for the oxidation-reduction reaction of a piece of solid copper wire immersed in an aqueous solution of silver nitrate

According to the activity series, copper is more reactive than silver. Therefore, the copper is oxidized, and the silver is reduced. Write the half-reactions:
oxidation: $Cu → Cu^{2+} + 2e^-$.

reduction: $Ag^+ + e^- → Ag$.

Multiply the reduction half-reaction by 2 to balance the number of electrons:
oxidation: $Cu → Cu^{2+} + 2e^-$.

reduction: $2Ag^+ + 2e^- → 2Ag$.

Cancel the electrons and combine the two half-reactions into the net equation:
$Cu + 2Ag^+ → Cu^{2+} + 2Ag$.

Finally, add the symbols to indicate the state of each reactant and product:
Cu (s) + 2Ag^+ (aq) → Cu^{2+} (aq) + 2Ag (s).

Note that this equation is also classified as a single-displacement reaction:
Cu (s) + $2AgNO_3$ (aq) → $Cu(NO_3)_2$ (aq) + $2Ag$ (s).

This single-displacement reaction has the same net ionic equation after canceling out the spectator ions.

Water

The vast majority of cells are mostly comprised of water and reside in water-rich environments. Because of how prevalent it is, the uniqueness of water is often overlooked. Water is composed of two hydrogen atoms and one oxygen atom, bonded together by covalent bonds, and forming a V-shaped molecule. This V-shape is a result of water being a polar molecule. Polar molecules are those which have an uneven distribution of electrons in their orbits or shells (this uneven distribution results in having the positive charges on one side of the molecule and the negative charges on the other). Oxygen possesses an electronegativity and a large positively-charged nucleus, both of which contribute in pulling the hydrogen electrons closer to the oxygen atom. This 'closeness' results in the hydrogen atoms being slightly more positively charged while the oxygen atom is slightly more negatively charged. In water, these molecules continually interact and link up very briefly due to weak intermolecular bonding, resulting in *hydrogen bonds*.

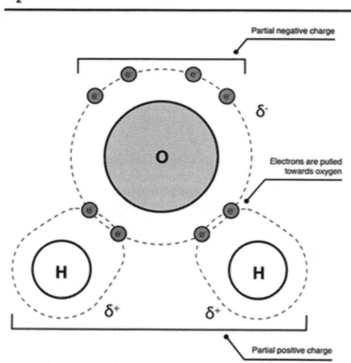

Water possesses many important attributes, namely its cohesive and adhesive properties, its ability to moderate temperature, the fact that it expands when it freezes, and its use as a versatile solvent.

Cohesion, or the attraction of molecules to other molecules of the same type, occurs when hydrogen bonding is occurring between water molecules. This bonding that occurs allows the water molecules to attach to one another, even working against gravity at times, as in the case of water being transported upward through a stem to the top of a plant. This is accomplished by an entire network of water-conducting cells, pushing water from the roots up and out to the plant's leaves. Another example of how we can see and experience the cohesive properties of water is in surface tension. Slightly overfilling a glass of water results in water being above the rim of the glass without running over. This is only possible because of the unique bonding that occurs between water molecules-due to water's cohesive properties, it is able to remain attached to itself and run over. Raft spiders take advantage of water's cohesive properties as well, using surface tension to actually walk across small bodies of water. In contrast to cohesion (the attraction of the same type of molecules to each other), adhesion is the attraction of two different types of molecules. One way this happens in nature is where water molecules form weak hydrogen bonds with plant cell walls in order to help fight gravity.

As mentioned earlier, water also possesses an ability to moderate temperature. Water has the unique ability of being able to release and absorb immense amounts of heat while only undergoing a small change in temperature. With this ability, water is able to moderate air temperature by absorbing or releasing stored heat into the air. All of this is because water has a high specific heat, or the amount of heat required to change a unit mass of a substance by one degree Celsius. Water's specific heat is one calorie per gram per degree Celsius. This means that for each gram of water, it takes one calorie of heat to raise the temperature by 1 degree Celsius.

Another unique property of water is that when it freezes it expands instead of contracts. With other liquids, freezing causes the water molecules to move more slowly and stay closer together (similar to how people huddle together to stay warm in colder temperatures). Water molecules, on the other hand, form hydrogen bonds with each one another as they move closer together. As the temperature gets colder and colder these hydrogen bonds grow stronger and stronger, and when the water has fully frozen into ice, these strong hydrogen bonds are frozen as well, taking up about 10 percent more volume than they do in their liquid state. Because the same amount of water molecules as before are now taking up more space in their frozen state, the resulting ice is less dense than the water it originated as, causing it to float to the top of a glass of water.

Hydrogen bonds

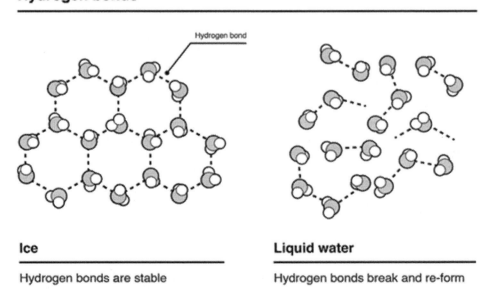

Ice

Hydrogen bonds are stable

Liquid water

Hydrogen bonds break and re-form

- 107 -

Finally, the previously mentioned polarity of water molecules also means that water possesses diverse uses as a solvent. A solvent is a substance in which a solute is dissolved, and solutes like salt are easily dissolved in water because it is made up of positively and negatively charged atoms known as cations and anions, known as ionic compounds. These cations and anions dissolve so easily because they are attracted to the slightly positive charge of hydrogen atoms and the slightly negative charge of the oxygen atoms. Water molecules then separate the individually charged atoms, preventing them from bonding to each other again and thus creating a homogeneous solution of the cations and anions. Non-ionic compounds like sugar are also easily dissolved in water because they have polar regions. Water molecules form hydrogen bonds with the polar regions (hydroxyl groups) of these compounds, resulting in a homogenous solution. Substances that are attracted to water are called hydrophilic while substances that repel water a called hydrophobic.

Concepts of acids and bases

Every liquid has traits that are either acidic or basic. Hydrogen ions (H+), when released in a liquid, become acidic. On the other hand, when hydroxide ions (OH-) are released in a liquid, it becomes basic. These ions (hydrogen and hydroxide) are the two that determine a solution's status as acidic or basic.

Brønsted–Lowry Approaches
The *Brønsted–Lowry Theory* of acids and bases states that the *acid* is a proton donor (a hydrogen atom, H+) and that the base is a proton acceptor. The pH scale is used to describe acids and bases, ranging from 0-14 with 7 being the middle of the scale, known as neutral. Values less than seven are considered to be acidic while values greater than 7 are considered to be basic (or alkaline).

Acids and bases are also divided into two categories: strong and weak. An acid's strength is measured by the following equation:

$$K_a = \frac{[H^+]\,[A^-_{weak}]}{[HA_{weak}]}$$

When K_a is a large number, it is considered to be a strong acid (e.g. hydrochloric acid, or HCl, has a K_a value of to 1.3×10^6). Acids that have a small K_a are considered to be weak (e.g. water, or H_2O, has a K_a value of 1×10^{-14}).

A base's strength is measured by the following equation:

$$K_b = \frac{[HB^+][OH^-]}{[B]}$$

The Brønsted–Lowry Theory of acids and bases holds that every acid has as conjugate base and that every base has a conjugate acid.

Lewis Theory
The Lewis Theory of acids and bases states that bases can donate pairs of electrons and that acids can accept pairs of elections. A Lewis acid is any substance that can accept a pair of non-bonding

electrons. A hydrogen ion (H+) is a good example of a Lewis acid because it can only accept one pair of electrons.

A Lewis base, on the other hand, is any substance that can donate a pair of electrons to a Lewis acid. A hydroxide ion (OH-) is a good example of a Lewis base because it can only donate one pair of electrons. The combination of Lewis acids and bases results in the formation of a Lewis adduct.

Solution and solubility

<u>Different types of solutions</u>
A solution is a homogenous mixture of more than one substance in which a solute is uniformly dissolved within a solvent. A solution (the result of a solute being dissolved into a solvent) is said to be diluted if only a small amount is dissolved, while a solution is said to be concentrated if a large amount is dissolved. One example of a diluted solution is water that comes from an unfiltered house tap because it contains very small amounts of some minerals.

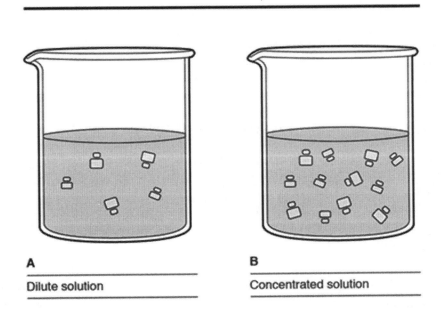

Solution Concentration

A

Dilute solution

B

Concentrated solution

A solution is considered to be saturated when a solute is no longer dissolving in a solvent. An example of this can be found in a simple hummingbird feeder. Hummingbirds prefer to eat a sugar-water solution that is as sweet as possible. When dissolving sugar in water, there will be a point at which sugar crystals will no longer dissolve and instead will remain as whole pieces floating around in the solution. It is at this point that the sugar-water solution is considered saturated as it can no longer dissolve sugar crystals. The level of a solvent at which it can no longer dissolve any more solute is known as the saturation point. In some cases, however, it is possible to force more solute to be dissolved into a solvent, resulting in what is known as crystallization. Just before crystallization takes place there is a point at which a solution becomes supersaturated. Supersaturation can also occur in a seemingly stable solution if the solution is disturbed, resulting in the start of the crystallization process.

Terms like diluted, concentrated, saturated, and supersaturated are certainly help in qualifying a solution, a chemical necessitates a more precise, quantitative description, and this is especially true when mixing strong acids or bases. In order to calculate the concentration of a solution, we must first find the solution's molarity. Molarity, or the amount of solute per unit volume of solution, is sometimes measured in parts per million (or ppm), as is the case in environmental reporting. Parts per million is the number of milligrams of a substance dissolved in one liter of water. In order to find the molarity of a solution, the following formula is used:

$$c = \frac{n}{V}$$

In the above formula, c is the molarity of a solution, n is the amount of solute measured in moles, and V is the volume of the solution measured in liters.

Example 1
Find the molarity of a solution in which 2.0 grams of NaCl are dissolved into enough water to make 100 mL of solution.

In order to solve this, we must calculate the number of moles of NaCl.

In order to find the mass of NaCl, we must first calculate the mass of each of the molecule's atoms by adding them together:

23.0g (Na) + 35.5g (Cl) = 58.8g NaCl

Next, the combined total mass of NaCl (58.8g) must be multiplied by one mole per total mass of the substance:

2.0g NaCl × (1 mol NaCl/58.5g NaCl) = 0.034 mol NaCl

Lastly, divided the moles by the number of liters of the solution:

(0.034 mol NaCl)/(0.100L) = 0.34 M NaCl

In order to prepare a solution of a different concentration, the molarity of the solution must be used to calculate what is known as the *mass solute*.

Example 2
Prepare 600.0 mL of 1.20 M solution of sodium chloride.

Here's how we solve this:

1.20 M NaCl = 1.20 mol NaCl/1.00 L of solution

0.600 L solution × (1.20 mol NaCl/1.00 L of solution) = 0.72 moles NaCl

0.72 moles NaCl × (58.5g NaCl/1 mol NaCl) = 42.12 g NaCl

The answer, then, is that we must dissolve 42.12 g NaCl in enough water to make 600.0 L of solution.

Factors affecting the solubility of substances and the dissolving process

There are a number of factors that affect the rate at which dissolving occurs, including particle size, temperature, pressure, and agitation (or rate of stirring). Recall the ideal gas law which states that $PV = nRT$, where P is pressure, V is volume, and T is temperature. If any of these three properties are affected (pressure, volume, and/or temperature), the entire system will also be affected. These effects of these changes play out as follows: an increase or decrease in any of the above-mentioned factors (particle size, temperature, pressure, or agitation) will result in an increase or decrease in the dissolving rate, respectively, because each of these factors contribute to the breaking apart of held-together intermolecular forces. Once these forces are successfully broken apart, the solute particles will link to particles in the solvent, resulting in the solute being dissolved.

A solubility curve is a graphic representation of the relationship between temperature and the solubility of a given substance in a given solvent. If a given reading falls below the solubility curve, the solvent is said to be unsaturated and can thus hold more solute. If a given reading falls on the solubility curve, the solvent is said to be full (or saturated) and thus cannot hold more solute. If a given reading falls above the curve, the solvent is said to be unstable (or supersaturated) because it is holding more solute than it should.

A solvent is said to be polar if it has different electronegativities, or partial charges. As mentioned earlier, water is an example of a polar solvent. A solvent is said to be non-polar if it has similar electronegativities, or lacking partial charges. Benzene is an example of a non-polar solvent. Knowing a solvent's polarity is crucial when attempting to dissolve solutes. Polar solutes will dissolve in polar solvents, and non-polar solutes will dissolve in non-polar solvents ("like dissolves like" is a helpful phrase to remember here). The resulting solid from a reaction is called a precipitate. Salt (an ionic compound resulting from a neutralization reaction) can be removed from a solvent such as water by a precipitation reaction. This precipitation reaction, when specifically involving water, is a process known as ionization.

A freezing point depression occurs when a solute is added to a solvent in order to lower the solvent's freezing point. When applied in colder temperatures, this can prove to be an especially useful process. One example of this is in the application of salt to ice in winter, which allows the ice to melt at a much lower temperature than normal, resulting in safer driving conditions (note: this only works down to a certain degree as salt becomes ineffective when the temperature is too low). Another example of this can be found in the mixing of water and ethylene glycol, a mixture used to keep radiator fluid (antifreeze) from freezing in colder temperatures.

Titration

Solution stoichiometry

Solution stoichiometry deals with the quantities of solutes within chemical reactions occurring in solutions. The quantity of a solute in a solution is derived by taking the molarity of the solution and multiplying it by the solution's volume (the total number of moles of the elements making up the solute should be equal on either side of the equation).

If the concentration of a specific solute in a solution is not known, a titration can be used. A titration takes the solution with the unknown solute and combines it with a standard solution in which the solute concentration is already known. The equivalence point, then, is the point at which the unknown solute has completely reacted with the known solute. Using what is known about the standard solution (its concentration and volume) and the volume of the unknown solution, we can determine the concentration of the unknown solute by utilizing a balancing equation. One example of this can be found in the combining of acids and bases: the equivalence point is only reached when the rendered solution is neutral. When HCl, an acid, is combined with NaOH, a base, the resulting solution is not neutral because there are an unequal number of cations and anions.

Precipitation titrations

A precipitation titration is a titration in which the endpoint is determined by the formation of a precipitate. Argentometric titrations are the most common precipitation titrations (Argentum means silver in Latin), which involve reactions between a silver ion and a titrant of silver nitrate ($AgNO_3$). Because it reacts so quickly, silver nitrate is seen as a very useful titrant. The resulting products of all titrimetric precipitations are silver salts. A simple argentometric precipitation titration can be performed in order to determine the amount of chlorine in seawater. The reaction appears as follows:

$$AgNO_3\ (aq) + NaCl\ (aq) \rightarrow AgCl\ (s) + NaNO_3\ (aq)$$

Silver chloride, which precipitates out of a solution, is almost entirely insoluble in water. Potassium chromate (K_2CrO_4) is a selective indicator and can be added in order to discover when the reaction will be complete. Once all chloride ions from the sample have precipitated, silver ions will then react with chromate ions, forming the orange-colored Ag_2CrO_4. Having the sample volume, the amount of titrant necessary to complete the precipitation, the reacting species' molar mass, and the sample's density proves to be all the information needed in order to calculate the concentration of chloride ions.

A titration curve can be useful because it conveys a visual representation of what occurs before, during, and after the equivalence point. An argentometric titration curve is sigmoidal when the reagent volume is plotted on the x-axis and the concentration function is plotted on the y-axis. Here's an example:

Sample Titration Curve

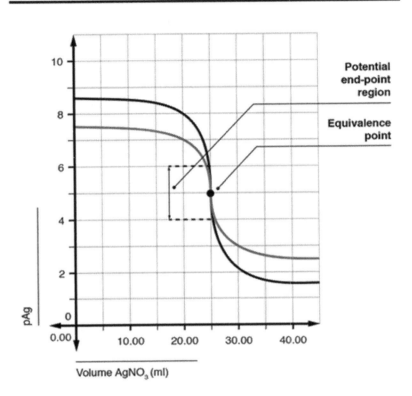

There is an obvious drop in reagent concentration at the equivalence point, but beyond it the concentration decreases more gradually. Small amounts of added titrant around the equivalence point caused dramatic changes in the concentration of both the analyte and the reagent. The above example also shows that at the point of equivalence the molar concentrations of sample cation/titrant anion and sample anion/titrant cation are equal.

Nature of Molecules and Intermolecular Interaction

Ionic substances

Ionic compounds are simply put, compounds which are held together with ionic bonds. Ionic bonding results from the transfer of electrons between atoms. A cation or positive ion is formed when an atom loses one or more electrons. An anion or negative ion is formed when an atom gains one or more electrons. An ionic bond results from the electrostatic attraction between a cation and an anion.

One example of a compound formed by ionic bonds is sodium chloride or NaCl. Sodium (Na) is an alkali metal and tends to form Na^+ ions. Chlorine is a halogen and tends to form Cl^- ions. The Na^+ ion and the Cl^- ion are attracted to each other. This electrostatic attraction between these oppositely charged ions is what results in the ionic bond between them. Rocks and minerals are usually ionic compounds.

$$Na \cdot + \overset{\times \, \times}{\underset{\times \, \times}{\times Cl}} \overset{\times}{\times} \longrightarrow [Na]^+ [\overset{\times \, \times}{\underset{\times \, \times}{\cdot Cl}} \overset{\times}{\times}]^-$$

electron transfer from
sodium to chlorine

Lattice geometries

Ionic compounds have an endlessly -repeating pattern holding them together. This pattern is known as a lattice and is dependent on the ions which are present. The number of single molecules present determines the size of the lattice. For example, each grain of table salt is a crystal which is a repeated structure of sodium chloride (NaCl) molecules. The ions of sodium and chloride alternate with one another in three dimensions to form a cube structure.

Sodium Chloride Lattice

6:6 Coordinated

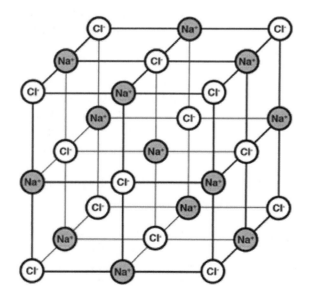

The lattice previously depicted has a centered sodium ion. This sodium ion is connected to six chloride ions, however, if the chloride ion were centered, it would have six sodium ions connected to it as well. This means that sodium chloride is described as 6:6 coordinated.

The lattice structure is determined by potential attractions between ions. Sodium ions can accept only six chloride ions. If more chloride ions were present, they would begin to repel one another and destabilize the crystalline structure.

As mentioned before, lattice structure is able to vary with other ions present. Zincblende (ZnS) has a coordination of four per ion, and is, therefore, 4:4 *coordinated.*

Lattice energies
Opposite charges attract one another and allow for bonding in ions. Lattice energy refers to energy that is released when two oppositely-charged ions bond. Single ions require less energy to stay together in crystal lattices. Lattice energy is primarily affected by the ionic charges and the ionic radii. Bonds become stronger as ionic charges increase in magnitude. A bond that has a -2 anion and a +3 cation is much stronger than a bond between a -1 anion and a +1 cation.

Lattice energy (U) is always positive and can be calculated using the following formula

$$U = k' \frac{(q_1)(q_2)}{r_o}$$

K is the constant and depends on valence configurations and lattice structure. (q_1) and (q_2) refer to the charges on the ions, and r_o is the internuclear distance. Ionic compounds can have different lattice energies despite having the same arrangement. This is due to having ionic charges of higher magnitude. For instance, magnesium oxide has two +2 cations which are bonded to -2 ions. This has a similar structure to sodium chloride, but will have a much stronger lattice energy due to the greater magnitude of the bonds.

Ionic radius size
The ionic radius size increases down a group of the periodic table. This is due to the increasing energy levels and the fact that electrons are orbiting farther and farther from the nucleus. The trend seen across the periods of the periodic table is due to the formation of cations or anions. Metals form cations or positive ions. Cations are smaller than their neutral atoms due to the loss of one or more electrons. Nonmetals except the noble gases form anions or negative ions. Anions are larger than their neutral atoms due to the gain of one or more electrons.

Radius/Ratio Effects
Radius ratio refers to the ionic radius of the smaller ion divided by the ionic radius of the larger ion. Usually the larger ion will be the anion and the smaller ion will be the cation. The lattice structure in crystals of 1:1 compounds, such as sodium chloride (NaCl) depends on the radius ratio. If the radius of the positive ion is calculated at greater than 73%, an 8:8 coordination is possible. If the calculation ranges between 41% and 73%, a 6:6 coordination is possible.

Covalent molecular substances

Covalent bonding results from the sharing of electrons between atoms. Atoms seek to fill their valence shell and will share electrons with another atom in order to have a full octet (except hydrogen and helium, which only hold two electrons in their valence shells). Molecular compounds have covalent bonds. Organic compounds such as proteins, carbohydrates, lipids, and nucleic acids are molecular compounds formed by covalent bonds. Methane (CH_4) is a molecular compound in which one carbon atom is covalently bonded to four hydrogen atoms as shown below. Covalent bonds are very strong and occur between two or more nonmetal atoms.

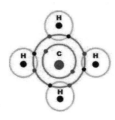

Lewis diagrams

Lewis diagrams—also called electron dot diagrams—are a symbolic representation of covalent bonds. Gilbert Lewis first discovered the structure of covalent bonds, and this form of diagram is named after him. Lewis diagrams show electrons in the valence shell, which are electrons available for covalent bonding. To draw a Lewis diagram follow the following procedure:

    Determine the number of available electrons.
    If the compound has more than two atoms, the least electronegative atom goes in the center—remembering that hydrogen (H) must go on the outside.
    Include all chemical bonds. Two electrons forming chemical bonds are usually represented with a dash.
    Make sure to complete the octets of electrons on the outside of the atom. Hydrogen only needs two electrons in the valence shell. All other atoms need eight electrons in the valence shell. There are some exceptions to this rule; for example, beryllium (Be) only needs four electrons in its valence shell and boron (B) needs only six electrons in its valence shell.
    Finally, Electrons can be moved from outer atoms, forming double or triple bonds if all of the electrons are used up but the octets still haven't been filled.

A good example to follow is the common molecule, CO_2, or carbon dioxide. Carbon is in the periodic group 14, and therefore has four valence electrons. Oxygen is in Group 16 and has six valence electrons. The total is 10 valence electrons. Carbon is the lower electronegative atom and therefore must be in the middle of the Lewis diagram with the two oxygen atoms on the side. Covalent bonds are formed between the oxygen atoms and the carbon, and two of the ten electrons should be placed in between each oxygen atom and the carbon. After the two electrons are taken out, the rest of the valence shells should be filled. There are not enough electrons in carbon dioxide, but using double bonds fills the valence shell and completes the following Lewis Dot structure.

Lewis Diagram

$$\overset{\cdot\,\cdot}{\underset{\cdot\,\cdot}{O}} = C = \overset{\cdot\,\cdot}{\underset{\cdot\,\cdot}{O}}$$

- 116 -

Valence bonds

The model for valence bonds has been supplemented in recent times with the molecular orbital model. This model illustrates the atoms being brought together and the formation of hybrid molecular orbitals by an interaction with atomic orbitals. The molecular orbitals are a cross between original atomic orbitals and usually will extend between two bonding atoms. Quantum mechanics, which is the modern theory of action that is applied on very small scales, can be used to calculate the electronic structure, bond angles, bond distances and energy levels of simple molecules with great accuracy. Bond distances can be determined with as much accuracy as measurement provides. Energy calculations for small molecules are accurate enough to be used in determining thermodynamic heats of formation.

The effects of overlapping of the orbitals and the potential energy changes in a molecule with distance need to be considered when discussing valence bond theory. The Lewis structure of H_2, for example, would be H – H, but a simple diagram like this fails to demonstrate the bond strength. The electron cloud in the nucleus of one atom is interacting with the electrons in another atom's nucleus. Potential energy must be mapped out as a function of distance between two atoms as demonstrated below:

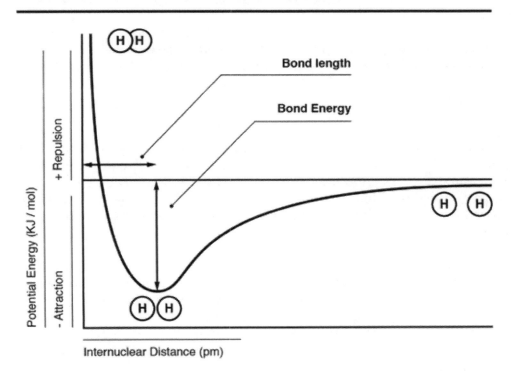

The minimum distance which two atoms approach may be referred to as the bond energy. The corresponding link is known as the equilibrium bond length, which is a happy medium that corresponds to a minimum in potential energy. This minimum is achieved when orbitals overlap and contain two spin-paired electrons. More energy is necessary to separate overlapping atoms.

Molecular orbitals

<u>Orbits and orbitals</u>
An orbit is a definite path, but an orbital is a region in space. The Bohr model described electrons as orbiting or following a definite path in space around the nucleus of an atom. But, according to the uncertainty principle, it is impossible to determine the location and the momentum of an electron simultaneously. Therefore, it is impossible to draw a definite path or orbit of an electron. An orbital as described by the quantum-mechanical model or the electron-cloud model is a region in space that is drawn in such a way as to indicate the probability of finding an electron at a specific location. The distance an orbital is located from the nucleus corresponds to the principal quantum number. The orbital shape corresponds to the subshell or azimuthal quantum number. The orbital orientation corresponds to the magnetic quantum number.

<u>Quantum numbers</u>
The principal quantum number (n) describes an electron's shell or energy level and actually describes the size of the orbital. Electrons farther from the nucleus are at higher energy levels. The subshell or azimuthal quantum number (l) describes the electron's sublevel or subshell (s, p, d, or f) and specifies the shape of the orbital. Typical shapes include spherical, dumbbell, and clover leaf. The magnetic quantum number (m_l) describes the orientation of the orbital in space. The spin or magnetic moment quantum number (m_s) describes the direction of the spin of the electron in the orbital.

<u>Aufbau principle</u>
The Aufbau principle is named from the German word for "building up," and it describes how electrons fill the energy levels or shells of an atom. In general, electrons will fill the n = 1 energy level before filling the n = 2 energy level, and electrons will fill the n = 2 energy level before filling the n = 3 energy level. The s subshell of an energy level will fill before the p subshell, which fills before the d and f subshells.

<u>Hund's rule</u>
Hund's rule describes how electrons fill the orbitals in a sublevel. Less energy is required for an electron to occupy an orbital alone than the energy needed for an electron to pair up with another electron in an orbital. Therefore, electrons will occupy each orbital in a subshell before electrons will begin to pair up in those orbitals. For example, in the $2p$ subshell, one electron will occupy each of the three orbitals before pairing begins. In the $3d$ subshell, one electron will occupy each of the five orbitals before pairing begins.

<u>Pauli exclusion principle</u>
The Pauli exclusion principle describes the unique address or location of each electron in an atom. Each electron has a unique or exclusive set of four quantum numbers indicating the electron's energy level, subshell, orbital orientation, and magnetic moment. Every orbital can hold a maximum of two electrons, but even if two electrons occupy the same orbital resulting in identical energy levels, subshells, and orbital orientations, they must have opposite spins, which means that their magnetic moment quantum numbers will differ.

<u>Electron configuration and the periodic table</u>
Electron configurations show a direct correlation to the periodic table. The periodic table can be divided into blocks representing s, p, d, and f subshells. The energy level corresponds to the row or period of the periodic table. The subshells, s, p, d, or f are related to the block's group numbers. The s block corresponds to groups 1A and 2A. The p block corresponds to groups 3A–8A. The d block

corresponds to the 10 groups of transition metals, and the *f* block corresponds to the two rows of inner transition metals (14 groups) located at the bottom of the table.

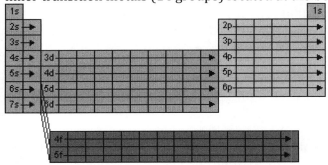

- The s orbital is the simplest of the orbitals. This is the innermost orbital of any atom and in hydrogen and helium is also the outermost orbital. The s orbital can contain two electrons and is spherical in shape.
- The p orbitals come after the s orbitals. There can be up to three p orbitals. One exists on each of the x, y, and z axes. Each of the p orbitals can contain two electrons, totaling six electrons.
- After the first and second *s* orbitals are filled, the *p* orbitals are filled. There are three *p* orbitals, one on each of the x, y, and z axes. Each *p* orbital can contain two electrons for a total of six electrons in the p orbitals.
- The d orbitals are filled after the p orbitals are full. There are five d orbitals which can contain two electrons each, totaling ten electrons.
- The *f orbitals* are next; there are seven *f* orbitals, which can contain a total of fourteen electrons.

Each shell containing the various orbitals has an increasing number of prerequisite subshells. This is demonstrated below:
- The first shell only has the one *s* subshell, so it has up to two electrons.
- The second shell has the *2* electrons in the s shell and *2p* subshells, so it has (2 + 6) eight electrons.
- The third shell has the *3s, 3p* and *3d* subshells, so it has (2 + 6 + 10) 18 electrons.
- The fourth shell has the *4s, 4p, 4d* and *4f* subshells, so it has (2 + 6 + 10 + 14) 32 electrons.

The formula $2n^2$ is used to determine the maximum number of available electrons per shell, where *n* is the shell number. The elements in the third period, for example, have three subshells. This provides them with up to 18 electrons, but will have only up to eight valence electrons because the d orbitals will not be filled.

The periodic table demonstrates the electron configuration of each element. Calcium (Ca), for example, is on the 4th period and has an atomic number of 20. It can, therefore, be written out as $1s^2 2s^2 2p^6 3s^2 3p^6 4s^2$. Transition metals are exempt to this rule because their quantum energy level rules allow their shells to remain unfilled.

Bonding, non-bonding, and anti-bonding orbitals are formed when atoms are brought together. This is referred to as molecular orbital theory. For N atomic orbitals in molecules, the result is N molecular orbitals. This can be described by wave functions.

An example of this is when a molecule that has two atomic orbitals, two molecular orbitals must be formed: one bonding and one anti-bonding. A certain energy would separate the molecular orbitals. A molecule with ten atoms would form five anti-bonding and five bonding molecular orbitals. A molecule that has three atomic orbitals would form one bonding, one non-bonding, and one anti-bonding molecular orbital.

Sigma bonds (σ bonds) are formed when atomic orbitals directly overlap. These are the strongest type of covalent bond. Sigma bonds are symmetrical around the bond axis. Common sigma bonds—where z is the axis of the bond—are s+s, p_z+p_z, s+p_z, and $d_z^2+d_z^2$.

Pi bonds (π bonds) are different and are usually weaker than sigma bonds. Pi bonds are a type of covalent bond where two ends of one p-orbital overlap the two ends of another p-orbital. D-orbitals can also form pi bonds.

Single bonds usually take the form of sigma bonds, and multiple bonds are usually one sigma bond plus one pi bond. A double bond is one sigma bond plus one pi bond. A triple bond consists of one sigma bond and two pi bonds. For example, ethylene has delta bonds (δ bonds) that are formed from four ends of one atomic orbital overlapping with four ends of another atomic orbital.

Hybridization

Orbital hybridization is the mixture, or shifting, of ground state orbitals within an atom which permits the formation of the necessary number of bonds to meet the octet rule. This is a widely accepted theory developed by Linus Pauling; it has great explanatory power, but does not correspond to actual physical processes. The theory predicts that a 2s electron becomes energized, or excited, and is "promoted" to a vacant 2p orbital; then, the half filled 2s orbital and the three half filled 2s orbitals combine to form the hybrid sp3 orbital which can then form bonds with other atoms. The ability of C to form a virtually infinite number of compounds despite its ground state electron configuration of $1s^22s^22p^2$ is explained by the orbital hybridization theory. Though C is the most striking application of the theory, N and O can also hybridize.

Bond energies

Bond energy describes the amount of energy needed to break one mole of covalently-bonded gases apart. Bond energies are measured in kilojoules per mole (kJ/mol). One mole is equal to Avogadro's number: $6.02214078 \times 10^{23}$.

To calculate the number of moles, some simple formulas can be used:

Moles = mass (g) / Relative mass (grams per mole).
Example: To calculate the number of moles in 30 grams of Helium, find the relative mass of helium on the periodic table. Helium's relative mass is approximately two.

On the periodic table, Helium's relative mass is approximately two. Using this information and the formula yields this result:
Moles = 30 / 2 = 15 moles

Some bonds are broken and others are formed in chemical reactions. These do not break or form spontaneously and chemical reactions always require energy to take place. The energy needed to break a bond is the *bond energy*. The usual rule is that the shorter the bond length, the greater the bond energy.

Energy is required for chemical reactions to occur and is released during reactions. One way to think of reactions is the breaking and formation of chemical bonds. Because chemical bonds have measurable strength, they tend to stay together unless acted upon by an external force, or energy; this energy is the reaction's activation energy. When bonds are broken or formed, energy stored in the bonds or substances is released. Energy on both sides of reactions occurs in various forms such as kinetic energy, heat, and light, and its measurement is an important part of understanding and balancing reactions and equations. Measuring the energy of reactants compared to that of products yields a difference in energy, or enthalpy, symbolized in equations by $\Delta H°$, which may be thought of as the "heat" of a reaction (though energy does not always take the form of heat).

Enthalpy can be calculated by using the bond energies in a reaction. For every chemical reaction, there will always be a change in energy. When energy is released, it indicates that bonds are created. The enthalpy or a bond being formed is positive and may be demonstrated by heat or light. Energy is also required to break bonds, and forms a negative enthalpy change. Conversely, energy is also required to break bonds. Thus, the enthalpy change within a system is negative because energy is released when forming bonds.

The energy gained or lost is determinable when looking at the two sides of a reaction. For example:

Two moles of water forming two moles of hydrogen and one mole of oxygen:
$2H_2O(g) \rightarrow 2H_2 + O_2(g)$

The sum on the reactant's side (2 moles of water) is equal to four lots of H-O bonds, which is 4 x 460 kJ/mol = 1840 kJ/mol. This is the input.

The sum on the product's side is equal to 2 moles of H-H bonds and 1 mole of O=O bonds, which is 2 x 436.4 kJ/mol and 1 x 498.7 kJ/mol = 1371.5 kJ/mol. This is the output.

The total energy difference is 1840 – 1371.5 = +468.5 kJ/mol.

The energy difference is positive, which means that the reaction is endothermic and that the reaction will need energy to be carried out.

Covalent and van der Waals Radii

Intermolecular forces, also called van der Waals forces for their 19th century Dutch discoverer, are the electrostatic (or ionic) attractions between molecules. Because molecules in gases move so fast and are so far apart, the intermolecular attraction in gases is not an important factor in reactions. These forces are strongest in liquids and solids where they may determine the alignment of the molecules. Dipole interactions occur when the negatively and positively charged poles of molecules are attracted to one another; if the attractions are strong enough, the molecules form loose bonds, with the resulting structure shaped by the way the poles attract one another. Tightly bound molecules form solids, while loosely bound molecules form liquids. Nonpolar intermolecular attractions may occur when the electrons within a molecule are momentarily attracted to the positively charged nucleus of another molecule.

The covalent radius (rcov) refers to half of the bond length when two of the same kind of atom are bonded through a single bond in a neutral molecule. Theoretically, the covalent bond length should be equal to the sum of two covalent radii from covalently bonded atoms.

$$rcov(AB) = r(A) + r(B)$$

Intermolecular forces may be either short range or long range and are responsible for the properties in some materials, such as viscosity and surface tension in liquids.
- Short-range forces: when the centers of molecules are separated by three angstroms or less and tend to be repulsive
- Long-range forces: when the centers of molecules are separated by more than three angstroms and tend to be attractive, also known as van der Waals forces

Separation and Purification Methods

Chemical separations

Often more robust extractions and separation methods are necessitated in order isolate a particular compound. These methods utilize disparities in the makeup of different types of matter. Differences in the following characteristics of analytes are used:

- Size
- Mass
- Polarity
- Density
- Electron affinity

These methods include:

- Solvent Extraction
- Chelation
- Filtration
- Distillation
- Electrophoresis
- Chromatography

Solvent extraction

Solvent extraction, also referred to as liquid-liquid extraction (LLE) is the process by which the components of a liquid are separated by using two immiscible (or non-mixable) liquids. The mixture to be separated, often aqueous, is put into a container that usually holds a non-polar organic solvent along with another liquid. Since compounds have different solubility characteristics, one component of the liquid will be extracted before the other. After this process concludes, the solvent can be removed via evaporation or distillation of the solvent.

Chelation

Chelation is the when metal compounds and polydenate ligands bond. Chelation is an aspect of a broader process called leaching that removes small amounts of metals from ore samples. The ore is treated in solutions of differing temperatures, pH levels, and chelating agents. Chelation also has medical applications. A chelating agent, put into the body, binds to toxic heavy metals in a person's system and then the body collectively excretes the agent/metal combination.

Filtration

Filtration, one of the more straightforward processes discussed here, is used to separate solids and liquids. A solid and liquid mixture is poured through a filter. The liquid passes through, while the solid components are caught in the filter. For example, when you pour a pot of spaghetti noodles and water into a colander over your sink, you are utilizing a filter. The noodles (solid material) remain in the colander (filter), while the water (liquid) passes through into the sink. In the world of chemistry, membrane filters have very tiny pores that are utilized to remove microscopic objects. The pore sizes range in size from 0.001 to 10μm.

Distillation

Distillation is performed by heating a mixture. Substances differ in their heat of vaporization. So when heated, one component of a mixture will generally vaporize before the other. The mixture is put in a flask that's then heated. The component with the lower heat of vaporization is the first to evaporate. A condensing tube circulates water to put the vapor in liquid form. Then the condensate is collected. The flask will contain the left over component(s) of the mixture.

Electrophoresis

Electrophoresis utilizes difference in molecule size to separate molecules. A gel matrix is used which is a small box containing an agarose gel. It also has an electric current supply. The electric current is turned on and the nucleic acids migrate through the agarose gel and out the tiny openings in the gel matrix. The short nucleic acids accomplish this more quickly than the long ones, thus causing separation.

Chromatography

Chromatography can be split into the categories of planar chromatography and column chromatography. It separates compounds by using the differences in the speed of movement of compounds through another medium. In chromatography, a mobile phase transports the compound mixture through a stationary phase. The stationary phase is responsible for the compound separation.

Planar chromatography

Planar chromatography, can be further subdivided into paper chromatography and thin layer chromatography. The former uses paper as its stationary phase and the latter uses a sheet of textile that's been treated with an absorbent compound. Capillary action moves the mixture through the mobile phase and stationary phase. A compound's interaction with the stationary phase in relation to the mobile phase, determines how far it will travel. Thus, the different compounds are separated.

Column chromatography

The mobile phase of column chromatography involves a liquid or gas which is moved by applied pressure or natural forces. The stationary phase is within a tube. The different types of column chromatography are as follows:

- Gas chromatography is used on materials that do not change physically when vaporized. The mobile phase is generally a neutral carrier gas like helium. Then the mixture goes through the stationary phase which is a column internally coated with an inert material (like glass or fused silica).
- Normal and reverse phase chromatography utilizes different polarities of analytes. In normal, the mobile phase involves a non-polar organic compound (like hexane), and the stationary phase consists of columns packed with hydrophilic polar materials. In reverse phase, the mobile phase is a polar solvent, and the stationary phase consists of columns packed with nonpolar materials. In normal, the least polar components will be eluted first and in reverse phase the opposite occurs.
- Size exclusion chromatography (SEC) uses differences in molecule weight and size to separate them. A uniformly porous column is utilized, and the column packing pore size is determined by the sizes of the compounds at play. Compounds too big to pass through the pores inside the column will elute first and the small compounds will elute last.
- Ion exchange chromatography (IEC) can be used to separate almost any charged molecule. The mobile phase consists of a buffer made of an inorganic salt plus other required stabilizers. The molecules are separated based on their attraction to the packing of the charged column and the extent of their ionic charge. IEC can be subdivided into anion-exchange and cation exchange. Anion uses positively charged column packing whereas cation uses negatively charged column packing.

- Chiral chromatography resolves enantiomers (also called optical isomers) from each other. Generally, the stationary phase has a chiral molecule. This will give one enantiomer an increased affinity to the stationary phase. That enantiomer, will in turn, elute first.

Structure, Function, and Reactivity of Biologically-Relevant Molecules

Biomolecules

Biomolecules are organic polymers that perform various functions in the human body which are necessary for humans, animals, and plants to function. Biomolecules perform various functions including the following:
- Provide a stable structure for the body
- Function as fuel and nutrients for cells
- Serve a role in various reactions as enzymes (biological catalysts)
- Serve to regulate body defense mechanism
- Control genetic functions through heredity

Biomolecules fall within one of the following classes:
- Carbohydrates - such as starch (in animals) and cellulose (in plants)
- Proteins - such as nucleoprotein, plasma protein, hormones, enzymes and antibodies
- Nucleic acids - such as ribonucleic acid (RNA) and deoxyribonucleic acid (DNA)

All biomolecules are polymers, which can be hydrolyzed into their base parts, called monomers. Polymers are all made up of bound monomers. Carbohydrates are represented by a general formula, $(C_6H_{10}O_5)_n$, where $40 \leq n \leq 3000$. Starches produce the monosaccharide glucose ($C_6H_{12}O_6$) when hydrolyzed. Glucose remains stored as glycogen in the liver and muscle. Some proteins are structurally synthesized with nucleic acids to form complexes called nucleoproteins.

Classification of carbohydrates

Carbohydrates are classified into three categories:
1. Monosaccharide: Monosaccharides are carbohydrate monomers and are the smallest unit of carbohydrates. They are represented by a general formula $(CH_2O)_n$, where $n = 3 - 6$. Glucose (dextrose), fructose, and galactose are common examples of monosaccharides.
2. Disaccharides: Disaccharides are made when two monosaccharides are joined together. Disaccharides can also produce two molecules of monosaccharides when hydrolyzed. For example, hydrolyzing sucrose yields one molecule of glucose and one molecule of fructose. Hydrolyzing lactose yields a molecule of glucose and a molecule of galactose. Lastly, hydrolyzing maltose yields two molecules of glucose.
3. *Polysaccharides*: Polysaccharides have a high molecular weight for carbohydrates. Polysaccharides can produce many molecules of monosaccharides when hydrolyzed. Examples of polysaccharides are starch, glycogen, and cellulose.

Monosaccharides

Monosaccharides are named based on the number of carbon atoms in the molecule, such as triose (C3), tetrose (C4), pentose (C5), and hexose (C6). Aldoses are the name for a monosaccharide with a group of aldehyde and ketoses are monosaccharides with a ketone group (e.g. fructose).

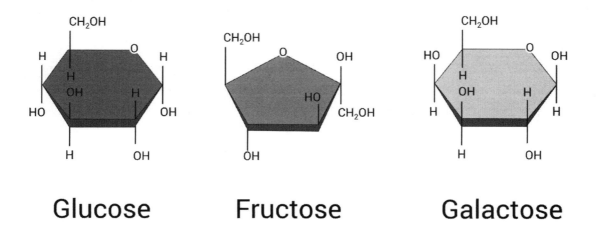

Glucose   Fructose   Galactose

Carbonyl compounds, aldehydes and ketones, can react with –OH group of an alcohol to form hemiacetal and acetal.

Glucose and fructose can form intramolecular hemiacetal to produce a cyclic structure because they contain both carbonyl and hydroxyl groups. This hemiacetal formation takes place between the C1 and C5 carbons to form a stable heterocyclic structure. A pyranose ring, is a six-membered ring consisting of five C atoms and one O atom, forms as a result of the cyclic structure. In a cyclic structure, C1 might have –OH group at the right or left side, and therefore may be termed α-D-glucose and β-D-glucose, respectively.

A reducing sugar is a sugar with a free aldehyde or ketone groups which can act as a reducing agent. All monosaccharides are reducing sugars, including glucose, fructose, and galactose. Many disaccharides are also reducing sugars including lactose and maltose (except sucrose). The reducing sugars are able to reduce Fehling's solution and Tollens' reagent.

Fehling's solution is made by mixing a solution of copper sulfate with potassium sodium tartrate in sodium hydroxide (NaOH). When treated with a reducing sugar, the deep blue color of Fehling's solution will fade and subsequently form a red hued precipitate.

Tollen's reagent will cause a silver precipitate when used to head a reducing sugar. The inner surface of the reaction vessel will also form a silver mirror.

Lipids

Lipids are a type of biological molecule which is naturally occurring and includes many types of nutrients including fats and vitamins. Lipids are defined as being hydrophobic, meaning they will not mix with water well and are unable to bond with the water. Fats, phospholipids, and steroids are the most important types of lipids.

Fats are made of glycerol and fatty acids. A molecule of glycerol is a chain of three carbon atoms with a hydroxyl group attached to each atom of carbon. Hydroxyl is one oxygen atom and an atom of hydrogen bonded together. This glycerol atom bonds with fatty acids to form fats. Fatty acids are made up of sixteen or eighteen carbon atoms, which are arranged into a backbone structure of long hydrocarbon chains. The carbon atom at the end of a fatty acid makes a double bond with one oxygen atom, using two of its four bonds. This is referred to as a carboxyl group. One of the other bonds is used to link to a hydroxyl group. Fats are made by joining three molecules of fatty acid and molecule of glycerol.

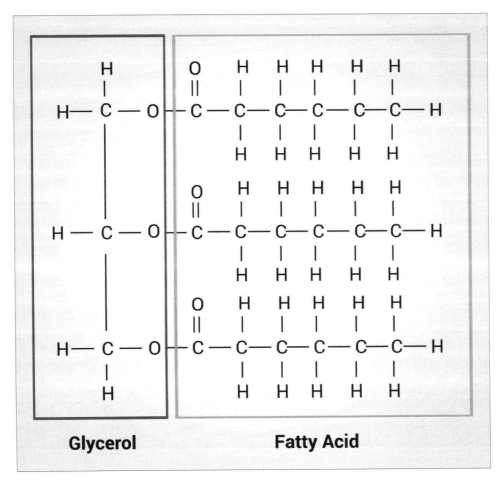

Glycerol   **Fatty Acid**

Phospholipids are a type of lipid made when a glycerol molecule is linked to two molecules of fatty acid. One phosphate group is attached to the glycerol molecule's third hydroxyl group. Phosphate groups consist of a single atom of phosphate which is connected to four atoms of oxygen, which results in an overall negative charge. Phospholipids have a peculiar structure resulting from a hydrophilic phosphate group head and a hydrophobic fatty acid tail. Phospholipids make two layered structures when mixed with water, called bilayers, which shield their hydrophobic sections from water. Phospholipids make up cell membranes which allow cells to mix with water-based solutions inside and outside. This forms a semi-permeable membrane around a cell, while also making a protective barrier.

Steroids are another type of lipid which is made of four carbon rings that have been fused together. Chemical groups that attach to these rings are what make steroids. Steroids are often found between phospholipid bilayers and help to reinforce the cell membranes while also helping with cell signaling (or communication). Cholesterol is a common example of a steroid found in animal cells.

Proteins

Proteins are a type of large biomolecule used for structure, function, and regulation of almost all functions of living beings. Proteins are necessary for a living being to function. The work protein traces its etymology to a Greek word for primary or first. Proteins are made from a large set of twenty amino acids which are linked together in un-branched polymers. Proteins are diverse because of a wide range of potential combinations. Amino acids form into polymers called polypeptides, which is derives their name from their peptide bonds. Polypeptides fold up to form coils of molecules used for biological functions. These molecules are called proteins. Proteins have four separate levels of structure:

- Primary – The primary structure relates to the sequence of amino acids, which can be arranged in various orders like letters in a word.
- Secondary – The secondary structure refers to beta sheets, or alpha helices, which are formed through hydrogen bonding in the polypeptide backbone, between the polar-regions.
- Tertiary – The tertiary structure refers to the molecule's overall shape resulting from the interactions between side-chains linked to the polypeptide backbone.
- Quaternary – The quaternary structure refers to the structure of the protein when it is made up of two or more polypeptide chains.

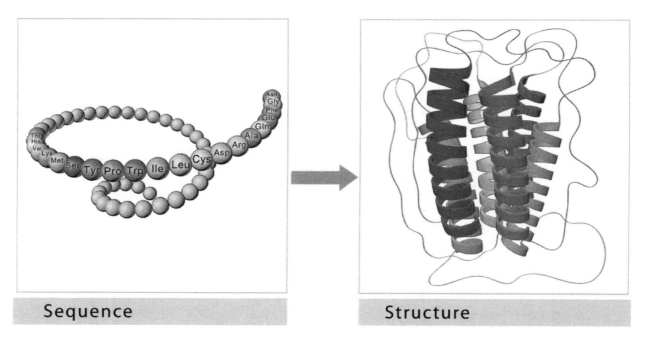

Sequence   Structure

Nucleic acids

Nucleic acids are also referred to as polynucleotide. This is due to the chains of monomers, called nucleotides, which make up nucleic acid. Nucleotides are made up of a nitrogen base, a phosphate group, and a sugar with five carbon atoms. Deoxyribonucleic acid (DNA) and ribonucleic acid (RNA) are the two forms which nucleic acid can take. DNA and RNA are used to store information about and to pass on genetic information to future generations. RNA comes in a single strand of nucleotides which fold onto itself, whereas DNA uses a double-helix structure to hold two strands of nucleotides.

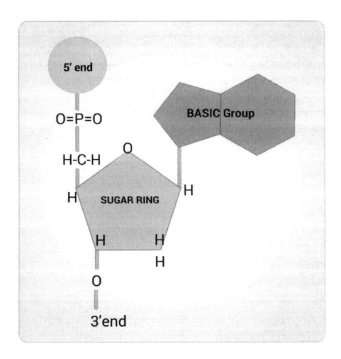

Principles of Chemical Thermodynamics and Kinetics

Gibbs free energy

Chemical reactions require energy. The force that precipitates chemical reactions is referred to as "free energy". Willard Gibbs did ground breaking work on this concept in 1873 and his name is now associated with the outcome of his work. Gibbs free energy, represented as G, corresponds to the thermodynamic work potential of a system at a constant pressure and temperature. Free energy used to be referred to as "available energy", or the "affinity" of one substance for another in chemical reactions. The vocabulary has become better defined and more precise over the years. Chemical reactions tend to cause a system to reach a state of equilibrium where free energy disappears. Gibbs free energy relates to measuring the amount of free energy available for reactions in a given system and the ability to measure the change over the time of the reaction at constant temperature and pressure. ΔG or the change in Gibbs Free energy can be found for both enthalpic (H) and entropic (S) systems. The changes in these systems correspond to the changes in free energy. The equations below illustrate this:

$$\Delta H_{reaction} = \Delta H_{products} - \Delta H_{reactants}$$
$$\Delta S_{reaction} = \Delta S_{products} - \Delta S_{reactants}$$

Spontaneous reactions are only possible if G is negative. Spontaneous reactions are defined as reactions that involve no external influence or outside force. G is dependent on entropy and enthalpy.

$$G = \Delta H - T\Delta S$$

Because T (temperature) is measured in Kelvin, it can never be negative.

Gibbs Free Energy (G)

$G = \Delta H - T \Delta S$

Summary   Spontaneous and Non-Spontaneous Reactions

	$\Delta H > 0$	$\Delta H < 0$
$\Delta S > 0$	**Spontaneity depends on T** spontaneous at higher temperatures	**Spontaneous at all temperatures**
$\Delta S < 0$	**Nonspontaneous** proceeds only with a continous input of energy	**Spontaneity depends on T** spontaneous at lower temperatures

Process	Products	Reactants	Sign	Meaning
Enthalpy	Lower #	Higher #	-	*Exothermic (energy released)*
Enthalpy	Higher #	Lower #	+	Endothermic (energy absorbed)
Entropy	Lower #	Higher #	+	*More disorder*
Entropy	Higher #	Lower #	-	Less disorder
BOLDED reactions are favorable				

In terms of collision theory:

- H > 0 and S > 0: Free energy tends to be used up or diminish to zero during endothermic reactions where low temperatures and high entropy exist. Slow particle movement combined with no energy invested in other chemical reactions leads to a complete consumption of free energy. However, if the temperature climbs high enough to increase particle motion, the extra kinetic energy will cause G to be negative leading to a spontaneous reaction.
- H > 0 and S < 0: In this case if enthalpy is high, but entropy is low, then extra energy will be needed to create a reaction. A low entropy endothermic reaction cannot proceed in this case without outside force. Because there are two unfavorable properties related to this particular reaction, it will never be spontaneous.
- H < 0 and S > 0: Here you have high entropy, but low enthalpy, and an exothermic reaction. In this case the reaction must always be spontaneous. Due to the two favorable properties, additional energy and outside force will not be required.

H < 0 and S < 0: Finally, if enthalpy is low and entropy is low, denoting an exothermic reaction with almost no random particle movement due to low temperatures, the reaction may not be spontaneous. The low and slow particle movement due to the low temperatures may keep the reaction from proceeding. However, if the temperature was to rise, or some other force was to increase movement speed of the particles, then the reaction could proceed.

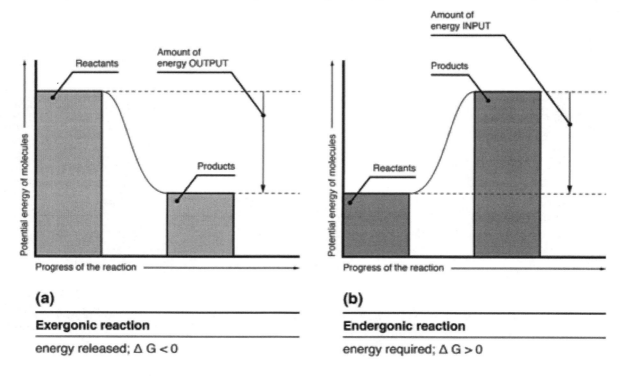

(a)

Exergonic reaction

energy released; $\Delta G < 0$

(b)

Endergonic reaction

energy required; $\Delta G > 0$

Helmholtz free energy

In a closed thermodynamic system with constant volume and temperature, the measure of available or "useful" work potential is called Helmholtz free energy. Helmholtz free energy is rarely used outside of explosives research. Gibbs free energy is the measure of the amount of total work a system can do at constant pressure and temperature, while Helmholtz measures the same thing under a constant volume and temperature. This distinction can be helpful when distinguishing between Gibbs free energy and Helmholtz free energy. Helmholtz free energy is symbolized by A and is found using the following equation:

$$A = U - TS$$

A= Helmholtz Free Energy
U= Internal energy
T= Temperature (in degrees Kelvin)
S= Entropy
A spontaneous reaction is only possible when A is negative.

Chemical potential

Chemical potential is the measure of a substance's tendency to give particles. This corresponds to the free energy of a system and is measured in G per number of moles or molar free energy. The more concentrated a substance is the higher chemical potential is possesses. Larger chemical potential is associated with higher concentration gradient. Lower temperatures cause a higher chemical potential because molar concentrations are highest. μ denotes chemical potential, which can be summarized in the equation:

$$\mu \equiv \left(\frac{\delta G}{\delta n}\right)_{T,p}$$

Chemical potential, then, is equal to the change in free energy over the change in number of moles with temperature and pressure constant.

This means that where concentration is low and particle motion is high, there will be low chemical potential. Conversely, where concentration is high and particle motion is low, there will be greater chemical potential.

Due to this, gases have relatively low chemical potential (low concentration and high particle motion) while solids (high concentration and low particle motion) have relatively high chemical potential.

As pressure increases, gases will change phase to liquid, and then change from liquid to solid. Temperature increases are the opposite; as temperature increases, solids will change phase to liquid, and then change from liquid to gas.

Chemical equilibrium

$$N_2 + 3H_2 \leftrightarrow 2NH_3$$

Some chemical reactions are reversible. They can work both ways. Sometimes they can work both ways simultaneously. When a chemical reaction happens in both directions (Forward reaction and Reverse reaction) simultaneously and the rate of reaction is the same on both sides, then a reaction is said to be in a state of equilibrium.

Chemical equilibrium can be influenced in different ways. If more reactants are added, then the reaction will be out of equilibrium until more products are produced and the same rate of reaction is achieved. Pressure can have a strong impact on chemical reactions. If gas is produced in one or both ways, then the side of the reaction with the greatest amount of gas will be more strongly affected by the increase in pressure. This increase in pressure on the side of the reaction with more gas will push the reaction in the direction of the other side, once again taking it out of equilibrium. Temperature can have a similar effect since temperature and pressure are directly proportional. Increasing temperature will always change the equilibrium constant (K) because K is dependent on temperature as shown in the equation below:

$$\Delta G = -RT \ln K$$

The forward reaction is favored if K is greater than one. And conversely, if the value of K is less than one, then the reverse reaction will be favored. The molar mass of each product can be used to determine the equilibrium constant, too. This is seen in the equation below:

$$aA + bB \leftrightarrow cC + dD$$
$$Kc = \frac{[C]^c[D]^d}{[A]^a[B]^b}$$

K reveals the equilibrium values. However, Q (also known as the reaction quotient) makes known the gap between current values and reestablishing equilibrium. When a reaction reaches equilibrium, then Q will be equal to K.

Partial pressure is used to measure Gas equilibrium, and not concentration. The equation for this is:

$$Kp = \frac{[PC]^c[PD]^d}{[PA]^a[PB]^b}$$

When a catalyst is added to a chemical reaction, the increase in the rate of the reaction is called *catalysis*. A catalyst increases the rate of a reaction while the catalyst itself is not changed by the reaction. A catalyst lowers the energy of activation necessary to produce the reaction. It becomes easier for the reaction to take place, thus speeding up the reaction. Z is the symbol used to denote catalytic activity in reactions. The measure of catalysis is mol/s. Catalysts can react with more than one reactant. As a catalyst works in a reaction, intermediates are formed. Catalysts are very helpful in that they can provide alternate states of transition and dramatically decreased activation energy of reactions.

Psychological, Social, and Biological Foundations

Sensation, Cognition, and Response

Sensory threshold

Sensory threshold is amount of strength needed for a stimulus to be perceived by an organism using one of the senses (sight, sound, taste, etc). For instance, if a person can hear everything above 20 hertz (Hz), but nothing below that frequency, their sensory threshold for sound would be 20 Hz. Different species, or even different organisms of the same species, may have different thresholds for the same stimulus.

Weber's Law

Weber's Law is based on the concept that an organism can sense a difference in a change in a stimulus. This change is known as the "just noticeable difference" and Weber's Law asserts that the proportion of this change must remain constant for the difference to be perceived, as opposed to the amount of change remaining constant. For instance, if you are waiting for your microwave popcorn to finish cooking, an extra 24 seconds added to the 2 minutes would be noticeable, a 20% increase in cooking time. However, if you were waiting 3 hours for a meal to finish cooking in the oven, the extra 24 seconds wouldn't be noticeable because the proportion of that difference in time is only .2%. Instead, you might notice a change in 36 minutes, because that would be a 20% increase in cooking time.

Signal detection theory

Signal detection theory explains methods for identifying a specific stimulus and being able to distinguish this signal from co-occurring signals that distort or disturb the desired stimulus. Using logic and probability through the signal detection theory, one should be able to identify the signal in question. Four possible outcomes determine whether or not a signal is present: hit, miss, false alarm, and correct rejection. If the signal is there and detected, hit. If the signal is there but undetected, miss. If the signal is not there but is detected, false alarm. If the signal is not there and is undetected, correct rejection. One example of the signal detection theory in action is when a doctor is diagnosing cancer. For instance, if the tumor is there but undetected, that would be a miss. But if the tumor is absent but detected, that would be a false alarm.

Sensory adaptation

In short, sensory adaptation is the process of getting used to something. If exposed to a constant stimulus over a period of time, an organism gradually adapts to this stimulus and the signal becomes weaker. An example of this concept would be jumping into a swimming pool. At first, the water may feel cold and it might be a shock to be suddenly submerged in this cold water. But after a short amount of time, the water feels pleasant because the skin has become less responsive to this stimulus.

Psychophysics

Psychophysics refers to the field of study concerning both mental and physical aspects of sensation. More precisely, it is the branch of psychology that explains the relationships between external stimuli and the physical and mental sensations that occur in response to these stimuli.

Sensory pathways

Sensory pathways allow the brain to receive sensory information from the rest of the body. This information travels either through the spinal cord or the thalamus and is delivered to the cerebral cortex or the cerebellum. Only the conscious cortex of the brain receives this information. Examples of these pathways may include pain and temperature information or touch and pressure information.

Sensory receptors

Sensory receptors are nerve endings that detect certain stimuli and respond to these stimuli by sending impulses to the brain. There are multiple types of sensory receptors and they are often classified by where they are located. Exteroreceptors are closer to the surface of the skin and respond to touch or other stimuli that occur outside the body. Interoreceptors are inside the body and respond to internal stimuli such as stomach pain. Proprioceptors detect unconscious stimuli such as body position and movement. Other types of receptors are classified by stimulus. Thermoreceptors respond to temperature, nociceptors respond to pain, and baroreceptors respond to pressure. Vibrations and touch are detected by mechanoreceptors, and chemical stimuli are detected by chemoreceptors, while light and visual stimuli are detected by photoreceptors.

Structures of the eye

The eye is composed of many parts that work together to send visual information to the brain through the optic nerve, translating the stimuli into images. The front of the eye is clear and called the cornea. This is where light travels through and into the pupil, which is the dark center of the iris. The iris is the color of the eye, such as brown, blue, or green, and filters the light that comes in. The clear, inside structure of the eye is called the lens, and it is responsible for focusing light on the retina. The retina is a layer of nerve cells, or photoreceptors, that respond to light stimuli. The ciliary muscles help focus this light by manipulating the shape of the lens. Lastly, the middle of the eye is filled with clear fluid known as vitreous.

Visual pathway in the brain

In order to process vision, eyes must send the information they receive to the brain. The photoreceptors in the retina capture the visual image and send nerve impulses through the optic nerve. Each eye sends its own messages that meet up at the optic chiasm and then split up on the way to the brain. Half of the left and right optic nerve travel to the left side of the brain, while the other half of each travel to the right side.

Parallel processing and feature detection

Parallel processing is when the brain is presented with different stimuli and must process these stimuli at the same time. An example of this would be when the brain is sent an image and it must determine the color, size, texture, and movement simultaneously. Feature detection is a theory that explains the reasons why seeing certain images or words may elicit different parts of the brain. It asserts that the nervous system is able to distinguish between significant features of the environment and irrelevant information in the background.

Structure and function of the ear

The three main parts of the ear are classified as the external ear, the middle ear, and the inner ear. The ear canal, which is what sound travels through, and the outside of the ear drum, or tympanic membrane, are in the external ear. The bulk of the ear drum resides within the middle ear and is what sound bounces off on its way to the brain. Also in the middle ear are the malleus, incus, and stapes or stirrup bones. These bones respond to sound waves by vibrating together, amplifying the sound and creating a wave in the fluid of the ear. This fluid is housed in the cochlea, the structure shaped like a snail containing hair cells that is located in the inner ear. The hair cells of the cochlea then send the auditory signals to the brain where they are then processed.

Hair cells
Hair cells are located in the cochlea of the ear and are auditory and vestibular sensory receptors. In response to movement, the hair cells bend and prompt a discharge of neurotransmitters that send signals to the brain. In humans, hair cells are unable to regenerate, so when they are damaged, hearing loss can occur.

Auditory processing and auditory pathways in the brain

Auditory processing is when sound enters through the ear and is delivered to the brain for interpretation. This sound passes through the ear canal and rebounds off the ear drum, creating vibrations in the cochlea, and is then transmitted via the auditory nerve. The message is sent to the brainstem where it can be translated into information regarding frequency, intensity, and position, and is then passed on through the temporal lobe, specifically the thalamus and auditory cortex. The auditory message is then interpreted to create a comprehensible meaning.

Somatosensation and receptor cells

When the body interacts with the environment, receptor cells transmit sensory information to the brain. This process is known as somatosensation. The following three types of receptor cells are involved in this process: mechanoreceptors, thermoreceptors, and nociceptors. Respectively, these receptors involve sensations of touch, temperature, and pain.

Sense of taste

Taste receptors pick up signals from specific tastes, which are sent to the brain and translated into flavors. These different tastes include salty, sweet, bitter, sour, and "umami," also known as savory. Taste occurs through taste buds, which are spherical-shaped growths on the tongue and are linked to taste receptors. Certain chemicals in food are related to these different tastes, and if present in food, allow the brain to recognize the flavors via the taste hairs covering the taste buds. For a food to be sensed as sweet, it would contain sugar, while umami foods are meaty. Both can be detected by T1R2 and T1R3 receptors. Salt would be present and detected via sodium channels to be distinguished as salty. For bitter foods, basic chemicals such as quinine are present, and for sour foods, acidic chemicals would be present. Bitter taste is transmitted through the T2R receptors and sour taste through the transient receptor potential (TRP) channel.

Sense of smell

Within the nasal cavity, olfactory cells detect smell, called olfaction. These cells are chemoreceptors and pick up on specific chemical stimuli in order to deliver messages to the brain about smell.

Olfactory pathways in the brain

When a person is exposed to something with a particular smell, this smell enters the nasal cavity. Inside the nasal cavity is the olfactory epithelium, close in proximity to the brain. Between the brain and the olfactory epithelium are the olfactory bulb and cribriform plate. The olfactory bulb has thousands of nerves and these nerves extend through the cribriform plate and into the olfactory epithelium. When a smell enters the olfactory epithelium, the cells at the end of these nerves detect the scent and send a message to the brain to interpret the particular smell.

Pheromones

Pheromones are a type of chemical that animals release, which work to communicate information to other animals of the same species. These pheromones help other animals avoid danger or find food by sending messages to their brain about the environment.

Kinesthetic sense

Kinesthetic sense is detected by the type of sensory receptors known as proprioceptors. These sense movement and body position through muscles, ligaments, and tendons in the body.

Vestibular sense

The ability to balance and perceive gravity is known as vestibular sense. This occurs through the hair cells within the inner ear. Because there is fluid within the cochlea, the body is able to sense when it moves and allows the brain to understand its position in space.

Bottom-up and top-down processing

Bottom-up processing is when the body is exposed to a stimulus and sensory receptors send information to the brain about this stimulus. Top-down processing is when a person is exposed to a stimulus but before the stimulus can send a signal to the brain, the brain remembers this specific stimulus and influences how the body reacts. The best way to explain these two different types of processing is through example. Imagine it is a hot day and you go to open your car door. When you touch the door handle, it burns your hand and sends a pain signal to your brain. This is bottom-up processing because the stimulus sent a signal that traveled from the hand to the brain. However, the next day is another hot day. You reach your car and remember yesterday when the handle burned your hand. You decide to use a jacket or other material to open the door in order to avoid burning your hand. In this scenario, you used top-down processing because the processing began in the brain when you remembered a previous experience with a hot door handle.

Perceptual organization

Perceptual organization is the way by which our brain recognizes objects and the structure of objects in order to interpret this information. Some ways that this occurs are through depth, form, and motion. Depth is how we are able to see the position of objects in a three-dimensional space.

Form is how we see the shape of the object, or its outline. Motion refers to the movement on an object. Using the knowledge that the word "gestalt" means "whole" in the German language, one can surmise that gestalt principles are related to perceiving something in its entirety. Understandably, the gestalt principles are a way of making sense of what our brains perceive in terms of its wholeness. For instance, when you are walking down a road, you perceive the street as a whole entity, as opposed to first seeing each pebble on the pavement, the texture of the road, and then the dark gray color of the street.

Selective and divided attention

Selective attention is when an individual must focus on a single event, task, or object when there are other things happening that are a distraction. For instance, if Joe needs to watch his daughter on the playground, he is using selective attention. He must focus on her playing and make sure she doesn't get hurt, without being distracted by the other children on the playground, other parents talking to him, or his phone. Divided attention is when an individual must focus on multiple things at once. In Joe's case, if he received an important phone call from work while he was watching his daughter, he would have to focus his attention on both of the tasks at hand.

Information-processing model

In the information-processing model, it is theorized that human memory works in a way similar to a computer. First the brain encodes sensory information that it receives and then it stores that information. When this information needs to be used, the brain has retrieval methods to bring that information to the mind once again.

Piaget's stages of cognitive development

According to Piaget, there are stages of development that all children move through at around the same ages. The first stage, sensorimotor stage, spans from birth to 2 years of age. In this stage the infant moves through the world using sensory information and his or her emerging motor skills. The second stage, preoperational stage, occurs between the ages of 2 and 7. During this stage the child learns to view the world using symbolic representations and language. In the concrete operational stage, from ages 7 to 11, the child is less egocentric and is able to think logically. The principle of conservation is developed as well, which is the idea that just because a substance has a different outer appearance, the amount of the substance is constant. The last stage, formal operational stage, starts at the age of 12 and extends into adulthood. The child in this stage has reached cognitive maturity and is able to think deductively, as well as to think through arguments and abstract ideas.

Cognitive changes in late adulthood

In adulthood, an individual will likely experience a decline in cognitive ability. Loss of memory, delayed reaction times, and difficulty speaking or following a schedule are common. This is due to the decline in information-processing abilities. The individual has difficulties encoding, storing, and/or retrieving information within the brain, and cognitive functioning is in turn negatively affected.

Roles of culture, heredity, and environment in cognitive development

Cognitive development can be influenced by culture and the environment in multiple ways. How one interacts with others and the environment changes how they think about the world. This can occur through language, social ties, socioeconomic status, disabilities, life events, and many other cultural and environmental experiences. Heredity also plays a role in cognitive development through genetic phenomena and family upbringing.

Biological factors that influence cognition

Biology plays a role in cognitive development in ways such as the formation of the frontal lobe, the hippocampus, and the amygdala. The frontal lobe is responsible for reason, organization, and future thinking. The hippocampus is pivotal in creating memories, while the amygdala gives humans the ability to sense danger while regulating emotions in response to certain stimuli.

Approaches and barriers to problem solving

Problem solving, or finding a solution for an issue at hand, can be approached in many different ways. Using the trial and error method, experimenting until you find a method that works, is often used, but may be inefficient and time consuming. Another approach is using an algorithm. Algorithms give step-by-step instructions for solving a problem, usually relying on a computer to arrive at a solution by calculating the answer. Heuristics are also used to solve problems, and involve following a general guideline for achieving a desired result. These heuristics are numerous and have different rates of success, but also may be a barrier to effective problem solving by leading to an incorrect solution due to a using an inappropriate or faulty shortcut. Other barriers include biases and fixation. Having an inherent bias when it comes to problem solving may lead to a wrong answer or ignoring a correct answer. Fixation refers to relying on information and solutions that worked in the past, but might not be appropriate for the situation at hand. This is also known as a mental set. Function fixedness is also a form of fixation and refers to the idea that certain objects can only be used in a particular way, without realizing that they could be used differently to help solve a problem.

Availability heuristic, representativeness heuristic, and confirmation bias

Availability heuristic refers to how easily one can call to mind an example of an event, and the assumptions that individual makes based on how the event is remembered. This might be based on how often the individual has heard of the event, how the media portray the event, or how significant the event might be to that individual. Representative heuristic is the idea that one may believe a certain sample shares the same qualities as the rest of the population, and assume certain characteristics about the population based on this sample. Confirmation bias refers to the idea that if you assume information about something and are very connected to this belief, you will recognize only the information that confirms that belief and not believe the opposing evidence. This is also known as belief perseverance.

Types of intelligence

Linguistic intelligence refers to the ability to understand language, including speaking, reading, and writing. Logical or mathematical intelligence is related to numbers and using logic to find answers. Musical intelligence refers to understanding how to play and read music. Spatial intelligence is when one understands the world through its relationship to and position in space. Body or kinesthetic intelligence refers to one's athleticism or bodily movement. Interpersonal intelligence is how a person interacts and understands other people. Intrapersonal intelligence refers to understanding oneself, also known as self-perception. Lastly, nature or natural intelligence is the understanding of the biological world in terms of patterns and object recognition.

Triarchic theory of intelligence

Triarchic theory of intelligence includes three different aspects of one's intelligence: practical, analytic, and creative. Practical intelligence includes physical activity, learning from the world around you, and applying that knowledge to your life. This is also known as contextual intelligence. Analytic intelligence includes mathematical operations, logical reasoning, and abstract thinking. This is the type of knowledge commonly evaluated through IQ tests. The third aspect is creative intelligence, or experiential intelligence. One is considered to have this type of intelligence when they are inventive and creative, thinking outside the box. People who design things or are able to create new solutions are considered creatively intelligent.

Influence of heredity and environment on intelligence

A common question in science is whether nature or nurture is responsible for a person's abilities or features. This concept also comes into play with intelligence. Although people have tried to pin down one or the other as the cause of intelligence, both have been found to influence this concept. Genetics play a large role in intelligence, as evidenced by twin studies, but this heritability of a trait is coupled with the effects of the person's environment. Experiences, culture, and learning have been shown to influence intelligence, especially negative events in one's life.

Variations of intellectual ability

Some individuals have variations in IQ, or intellectual ability, that are classified as either a form of intellectual disability or giftedness. Intellectual disability (previously called retardation) refers to someone with an IQ that is below average. Different forms of intellectual disability range from inability to perform academically past a sixth-grade level to being unable to function without a caretaker. This can be caused by both environmental factors and genetics. Another subset of the population is classified as intellectually gifted. These individuals have an IQ that is above average, or more than 2 standard deviations from the mean IQ score.

States of consciousness and alertness

States of consciousness occur when an individual is awake and aware of his or her surroundings. Being able to pay attention and respond to one's surroundings refers to the concept of alertness. Alertness can be affected by chemical substances or injuries to the head, as well as other medical conditions. Although one is in a state of consciousness, he or she may not necessarily be alert due to these various limitations. Examples of these circumstances are narcolepsy, sleep deprivation, or mental health conditions.

Stages of sleep and the sleep cycle

The first stage of sleep is when the individual is able to wake easily because he or she is in between sleep and consciousness. It is also the first part of the non-REM sleep when the eye movements are slower than in REM sleep. This stage may last around 5 to 10 minutes and is when activity occurs in the muscles. Stage 2 of non-REM sleep is more difficult to wake from because the individual is in slightly deeper sleep. The next two stages are also non-REM sleep and where sleep is deepest. This is when delta waves are active and the body is able to repair itself. An hour and a half into this non-REM sleep is when the REM stage occurs, as well as when dreaming happens. This sleep cycle repeats itself about 4 or 5 times throughout the sleeping period, with the REM cycle getting longer each cycle, from 10 minutes to an hour long, and the deep sleep getting shorter.

Circadian rhythms

In order to sleep, our bodies have a type of biological clock known as circadian rhythms. These rhythms control our sleep cycle by using light (both artificial and natural). This light sends information through the eye to the pineal gland in the hypothalamus. This gland releases hormones and enzymes, such as melatonin and adenosine, which cause sleepiness. Because of the important role light plays in the sleep cycle, one can reset these circadian rhythms by adjusting the light and dark cycles.

Sleep-wake disorders

Parasomnias are sleep disorders that involve the individual performing actions that are considered abnormal while a person is sleeping. Sleep walking, talking, and other actions are considered parasomnias. Dyssomnias also occur during sleep, but disturb a person's sleep cycle. Disruptions in breathing or falling asleep at abnormal times fit into this category with disorders known as sleep apnea and narcolepsy, respectively. Another disorder is called insomnia, which involves a person not being able to sleep when they need to.

Hypnosis and mediation

Hypnosis is the process by which a person is put into a state of consciousness that makes them more suggestible. This state of consciousness is induced by a hypnotist and may lead people to say or do things they would otherwise not do. However, this does not mean the individual will do things against their will or that they would be morally opposed to, simply that they experience the world differently. Although many people use this technique to elicit forgotten memories, this also means that the patient is more open to suggestion and it has been found that some of these memories are inaccurate. Meditation also attempts to induce a different state of consciousness by using breathing or thinking techniques, usually in order to diminish stress.

Consciousness-altering drugs and drug addiction

Consciousness-altering drugs, or psychoactive drugs, affect the brain by changing the way an individual experiences or behaves in the world. Different drugs have different effects on the brain; depressants, barbiturates, and opiates help a person relax, stimulants induce energy, and hallucinogens make the user hallucinate and/or experience a vast array of emotions. These drugs work by changing how the neurons in the brain fire and in turn affecting the nervous system. Using these types of drugs excessively can lead to drug addiction. Many of these drugs create a pleasurable sensation by triggering the reward pathway in the brain. Dopamine is released when drugs are used and because this happens in the pleasure center of the brain, an individual may try to recreate that sensation by using drugs more often. When this happens, an individual may use drugs so frequently that their body depends on the drug (addiction) and reacts unpleasantly when the drugs are taken away (withdrawal).

Encoding

Memory encoding is a process in which our brains are able to transform sensory information into storable memories. The types of encoding are acoustic, visual, semantic, and tactile. Acoustic encoding uses sound to convert auditory signals into memory. Visual encoding converts images into memory, semantic encoding uses meaning to code information, and tactile encoding uses physical touch to create a memory.

There are many ways to help the brain remember certain information by encoding memories. Repeating words or information helps encode memories. In addition, visualizing information, placing information into separate categories (chunking), creating a narrative about the information, and using acronyms aid in encoding memories. Assigning meaning to a topic or making information relevant to your own life also helps memorize information.

Memory storage

The different types of memory storage depend on how long information is stored in the brain. The first type of storage is sensory. This includes both iconic memory (also known as photographic memory) and echoic memory (sound memory). This type of memory is extremely short term and as soon as it is gone, it is replaced by a new sensory memory. The second type of storage is short-term, or working, memory. Using this sensory information, the brain often allows these memories to be stored for more processing. Performing math equations in your head, memorizing a list while you walk to the other room to write it down, or dialing a phone number that you were just given during another phone call all require this form of working memory. This type of memory only lasts for about 20 to 30 seconds. Long-term memories, on the other hand, can last anywhere from a few days to an entire lifetime. Long-term memory is also able to hold as much information as it needs, while the other forms of memory storage are more limited. Repeating information and focusing on the meaning of the information are some of the main ways to transfer short-term memories into long-term storage.

Semantic networks and spreading activation

Semantic networks are based on the theory that long-term memory is organized by connecting related information into a type of web network. These relationships between ideas help us understand different concepts by relating them to things we have experienced or learned in our past. When a specific idea triggers different memories and concepts, this causes spreading activation. When you think of one idea, food, for example, it triggers thoughts about types of food (like cheese or bread) and the details about those foods. This helps to remember various details of a specific topic or event.

Recall, recognition, and relearning

Recall is defined as the ability to retrieve a memory. Three different types of tasks use recall. Free recall is when you can remember information without being cued, or asked, for it. Cued recall is when you remember something after being asked. The third type of recall task is serial recall, which is when you remember a list or sequence of events in a specific order. Recognition is defined as being able to remember information once presented with the correct option within a collection or range of information. An example would be when you answer a multiple choice question, and can remember the information because you are presented with the correct answer among incorrect answers. Relearning is when you have already learned something, but have to familiarize yourself with the information once again.

Processes that aid in retrieving

One process that aids in retrieving memories is the use of retrieval cues. When trying to remember something, certain words, events, people, or images may trigger your brain to retrieve that memory. For instance, if you lose your train of thought and are trying to remember what you were thinking, it may help to retrace your steps by repeating topics or words that you were thinking of before this in order to retrieve your most recent train of thought. Another way to help retrieve memories is using emotion. It is easier to recall information when you have an emotion connected to it. For instance, if something makes you angry, feeling the emotion of anger again later may prompt you to remember this previous experience. By associating events and information with emotion it becomes easier to remember that material.

Effects of aging on memory

There are various and contradictory views on the effect aging has on memory. Many believe that the ability to recall information is hindered in late adulthood and that it is more difficult for older individuals to use free recall when retrieving a memory. Although this may be true and may be seen in the difference in brain structure as we age, it is also true that people who are older in age are still able to learn new information and recall old memories. Scientists and psychologists have also suggested ways to help people remember information as they age, including attributing meaning to new information and using other forms of memory aids.

Memory dysfunctions

Memory dysfunctions occur when damage is sustained to parts of the brain and it negatively affects the brain's ability to store and recall memories. During late adulthood, a form of memory dysfunction, called dementia, may occur. This term refers to the rapid loss of memory function and can have many causes, ranging from biological abnormalities to environmental factors. The most common cause of dementia is known as Alzheimer disease. This disease is characterized by slow and subtle change in memory and personality, but it is irreversible and may lead to physical disability in an individual, which may result in death. Another memory dysfunction is amnesia, which is found in two forms: anterograde and retrograde. Anterograde is characterized by an individual not being able to create new memories, while retrograde is when the individual can't remember things that have occurred in the past. Another memory disorder, called Korsakoff syndrome, happens when a person doesn't get enough vitamin B1. Commonly caused by alcohol abuse, this disorder negatively affects memory, coordination, and speech.

Decay and interference

Decay is defined as the fading of memory, especially short-term memory, due to the passage of time. The longer it is since you learned something or retrieved a memory, your ability to recall that memory is reduced. Long-term memory is less impacted by decay, likely because those memories are recalled more often, while short-term memories are new and less likely to be remembered after time has passed. Interference occurs when memories are unable to be retained because of a different memory. Proactive interference is when a new memory is impeded by an older memory and the new information is unable to be retained. The opposite is known as retroactive interference—when a new memory interferes with the ability to remember an older memory.

Constructing memories and monitoring sources

The main way individuals are able to construct a memory is through something called a schema. This schema is a way that we are able to understand the environment based on biology and external influences. This framework can act on memories by skewing information to fit into the schema. Another way that we construct memories is through false memories, which happens when our imagination fills in gaps in our memories. Misinformation also influences our memories; when we are told false information, this changes our memories or creates new memories based on this misinformation. Lastly, remembering the source of the information helps make our memories more precise. Source monitoring errors occur when we are unable to remember how, when, or where we attained the information, despite still remembering the factual content.

Neural plasticity

A person may experience many changes throughout his or her life that influence the brain's processes and abilities. The idea that the brain can adapt to these changes is known as neural plasticity. There are many different ways the brain is able to adapt to the changes. One way is through compensatory masquerade. This is when one area of cognitive functioning is negatively affected and the brain must find a way to compensate for this change. Another type of neural plasticity is cross-modal reassignment, which is when the brain is able to reorganize its processes or connections after one or more of the sensory systems is ineffective. For instance, if a person loses his or her sense of sight, the brain attempts to make up for this loss by strengthening other senses. Map expansion is another type of neural plasticity, and is the process of strengthening an area of the brain due to exposure or learning. An example of this is when a person takes a math class, the mathematical portion of the brain is strengthened. Lastly, homologous area adaption often occurs in early development when one area of the brain is damaged. In this type of neural plasticity, the function of the damaged area would be reassigned to another area of the brain, reorganizing and making room for these processes.

Memory, learning, and long-term potentiation

During the lifespan, an individual's brain is continually learning and growing. This growth does not take place in the literal sense of getting bigger, but it does strengthen the connections between different neurons with continued use. These connections are known as synapses and the processes of strengthening these synapses is known as long-term potentiation. The stronger the synapse, the quicker the brain is able to transmit information via this connection. This process is how we are able to learn new information and explains why we are able to do things at a faster pace when we have done something many times before.

Theories of language development

The main theories of language development explain how individuals acquire language. The nativist theory describes how individuals are born with genetic code that enables him or her to learn a language. This theory uses the idea of universal grammar to explain how different languages use similar rules of grammar and how children are able to understand language rules so easily. Another theory is the interactionist theory, which uses ideas from social and biological perspectives to explain how language is learned through a dependency on, and desire for, communication. In this theory, individuals learn through the environment and social interactions.

Language and cognition

The Sapir-Whorf hypothesis explains how language influences cognition by stating that our thoughts are determined by language. The way we express our words and the grammar and patterns that we learn change the way we perceive the world. The utilization of objects or concept of time can often be seen differently in different languages around the world. The areas that control the processes of language and speech are known as Broca's area and Wernicke's area. Broca's area controls speech and is found in the left frontal lobe of the brain. Wernicke's area is in the left temporal lobe of the brain and is in charge of language comprehension.

Components of emotion

Cognition, physiology, and behavior are the three components of emotion. The cognitive component includes how an individual thinks and evaluates different circumstances. Viewing a situation as dangerous, exciting, or another emotion is evaluated by using schemas and previous knowledge about the specific event. The physiological component of emotion is how your body experiences an emotion. Increased heart rate, sweating, or other bodily functions occur in certain situations in response to emotion. Lastly the behavioral component involves physical and vocal responses to an emotion. This component is observable and can include pacing, talking fast, or not talking at all.

Basic universal emotions and the adaptive role of emotion

The universal emotions are sadness, happiness, disgust, surprise, anger, and fear. Some may also include joy and contempt. Joy is conceptualized to be long-lasting and derived from selflessness or spiritual connections, which is different than the temporary emotion of happiness. Facial expressions of these emotions involve changes in one's eyes, cheeks, jaws, and mouth corners. Emotion can also be adaptive, helping one to better interact with the environment. For instance, when surprised or fearful, individuals often open their eyes very wide, which may help them see everything around them. In addition, having a moderate amount of emotion, as opposed to excessive emotions or none at all, is shown to improve one's abilities and performance.

Theories of emotion

The James-Lange theory of emotion endorses the concept that the cognitive component of emotion is directly influenced by behavior and physiology. For instance, if you have a fast heart rate and sweaty palms, this would lead you to think that you are fearful. On the other hand, Cannon-Bard theory states that behavioral aspects of emotion are the result of cognition and physiological emotion. Instead of interpreting your sweaty palms as evidence of fear, you would first interpret the situation as scary while also exhibiting physiological evidence of fear, and these would lead to screaming or running away from the scary situation. Lastly, Schachter-Singer theory focuses on the chronology of emotion being first physiological emotion, then cognitive emotion, and then experiencing an emotion. This means that an individual would have sweaty palms and a fast heart rate, and then think critically about the situation at hand. After having evaluated the situation, the emotion of fear would then be experienced.

Brain regions involved in generating and experiencing emotions

The major brain regions involved in generating and experiencing emotions are the limbic system and the autonomic nervous system.

Role of the limbic system in emotion

The limbic system consists of the amygdala, the thalamus, the hypothalamus, and the cingulate gyrus. The amygdala is involved in the emotions an individual experiences when presented with certain stimuli. The amygdala is also responsible for the "fight or flight" response and helps the body be prepared when faced with a frightening or upsetting situation. The thalamus and hypothalamus control the neurotransmitters linked to emotions. The amygdala transmits information to the hypothalamus and this part of the brain is responsible for the physiological aspects of emotion. Lastly, the cingulate gyrus is responsible for experiencing emotions related to memories. Happy memories are related to that emotion, while upsetting memories trigger negative emotions.

Relationship between emotion and the autonomic nervous system

The autonomic nervous system consists of 2 different aspects: the sympathetic division and the parasympathetic division. The former of these is responsible for the release of adrenaline when faced with a stressful or surprising situation. This adrenaline leads to physiological changes such as increased heart rate, dilated pupils, increased blood sugar and blood pressure, and slowed digestion. This is also what is in charge of the flight or fight response. The parasympathetic nervous system controls the resting and relaxing aspects of the body with regard to emotion. In other words, when you are calm and relaxed, this part of the nervous system controls the constriction of pupils, increased digestion, and decreased heart rate and blood flow.

Physiological markers of emotion

Emotion can be detected by different types of physiological markers. For instance, a person will exhibit different bodily responses when he or she is calm versus when frightened. Heart rate, blood pressure, respiration, and muscle tension are increased when a person is scared, but decreased when relaxed and happy. Blood flow to certain areas of the body, such as the face, are also related to emotions of anger and embarrassment, while crying is indicative of sadness.

Concept of appraisal in relation to the nature of stress

Although some events throughout the course of an individual's life may generally be considered stressful, many people experience frustration in response to situations that others may not deem stressful. This phenomenon occurs by way of cognitive appraisals. A cognitive appraisal is how an individual perceives an event and therefore influences how he or she responds to such an event. This appraisal could be based on past events, personal beliefs, culture, or various other reasons, and is representative of the schemas at work for this individual. For example, let's say that Susan is given a new car. Many people would believe that this should be exciting and they might be grateful for this gift. However, after being given the car, Susan is unable to sleep and becomes angered by the gift. Susan had been in a car accident when she was younger, and her mother was killed by a drunk driver. This previous event altered Susan's perception of driving and cars, and therefore her cognitive appraisal of the gift was that it was dangerous, which caused her to feel stressed.

Stressors

Many different types of stressors impact individuals during their lives. Some are more difficult to overcome, some are easy, and some are even joyous. Cataclysmic events are recognized as being unpredictable and catastrophic. Events such as these are large and devastating, such as natural disasters and wars. Personal events are another category of stressors and involve life changes that may either be joyful or upsetting. These events range from getting married and having children, to losing a loved one or losing a job. Daily stressors are events and activities that a person experiences throughout the day. These types of stressors, also called hassles, include things such as traffic jams, paying bills, working, or running errands, which cause distress on a daily basis.

Effects of stress on psychological functions

Stress can affect people in many different ways, from contributing to disease to causing psychological disorders. Stress can even help to increase productivity or motivation if experienced at a mild level. However, severe stress can lead to fatigue, depression, anxiety, post-traumatic stress disorder (PTSD), or lack of concentration.

Physiological responses to stressors

The body responds to stress in various ways. When experiencing a dangerous situation, the body may be triggered into the fight or flight response. This causes the heart rate to increase and releases glucose into the bloodstream. This in turn allows the individual to either "fight" against the stressor or run away ("flight"), as necessary. This is also the first stage when stress triggers the body to go through three stages of response: alarm, resistance, and exhaustion. Alarm is when adrenaline is pumped into the bloodstream and helps the individual respond to a situation. The resistance stage is when all of this adrenaline (or other hormones) is depleted and the body becomes fatigued. People are also likely to become ill at this stage because of the decreased resources. Lastly, the exhaustion stage is when these different side effects of stress (eg, depression, anxiety) are exhibited.

Emotional and behavioral responses to stressors

When stress occurs, our emotions and behaviors are changed. Because of the strain on biological resources experienced during stress, the body is exhausted and this can impact the mind. It is likely that the individual experiencing stress may feel depressed or anxious and this may lead to a decreased resilience to difficult experiences, resulting in feeling increased stress to less stressful situations. Stress may also lead to poor judgment or bad decision making. It is also possible that a person changes his or her eating habits or consumes more alcohol. Disturbed sleep patterns and increased irritability are also likely side effects of stress.

Managing stress

An individual can alter his or her behavior or mindset to manage stressful situations in many different ways. Eating healthier, sleeping more regularly, exercising, and avoiding alcohol and drugs help to keep stress away. It has also been shown that spending time doing pleasurable things with people that you enjoy leads to a reduction in stress. In terms of psychological changes a person can make to help manage stress, meditation is a common technique. Focusing on breathing and relaxing are common ways to reduce stress, as is working to increase patience and other positive emotions.

Influences on Behavior and Behavioral Change

Neurons and neurotransmitters

Neurons are essential parts of the nervous system and work to transmit information using electrical impulses. Neurons are cells that have an axon and dendrites to help transmit and receive these impulses. The axon carries the information, while the dendrites receive it. This is done by way of neurotransmitters, which are chemicals that the neurons use in order to send and receive these messages. Neurons also play a role in reflexes. This is by way of a reflex arc, which consists of a sensory receptor and various neurons. The neurons involved in this process transmit sensory stimuli from the receptor to other neurons to the effector. This process does not send information to the brain for processing, but instead creates an instantaneous response by the body. For instance, when a person touches something hot, the sensory receptors send information through the neurons to the effector, producing an immediate response, causing the person to quickly move away from the source of heat.

Peripheral nervous system

The peripheral nervous system is made of nerves and sensory organs that send sensory information through nerve impulses to the brain and spinal cord. These nerves and organs are found throughout the body, including everything outside the spinal cord and brain. The purpose of the peripheral nervous system (PNS) is to maintain communication with the central nervous system (CNS), but the PNS doesn't have the protection that the CNS has of bones that contain these vital organs. This means that the PNS is more susceptible to damage by environmental or biological factors.

Central nervous system

The central nervous system (CNS) is made of the brain and spinal cord. The spinal cord is a column of nerve fibers that connects the brain to the rest of the body, while the brain is a complex organ responsible for our thoughts, memory, and other vital processes. The CNS receives sensory information from the peripheral nervous system, where the information is then processed. The CNS is also able to send this processed information back out in the form of motor output. This means the CNS is responsible for bodily movement and cognitive processing.

Forebrain, midbrain, and hindbrain

The forebrain is vital to the processes of problem solving, emotion, logic, and mood. It also controls temperature and sleep regulation. This part of the brain includes the cerebrum, the limbic system, the hypothalamus, and the thalamus. The midbrain includes the tegmentum, tectum, and cerebral peduncles. It is located in the middle part of the brainstem and is responsible for motor control, dopamine production, and motivation. It also is associated with visual and auditory processing. The hindbrain, located in the rear of the brain, includes the cerebellum, pons, and medulla oblongata. The processes that the hindbrain takes part in are arousal, digestion, balance, respiration, and other vital motor functions.

Lateralization of cortical functions

Lateralization of cortical functions refers to the separation of the left brain and right brain. The left brain controls language, writing, positive emotion, and the right side of the body. The right brain controls the left side of the body, along with time and space processing, negative emotion, and nonverbal (facial and body movement) information.

Studying the brain

One is able to understand the brain in more detail by use of imaging and measurement of chemical activity. Some of the imaging used for this is through computerized tomography (CT) and magnetic resonance imaging (MRI) scans that capture the structure of the brain. Positron emission tomography (PET) and functional MRI (fMRI) scans can also be used to capture the functions of the brain, while computer scans are also used to better understand these processes.

Neuronal communication and its influence on behavior

Neurons play a role in influencing behavior by communicating and releasing neurotransmitters. When these neurons send messages for the purpose of performing a certain behavior, neurons communicate with one another via chemical signals. One type of neuron that is involved in this process is called a dopaminergic neuron, which releases dopamine and influences mood and behavior. However, if there are issues with these neurons, the dysfunction may cause certain degenerative diseases such as Parkinson or Alzheimer disease. This leads to a decrease in motor skills and memory, and is often found in older individuals.

Influence of neurotransmitters on behavior

Neurotransmitters are the chemicals through which neurons communicate with one another. Many different chemicals are involved in this process and each one is related to different behavioral functions. One of these chemicals, endorphins, plays a role in experiencing pleasure or pain, reducing or numbing the pain when necessary. Norepinephrine is a neurotransmitter involved in learning and memory, and also energy and alertness. GABA (gamma-aminobutyric acid) is an inhibitor of neurons. Too little GABA in the brain can lead to anxiety and depression. Serotonin plays a role in sleep and mood, which also leads to anxiety and depression when deficient. Dopamine influences one's ability to concentrate and learn. If too little or too much, it can cause Parkinson disease or schizophrenia, respectively. Acetylcholine impacts memory, learning, and sleep, causing depression or dementia when out of balance. Lastly, epinephrine, also known as adrenaline, is helpful during stressful situations as it intensifies moods and emotions, allowing the individual to act quickly during fight or flight situations.

Endocrine system

The endocrine system plays an important part in the body and impacts a person's behavior through its use of hormones and neurotransmitters. These aspects of the endocrine system influence reproductive behaviors and sexual arousal, as well as sleep and mood. The main component of the endocrine system is the hypothalamus; it is important in the coordination and activity of this system and helps to control the pituitary gland. This gland, also known as hypophysis, releases hormones for growth and reproduction, as well as neurotransmitters. The adrenal gland releases adrenaline, while the thyroid controls energy and metabolism throughout the body. The parathyroid regulates the parathyroid hormone (PTH) and is responsible for bone development.

The reproductive organs are also part of the endocrine system, and are responsible for either estrogen and progesterone or testosterone production, depending on the organs a person possesses. Lastly, the pineal gland connects the endocrine system to the nervous system, while controlling melatonin.

Genes, temperament, and heredity in relation to personality

Personality is a result of a variety of factors including the environment and genetics. Genes are the biological coding that a person is born with and they interact with environmental factors to determine personality characteristics and other important behaviors and conditions. Temperament refers to the mood and overall character a person is born with. Whether they are inherently energetic, quiet, or intense is determined by temperament. This is also impacted by environmental influences, but still remains a part of the individual's personality. Heredity also plays a role in genetic personality as a person inherits personality traits and behaviors from their parents.

Adaptive value of traits and behaviors

It is often necessary for individuals to alter their behavior due to the environment they are living in. Adaptation refers to the ability for the individual to adapt to the environment. Even though many traits and facets of personality are genetically determined, there is room for adaptation when needed. For instance, if Jane grew up not having to do the cooking or cleaning and her personality was somewhat lazy and entitled, then when she moved away to college she would have to adapt this personality to her new environment. She would need to learn to cook and clean for herself, and this would likely change her behavior, which in turn may have an impact on her personality.

Interaction between heredity and environmental influences

Environment and genetics both influence a person's behavior and personality, and these influences interact with one another as shown by twin studies. Twins who were raised separately shared more characteristics than two people unrelated. However, it was also shown that they had different personalities, giving evidence that environmental factors also have a significant influence on personality and behavior. For instance, a set of twins who were adopted by different parents may enjoy the same types of food, like the same clothes, or even have a similar haircut. However, despite having similar tastes, one may enjoy skiing, while the other would rather surf. These different preferences and behaviors contribute to personality and are impacted by multiple factors that interact with one another.

Influences of experience and genetics on development of behaviors

Experiences in an individual's life are often the cause of a change in behavior. For instance, if Billy was in a foreign country and his wallet was stolen by a robber, he may decide not to go back to that country, or begin to be more aware of his surroundings after. Also, because environmental and genetic factors both contribute to personality and behavior, there are instances where one can impact the other. Experiences can greatly influence a person's genetic code, while this genetic code may affect that person's behavior. In addition, genetics play a large role in how an individual behaves, and these genes may be expressed in different ways. Regulatory genes control how other genes are expressed, while epigenetics modify how a gene is expressed (a phenotype) without actually changing the genotype (genetic code). These epigenetics are influenced by experiences and environment, but also may be hereditary.

Genetically based behavioral variation in natural populations

In natural populations, certain genes encode for certain behaviors. These genes are not found in all members of a particular species, group, or family, which means that there will inherently be differences in behavior for all of these individuals. These behaviors are likely to vary for a number of reasons, including social factors, the environment, and individual experiences.

Prenatal development

Before a child is born, it goes through a process of development that begins with conception. After being fertilized by the sperm, the egg becomes a zygote, and then develops into a blastocyst. This then leads to an embryo, during which time the embryo develops organs and the cardiovascular system is grown. The next step is the fetus. During the fetal development, tissues and organs mature and the body of the fetus grows larger. Once the fetus is developed (or prior to this, depending on the circumstances of pregnancy), the baby is born.

Motor development

Once a baby is born, he or she develops motor skills in order to better navigate and understand the world. First, the child learns how to roll over; this usually occurs after 4 months. After 6 months, it is common that the child is able to sit without needing assistance, and once he or she is a year old, walking skills are often developed. Being able to jump in place is the next milestone a child accomplishes, and this happens when the child is about 2 years old. Other motor skills continue to be developed after this time, including dexterity and being able to use utensils and scissors, using all of the fingers to hold an object, and being able to write and draw.

Developmental changes during adolescence

During adolescence, an individual will go through developmental changes, also known as puberty. This change is the signal of adulthood beginning and a time when both girls and boys are able to learn abstract problem-solving skills while discovering their identities and independence. For girls, the physical changes during puberty involve menstruation, growing hair on her underarms and pubis, acne, developing sweat glands, and breast formation. For boys, the voice begins to change and deepen, hair is grown around the pubis, underarms, and face, acne develops, and the testes and scrotum grow.

Personality theories

Psychoanalytic theory
Psychoanalytic theory was developed originally by Sigmund Freud in order to understand how our unconscious influences our behavior and personality. He developed a theory about the unconscious that included 3 major aspects: the Id, Ego, and Superego. The Id is believed to be the undeveloped part of the unconscious that is driven by basic instinct for survival and pleasure. The Ego regulates the Id and understands how to achieve goals realistically. This part of consciousness is rooted in the unconscious, but interacts with reality. The Superego is the conscience of a person and it is developed through learning morality from authority and parental figures. The Superego is based in the outside world and is considered a conscious entity. Psychoanalytic theory is also largely thought to revolve around psychosexual development. These development stages include the oral, anal, phallic, latency, and genital stages, which explain how an individual's personality is developed based on whether or not he or she successfully moved through these stages.

Humanistic theory

Humanistic theory maintains that humans have control over their lives and are able to become self-actualized and aware of their behaviors if they put in the work to do so. This perspective is more optimistic in its view of the individual and was developed by the psychologists Abraham Maslow and Carl Rogers. Maslow believed that there was a hierarchy of needs that all people experienced, and that if basic needs such as food, shelter, and safety were unmet, the individual would not be able to move onto higher order needs, such as intimacy, work fulfillment, or self-actualization. Rogers developed a style of therapy known as person-centered, which allowed the therapist and client to develop a relationship in order to influence the client's personality and/or behavior. He stressed the importance of maintaining a self-concept that is congruent to reality in order to better understand one's identity.

Trait theory

Gordon Allport and Raymond Cattell were the main contributors to the trait theory of personality, which endorsed the idea that traits and sequences of traits were better means to understand a person's personality, and that these traits were stable and observable. Allport theorized that the conscious was more useful than the unconscious in terms of assessing personality, and he explained the three different types of traits: cardinal, central, and secondary. The cardinal traits were the most important and overarching traits that a person exhibited, while central traits were more common among the rest of the population. Secondary traits were thought to be how a person responded to an event. Cattell proposed that the many different traits exhibited by people could be condensed into just 16 different factors of personality. He based this concept on his knowledge of statistics using factor analysis and created these factors, such as intelligence, discipline, assertiveness, and friendliness, to better understand personality.

Social cognitive theory

Social cognitive perspective theorizes that personality and behavior are determined by social and environmental influences. This theory proposes that observing the behavior of others, being told how to act, and understanding the motivations of our peers affects our own behavior, as do the situations we experience. Albert Bandura is the main contributor to this perspective, experimenting with children and their toys to better understand aggression. He showed that children learned how to be aggressive when exposed to someone modeling aggressive behavior, while the opposite was true of the children exposed to non-aggressive behavior. This theory also explains how cognition, behavior, and the environment are interconnected and affect one another to cultivate personality.

Biological theory

The basis of the biological theory of personality is that our personality is somewhat determined by our genes and biology. Temperament and heritability are large parts of this theory, acknowledging that these are determined by how our genes and bodies are composed. This theory also includes the idea that behavior is influenced by the part of our brain responsible for reward and punishment, shaping our motivation based on what gives us pleasure or pain. Hans Eysenck is a main contributor to this theory and believed that genetics and the limbic system play a large part in personality. He suggested the three-factor model of personality that describes extraversion, neuroticism, and psychoticism as the aspects of a person's personality that are influenced by the various biological processes in the body.

Behaviorist theory

The behaviorist approach to personality suggests that our behavior can be manipulated and influenced by observation and learning. The two main psychologists associated with this theory are

B.F. Skinner and Ivan Pavlov. Skinner believed that our environment affects our behavior through operant conditioning. Being rewarded or punished for a specific behavior will lead to an increase or decrease in this behavior, respectively. Skinner's view on childhood and personality were notable for his time, as he didn't agree with other psychologists that the events of one's childhood shape personality. He also maintained that personality changes over the lifespan and that different events and experiences help to shape personality. Pavlov did not consider himself a behaviorist, but his contribution of classical conditioning was prominent in this perspective of psychology. He proposed that pairing a neutral stimulus with an unconditioned stimulus would create a conditioned response. For instance, imagine a person is afraid of loud noises, but feels indifferent towards dogs. If a dog approached that person at the same time a loud noise erupted, and this happened many times, the person would likely become afraid of dogs in addition to the loud noise.

Situational approach to explaining behavior

The situational approach is related to the trait theory of personality. This concept explains that the way a person reacts to a situation is determined by both their personality as well as the situation. Some people will react to the same situation in very different ways, but there are also situations that tend to elicit a similar reaction from very different individuals. This approach also explains that a person will react differently from one situation to another depending on both the situation and the personality of that individual. Fritz Heider also contributed to this concept by proposing attribution theory. This theory is when people tend to interpret information about the world based on attributions. This tendency to interpret leads to people behaving differently because of the attributes of a situation or relationship.

Biomedical and biopsychosocial approaches to psychological disorders

In the biomedical approach to psychological disorders, the main concern is a focus on the body and bodily processes. This approach holds that illness can be traced back to biological causes, meaning there will be a biological treatment for such an illness. This approach does not believe social or psychological factors are important to diagnosing disease and the mind and body are considered unconnected. The biopsychosocial approach to psychological disorders is quite different. Instead of simply considering biological causes and treatments for illnesses, psychological and social factors are also thought to be significant. In addition, the mind and body are considered to be inseparable, influencing and changing one another.

Classifications and rates of psychological disorders

Psychological disorders are classified in two main ways: using the International Classification of Diseases, Tenth Revision (ICD-10) from the World Health Organization or using the *Diagnostic and Statistical Manual of Mental Disorders, Fifth Edition* (*DSM-5*) from the American Psychiatric Association. The ICD-10 is based on 10 main groups of psychological disorders, including organic disorders, substance use, schizophrenia, mood disorders, neuroticism, behavioral syndromes, personality disorders, intellectual disability, psychological development disorders, and emotional disorders. The *DSM-5* now uses nonaxial documentation of diagnosis to identify psychological disorders that include clinical disorders, personality disorders and mental disability, general medical conditions, psychosocial and environmental problems, and the global assessment of functioning. It has also been found that about one-quarter of adults will experience some form of psychological disorder in their lifetimes. Age has an effect on psychological disorders, with prevalence increasing as people age and Alzheimer disease and dementia are the most common. Depression is also considered to be prevalent with between 6% and 8% of the population experiencing this disorder in their lifetimes. Anxiety rates are also high, with between 11% and 12% of people reporting anxiety in their lifetimes.

Anxiety, obsessive-compulsive, and trauma- and stressor-related disorders

Anxiety disorders are defined as a fear or worry about certain objects or situations. This fear or worry interferes with someone's ability to function in everyday situations and can cause different biological symptoms such as lack of sleep and indigestion. Anxiety disorders are categorized by type of disorder including panic disorder, phobias, and social anxiety disorder. Obsessive-compulsive disorder is also included under the umbrella of anxiety disorders and is defined as obsessive thoughts and compulsive behaviors revolving around a certain anxiety. Trauma- and stressor-related disorders are related to anxiety disorders as well, due to the anxiety symptoms (as well as depression symptoms) that are experienced after going through a traumatic or stressful event. A common disorder associated with this category of disorders is post-traumatic stress disorder (PTSD).

Somatic symptom disorders

Somatic symptom disorders are characterized by the physical problems and illnesses that are caused by psychological stressors. Having emotional difficulties or mental health issues, or experiencing a stressful event can trigger these physical symptoms, though there is no method of deriving the exact cause. If someone is experiencing a somatic symptom disorder, common symptoms the person will exhibit are difficulties speaking or using his or her senses, loss of strength, lack of balance, or difficulty moving certain parts of the body. Examples of these disorders are hypochondriasis, body dysmorphic disorder, conversion disorder, and pain disorder.

Depression, bipolar disorder, and other related mood disorders

Mood disorders are characterized by mood disturbances, changes, or difficulties. Depression is a mood disorder in which a person experiences feelings of extreme sadness, worthlessness, and a loss of hope for at least 2 weeks. This disorder may also lead to suicidal thoughts and actions. Bipolar disorder is another type of mood disorder in which individuals experience extreme mood swings and emotional instability. Those with bipolar disorder will have periods of depression or extreme sadness, followed by manic episodes with higher energy, positive thoughts, and increased activity levels, along with possible irritability.

Schizophrenia

Schizophrenia is a mental disorder that causes psychotic symptoms in an individual. These symptoms can include delusions, visual and auditory hallucinations, paranoia, unorganized speech and thinking, or difficulty with motor functions. This specific disorder causes the individual to lose touch with reality and is thought to be caused by a combination of genetics and environmental factors. Development of this disorder usually occurs in young adulthood, often when the individual is going through many social and physical changes.

Dissociative disorders

Dissociative disorders are diagnosed when individuals have symptoms of memory loss, an altered view of their identity, are detached from the world and themselves, or exhibit depression and/or anxiety symptoms along with a dissociative state. This disorder is often marked by a traumatic life event, causing the individual's mind to protect him or her from psychological stress. Dissociative identity disorder (previously known as multiple personality disorder) is an example of such a disorder, characterized by different identities emerging from one individual, with each identity often having different memories or personalities to help cope with a stressful situation.

Personality disorders

Personality disorders are a type of psychological disorder that are enduring, maladaptive, and rigid patterns of thoughts and behavior that make it difficult for an individual to function in a socially acceptable manner. Various types of personality disorders share these characteristics, often thought to be caused by life experiences and/or genetic abnormalities. Individuals with personality disorders have difficulties carrying out everyday behaviors or interacting with others and maintaining relationships. Examples of personality disorders include narcissistic personality disorder, in which a person has an inflated sense of self; paranoid personality disorder, in which a person is highly suspicious of those around him or her; schizoid personality disorder, in which a person avoids others and has little interest in establishing relationships; and obsessive-compulsive personality disorder, which differs from OCD in that a person is obsessively detail-oriented and strives for perfection, but does not exhibit obsessions and compulsions due to anxiety.

Biological bases of disorders

Schizophrenia

With schizophrenia, individuals are likely to have a genetic predisposition to the disorder. This means that if there is a predisposition, the individual is not guaranteed to be diagnosed with schizophrenia, but there are environmental factors that may contribute to developing the disorder because of the genetics involved. Schizophrenia is also thought to be related to elevated amounts of dopamine within the brain. Due to the effectiveness of antipsychotic drugs that block dopamine receptors, it is thought that dopamine dysregulation may be a biological basis for schizophrenia. The disorder is thought to be more likely associated with high numbers of dopamine receptors, as opposed to excessive levels of dopamine production. Brain abnormalities within the prefrontal cortex and the limbic system are also associated with schizophrenia and thought to be a cause for the disorder.

Depression

Depression has been shown to be associated with irregularities in neurotransmitters, such as serotonin, as well as abnormal levels of dopamine, norepinephrine, and cortisol. Serotonin is key in regulating mood, which leads scientists to believe that the abnormal levels of this neurotransmitter are related to the development of depression. In addition, antidepressants often increase serotonin levels, frequently leading to regulation in mood. It is also believed that some people are genetically predisposed to developing depression, meaning that those with this predisposition will not necessarily be diagnosed with depression, but environmental factors may influence the development of the disorder.

Alzheimer and Parkinson diseases

Alzheimer disease is a nervous system disorder that is degenerative in nature and affects an individual's memory and functioning. Within the brain, plaques and tangles are formed that negatively impact the brain cells of a person. Plaques are likely to contribute to the death of brain cells and cause damage due to clusters of beta-amyloid protein. Tangles occur when strands of proteins are tangled within brain cells, preventing the essential nutrients needed for the brain from being transported. Parkinson disease is also degenerative in nature and negatively impacts motor function and mental processes. This occurs when the nerve cells within the brain (substantia nigra) are weakened. These nerve cells produce dopamine and the decline in functioning of these nerve cells leads to a drop in dopamine, affecting the ability for these nerve cells to communicate with the corpus striatum. The production of dopamine normally is how individuals are able to have coordination and muscle function, which is why Parkinson disease develops when the substantia nigra are weakened.

Stem cell–based therapy to regenerate neurons

Many degenerative diseases are shown to be caused by the deterioration of neurons. Being about to regenerate these neurons would be essential to treating these diseases, such as Parkinson disease. Studies have shown that stem cells may be an effective tool in accomplishing this goal due to their ability to renew themselves, due to their efficacy in studies on animals. Brain cells are thought to be able to be restored by using neural stem cells, essentially repairing the damage caused by neurodegenerative diseases. These stem cells can be used to generate a significant amount of dopaminergic neurons, thus being a useful tool for this endeavor.

Influence of instinct, arousal, drives, and needs on motivation

Instinct is behavior that is unlearned, but derived from biological influences. This behavior occurs throughout animals of the same species. The concept of arousal is seen as a level of awakening when an individual (or animal) is alert and stimulated, allowing him or her to be the most productive. Drives are known as mental and physical states that come from within the individual. These drives are helpful in creating a sense of urgency to carry out a specific behavior based on the drive involved. Hunger, thirst, exhaustion, and pain are all different types of drives that act in this manner. Lastly, needs are also internal states that influence behavior. Although needs may include different types of drives (needing to eat something, for instance, is an innate need), they can also incorporate higher level needs and learned goals in order to influence behavior. Wanting to earn money or power are examples of these learned needs, leading the individual to behave in ways that get him or her closer to this goal.

Drive reduction theory and incentive theory

Drive reduction theory uses the concept of drives to explain how motivation influences behavior. This theory suggests that humans will engage in behaviors that contribute to a reduction in drives. The discomfort involved in the drives motivate someone to find a way to reduce this discomfort, leading to the execution of certain behaviors. An example of this would be if someone is hungry. This hunger is a drive that creates a certain amount of discomfort, either psychologically or physically, and the individual experiencing this hunger will want to quell such a drive. In order to do this, the person decides to eat a sandwich, which in turn reduces his or her hunger. Incentive theory is thought to work in a similar way, but instead of being motivated by internal experiences, the individual is motivated by external sources. In this theory, it is proposed that the person is offered an incentive in some way to either increase or decrease a certain behavior. For instance, being rewarded with one's favorite food might be an incentive for that person to clean the house.

Cognitive and need-based theories

Expectancy theory and goal-setting theory are examples of cognitive theories of motivation. Expectancy theory explains that individuals consciously behave in ways that they believe will decrease pain and increase pleasure. Goal-setting theory explains how individuals behave when they set goals for themselves. It proposes that when goals (even small goals) are accomplished and the individual receives positive feedback, this increases his or her performance later on. Need-based theories are also used to explain motivation and behavior. One example of this type of theory would be Maslow's hierarchy of needs. This theory explains how humans have 5 basic needs that include physiological needs, safety, social, esteem, and self-actualization. These are supposedly inherent needs, but in order to achieve the higher level needs (esteem and self-actualization) one must first meet his or her physiological and safety needs, such as food, water, and shelter.

Biological and sociocultural motivators that regulate behavior

Certain behaviors, such as eating, having sex, and using substances, can be explained by both biological and sociocultural motivations. Eating, for instance, is necessary to survival, and the brain, digestive system, and hormones help to regulate this behavior. Hunger is signaled within the brain, leading a person to eat food. When full, the feeling of satiation comes from the ventromedial nucleus of the hypothalamus. Hormones, such as leptin and insulin, also aid in the digestion of the food. However, sociocultural motivators will also regulate eating; wanting to appear thinner or be healthier may lead a person to stop eating before they are full, or to wait to eat even when they are hungry. Sex is another behavior that is biologically influenced; hormones and sensory information may lead to an individual wanting to have sex. However, these desires may also be influenced by culture, social pressure, age, and emotion. Lastly, drug and alcohol behavior may be increased or decreased based on biological symptoms and experiences, such as dopamine levels or withdrawal symptoms. However, drug use may also be encouraged or discouraged based on the culture one is exposed to, curiosity, or events that they experience.

Components of attitudes

Attitudes are composed of three different aspects: cognitive, affective, and behavioral. The cognitive aspect of attitude is how the individual thinks about something. Beliefs and knowledge about certain events or subjects fall into this category. For instance, if Jane knows that snakes are able to kill someone with just one bite, this may lead her to not like snakes, and possibly fear them. The affective aspect of attitude is how an individual feels about something. The feeling of love falls into this category; if Bob loves his wife, he is likely to have a positive attitude towards her. Lastly, the behavioral aspect of attitude is how someone acts in response to something. If a person has a negative attitude towards an issue, this will likely lead to that person behaving in a manner that exhibits this attitude. For instance, if Joe doesn't like Elaine and has a negative attitude towards her, this may influence his behavior in her presence. He may avoid her, or speak to her differently because of his dislike towards her.

Influence of behavior on attitudes

Behavior is a significant component of attitudes, and is likely to influence these attitudes. Foot-in-the-door phenomenon is one way in which behavior influences someone's attitude and works through the concept of compliance. When asked to do something simple, an individual may agree and fulfil this request. By engaging in this behavior, the individual is likely to agree to the next task, even if it is more difficult. After agreeing to these requests, the individual is likely to have a more positive attitude towards the person asking. Another way that behavior influences attitude is through role-playing effects. When asked to act in a way consistent with a type of person or character, the individual may internalize the behavior and have this influence his or her attitude. The most famous example of this is the Stanford prison study, when students were asked to act as either prisoners or prison guards. The student prisoners began to feel helpless or rebellious in face of their new role, while the prison guards began to feel more powerful and tough. The students had internalized these roles so extensively that the study was shut down after only 6 days.

Influence of attitudes on behavior

Often, a person acts in a certain way due to the attitudes he or she has about a situation. These attitudes can be influenced by personal experience, knowledge about a subject, or an expectation of a specific outcome. Icek Ajzen's theory of planned behavior is one way in which this process is explained. This theory holds that a person has a set of beliefs about a certain behavior, which influences his or her attitude towards that behavior. This in turn leads to the individual behaving in a way that coincides with this attitude. For example, if a student believes that she should be sitting quietly and alert in a class, it would make her happy to engage in this behavior, and she would sit quietly and alert in class. Another theory, the attitude-to-behavior process model, explains that a person's perception of an event will lead him or her to behave in a way that coincides with this perception. It also says that social norms are likely to affect a person's behavior. In this model, the event or situation prompts him or her to have an attitude about the situation, which in turn affects the social norms or individual perception of the event.

Cognitive dissonance theory

A common theme in our lives is thinking or feeling a certain way, but acting differently. Cognitive dissonance is the psychological explanation of this theme and can lead to anxiety if unresolved. This concept is best explained by an example. If George wants to lose weight, it would make sense that he would try to eat healthier. However, George loves ice cream, pizza, and other unhealthy foods. George may start to feel frustrated and angered at himself if he indulges in his favorite foods because of his goal of losing weight. These two opposing thoughts or feelings create a cognitive dissonance within George's psyche. Similarly, if George were to eat in an unhealthy manner while trying to lose weight, he may feel a certain tension within his mind. In order to resolve this cognitive dissonance, George would need to do one or more of three things: change his thoughts, change his behaviors, or introduce a new thought. George could either change his desire to lose weight, cease his indulgence in unhealthy foods, or decide to incorporate exercise into his routine. By making these alterations, George would resolve the tension created by his opposing thoughts and or behaviors, therefore alleviating his cognitive dissonance.

Social facilitation

Social facilitation refers to how an individual performs better when there are other people around. Doing group activities, studying, exercising, and other simple tasks are often done better or more easily when done with two or more people. Having someone watch you or do an activity with you is likely to increase arousal/stimulation for that activity, making you work harder or more quickly on a simple task. However, because it increases arousal, this only works for easy behaviors; more complicated or difficult activities are done less easily when in the presence of others as it may make the individual more nervous and less able to focus on the task at hand.

Deindividuation

Deindividuation occurs when an individual is among a crowd and that individual loses his or her sense of self-awareness. A common term for this concept is also "mob mentality." When part of a "mob" or crowd, the individual may not feel responsible for his or her actions and participate in the actions of the group. This means that things that the individual would never do when he or she is alone may be easier to do when the rest of the group is doing it. For instance, Harold would never scream at a police officer when he is on his own, but when a crowd of people is yelling at the police in a protest, Harold also participates in the protest by yelling. Due to the anonymity and diffused responsibility, an individual is likely to feel more comfortable participating in the group activity than if he or she were alone. Not being able to be picked out of a crowd or held responsible for his or her actions may contribute to which behaviors the individual takes part in. The larger the group, the more anonymous the person is and the less responsibility her or she is likely to feel, and the more likely he or she will partake in the group behavior.

Bystander effect

When something bad is happening in front of a large number of people, bystander effect may come into play. If someone is robbed in plain view of a group of people, and none of the people help or call the police, this is a bystander effect. This concept becomes more likely when there are more people around. For instance, if a single person is walking down the street and he or she witnesses a crime, he or she is likely to call for help or help the victim of the crime because there is no one else around. However, the more people are around to witness the crime, the less responsibility each individual person is likely to feel. Each person may assume that because there are so many people around someone else is likely to call the police. However, if everyone in the group assumes that someone else will take responsibility, then no one will actually help the victim, creating a bystander effect.

Social loafing

When a group is given a project, each participant is likely to contribute less to the project than they would on their own. This concept is known as social loafing. Larger groups of people are more likely to lead to social loafing because each individual may feel as though they do not have as much responsibility when there are more people. In addition, if there is conflict within this group, group members are likely to contribute less to the project. Individuals also may fit into different categories when working on a group project. The in-group is comprised of individuals who are working hard and putting in more effort to finish the project. The out-group is comprised of individuals who aren't putting in as much effort and not taking responsibility for their part of the project. In order to reduce the phenomenon of social loafing, it is necessary to have smaller groups, as well as delegate responsibility to each individual member of the group.

Social control

Social control is how society creates normative behaviors and formal rules for the way people should behave in order to prevent chaos. Informal social control is the category that unwritten social norms fall under. Not disrupting a funeral or not picking your nose in public are examples of informal social control that help keep society more organized. Formal social control refers to the laws placed on a society in order to keep society controlled. Behaviors that fall into this category are not committing crimes of murder or robbery because the individual will go to jail or be otherwise punished for disobeying these forms of formal control.

Peer pressure

Peer pressure is when the people around you encourage you to participate in certain behaviors or decisions. This peer pressure can either be positive or negative depending on the behaviors performed. The people who are referred to as peers can be friends, family members, coworkers, team members, or other people who you relate to and want to spend time with. Peer pressure occurs when an individual doesn't necessarily want to participate in an activity or behavior, but feels pressured to do so by peers in order to "fit in" or follow norms of a certain group. Positive forms of peer pressure can include going to sporting events, volunteering, or other positive group activities. Negative forms of peer pressure include behaviors such as using drugs, committing crimes, or drinking alcohol illegally.

Conformity

Conformity is a way that individuals change their behaviors in order to be accepted into a group. Behaving in such a way is likely in response to feeling pressure to do so, but this pressure can be either real or imagined. The members of the group may explicitly tell the individual that participating in certain activities will make them fit into the group, but the individual may also infer from the group behavior how he or she is expected to act and subsequently feel pressured to act the same. Examples of conformity can include changing the way one dresses, engaging in risky behaviors such as drug and alcohol use, acquiring new hobbies, or going to events that the individual would normally not attend.

Obedience

Obedience can be defined as changing one's behavior in response to authority. This means that the individual may not normally engage in certain behaviors, but because they are being pressured by an authority figure to do so, the individual changes his or her behavior to obey. This occurs when an authority figure such as a boss, parent, teacher, or otherwise imposing person asks, commands, or instructs a person to perform a certain behavior, and the individual feels forced to comply with these instructions. Obedience can be viewed positively or negatively, depending on the context. For instance, obeying one's parents or a police officer may be considered socially acceptable or even required in order to maintain a sense of control or morality within a society. However, at times individuals may feel required to obey a person of power in order to keep their jobs or not be punished, which may lead to obeying orders that may be immoral or otherwise wrong.

Group polarization

Group polarization is a concept that refers to groups of people making extreme decisions that don't necessarily align with the individual's original ideas. As an example, imagine that Joe originally felt that the pizza place should warn its customers that there are anchovies in certain menu items. However, when in the midst of a group of customers who also want a change in the menu items, they all decide that anything with anchovies should be taken completely off the menu. Joe originally did not want anchovies taken off the menu, but because of group polarization, the group made a more extreme decision. This concept also refers to the inclination of individuals to take greater risks when part of a group of like-minded individuals. Being part of this type of group may lead people to believe they share qualities and characteristics of a specific category of people, influencing the way they think and behave when part of a larger group.

Groupthink

Groupthink occurs when the members of a group agree to or accept the ideas and decisions of the larger group without bringing up their own individual ideas. This often leads to bad decisions made by the group because the decisions are not questioned or altered. For instance, imagine a group of people are trying to decide how to deal with a situation of unhealthy options at a fast food

Copyright © Mometrix Media. You have been licensed one copy of this document for personal use only. Any other reproduction or redistribution is strictly prohibited. All rights reserved.

restaurant. Someone proposes the idea that they should take drastic action and vandalize the restaurant. Although this is a bad idea and one of the members, Sam, disagrees with this idea and thinks they should instead write a letter asking for healthy alternatives, everyone else in the group agrees with the idea of vandalism. This leads Sam to feel that he shouldn't disagree with the group and decides to support this proposal. The group then decides to vandalize the restaurant and the members of the group are arrested. This example of groupthink led to a bad decision even though there may have been better alternatives. Groupthink tends to occur when the group is more cohesive and lacks diverse opinions. In addition, strong group leaders also contribute to groupthink because people are less willing to disagree.

Sanctions

In society, people are expected to follow rules, whether explicit or implicit. These rules are called social norms and they can be laws that society has put in place or they can be unwritten rules that people have learned over the course of time. For these rules to work, there need to be punishments or consequences for individuals who fail to abide by these social norms. These punishments are known as sanctions. Sanctions can be punishments that individuals must endure for illegal behavior, such as jail time or being fined, but they can also be responses to violations of legal, but unwritten social norms, such as shame or ridicule from other members of a society. For instance, if someone were to wear a colorful and extravagant outfit to a funeral, instead of the traditional black clothing, that person may be judged by his or her peers or shamed into leaving early. These sanctions work to uphold the social norms and help people learn how to act in social settings.

Folkways, mores, and taboos

Multiple types of social norms are in place that individuals in a society must adhere to in order to maintain cohesion and control within the society. Three different types of social norms, folkways, mores, and taboos are used within a society to prevent chaos. Folkways are casual social norms that, if violated, cause less of an outrage than when more severe social norms are violated. For instance, wearing casual clothing to a formal event would be a violation of a folkway. Doing so may cause other people to stare or internally judge the individual, but consequences larger than that would be disproportional to the action. Mores are social norms that, if violated, lead to more severe social sanctions and stigmatization. The word "more" is derived from "morality," which helps understand what mores are: social norms based on a moral code. An example of a more would be living with a romantic partner before getting married. This type of more goes against certain religious moral codes that say couples must be married before cohabitating. Taboos are also a type of social norm that, when violated, elicit a strong response from society such as disgust or rejection. An example of a taboo is incest, which is not tolerated in certain societies and leads to extreme responses from society when it occurs.

Anomie

Social norms exist in order for a society to function in a controlled and predictable manner. However, when these social norms don't exist or when they are lacking, this concept is known as anomie. Anomie occurs when the social constructs of a community or group are broken down and the society no longer provides moral codes or laws for individuals to live by. Anomie can also refer to the phenomenon of individuals no longer accepting or abiding by the social norms, by way of individualism or isolation. Some believe that this is a form of anarchy and that the society can no longer exist with harmony among its citizens, while others may see it as freedom from oppression.

Deviance

Deviance can be defined as behavior that does not abide by social norms within a group. This deviance varies from culture to culture due to the various social norms that exist within each society. Something that is considered deviant in one culture does not necessarily mean that it is deviant in another. Some deviant behavior is against the law, while others may just be considered impolite or abnormal. Different theories also exist regarding deviance, including differential association, labeling theory, and strain theory. Differential association refers to the idea that when a person is associated with individuals who are considered deviant, that person will also be considered deviant. This form of deviation is thought to contribute to social change through more and more individuals becoming part of the deviant group, thereby changing how that behavior is viewed. Labeling theory refers to the idea that labels can influence how people view themselves, thereby potentially influencing their behavior. If someone is told he is an overachiever, for instance, he may either reject the label and become less motivated, or accept the label and embrace the motivation. Lastly, strain theory refers to how society is structured, and how it may put excessive pressure on individuals that lead to deviant behavior. For instance, if society is structured in a way that makes it difficult to afford rent or food, people may feel that robbery or committing other crimes is the only option for survival.

Collective behavior

When large amounts of individuals engage in the same behavior, this is known as collective behavior. Collective behavior can include things such as fads, mass hysteria, and riots. Fads are defined as temporary trends that many people in a society follow. Collecting a specific item (Beanie Babies or Silly Bandz), saying certain phrases or words (selfie or psyche), or watching certain television shows (Care Bears or Jersey Shore) all fall under the category of a fad. Mass hysteria refers to a large amount of people worried about the same thing, whether real or imagined, due to media coverage or through rumors. An example of mass hysteria would be the Salem witch trials in the 1600s. Riots are also a form of collective behavior and can be in response to either positive or negative societal events. Riots may happen in a city where a professional sports team wins a national championship, or if there are accusations of racism in societal structures.

Socialization

Socialization can occur through many different societal structures with the goal of an individual learning the social norms of the community. The primary agent of socialization is family. This is the first place where an individual learns how to behave, and the different features of the family influence the individual's personality and belief system. How large the family is, how religious they are, and what culture they are part of are each part of the familial socialization. Another agent of socialization is the mass media. This is often where people get information about the world and how to perceive this information. Mass media includes television, Internet, radio, and other forms of communication and entertainment. These sources of media give individuals information about politics, religion, culture, and much more. Peers are also a way for an individual to learn social norms. How the peers are raised by their own family, their experiences and beliefs, and their interests influence how the individual perceives the world and their own interests. Peers are usually of the same age and share various interests that bring them together. Peers can be positive or negative depending on the behaviors they encourage, and are most influential during adolescence when the individual is attempting to create his or her own identity. Lastly, the workplace is also a main agent of socialization, and it is where individuals learn behaviors and knowledge that help them become a part of the workforce. Ethics, professionalism, and how to work in stressful situations are just some of the things an individual learns in the workplace in order to follow social norms.

Neutral, conditioned, and unconditioned stimuli

The concept of classical conditioning uses specific terms to explain how behavior is learned through a biological response. A neutral stimulus is one that does not naturally produce a response from an individual, such as a bell ringing or a light flashing. An unconditioned stimulus is one that triggers a natural response, such as how a frightening loud noise causes an individual to feel scared, or how the smell of delicious food causes one to salivate. A conditioned stimuli is one to which an individual has developed a learned response. An example of this would be Pavlov's dogs: the dogs had no reaction to a ringing bell originally (neutral stimulus) and they would salivate when they smelled their food (unconditioned stimulus). Pavlov would ring the bell and serve the food at the same time, causing the dogs to become conditioned to this neutral stimuli. The conditioned stimuli became the ringing bell, which would cause the dogs to salivate before they could smell their food.

Conditioned and unconditioned responses

In the theory of classical conditioning, individuals are believed to learn certain behaviors through acquisition of conditioned responses to different stimuli. An unconditioned response is a naturally occurring response to an unconditioned stimuli. For instance, a natural reaction to a sudden loud noise would be fear or surprise. A person's response to that may be screaming, jumping back, or even running away. These responses are unconditioned responses to this specific stimulus. A conditioned response is one that does not occur naturally and the individual has acquired this response to a once-neutral stimulus through conditioning. An example of this would be Pavlov's dogs: The dogs in his study would salivate whenever they smelled their food. This salivation would be considered an unconditioned response because it is naturally occurring. The dogs originally had no response to a bell ringing (a neutral stimulus), but Pavlov decided to ring a bell at the same time he gave the dogs their food. Over time, because of the consistent pairing of the food with the bell, the dogs salivated when they heard the bell ring, even when there was no food. This salivation in response to the bell ringing is an example of a conditioned response.

Processes of classical conditioning

Classical conditioning explains the process of acquiring certain behaviors in response to certain stimuli. The process of learning the associations between certain stimuli is known as acquisition. Acquisition refers to developing a conditioned response to a stimulus through the pairing of a neutral stimulus with an unconditioned stimulus. However, if this pairing stops occurring, after a while extinction will occur. Extinction refers to the loss of the association of these stimuli. For instance, if a dog learns that a bell ringing signals food coming, he salivates in response to the bell (even when no food is presented). This is the acquisition of a conditioned response. However, if the bell rings consistently with no food presented, the dog may no longer salivate when the bell rings. This is known as extinction. After a response is extinguished, if there is a rest period (a couple hours or a day) where the bell does not ring, the next time the bell rings may elicit the same conditioned response: salivation. This reappearance of the conditioned response after extinction is known as spontaneous recovery. In addition, if the dog learns that the bell ringing means food, and therefore salivates, the dog may also salivate when the doorbell rings, or when a similar sound occurs. This is called generalization. However, there is also the possibility that the dog is able to distinguish between the bell ringing and the doorbell, which would be called discrimination. This is when the dog does not salivate when he hears a similar noise because he does not associate it with being given food.

Shaping and extinction in operant conditioning

Operant conditioning is a theory in which behavior can be learned through punishments and rewards. When a behavior is learned through reinforcement, this is known as shaping. However, if the individual learns this behavior, but it is no longer being reinforced, the individual may not exhibit this behavior anymore. When this behavior declines, this is referred to as extinction.

Types of reinforcement

Positive, negative, primary, and conditional
In operant conditioning, one way of learning behavior is through reinforcement. There are different types of reinforcement, positive and negative, and they are used in order to increase a specific behavior. Positive reinforcement is when an individual is given a reward in order to encourage an increase in that behavior. For instance, if a parent wants a child to clean his or her room, the parent may reward a clean room by giving the child candy. The child then cleans his or her room more often in order to get more candy. Negative reinforcement is a bit more complex. Contrary to what one may think, negative reinforcement does not refer to a punishment; instead it refers to taking something away in order to increase a certain behavior. Using the example above, the parent may encourage the child to clean his or her room by saying that they will not make him or her clean the bathroom. Because the child does not want to clean the bathroom, he or she cleans the bedroom in order to avoid this extra chore. Primary and secondary reinforcers are rewards to help increase behavior. Primary reinforcers are rewards that a person desires naturally: food, water, and other pleasure, while secondary reinforcers are rewards that a person learns to desire, such as money or toys. These secondary reinforcers are not natural rewards, but instead things that a person has associated with a primary reward and learned to desire.

Fixed-ratio, variable-ratio, fixed-interval, and variable-interval
In order to reinforce a behavior through operant conditioning, there are different schedules that this reinforcement can occur in, and these schedules may have different efficacy. Fixed-ratio schedules are when behavior is rewarded in a specific pattern. This could mean that each time the behavior occurs, it is rewarded, or it could mean that every fifth time the behavior occurs it is rewarded. This schedule is fairly predictable, especially compared to variable-ratio schedules. In this type of schedule, the behavior is rewarded at a different rate each time. For instance, instead of being rewarded for a behavior every time it occurs, the behavior is rewarded the first time, and then it is rewarded after 5 times, and then it is rewarded again after the fourteenth time. Another schedule of reinforcement is called fixed-interval. Similar to fixed ratio, the behavior is rewarded predictably after a certain amount of time has passed. For instance, the behavior is rewarded, and then it won't be rewarded again for another minute each time. Variable-interval schedule is similar to the variable-ratio, in that it is unpredictable; the behavior may be rewarded immediately, but then rewarded 4 minutes later, and then again 3 minutes later.

Punishment in operant conditioning

In operant conditioning, punishment is one way to shape a person's behavior. However, unlike reinforcement, punishment seeks to decrease a behavior. For instance, if a child is screaming, a parent may want to decrease this behavior through punishment. One type of punishment, positive punishment, introduces a stimulus in order to decrease a behavior. This means that the parent might spank his or her child, or scold them. This causes the child to stop screaming in order to avoid this punishment. Negative punishment works by taking something away in order to decrease a behavior. In this example, the parent might decide to take away the child's dessert in order to decrease his or her screaming. Because the child wants dessert and doesn't want to lose it, the child learns to stop screaming in order to avoid the punishment.

Escape and avoidance learning

Individuals often learn how to approach the world based on learning experiences that shape one's view of the world. For instance, escape and avoidance learning are ways that individuals learn about things that might do them harm or cause them discomfort. If something hurts a person, that person will likely try to get away as fast as possible. This is represented by the concept of escape learning. The next time the individual interacts with this thing that previously hurt them, they will try to avoid it. This concept is known as avoidance. The two concepts work together in escape and avoidance learning, and the individual learns that this thing must be avoided in order to evade discomfort. An example of this is if a person sees a cactus and decides to touch it, she may prick a finger. She reacts to the pain by jumping away from it, or escaping it. The next time she sees the cactus, she remembers being pricked by it previously and avoids touching it.

Associative learning

Cognitive processes
Associative learning is when a person learns that two things are associated and produce a specific response. Operant and classical conditioning are two ways that associative learning can occur. There are also different cognitive processes that influence associative learning including latent learning, problem-solving, and instincts. Latent learning is a passive type of association in which an individual is not rewarded for a behavior but learns to behave in this way naturally. Problem-solving is a process in which a person encounters a problem and must step back, observe the situation, think about it, and then decide how to solve the problem. Instincts are genetic or biological behaviors that are naturally occurring and difficult to change. Animals, especially mothers, have instinctual protectiveness of their young, making it difficult to teach these animals otherwise.

Biological processes
Associative learning is a process of acquiring certain behaviors through learning, but this process may also be influenced by biology. One way this occurs is through instinctive drift. If an animal, for instance, has instincts that lead it to hunt for food in order to survive, this is the natural way for that animal to behave. However, if the animal in question is a domestic cat, a human may try to train the cat to stay at home, eat canned cat food, and sleep all day. However, the cat still has instincts to hunt, and when let outside, the cat reverts to these basic instincts and hunts and eats a mouse. This reversion back to hunting after being domesticated is known as instinctive drift. An individual or animal may also have biological predispositions that influence how they behave. This predisposition may make the individual more likely to develop certain diseases or various characteristics. An example would be a person who has parents who are alcoholics. This individual may be more likely to develop alcoholism based solely on this biological predisposition, in addition to being exposed to an environment and family that encourage drinking. Other examples would be personality traits, intelligence, diseases, and other similar behaviors.

Observational learning

Modeling

Modeling is a process by which an individual learns how to do certain behaviors by watching other people engage in this behavior. Parents, teachers, friends, and other individuals that the person either relates to or is exposed to often can serve as these models of behavior. When an individual sees another person successfully engaging in a certain behavior, it increases the confidence of the individual also performing that behavior successfully. Being able to mimic another person's behavior through modeling allows the observer to understand how and when to act a certain way and increases the likelihood of successfully following in his or her footsteps.

Brain, mirror neurons, and vicarious emotions

In observational learning, there are different biological processes that impact learning different behaviors. Mirror neurons are one example of such a process; they originate in the frontal and parietal lobes of the brain and are activated when an individual is performing a certain behavior or exhibiting a certain emotion and that individual observes another person engaging in the same behavior. This allows an individual to learn how to perform certain behaviors and understand another person's feelings. The brain allows the individual to also feel emotions, despite not sharing the same emotion. Empathy is one way in which this occurs, and involves two individuals sharing an emotion and feeling that emotion together. Emotions can also be felt vicariously. This refers to the idea that even though two individuals don't share a certain emotion or experience, both feel the same emotion. For instance, if Rachel's friend gets married and is happy, Rachel may feel the same emotion because she is vicariously experiencing the happiness of her friend.

Applications of observational learning to explain individual behavior

Individual behavior is often impacted by learning through observation. These observations are usually through family interactions, but may also refer to friendships, school life, the workplace, media, and other social environments. Some applications of this may be when a person is a part of an abusive family and they themselves develop an abusive personality and behavior, or if the individual has friends who are very loving and welcoming, the individual may learn to also be loving and welcoming through observation.

Elaboration likelihood model

The elaboration likelihood model explains the ways that people tend to make decisions. Taking time to think about a decision or following other peoples' decisions are ways in which people make a decision and these ways are explained in the elaboration likelihood model. The model evaluates how likely a person is to use either one of these methods for making a decision. Central route processing is the tendency for an individual to think hard about a decision. This person would read articles, talk to other people, and carefully examine each aspect of the decision at hand. Peripheral route processing refers to a person who is only paying attention to information that is not central to the decision at hand. This person would be more likely to look at how attractive something is to them, what their friends are doing, or what people tell them to do. An example of the elaboration likelihood model is when someone is deciding which computer to buy. A person using central route processing is more likely to pay attention to user reviews, the amount of hard drive, and the speed of the computer. Someone using peripheral route processing may be more likely to make a decision based on commercials, which computer looks better, or what a friend of theirs has.

Various factors that affect attitude change

Attitudes can be changed by different aspects. For instance, if a person's behavior were to change, this would be observed by others and then this would influence that person's attitude. An example of this would be if a person buys a new sweater, but then people don't compliment the sweater or they make fun of it, this may cause the individual to no longer like the sweater. Messages from others and the media also influence attitudes. These messages influence how the person feels about something, thereby affecting his or her attitude. In this scenario, the characteristics of the message and who the message is targeting would change a person's attitude. If that person were to see a movie and like it, he might change his attitude if he hears that other people didn't like it or he reads negative reviews about the movie. Attitudes can also be changed by social factors and the environment. For instance, if a person were to have friends that like certain types of food and going to specific social events that she originally didn't like, she may learn to like it or change her attitude to fit in with the friend group.

Self-Identity and Social Influences

Self-concept and self-identity

Role of self-esteem
Self-esteem refers to how much an individual accepts and values themselves. People may have high or low self-esteem, and this influences their self-identity or self-concept. A person with high self-esteem may feel more confident and view themselves in a positive manner. This person is less likely to worry about what others say about him and other people's opinions are less likely to influence his self-identity. However, a person with low self-esteem is the opposite. This person does not view himself in a positive light, and has less confidence in how he is as a person. Other people's opinions of him are highly influential on how he sees himself, and this has a negative impact on his identity.

Role of self-efficacy
Self-efficacy can be defined as a person's belief in his or her ability to be successful or achieve a specific goal. Different tasks and circumstances are viewed to have different levels of self-efficacy for a person, and this level of self-efficacy can be either positive or negative. A person with high self-efficacy is more likely to have a positive view of the task at hand and have more confidence completing this task. This type of individual is also less fearful in taking risks and is able to evaluate themselves more accurately. However, a person with low self-efficacy is more prone to negative thoughts regarding a specific task and has more doubts and fears of his or her ability to accomplish a goal. This person is less likely to take risks and believes she will fail, even when this evaluation of her abilities is incorrect

Role of locus of control
A person's self-concept and self-identity can be influenced by his locus of control. This phrase refers to how a person views his control of a situation and impacts the attitudes and behavior that are related to this situation. There are two different categories of locus of control: external and internal. A person with an external locus of control views the situation as being controlled by outside forces, and he doesn't believe that he has control over what happens. People who have this external locus of control tend to blame others or external causes for what happens, or feel hopeless about the situation. They may also say that if a problem is solved successfully, it was lucky or a fluke. Individuals with an internal locus of control have the opposite view of situations. These people tend

to blame themselves if something goes wrong because they believe that they are able to control what happens. This type of person may also take more control over situations and work tirelessly to accomplish a goal because they have more confidence in their ability to control the situation.

Identity types

People are likely to identify themselves in terms of different groups that they fit into. These groups form a basis for an individual's identity and can range from cultural identities to age or gender. Someone's racial or ethnic identity signifies their heritage or cultural background based on skin color or country of origin. Gender is another identity: males, females, transgendered people, and other groups fall under the category of gender. Age can also be an identity, not just by how old a person is, but by how old they act or feel internally. A person's religion, sexual orientation, or social class also signifies identity and may impact how an individual views him or herself.

Theories of identity development

There are many theories about the development of identity and they differ based on psychological fields of study and the theory's main focus. One theory, by Lawrence Kohlberg, is based on morality. This theory focuses on how an individual develops a sense of morality through cognition and resolution of moral dilemmas. This theory explains these moral dilemmas through consequences of certain actions, social order, and rules of social relationships throughout the lifespan. Freud also developed a theory of identity based on the different psychosexual stages. This theory explains that children go through a series of these psychosexual stages (oral, anal, phallic, latency, and genital) as the child ages, and if the child does not successfully move through these stages, he or she may become fixated at a certain stage, resulting in the formation of an identity or personality that is shaped by this fixation. Erik Erikson's theory of psychosocial identity development describes different stages of the lifespan wherein the individual must successfully resolve the conflict at each stage. These conflicts range from trust and autonomy to identity and intimacy. These different stages are different parts of an individual's psychology and formed through social interactions. Conflicts not fully resolved in this theory create difficulties in a person's life throughout time.

Influences on identity formation

Individuals
A person's identity is formed through individual aspects in different ways. For instance, imitation is one way that a person can be influenced by the individuals around her. Mimicking the behavior of parents, siblings, friends, or other people in a person's life is the definition of imitation. These behaviors often occur because the person represents traits that you identify with and help to build your own identity. The looking-glass self is also a way that individuals shape another person's identity. For instance, if a Jon has friends who view him as fun, but his parents see him as a lazy person, these ideas shape the way that Jon thinks of himself, and therefore form his identity. Another way that individuals affect a person's identity is when the person takes on the roles or identity of the other individual. If Jon, for instance, pretends to be like a police officer on television, he is experimenting with that person's identity. By pretending to be someone else, this helps an individual figure out how his own identity coincides with that of another person.

Groups
Groups can have a large impact on how a person's forms his or her identity. The main way this occurs is through the use of reference groups. This means that an individual is exposed to groups that have different characteristics, interests, and personalities, and draws conclusions about these

groups based on these traits. The individual is then able to see how his own identity fits into these groups to determine more information about his identity. An example of this would be Penny. Penny sees a group of girls at school who are very quiet and read many books. This group isn't very popular but they are very friendly and helpful to other people. Another group of girls at school is very popular and the girls in that group play sports and go to a lot of social events. However, this group isn't as friendly as the first group and they don't always treat people nicely. Penny doesn't play sports, but she does read a lot of books. This leads her to identify more with the first group of girls and use them as a reference group. This may shape more of her identity if she sees more things about this group that she can identify with. If Penny identifies with this group and they are very good students, she may also strive to be a good student and evaluate her own test scores on what the test scores of that group are.

Culture and socialization

A person's identity may be influenced by the culture he lives in as well as the ways in which he socializes. Culture is often defined as the way people live and act within a certain group. These groups share characteristics such as religion, race, sexual orientation, ability, and language. These characteristics of a culture help individuals define themselves in relation to this culture, but also within a variety of cultures that they identify with. For instance, a person may have Japanese heritage and share characteristics of Japanese cultural groups, but also be sexually attracted to someone of the same sex, which would lead them to identify with homosexual groups. Some of these cultures may range in how accepted they are within a larger society, which may also shape the way an individual identifies with that culture. Socialization is also a way in which a person forms his or her identity based on their social experiences throughout the lifespan. This person may have to learn different rules and skills for maneuvering this society and also use others as a reference for how to behave.

Attributional processes

Attributional processes happen when a person assigns meaning to behavior and events, and these meanings, or attributions, influence and represent the cognitive processes and actions of that person. There are different types of attributions: internal and external. Internal attributions are when a person attributes meaning based on internal motives such as beliefs and emotions. External attributions are more situational and assign meaning based on the events and external characteristics. Fundamental attribution error is a process that occurs when an individual uses internal attribution for something that is a cause of the environment or situation. For instance, if Bill is angry and yells at Karen, Karen may believe this is because Bill is simply an angry person. However, Karen was unaware that Bill was angry because he had been fired from his job that day. This is an example of fundamental attribution error. Culture also plays a role in attributions; some cultures are more individualistic and may attribute more behaviors to internal processes such as personality, while other cultures are more collectivist and are more likely to attribute behaviors to external sources.

Influences on our perceptions of others

Self-perceptions

Self-perception can be defined as how an individual sees themselves. They use their own experiences and beliefs, as well as cultural characteristics to better understand how they behave and interact with others. These self-perceptions also come into play when perceiving others. This means that how a person views his or her own behavior, morals, or social roles influences how he or she understands the behavior, morals, or social roles of another person. For instance, Jim believes that he is smart because he reads a lot of books. If Jim were to find out that his friend doesn't read as many, this may lead him to believe that his friend is not very smart.

Perceptions of the environment

Perceiving others can be influenced by a variety of factors. The environment we live in can affect how we see others, how they see us, and how we behave. Different environments (eg, work, school, parties, funerals) may have different sets of social rules that people are expected to follow in order to maintain cohesion and understanding. How individuals see this environment may depend on the different social rules they understand, as well as other factors such as time and place. For instance, Gary thinks that wearing bright colors to a dance club or party is normal and expected of most people. But Gary also has come to understand that these outfits are not appropriate for all settings. If Gary were to see Wendy wearing a bright pink dress at a club, he may not even notice, but if she wore the same outfit to a funeral, his perception of Wendy would change. In addition, how a person feels in a certain situation may also influence their perception of others. If a person is comfortable, they may perceive others more positively than if they were in an uncomfortable environment.

Contributing factors to prejudice

Power, prestige, and class

Having power often refers to being able to control situations and other people. This ability is also a factor that contributes to prejudice. Prejudice is when a person has different opinions about a person or group of people based on the social, cultural, or other marginalized group they belong to. Political power, economical power, and personal power are different examples of these and each may contribute to prejudice by putting the needs of oneself in front of others. Having one's own opinions and being in a position of power make this easier and it is more likely to let biases control one's thoughts and behaviors. Prestige is also a contributing factor to prejudice and refers to the amount of recognition or fame a person has. Different occupations (e.g., doctors, lawyers) have more recognition and better reputations than others, giving them more prestige and different perceptions of the world. These perceptions may contribute to prejudicial opinions. In addition, social or economic class may also contribute to prejudice because of how a person views others. For instance, people with more money may view those of lower economic classes less intelligent or lazy simply based on the amount of money they make.

Emotion

Prejudice can be influenced by a variety of factors, such as emotion. Having stronger emotions, or being emotionally aroused, when something happens contributes to how one feels about that event. If someone were to be physically assaulted by someone of a different race or a different social class, this would likely trigger strong emotions during the assault. Seeing people who share characteristics with the assailant may also trigger those same emotions in other situations. This strong emotion may lead to prejudicial opinions based on the event.

Cognition

Cognition is defined as the thought processes that an individual has, and can be an influential factor in prejudice. When you hold certain beliefs or learn different information, this may influence your perception of others. Race, class, culture, and other characteristics are ways that people define others, and if we have certain beliefs and understandings of these characteristics, it is likely that we will jump to conclusions about others based on these cognitive processes. For instance, if Harry reads that certain races are arrested for more crimes than other races, this may lead him to believe that particular race is more prone to criminal behavior. Because of this knowledge, Harry may also treat people of that race differently.

Stereotypes

Stereotypes are a way that people can understand others based on generalizations about that person's class, gender, race, culture, religion, or other category. Although these stereotypes allow people to process information about groups of individuals more quickly and predict behavior, they also may be based on incorrect information or lead to people ignoring individual differences. These stereotypes are often based on specific experiences and are shared by many people. There can be positive or negative stereotypes, but both types can be detrimental to the understanding of different cultures and groups of people. Positive stereotypes explain the good characteristics of groups, such as being smart or talented based on which group one belongs to. Negative stereotypes focus on the bad characteristics and may lead to prejudice and discrimination.

Stigma

A stigma refers to the idea that a person, or group of people, views someone else negatively based on that person's beliefs, behaviors, or other qualities. These qualities often differ from social and cultural norms, and can be characteristics such as religious views, money problems, sexual orientation, or even disease. Many things that are stigmas are thought to be the fault of that person and lead to the dislike or mistrust of a person because it is believed they can control it. However, mental disorders that are out of a person's control, or problems that are caused by external circumstances, can also be stigmatizing and thought to be shameful or disgraceful.

Ethnocentrism

Ethnocentrism is the idea that a specific culture or ethnic group is better than another. This often occurs when a specific individual views his or her own culture or ethnic group as superior because of his or her own biases surrounding this topic. If a person believes that they are better than others, they may judge people based on their culture and ethnicity, leading to prejudice and discrimination. There are also concepts that help explain ethnocentrism: in-groups and out-groups. An in-group is a group with which a person identifies and claims membership, while an out-group is one with which an individual does not identify. Out-groups are viewed as "others" and as threats to the in-group's superiority. An example of this would be a person who identifies as Christian and views other religions as inferior to his own. Because this person believes that he is right about religious topics and thinks that Christianity is the best religion, he may treat people from other religions with contempt and view other religions as morally wrong.

Cultural relativism

Cultural relativism is the idea that all cultures and ethnicities are equal and that no group is better than another. This is the opposite of ethnocentrism and proposes that no culture is at the center of the universe, nor one more morally correct than another. In this view, people don't discriminate against others based on language, religion, race, or other cultural differences, and instead embrace the idea that these differences do not pertain to morality or truth.

Self-fulfilling prophecy

Self-fulfilling prophecy is a way in which a person's behavior is shaped by the way people see them. If a person is viewed negatively, people may treat them in a way that reinforces this view and causes that person to behave in a way that confirms this negative view. An example of this would be a teacher who thinks that a student is a troublemaker based on either a stereotype, or unconscious bias that the teacher holds. Due to his or her opinion, the teacher treats the student as a troublemaker by expecting the student to misbehave, getting mad at the student for minor mishaps, or paying more attention to this student than the others. This treatment is likely to elicit bad behavior, and because of this, the student may misbehave more and more, thereby confirming the original view of the teacher.

Stereotype threat

A stereotype threat is the idea that a person's awareness of a stereotype about his or her own race, gender, or other characteristic may cause anxiety and fear of confirming this stereotype. This anxiety and fear may also negatively influence one's ability to perform well on certain tasks, putting the individual at risk for confirming the stereotype simply by being defensive or worried about it. An example of this would be the stereotype that females have poor mathematical skills. If a girl wants to disprove this stereotype, it may cause her anxiety about her performance. Because of this anxiety, when the girl takes a math test, she may not perform very well, and confirm the stereotype she was so worried about in the first place.

Types of status in relation to social interaction

A person's status describes where that individual fits into society. Two types of status describe this position in society, and they interact with one another to determine this position. Achieved status is one that is earned by different accomplishments and events. Examples of this type of status would be getting an education, getting married, or getting a job. Within this status, there are different levels, such as income, fame, or social status. The second type of status is known as ascribed status. Ascribed status is something an individual is born with and they inherit through birth. Examples of this would be gender, race, sexuality, or socioeconomic status.

Role conflict and role strain

A social role is something that an individual is assigned or chooses to be a part of, and it is defined by a set of rules and normative behaviors. As a member of society, each individual has a role based on lifestyle, occupation, or relationship. When a person has trouble following the rules and responsibilities of her role, this is known as role strain. An individual may, for instance, feel that her role of being a leader of a group is too much of a responsibility and she doesn't have enough time to fulfill this role. An individual may also have two different roles that she must adhere to. When these different roles interfere with one another, this is known as role conflict. If an individual is a mother, for example, but also has a full-time job, she may feel conflicted when she has to choose between going to a meeting and taking her child to a school event.

Role exit

Social roles are helpful in understanding one's position in the world and how he or she is expected to behave. However, when a role is too demanding or conflicts with another, a person may choose to give up a role. This concept is known as role exit. An example of this would be a father who feels conflicted in his role as a father and as a full-time employee. He may decide that, because one role is more important, or because he no longer wants to adhere to a certain role, he must exit one of his roles. By choosing to be a stay-at-home dad and quitting his job, the father may decide to exit his role of being a full-time employee.

Primary and secondary groups

Throughout the lifespan, a person may fit into many different groups based on their social interactions and environment. There are two main types of groups that explain the differences in these relationships, called primary and secondary groups. Primary groups are groups in which a person has a long-term relationship and/or interaction with the members of the group. These groups spend significant amounts of time together and interact over lengthy spans of time. Examples of primary groups would be a person's immediate family, core group of friends, or spouse and children. Secondary groups are more temporary and don't spend as much time with one another. These groups have a specific purpose and are not as deep or personal. Examples of these groups are a person's classmates, coworkers, or a client in a professional setting.

In-group and out-group

Individuals often perceive the world according to the groups they fit into. These groups can be based on characteristics such as gender, race, sexual orientation, or other cultural differences. People often view the world based on in-groups and out-groups as well. An in-group is one with which the individual identifies in which he feels that he belongs. An out-group is a group that the individual does not feel as though he belongs to, and he may hold different opinions or prejudices towards this group.

Group sizes

A person may identify with various types of groups. Different sizes of groups may influence the relationship or help to strengthen the bonds between the group members. A dyad is a group that is made up of two individuals. These groups may be very close and connected, such as a husband and wife, or father and son, but they may also be less interpersonal, such as a doctor and patient, or a salesman and a customer. Another type of group size is a triad. This type of group has three members. An example of a triad would be two parents and a child, or a single parent and two children.

Networks

People have many different methods of interacting with others, and one way of doing this is through the use of networks. Networks are made up of connections between different individuals and groups of people. These networks can be made of connections based on culture, environment, interests, and various other ties that connect people socially. The structure of most societies is based on these networks and help people interact with one another. The terms used for the different aspects of networks are nodes and ties. Nodes are the individuals or groups that exist in a larger group. These nodes are connected to one another via ties, and these ties can either be weak or strong. Weak ties connect individuals who are not as close personally, and can be used to expand one's network. Stronger ties help connect people and create close, personal bonds with one another. The negative aspect of stronger ties, however, is that these connections help connect people of similar interests and backgrounds, creating less diversity, which may impede creative endeavors.

Formal organization

Organizations are a social structure in which people are connected through a professional association and work together to achieve a common goal. These organizations are a singular unit that has its own culture and structure to help the members accomplish their goals. Within these organizations exist methods of containing this structure and holding members responsible for their actions. This can be through the use of committees or judicial entities, and it is also through the use of a hierarchical system to maintain order. Formal organizations are a type of organization made of less personal connections and the individuals serve a specific purpose of the group. Examples of these formal organizations are government departments, public or private universities, healthcare networks, or private companies.

Ideal bureaucracy

An ideal bureaucracy is one that successfully carries out the responsibilities of the government through the use of government officials. These officials are not elected representatives, but they make decisions for the system of government they serve. An ideal bureaucracy consists of a hierarchical authoritative system with promotions based on merit or achievement. This system is efficient, impersonal, and effectively divided in order to accomplish the goals set forth by the system. Explicit rules concern behavior, goals, and methods for accomplishing these goals.

Perspectives on bureaucracy

Bureaucracy can be approached in a variety of methods in order to achieve success. One such perspective is known as the iron law of oligarchy. In this theory, it is believed that there will inevitably be a tendency for individuals in elite positions to rule the government. These systems start out as democratic, with elected officials, and grow further and further away from this concept, turning towards a system controlled by a selected number of individuals. Another perspective on bureaucracy is that of McDonaldization. This concept refers to the McDonald's-type fast food restaurants and the efficiency of such businesses. McDonaldization is the idea that it would be easy and efficient to use these business structures as a guideline for bureaucracy and strive for more efficiency, more predictability and standardization, and the ability to calculate and control behaviors and productivity.

Role of gender in the expression and detection of emotion

Expressing and detecting emotions can differ due to multiple variables, including gender. Gender plays a significant role in this process through an individual expressing emotion, but also in the detection of that emotion based on that individual as well as the observer. Masculine individuals are more likely to exhibit aggressive and forceful emotions, while femininity is related to gentle and expressive emotions. Because of these gender-based expectations, this may cause an individual to express emotions based on his or her gender. For instance, boys are expected to be tough and are less likely to cry or exhibit any signs of weakness, while girls are supposed to be "lady-like" and not behave aggressively. It is also thought to be easier for females to detect emotion because of their tendency to express more emotions than males.

Role of culture in the expression and detection of emotion

Some cultures express emotion differently and are able to detect different emotions more easily. In societies that are more individualistic (Western countries), individuals are more likely to express emotions, such as pride or jealousy, because these are emotions focused on the individual as opposed to the rest of society. In addition, individualist countries may encourage the expression of emotions more than in other societies, allowing people to feel more comfortable expressing these emotions. In collectivist cultures (countries in Asia or Africa), individuals may be more likely to express feelings based on group dynamics, such as shame or friendliness, because these emotions are felt in relation to society. In these collectivist countries, people may also be less likely to express personal emotions because of the effect it may have on those around them. Detecting emotions also varies based on cultures, as culture may influence which emotions an individual pays attention to, such as the idea that Americans may be more likely to detect the emotion of another individual easily, but someone from Japanese culture may be more likely to detect the emotions of background figures or other group members more easily.

Impression management in relation to presentation of self

Individuals are likely to present themselves in such a way that purposefully influences those they interact with. How a person dresses, what they say, how they say it, and how a person acts are all ways in which people present themselves to others according to the way they wish to be seen. For instance, a doctor may want to dress professionally and wear a lab coat in order to demand respect and authority with his or her patients. If a person wants to be seen as friendly and sociable, he or she may decide to speak to strangers or pretend to like something that the other person likes in order to achieve this goal.

Front stage and back stage self

The concept of a frontstage self and a backstage self is a dramaturgical approach to describe how people interact with one another in society. This approach uses theater as a metaphor for explaining how people present themselves. The frontstage self is one in which the individual knows people will be watching and "performs" for these people. He or she follows rules for how to act in society and performs in a way that fulfills the expectations of the observer. The backstage self is when the individual is able to behave in a way that aligns with his or her true self and doesn't have to perform for others. This is when the individual is by him or herself and can regroup and prepare for the next "performance."

Verbal and nonverbal communication

People are able to communicate their emotions and feelings to others though various methods. Verbal communication, in addition to nonverbal communication, work to express thoughts and emotions in order for an individual to be better understood by his or her peers. Verbal communication consists of words and language that are spoken to others, or written down in order to convey a message. This type of communication can be in person, over the phone, through media outlets, or in a written note. Nonverbal communication can consist of facial expressions, body language, and other methods of conveying information without directly expressing it. For instance, someone may initiate eye contact with another person in order to send a message to that person. Crying, gesturing, or emoting in other ways also uses nonverbal communication to interact with others. Verbal and nonverbal communication can work together or even contradict one another, and they also both may be misinterpreted if the meaning is unclear.

Animal signals and communication

Animals can communicate with one another in similar ways as humans, in that they may use sounds to express themselves as well as body language and physical touch. However, animals may also communicate in additional methods that better convey their meaning. Some animals sing to one another during mating rituals, while others use auditory methods of displaying aggression and hostility. Physical touch and body language, such as cuddling or baring teeth, also work to convey messages to other animals. In addition to these methods, visual displays of information, such as size, shape, color, facial expression, and movement, also help to signal signs of danger, food sources, or different emotions. Animals also emit different chemical odors in various methods to communicate; pheromones and urine are two ways that this occurs. Animals not only interact with others within their own species, but also other animals in order to convey warnings or deception. For instance, some insects disguise themselves through different colors and symbols on their bodies in order to avoid being attacked by predators.

Attraction

Individuals behave differently in social situations due to various factors. One of these factors is attraction. Attraction is defined as feeling positively about a person based on different characteristics. Physical attraction occurs when someone views another as visually appealing, while sexual attraction refers to being aroused sexually by another. Attraction can also be the result of personality traits and behaviors, along with shared interests and other similarities. Being attracted to another person may establish relationships and continue into loving feelings when this attraction is strong. How much a person is attracted to another can be based on the physical traits, personality, and/or sexual attraction, but proximity and continued interaction also contribute to this. Being exposed to another is, in itself, often enough to develop attraction and the longer and more consistent this exposure, the more likely a relationship is able to form.

Aggression

Aggression is one way in which individuals may behave in certain social situations. The purpose of aggression is to harm another person either physically or emotionally, but it also may be an expression of anger or fear, as well as an intimidation technique to assert dominance. Different types of aggression may be exhibited within social interactions: indirect, direct, emotional, and instrumental. Indirect and direct aggression is a person's intent to harm someone; direct refers to the interaction being face-to-face, while indirect is not. Emotional aggression is a result of feelings of anger and the intent to hurt someone is not necessarily present. Instrumental aggression serves the purpose of achieving an objective that is not considered aggressive in nature. All these different types of aggression share the characteristic of wanting to hurt another individual, though the method or emotion behind the behavior may vary.

Attachment

Attachment refers to the idea that two (or more) people are connected emotionally and often is described in reference to parent-child interactions. In this type of attachment, the relationship is said to develop during the first 2 years of a child's life. This was studied by Harry Harlow through the parent-child relationships of monkeys. This psychologist found that the relationship between a mother and her infant is very important to the survival of the infant. However, he also found that this relationship was not based solely on necessities such as food and water, but instead based on the comfort and warmth from the mother. In John Bowlby's attachment theory, there are different forms of attachment for young children: secure, avoidant, ambivalent, and disorganized. Secure attachment is what should be strived for and is considered normal; in this bond, the child trusts the parent and prefers him or her to strangers. Avoidant attachment refers to a child who doesn't share a unique bond with the parent due to the uncaring nature of the mother or father, and the child is likely to treat the parent as he or she would another stranger. Ambivalent attachment occurs when a child has an inconsistent parent and doesn't trust the parent to return when he or she leaves. The child is often upset when this happens and cannot be comforted upon the parent's return. Lastly, disorganized attachment is when a child is abused by the parent and behaves unpredictably whether the parent is there or not.

Altruism

Altruism is the idea that a person will help another despite this assistance possibly impeding upon his or her life. Another term for this concept is selflessness, as it refers to the idea that the individual doesn't think about him or herself before helping someone else. This type of behavior is not something that the individual feels obligated to do; instead the motivation comes from the person's desire to help someone else. Evolutionarily, altruism is sometimes explained by the desire to indirectly help oneself through the continuation of his or her genes. For instance, it is more likely for a person to help someone who is biologically related to them, as opposed to someone who does not share their genes. It is also likely for a person to benefit indirectly from altruistic behavior through the idea that if a person helps someone else, that other person may return the favor in the future.

Social support

Social support can be defined as the emotional or physical assistance and/or reinforcement of individuals within one's social network. This can include friends, family, coworkers, or anyone else who offers support. Often this support is in reaction to an individual experiencing a difficult situation or crisis when he or she needs the help and comfort of those around him or her. This social support is useful in times of need in order to reduce stress and frustration concerning the situation. Types of social support include emotional, instrumental, and informational. Emotional support is a way that the individual feels included or important to the people in his or her life, as well as within society as a whole. Emotional support may come in the form of listening or simply just spending time with the individual. Instrumental support is when a tangible form of assistance is provided, such as money, physical assistance, or food. Informational support is when someone in a person's social network offers advice or information pertinent to the situation at hand in order to problem solve.

Foraging behavior

Certain behaviors in animals can be explained through biology, including foraging behavior. Foraging behavior is the act of looking for food in order to eat and survive. Different animals may do this in different ways, but the purpose is the same: to survive and reproduce. Some of these behaviors may include foraging alone or within a group, using sticks or other tools, or storing food for the future. The main goal of these foraging behaviors is to allow the animal to gather and eat the most amount of nutrients with the least amount of effort. Variables also influence an animal's ability to forage, including how they learn, genetics, the presence of predators, or parasites that may be lurking in food sources. Animals work to decrease the risks to foraging, such as avoiding parasites and predators, in order to increase their chance of survival.

Mating behavior and mate choice in animals

One way in which animals strive to keep their own species alive is by mating. They may do this by mating with a single animal or they may have multiple partners. In addition, animals may also differ in how they select their mates. This may vary based on species or even gender. Some species prefer to mate with any partner they are able, known as random mating, while others prefer those with similar characteristics, known as assortative mating. However, when assortative mating occurs, this may lead to increased instances of inbreeding, which may negatively influence later generations. There is also the concept of non-assortative mating, which is when animals with different characteristics mate with one another. Non-assortative and random mating lead to more diversity and don't have as many limitations or consequences as assortative mating. It has also been found that females are more particular about the mate that they choose and it is said that the females look for more superior characteristics such as genetics or survival when choosing a male to mate with. Males on the other hand may not be as simple: there is controversy surrounding how males choose mates, and it is said that they often are more particular when there is more diversity within potential mating pools.

Game theory

Game theory is the idea that one can use mathematics to better understand how decisions are made. This theory explains that every decision has a ratio of the costs and benefits, and the decision with the best ratio is the one that is chosen. When this is applied to animal behavior, it allows for the ability to describe how animals are able to survive and reproduce. This is done by analyzing the offspring as a benefit, or signal of better fitness. When a species has an increase in offspring while other species have less in comparison, this is a sign of fitness. Game theory helps humans to better analyze and understand choices of optimal behavior and to see how changes occur.

Inclusive fitness

Altruism is the idea that an individual will voluntarily help another individual, even if it comes at the expense of their own livelihood. This is often a characteristic of people who are selfless, but with humans, this may also lead to positive feelings that help drive this personality trait. With animals, on the other hand, altruism can be described evolutionarily; animals are likely to participate in altruism because they expect tangible and beneficial results from such behavior. For instance, a mother bear will protect her young in order to carry on her own genes, or may help another bear in the expectation of reciprocity. This phenomenon is known as inclusive fitness, also defined as altruistic behavior that indirectly benefits an animal by helping to increase its chances of survival in terms of itself or its kin. In other words, the selfless behavior is detrimental to the animal's own fitness, but benefits the fitness of the other. In this sense, the animals share this fitness in order to indirectly improve survival and reproduction.

Discrimination

Individual versus institutional discrimination
Discrimination is the act of treating a group of people (or single person) differently due to characteristics such as ability, age, religion, race, gender, or sexual orientation. When a singular person participates in discriminatory behavior, this is known as individual discrimination. This can occur when the person behaves differently towards a person on the basis of one of these traits, and treats them in an undesirable manner. Discrimination can also happen at an institutional level, also known as institutional discrimination, and it occurs when a system put in place by the government or organization inherently treats people differently based on the qualities they possess that were previously mentioned. This leads to biased views and actions towards these groups by others, and how visible this discrimination is can range from blatant abuse to subtle differences in access to various opportunities. Examples of this might be a person of color being refused admission to a university or refusal of a marriage license due to sexual orientation.

Relationship between prejudice and discrimination

Prejudice can be defined as having a negative or unwarranted attitude towards another person or group of people based on qualities these groups possess, such as race, religion, sexual orientation, social class, or age. This differs from discrimination, as discrimination is the act of behaving differently towards these people based on the group they belong to. Although these concepts differ (one is an attitude and the other is behavior) each can lead to the other in a cyclical relationship. If a person has prejudicial views towards individuals of a different group, he or she may behave in a way that reflects this attitude. On the other hand, if discrimination occurs through either governmental institutions or through chance by an individual, this may lead to negative views about a group of people. Discrimination can also occur through the behavior of others; if the individuals in one's social group discriminate towards people of a different group, this may lead that person to also act in this manner, possibly leading to his or her own prejudices being formed.

Power, prestige, and class

Being in a position of power gives a person control over the lives of others. Having this power can contribute to treating others differently and creating a larger gap between those in power and the rest of society. Individuals with power are able to use this power in order to make the world work in a way that favors people in majority groups, leaving marginalized populations to become increasingly less powerful and more separated from those in power. Having prestige, or a good reputation, is also a way that influences discrimination. People with more education or more achievements are given more opportunities, leaving those with less prestige to become more marginalized and have less ability to overcome this discrimination. Social and economic class also impact discrimination, as those with more money and higher social status are able to get what they want more easily than those with a lower status. This causes people in high classes to treat others in a more negative manner, discriminating against people simply because of their social status.

Social Structure and Demographics

Microsociology and macrosociology

In sociology, there are two different main fields of study when it comes to understanding social structures: microsociology and macrosociology. Both of these concentrations are important to understanding social behavior and motivation, but they are quite different in terms of how this topic is studied. Microsociology is the study of the individual social interactions, while macrosociology is the study of the larger social systems and structures such as governments and organizations. While microsociology focuses on personal values, beliefs, and behaviors, macrosociology focuses on shared cultures, languages, and social roles. An example that illustrates this difference is the impact of socioeconomic status on behavior. At the individual level, microsociology would be focused on how a person is treated based on this status. If the person is of a lower socioeconomic status, microsociology would look at the patterns of behavior and beliefs of those who interact with this individual. Macrosociology would, instead, look to the institutional level and evaluate the differences in policies and cultural norms that influence socioeconomic status.

Functionalism

Within societies, there are structures in place that can be studied and explained. This is known as functionalism. Functionalism is a theory developed by Emile Durkheim in order to describe the structure of society and how it functions. This theory holds that society is complex but each part contributes to the whole by working together and creating unity; when one part of society fails, this leads to unwanted change and chaos. Functionalism works because there is harmony and understanding between the different parts of society, which creates a united social structure. However, this theory doesn't acknowledge the negative consequences that conformity can produce and ignores the individuals of the society in terms of activism and social justice.

Conflict theory

Conflict theory is an idea put forth by Karl Marx that explains how conflict within a society arises through the competition of resources, both economically and socially. Because different groups of society maintain different levels of wealth or power, there is inherently conflict between these social groups. There is a lack of harmony between these groups of people and the control of society is maintained by those in power. This leads to the exploitation and discrimination of those with less power and of lower social or economic classes. Although there are discrepancies in benefit and a lack of mutual aid, this unequal distribution of power is also theorized to be the reason social order is possible. Because of the vast amounts of control these groups of power have, there is more ability to keep order and control unwanted behavior.

Symbolic interactionism and social constructionism

Symbolic interactionism is the idea that groups of people interact using symbols to convey meaning. Different groups of people have different interpretations of these symbols, however, and people act on these symbols based on their interpretations. For instance, one culture may view a gesture positively, while another views it negatively. In America, holding up two fingers is a way to convey peace, while in England, this is an offensive gesture. Social constructionism is the idea that meaning comes from the constructs set forth in a society. These constructs can be perceived as reality, or even questioned by people within the society, which creates an ongoing and fluctuating reality that is both subjective and objective. An example of a social construct is money. Pieces of metal and paper may not literally have value, but people place value on these objects, creating a socially constructed method of currency. There are two main types of social constructionism: weak and strong. Weak social constructionism is when facts are the basis for reality, while strong social constructionism relies on language and behaviors.

Exchange theory and rational choice theory

Exchange theory and rational choice theory are part of a concept known as exchange-rational choice. Exchange theory is the idea that exchanges of goods and/or services create relationships and these relationships explain social change and stability. In this theory, both sides of the exchange benefit from this negotiation, driven by a process of costs and rewards to each party. Rational choice theory, or rational action theory, explains that the choices and exchanges a person makes work through a process of minimizing costs and maximizing rewards. The decision that the individual makes is based on this idea, allowing him or her to make the most rational choice.

Feminist theory

Feminist theory is a concept that describes the roles and rights of women in society. This theory examines the inequality of the genders based on ideas such as gender roles and objectification, as well as systemic sexism within government organizations. Feminist theory has various forms that have developed throughout history and range from liberal feminism to radical and Marxist feminism. Each type examines a different facet of the gender divisions such as gender characteristics, inequalities, oppression, and structural persecution.

Education, hidden curriculum, teacher expectancy, and educational segregation and stratification

Education is a social institution that revolves around learning and acquiring knowledge of a broad range of topics. In the United States, this institution is divided into different levels of education that an individual may move through during his or her lifespan. The system includes early childhood education such as preschool and kindergarten, primary school, secondary school, college or university, and graduate school. During these levels, the schools impose curriculums that are believed to help the child succeed later in life. However, there is a concept known as hidden curriculums which are topics that are not explicitly taught, and are instead implied or mistakenly communicated. For instance, the relationships between a teacher and his or her students may dictate how the students are expected to act. If the teacher reacts negatively to lots of questions, the students may think that asking questions is bad, leading to a continuation of this behavior later in life. This also relates to the idea of teacher expectancy; if a teacher expects a child to behave a certain way, this may inadvertently influence his or her behavior towards the child, resulting in the child behaving in a way that confirms the teacher's expectations. Lastly, educational segregation and stratification refers to the differences in quality of education in various regions and schools because of the financial aspects of that area. Namely, if a school is underprivileged, the students will not have a worthwhile education.

Family structure and forms of kinship

A family is a social group that is connected through marriage and ancestral relationships. There are various forms of families, but the main structure of a family includes parents, grandparents, siblings, children, spouses, and extensions of these relationships. Primary kins are related directly, through connections such as spouses, children, and siblings. Secondary kins are separated by one family member. Examples of these are grandparents, aunts, and uncles. For instance, your mother's sister is separated from you by one family member: your mother. Tertiary kins are separated by two relatives. A common example of a tertiary kin is a cousin. This would be your mother's sister's children, for example, separating you and your cousin by both your mother and your aunt.

Family structures may differ in many ways. Adoption, divorce, family death, families with same-sex parents, or families with step-parents are all different forms of relationships that occur. Within these structures are concepts such as marriage and divorce that tie families together. Marriage is a legal concept that allows individuals to be connected through the law. This is often helpful in healthcare decisions, as married individuals are able to make these decisions or are named next-of-kin when one person in the marriage is ill or passes away. In the instance of divorce, these marriages are terminated and the individuals are able to separate these responsibilities and legal ties. A divorce may also allow the individuals to move forward and marry again, thereby creating step-parents to any children involved in the previous marriage.

Violence within families

An important concept when discussing families is violence within these relationships. Members of a family may report abuse from other members of the family, such as spouses, children, parents, or members of the extended family. This violence can come from any member of the family and target any other member, regardless of age or gender. This violence may not always be in the form of physical abuse, with some abuse being emotional or sexual. Common examples describe a male family member abusing younger children or a female spouse; however, female family members are also known to be abusive at times. In addition, elder abuse is also a form of family violence, with children extorting or physically abusing older parents and relatives.

Religiosity and religious organizations

Religion is a significant aspect of society and can influence these societies in many ways. How religious a person is can be referred to as his or her religiosity, which helps to explain how a person views the world, their sense of purpose, and the concept of a higher power. Different types of religious organizations include churches, sects, cults, and denominations. Churches are a structured, stable, and government-aligned organization that teach its members about specific religious beliefs. These beliefs can be from religions such as Judaism, Christianity, Islam, or Hinduism, but there are also many others. Denominations are independent branches of a religion, but still recognized by that church. Sects are organizations that have broken off from the church's teachings in order to promote a version of that religion that is more in line with traditional belief systems. Cults are also organizations that have broken from the church, but instead of upholding traditional teachings, cults are considered to teach innovative and new beliefs and are often led by an individual who is enigmatic and confident.

Relationship between religion and social change

Religion can play an important role in society, especially in reference to social change. Social change and religion influence one another and together have an impact on society as a whole. Modernization is an example of this as a vehicle of social change. Modernization refers to the concept that as society learns and creates new technology, that society becomes more modern. This transition and/or continuous process of change can also lead to a change in beliefs and in turn can impact religious views. In some cases, this can lead to religion having a reduced impact on people, known as secularization. This concept explains how religion becomes less important in societies, influencing how people learn to view the world and their own purpose in this world. Fundamentalism is also a way in which religion and social change are related. This concept refers to the process of religious teaching becoming more traditional or literal in terms of interpretations of religious texts. This fundamentalism may be in response to social change, but also may lead to social revolution in order to bring religion back to the forefront of society.

Power and authority in government and economy

Power and authority are two of the ways in which a government is able to function in society. Governments make and enforce the rules of this society for the purpose of maintaining order, which gives the government a significant amount of power. This power is maintained by money and systemic measures put in place to govern the people of a society. With threats of punishment and conformity of the members of a society, this power is kept intact. In other words, in order for the government to maintain its status quo, the individuals of the society must accept the authority of this structure and follow the rules set forth. If the government lost its ability to follow through with threats when laws are broken, or if many people fight against this authority, the government has the potential to be overthrown and cease to function as intended.

Economic and political systems

While the government creates and enforces the rules of a society, the economy refers to how the people of a society are able to get the things they need, such as money and goods. Different systems can be utilized to impact both government and the economy simultaneously. In other words, certain methods of governing influence the economic systems that bolster society. The two main systems are known as capitalism and socialism. Capitalism is a concept that describes how privately owned companies produce and distribute resources in order to make a profit. This type of system is self-sufficient and relies solely on consumers in order to prosper. Socialism on the other hand is a system where these resources are produced and distributed through the government and are not owned by a sole company or individual. These goods are owned by the government and regulated as such in order to evenly distribute the resources to society. A system known as mixed-economy uses a combination of capitalism and socialism to regulate and distribute resources in order to support the economy.

Division of labor

Division of labor refers to the idea that each individual in a society contributes to society in a different manner. For instance, one person is trained in farming, while another practices medicine. These two individuals are experts in their respective fields, but may not know anything about the other person's field of work. These two people work together and provide services for one another (the doctor treats the farmer's illnesses, while the farmer provides food to the doctor) and benefit from the other person's knowledge. This division of labor allows individuals to become experts in a single topic and be able to live a full life, without knowing everything from each different field of work. If the doctor was instead required to farm his own crops, build his own house, and make his own clothes, he wouldn't need the farmer, or anyone else, but he also may not be efficient or even skilled at any of these different trades. The division of labor allows for more efficiency and expertise within a society.

Medicalization and the sick role

Medicalization is the process of classifying human conditions as treatable illnesses. These conditions are seen as separate from the individual and can be studied in order to develop treatments for such conditions. For instance, if a person is sick, he will go to the doctor who will diagnose him with an infection. The doctor then prescribes the patient antibiotics in order to get rid of the infection. Within this process of medicalization is also something called the "sick role." Someone who is sick is thought to have the right to disengage from his or her normal social roles because he or she is not at fault for such an illness. The person is also expected to try to get better by seeing a doctor or taking medicine. However, medicalization is also common for psychological conditions that are more difficult to deal with. A person with depression may be prescribed antidepressants, but this may not address the underlying cause of the depression. By medicalizing mental illness, patients may not be given the proper counseling or care required to help them, and because they are classified as sick, a person with depression who does not get better on medication may be told that she is not fulfilling the obligations of the sick role by trying to get better. This person may in turn be blamed for her illness or stigmatized, which may lead to her not wanting to be classified as sick.

Illness experience and delivery of health care

When a person is sick, he or she has something called the "illness experience." The illness experience is the process of experiencing an illness and going through certain steps in order to get better. An example would be if Joe were experiencing stomach pain. First, he would have the pain symptom, and then he would label himself as sick, taking on the sick role. Once he labeled himself as sick, Joe would go to a doctor seeking treatment for his illness. While at the doctor, Joe would develop a relationship with the doctor, where the doctor would help relieve Joe of his stomach pain. This might include performing surgery, prescribing medication, or advising Joe to stay away from certain foods or activities. After this Joe would follow the doctor's instructions and begin to recover from his illness. Within this illness experience is the healthcare system. Delivery of health care involves a primary care doctor who helps the patient or refers him or her to a specialist in order to better treat the illness. Different types of medical staff help in this process, including doctors (who diagnose and treat the illness), nurses (who monitor the patient and administer treatments), and emergency responders (who care for the patient on the way to the hospital).

Social epidemiology of health and medicine

Epidemiology refers to the study of illnesses by understanding how many people are affected, who develops the disease, and how to control the disease. Disparities and social factors also impact illnesses, which are studied through social epidemiology. This branch of medicine determines how society influences the health of a population and how to better control the disease based on this information. For instance, people with poor living conditions and lower socioeconomic status may be more prone to disease, or develop specific diseases because of where they fit into society.

Elements of culture

Culture has influence on many aspects of life and society, but it is also somewhat difficult to define. Culture is a wide-reaching concept that encompasses many different elements in order to better explain collective groups of people. The elements involved in culture include language, customs, rituals, social patterns, organization, religion, artistic expression, government, economy, and values. These elements differ between cultures and influence how the individuals who identify with a certain culture behave, speak, think, and feel about a vast number of topics. In addition, these different elements fit into two separate categories: material and symbolic culture. Material culture refers to physical or concrete elements of society such as clothing, buildings, or technology. Symbolic culture is more elusive and refers to the elements of culture that are not visible or well-defined, such as language, values, and traditions.

Culture lag and culture shock

Culture lag refers to the idea that different forms of culture change over time while other forms of culture are slower to adjust to these changes. The two main forms of culture in this theory are material and non-material, or symbolic, culture. This concept states that material culture, such as clothing, technology, and other physical types of culture, are the first to change over time, while non-material culture, such as religion, values, and traditions, are slow to follow suit. Culture shock is the idea that a person is surprised by the differences in different cultures when being exposed to a new culture. For instance, if a person comes from a small, quiet town where everyone knows each other, that person may experience culture shock when she moves to a big city, such as New York.

Assimilation and multiculturalism

When a person moves to a new city or experiences a new culture, he may have to integrate and learn how to live in a manner consistent with this culture. This is known as assimilation. An example would be if a person moves to a new country and learns the language, engages in that country's traditions and rituals, and learns to how interact with the citizens of that country. If the person was unable to do these things, he may have trouble assimilating to the new culture. Some people and places, however, do not have just one culture, and instead have a melting pot of different traditions, languages, and beliefs. This is known as multiculturalism. New York is a great example of multiculturalism with the many different people living there who come from all over the world.

Subcultures and countercultures

Within larger cultures often exist smaller cultures known as subcultures. These subcultures are distinct from the larger culture and add to the variety and complexity of a society. Some of these subcultures may develop through sociological changes and advancements, while others fade after a period of time. These subcultures include variation in style of clothing, music, traditions, and other beliefs and behaviors. Examples of subcultures can include emo or gothic cultures, or even religious traditions such as wearing a hijab in an American society. Some subcultures are vastly different from the predominant culture and may oppose this way of life; these are known as countercultures. Countercultures are forms of subcultures that don't fit into the mainstream society and don't share the values of this society. An example of a counterculture would be in the 1960s when American hippies were prevalent. This group of people opposed the government, listened to different music, and created their own communities apart from the American mainstream culture.

Mass media and popular culture

Popular culture is the mainstream and predominant culture within a society. This can refer to the types of fashion, music, or activities associated with a culture that are common at a certain point in time. This culture is widely accepted, but also can be criticized by others who don't participate in the popular culture. In addition, popular culture is often greatly influenced by mass media. Mass media refers to the abundant and various forms of media that work together to inform the public. These forms of mass media include movies, television, newspapers, radio, websites, and more. By reporting on a specific cultural phenomenon, these forms of mass media broadcast the ideas of a culture to make it more popular and widespread.

Relationship between evolution and human culture

Evolution can influence culture, but it can also be a product of this culture. Culture is a way in which each generation can pass information and traditions to future generations. Society has also evolved over time and the cultures of such societies can depend on this evolution. For instance, when societies are smaller they may be community oriented, with each member helping the others and contributing where they are needed most. This type of culture is dominant because it is necessary for survival in a society so small. However, with evolution of technology and society as a whole, this culture may need to change in order to work for the majority of the population. Developing currency and trade may be necessary in this case, and warfare may emerge through this evolution, altering the dominant culture. These are ways in which evolution influences culture, but culture may also impact evolution through new technologies and resources. With technological advances, a society may need to evolve to accommodate these changes. In addition, humans have evolved as a result of cultural changes by needing less body hair and less muscle mass than previous generations.

Transmission and diffusion

Culture is important to different groups of people and, as such, people feel that it is necessary to distribute and communicate these cultures to others. This can happen in one of two ways: transmission and diffusion. Transmission is the process of passing cultural beliefs and traditions to future generations from parents to their children, who pass it to their own children. Culture can also be disseminated to people in other parts of the world. This is known as diffusion. When a society wishes to educate or enlighten others about their own culture, they may travel to other parts of the world or otherwise distribute these ideas and ways of living to others as they see fit. This diffusion may help to advance other societies in a positive way, but may also be detrimental and displace the cultures and well-being of other societies.

Aging and age cohorts

As people age they experience different life events and new challenges, often directly associated with aging. These challenges that result from aging can include retirement, lack of independence, and a reliance on government assistance. This is significant because the aging community must put their faith in the younger generations to pay into social security or take care of them as they become more dependent on others. Imbedded in this ongoing relationship between the elderly and the younger generations is the concept of age cohorts. Cohorts are groups of people who experience similar life events and experiences at the same time due to their age. For instance, Millennials and Baby Boomers are two examples of popular age cohorts discussed in the media. Millennials include those who were born after the year 1980, while Baby Boomers were born following World War II. Baby Boomers are now between the ages of 50 and 70 years old and are a very large population due to the increased birth rate after the war. This means that Baby Boomers are going to be in need of substantial assistance from Millennials in future years, making the process of aging socially significant.

Gender

The concept of gender is derived from the idea that being a certain biological sex dictates how a person feels or behaves. Because individuals are characterized as either male or female at birth due to their anatomical features, gender is considered a binary construct as well. However, because biological sex is difficult to determine directly from appearance, there is a reliance on physical or behavioral attributes that are deemed either masculine or feminine and correspond respectively with male and female genders. For instance, long hair, makeup, and skirts are considered feminine characteristics, and therefore attributed to females. This binary description of males versus females also results in gender segregation, such as separate bathrooms or sports teams.

Race and ethnicity

Each individual has a complex heritage and may have their ancestry traced all over the world. However, many people may not identify with these various cultures, and instead identify with a select few. These cultures that a person identifies with are known as his or her ethnicity. Some of these ethnicities are associated with different physical characteristics, leading others to classify people based on these appearances. This physical appearance is known as a person's race. Race is a socially constructed concept that allows individuals to be grouped together based on this appearance and may or may not align with one's ethnicity.

Racialization and racial formation

Racialization is the process of assigning a person a racial identity. This racial identity may or may not be consistent with a person's own ethnicity or identity, and is often stereotyped or generalized. Racialization may also lead to discrimination or even preferential treatment in certain situations. In job settings and education, certain races are given privileges while others are forced to exert extra effort in order to be given the same opportunities. Racial formation is the idea that race is not a concrete or stable concept and can change as societies and individuals evolve. This means that race is a social construct that helps society justify discriminatory behavior and how people of different races interact with one another.

Immigration

Immigration is the process of a person moving to a new country and can be a result of various situational factors. A person may immigrate to a country for personal reasons such as family or relationships, for education, or for economic reasons, such as better jobs or better working conditions. Immigration refers to people who are coming to a specific country to which they are not native and it may involve learning how to adapt to a new culture and society. In this process it is also possible that individuals will, over time, lose their connections to their native culture and identity by assimilating to the new country. In the United States, immigration has increased in recent years, with many people coming from Mexico, the Caribbean, or India.

Intersections of race and ethnicity

Due to the differing definitions of race and ethnicity, these two concepts can overlap or be separate entities. Race is often separated into 6 categories: white, black, Asian, Hispanic/Latino, Native American, or Pacific Islander. However, a person can fit into more than one of these categories based on their family's racial identities. In addition, ethnicity refers to both country of origin and family heritage, which means that this can either be separate from or combined with one's racial identity. For instance, a person who is white could have different ethnicities such as American, English, or German, while a person who is black may have grown up in England, and identify with that particular ethnicity.

Sexual orientation

One demographic variable that is often difficult to ascertain is sexual orientation. Many research questions either do not address this topic or are unable to fully capture the complexity of one's sexual orientation. However, three categories of sexual orientation are most commonly referred to: heterosexual, homosexual, or bisexual. Heterosexual refers to someone being attracted to individuals of the opposite sex, homosexual refers to one who is attracted to same-sex individuals, and bisexual refers to someone who is attracted to people of either sex.

Theories of demographic change

The two main theories regarding demographic change are Malthusian theory and demographic transition. Malthusian theory is the idea that the population of a society will grow exponentially over time and, eventually, the world will not be able to sustain the number of people with the available resources. This theory explains that there are different types of checks that help to alleviate this excessive population growth: positive checks and preventative checks. Positive checks are phenomena such as war, famine, or disease that bring the population down through death. Preventative checks are measures that are put in place to prevent overpopulation such as taxation and contraceptives. Demographic transition, on the other hand, explains that birth rates and death rates fluctuate based on societal transitions and development. This theory outlines four stages of transition: pre-industrial age (where birth rates and death rates are both high), urbanization or industrialization (where technology improvements help to decrease the death rate), the mature industrial age (where birth rates decrease due to increased access to contraception), and post-industrial age (when population is high, but the birth and death rates are both low).

Population growth and decline

Population growth refers to the idea that the birth rate of a population is higher than that of its death rate, while population decline refers to when the death rate is higher than the birth rate. These rates are likely to fluctuate over time, but there are also ways in which researchers are able to estimate and visualize these rates. Population projections help to estimate the future population based on current data, while population pyramids allow individuals to see the differences in certain populations. When these pyramids are larger at the bottom, this shows population growth, but when it is larger at the top of the pyramid, this displays population decline. In addition, these pyramids are able to show differences in gender by representing gender on the sides of the pyramid. If there is a skew to either side of the pyramid, this represents a discrepancy in gender within a population.

Fertility and mortality rates

Fertility refers to the ability to have children and there are gender differences with this fertility. Men, for instance are able to reproduce throughout the lifespan, while women are only fertile from puberty to menopause. Fertility rates are calculated as the number of children for each parental unit. Mortality rates, on the other hand, refer to how frequent death is in a certain population. For instance, females tend to have lower mortality rates than males, while babies who were just born have a higher mortality rate, but this rate decreases as time passes. Certain patterns also exist within fertility and mortality rates for different countries. For instance, countries that are more developed have lower fertility and mortality rates, while the opposite is true of underdeveloped countries.

Push and pull factors in migration

The term migration refers to the relocation of a person or group of people to a new city or country. The reasons people choose to migrate are often known as push and pull factors. Push factors are the reasons a person leaves a place of residence, such as bad living conditions or poor work opportunities. Pull factors are the reasons that a person wants to go to a specific place, such as a better job, relationships, or other positive factors. Migration also is analyzed through positive and negative values of net migration, referring to the rates of people leaving or coming into an area. When these values are positive, this means more people are coming in than are leaving, while the opposite is true of negative values of net migration. Migration may be temporary or permanent depending on the reasons for migrating to a new place, and these reasons can differ based on money, personal relationships, or environmental factors.

Social movements

Social movements are started when a group of people joins together to support a specific cause that relates to their political or social values. These movements can be very small or extremely large and may vary in terms of formality. Many movements are based on the idea of relative deprivation, which refers to the concept that individuals compare their own situations to those in our immediate vicinity, as opposed to people across the world. This means that, in fighting for certain rights, individuals are less concerned with someone's rights in another country, and more concerned with how they compare to the person down the street from them. Some movements are proactive and seek to promote specific change, such as the civil rights movements and animal rights movements. Reactive movements, on the other hand, are social movements that are fighting back against changes; anti-war movements, for instance, are reactive. Different organizations, such as civil rights organizations or animal rights organizations, also help to enable these movements and provide opportunities for activism. Advertising, creating new organizations, or participating in protests are examples of various movement strategies and tactics that help bring recognition and support to social movements.

Globalization

Globalization is the process of interacting with and incorporating different countries through trade, technology, information, and migration. Advancements in technology allow globalization to occur more easily and help to facilitate the economic interdependence of different countries as well as the ability to communicate rapidly with individuals around the world. Globalization has been touted as a positive asset to many countries, with advancements in underdeveloped countries as well as a growing worldwide economy; however, there are also criticisms of globalization. These criticisms include arguments that globalization leads to colonialism and the disenfranchisement of indigenous peoples. Globalization is also believed to create larger gaps in inequality and force the cultural assimilation of populations that may not benefit from these changes. These inequalities and cultural disadvantages have triggered social changes as well as civil unrest and terrorism, which threaten political and economic stability.

Urbanization, industrialization, and urban growth

When large numbers of people move into densely populated cities from rural areas, it is known as urbanization. This process can be driven by multiple factors, including social and economic changes, such as jobs, housing, or transportation. Many of these changes are a result of modernization or industrialization, meaning more jobs in large cities creates a demand for a localized workforce. This process then results in urban growth and increases in migration to urban areas, but these changes also influence industrialization as well. For instance, as urbanization occurs, the cost of living also increases, resulting in changes in economy and living situations.

Suburbanization and urban decline

Although job availability and social changes lead to urbanization, this process also leads to an increased cost of living and a higher demand for more affordable housing options. Due to these reasons, and the availability of better technology and transportation, suburbanization is likely to occur in response to urbanization. Suburbanization is the process of more people moving outside of the city to suburban areas in order to avoid crime and other undesirable city living conditions. Suburbanization also may lead to urban decline due to the abandonment of certain urban areas.

These areas then experience high unemployment rates, poverty and a decline in the physical environment of the city.

Gentrification and urban renewal

When city areas experience urban decline, those areas are less populated and often are inhabited by people in poverty. This can sometimes result in selling large amounts of property in the area to wealthy individuals. This process is known as gentrification. Gentrification often leads to wealthy individuals raising rent prices or property values, which displaces those poorer individuals who are unable to afford better housing. Many times, gentrification also leads to urban renewal. Urban renewal, otherwise known as urban regeneration or revitalization, is the process of redeveloping those previously poor areas of cities and cleaning them up in order to make the areas more appealing or attractive.

Social Inequality

Residential segregation

Residential segregation is the idea that different groups of people are separated into different residential neighborhoods in an area. These different groups can be based on wealth, race, or other demographics. Often, this occurs through the availability of housing and the segregation is maintained because of the inability or undesirability of relocation. This can create less desirable outcomes for marginalized groups of people, such as poor living conditions, high crime rates, or lower performing school systems. In the United States, the most segregated groups are minorities, with black Americans at the top of this list and Hispanic Americans second. These segregations are found most often in the larger urban areas, such as Los Angeles and New York. In addition, income is also known to be a factor in residential segregation, and most of these low-income individuals are also minorities.

Environmental justice in terms of location and exposure to health risks

Due to residential segregation, there are many discrepancies in the availability of resources in different neighborhoods. In less wealthy communities, segregation is sustained because rent is cheaper due to undesirable living conditions. For instance, there is often more pollution, higher crime, and/or less health care available in poor neighborhoods in comparison to wealthy neighborhoods. Because individuals in these areas are less financially able to relocate to a safer area, they are exposed to more health risks and are less able to get the care they need to manage these risks. Due to the increased health risks, there are social movements committed to demanding equitable distribution of health care and fewer environmental risks to people residing in poor neighborhoods.

Social class and socioeconomic status

A person's finances and economic status have a great deal of importance in society. Living situation, wealth, and job status are just a few factors that are influential in society and that combine to explain a person's social class and socioeconomic status. Social class refers to where someone came from; someone who grew up in poverty would have low social class. Socioeconomic status refers to a person's current situation; a person who won the lottery would have high socioeconomic status while a person who went bankrupt would have a lower status. A person's social class will be constant, but may contribute to socioeconomic status. On the other hand, someone's status may constantly fluctuate and can change quickly. Being aware of your own social class and the current issues at hand in this class is known as class consciousness. However, if you are only aware of your own situation and believe that you are representative of an entire class, this is known as false consciousness.

Cultural capital and social capital

Although financial and economic means are significant factors in achieving a higher socioeconomic status, there are also social and cultural factors that influence this as well. Cultural capital refers to the idea that cultural factors, such as education, physical appearance, or language, influence how easily a person is able to get a job or move up in society. Social capital is similar, but instead of cultural factors, it explains how social factors contribute to socioeconomic status. Social factors may include family and friends, networking abilities, location, or other relationships and connections.

Social reproduction

Social reproduction is a concept that describes how people inherit their parents' social class, including social inequalities or privileges. For instance, a child born into a poor family will likely also experience the negative effects of being poor and may also grow up and continue to live in poverty. This works through factors such as living situation, race, ethnicity, finances, and health risks. The same child that was born into a poor family may have grown up in a poor neighborhood with no access to a quality education and have no friends with high social class. The lack of opportunities and connections will likely make it difficult for this child throughout life and he or she may never be able to overcome those difficulties without significant help.

Power, privilege, and prestige

Power, privilege and prestige are factors that influence a person's abilities to accomplish greater goals and having one or more of these things makes it easier to achieve a higher socioeconomic status. Power is the idea that a person has influence or control over another person and can manipulate them in a way that benefits him or herself. Privilege refers to the benefits and advantages that a person gains based on who they are or which group they are associated with. Prestige is also known as a person's reputation. This prestige influences how other people feel about a particular individual and is associated with more respect and admiration based on how an individual is perceived.

Intersectionality

is a concept that describes the various social categories that a person fits into. Having more than one marginalized identity, such as being black, being gay, or being female, is studied through intersectionality and this idea helps explain the complexity of a person's experience based on these various identities. For instance, a black person and a gay person may experience very different things throughout their lifetime in terms of discrimination and prejudice, but a person who is both black and gay may experience these things more intensely or in a different way.

Socioeconomic gradient in health

Although people from all different backgrounds, social classes, races, or genders are in need of health care, there are inequities that exist within the healthcare system. One of the main inconsistencies is in regard to socioeconomic status. There are many more people who are in need of health care or who don't have access to quality health care who are lower in socioeconomic status than those who are financially secure. This concept is known as the socioeconomic gradient because there is a spectrum of social classes and the health disparities among these classes are significant. Not only does this occur among the various social classes of the United States, but countries with a lower socioeconomic status also have poorer health care than more wealthy countries.

Global inequalities

Inequalities in health care, education, and other social and cultural factors impact not just individuals or groups of people but also entire countries. Developed countries have better access to resources and are able to create more opportunities for the citizens of those countries than underdeveloped nations. Because of the power and resources available to the more developed countries in the world, these countries are able to take shortcuts and treat less developed countries unfairly, especially when it comes to trade agreements and practices. These unfair practices then create large disparities in the economies of these various countries and lead to poorer living conditions for the citizens of underdeveloped countries.

Social mobility

Social mobility refers to the idea that a person can move up or down in terms of socioeconomic status. This can happen in a variety of ways, including generationally, individually, and through achievement. Intergenerational mobility is when the socioeconomic status of a child is different than his or her parents; the child either was able to move farther up the social ladder than his or her parents, or he or she fell below them for some reason. An individual may also move between socioeconomic classes throughout his or her lifetime; this is known as intragenerational mobility. These changes can also be ether vertical or horizontal. Vertical mobility is when a person moves up or down in terms of socioeconomic status, while horizontal mobility is when a person moves within the same socioeconomic status; getting a new job in the same social class would be an example of horizontal mobility. Lastly, a person experiences social mobility because of meritocracy. Meritocracy refers to the idea that a person's mobility or success is based on his or her achievements and talents, as opposed to privilege or prejudice.

Poverty

Poverty is a term that means a person is very poor and financially inferior. However, there are different ways in which poverty can be explained. Relative poverty, for instance, refers to a person who is poor when compared to others in his or her society. This type of poverty means that the person is unable to afford a lifestyle consistent with those around them. This is, however, different than absolute poverty, which refers to a person who is unable to afford to meet his or her basic needs, such as food and shelter, due to an insufficient income. In addition to these poverty definitions regarding how much money a person makes, social exclusion is also a contributing factor to a person being unable to afford a basic lifestyle. This concept of social exclusion refers to when a person's access to opportunities, resources, or basic rights is obstructed, despite other groups being able to access the same resources without difficulties.

Disparities in health in relation to class, gender, and race

Although people from all different backgrounds may suffer from the same health issues, certain health problems are more common in certain populations. For instance, people in lower social classes are more likely to experience negative health concerns than people in higher classes. Certain minorities, especially those living in less populated areas, are also more prone to HIV/AIDS, heart disease, diabetes, or other diseases than white individuals. White people, on the other hand, are more likely to develop skin cancer or cystic fibrosis. Women are more likely than men to develop chronic, but non–life-threatening diseases, while men are more likely to develop serious, life-threatening illnesses or die at a younger age.

Disparities in health care in relation to class, gender, and race

Healthcare access, although becoming more accessible to marginalized populations, is still insufficient and unequal among these communities. People living in poverty and in poor neighborhoods are likely to be more exposed to health risks, and yet unable to afford quality health care. These populations are also less likely to have insurance, so they may be overwhelmed by enormous medical bills when they are inevitably admitted to a hospital. This is similar to some people of minority races, such as blacks and Hispanics, who are also unable to access quality health care. In addition, many minority individuals may fear discrimination and refuse to seek help, and the same is true for people who are not heterosexual. Women and men also differ in terms of health care; women are shown to be more likely to see a doctor when experiencing a health concern than men. However, women are also more likely to be responsible for a child, and when they are forced to choose between their own health care and their children's, this negatively impacts their well-being, either financially, mentally, or physically.

Critical Analysis and Reasoning Skills

The Verbal Reasoning Test consists of reading selections each followed by a series of questions. There will be several passages on the Verbal Reasoning section of the MCAT, and you can spend a little over eight minutes per passage and still finish within the time limit.

Reading Comprehension

Important Skills

One of the most important skills in reading comprehension is the identification of **topics** and **main ideas.** There is a subtle difference between these two features. The topic is the subject of a text, or what the text is about. The main idea, on the other hand, is the most important point being made by the author. The topic is usually expressed in a few words at the most, while the main idea often needs a full sentence to be completely defined. As an example, a short passage might have the topic of penguins and the main idea *Penguins are different from other birds in many ways.* In most nonfiction writing, the topic and the main idea will be stated directly, often in a sentence at the very beginning or end of the text. When being tested on an understanding of the author's topic, the reader can quickly *skim* the passage for the general idea, stopping to read only the first sentence of each paragraph. A paragraph's first sentence is often (but not always) the main topic sentence, and it gives you a summary of the content of the paragraph. However, there are cases in which the reader must figure out an unstated topic or main idea. In these instances, the student must read every sentence of the text, and try to come up with an overarching idea that is supported by each of those sentences.

> ➤ **Review Video: Topics and Main Ideas**
> *Visit mometrix.com/academy and enter Code:* **371666**

While the main idea is the overall premise of a story, **supporting details** provide evidence and backing for the main point. In order to show that a main idea is correct, or valid, the author needs to add details that prove their point. All texts contain details, but they are only classified as supporting details when they serve to reinforce some larger point. Supporting details are most commonly found in informative and persuasive texts. In some cases, they will be clearly indicated with words like *for example* or *for instance*, or they will be enumerated with words like *first*, *second*, and *last*. However, they may not be indicated with special words. As a reader, it is important to consider whether the author's supporting details really back up his or her main point. Supporting details can be factual and correct but still not relevant to the author's point. Conversely, supporting details can seem pertinent but be ineffective because they are based on opinion or assertions that cannot be proven.

An example of a main idea is: "Giraffes live in the Serengeti of Africa." A supporting detail about giraffes could be: "A giraffe uses its long neck to reach twigs and leaves on trees." The main idea gives the general idea that the text is about giraffes. The supporting detail gives a specific fact about how the giraffes eat.

> ➤ **Review Video: Supporting Details**
> *Visit mometrix.com/academy and enter Code:* **396297**

As opposed to a main idea, themes are seldom expressed directly in a text, so they can be difficult to identify. A **theme** is an issue, an idea, or a question raised by the text. For instance, a theme of William Shakespeare's *Hamlet* is indecision, as the title character explores his own psyche and the results of his failure to make bold choices. A great work of literature may have many themes, and the reader is justified in identifying any for which he or she can find support. One common characteristic of themes is that they raise more questions than they answer. In a good piece of fiction, the author is not always trying to convince the reader, but is instead trying to elevate the reader's perspective and encourage him to consider the themes more deeply. When reading, one can identify themes by constantly asking what general issues the text is addressing. A good way to evaluate an author's approach to a theme is to begin reading with a question in mind (for example, how does this text approach the theme of love?) and then look for evidence in the text that addresses that question.

> ➤ **Review Video: <u>Theme</u>**
> *Visit **mometrix.com/academy** and enter **Code: 732074***

Purposes for Writing

In order to be an effective reader, one must pay attention to the author's **position** and purpose. Even those texts that seem objective and impartial, like textbooks, have some sort of position and bias. Readers need to take these positions into account when considering the author's message. When an author uses emotional language or clearly favors one side of an argument, his position is clear. However, the author's position may be evident not only in what he writes, but in what he doesn't write. For this reason, it is sometimes necessary to review some other texts on the same topic in order to develop a view of the author's position. If this is not possible, then it may be useful to acquire a little background personal information about the author. When the only source of information is the text, however, the reader should look for language and argumentation that seems to indicate a particular stance on the subject.

> ➤ **Review Video: <u>Author's Position</u>**
> *Visit **mometrix.com/academy** and enter **Code: 827954***

Identifying the **purpose** of an author is usually easier than identifying her position. In most cases, the author has no interest in hiding his or her purpose. A text that is meant to entertain, for instance, should be obviously written to please the reader. Most narratives, or stories, are written to entertain, though they may also inform or persuade. Informative texts are easy to identify as well. The most difficult purpose of a text to identify is persuasion, because the author has an interest in making this purpose hard to detect. When a person knows that the author is trying to convince him, he is automatically more wary and skeptical of the argument. For this reason persuasive texts often try to establish an entertaining tone, hoping to amuse the reader into agreement, or an informative tone, hoping to create an appearance of authority and objectivity.

> ➤ **Review Video: <u>Purpose</u>**
> *Visit **mometrix.com/academy** and enter **Code: 511819***

An author's purpose is often evident in the organization of the text. For instance, if the text has headings and subheadings, if key terms are in bold, and if the author makes his main idea clear from the beginning, then the likely purpose of the text is to inform. If the author begins by making a claim and then makes various arguments to support that claim, the purpose is probably to persuade. If the author is telling a story, or is more interested in holding the attention of the reader than in making a particular point or delivering information, then his purpose is most likely to entertain. As a reader, it is best to judge an author on how well he accomplishes his purpose. In other words, it is not entirely fair to complain that a textbook is boring: if the text is clear and easy to understand, then the author has done his job. Similarly, a storyteller should not be judged too harshly for getting some facts wrong, so long as he is able to give pleasure to the reader.

The author's purpose for writing will affect his writing style and the response of the reader. In a **persuasive essay**, the author is attempting to change the reader's mind or convince him of something he did not believe previously. There are several identifying characteristics of persuasive writing. One is opinion presented as fact. When an author attempts to persuade the reader, he often presents his or her opinions as if they were fact. A reader must be on guard for statements that sound factual but which cannot be subjected to research, observation, or experiment. Another characteristic of persuasive writing is emotional language. An author will often try to play on the reader's emotion by appealing to his sympathy or sense of morality. When an author uses colorful or evocative language with the intent of arousing the reader's passions, it is likely that he is attempting to persuade. Finally, in many cases a persuasive text will give an unfair explanation of opposing positions, if these positions are mentioned at all.

An **informative text** is written to educate and enlighten the reader. Informative texts are almost always nonfiction, and are rarely structured as a story. The intention of an informative text is to deliver information in the most comprehensible way possible, so the structure of the text is likely to be very clear. In an informative text, the thesis statement is often in the first sentence. The author may use some colorful language, but is likely to put more emphasis on clarity and precision. Informative essays do not typically appeal to the emotions. They often contain facts and figures, and rarely include the opinion of the author. Sometimes a persuasive essay can resemble an informative essay, especially if the author maintains an even tone and presents his or her views as if they were established fact.

> **Review Video: Informative Text**
> *Visit **mometrix.com/academy** and enter Code:* **924964**

The success or failure of an author's intent to **entertain** is determined by those who read the author's work. Entertaining texts may be either fiction or nonfiction, and they may describe real or imagined people, places, and events. Entertaining texts are often narratives, or stories. A text that is written to entertain is likely to contain colorful language that engages the imagination and the emotions. Such writing often features a great deal of figurative language, which typically enlivens its subject matter with images and analogies. Though an entertaining text is not usually written to persuade or inform, it may accomplish both of these tasks. An entertaining text may appeal to the reader's emotions and cause him or her to think differently about a particular subject. In any case, entertaining texts tend to showcase the personality of the author more so than do other types of writing.

> **Review Video: Entertainment Texts**
> *Visit **mometrix.com/academy** and enter Code:* **532184**

When an author intends to **express feelings,** she may use colorful and evocative language. An author may write emotionally for any number of reasons. Sometimes, the author will do so because she is describing a personal situation of great pain or happiness. Sometimes an author is attempting to persuade the reader, and so will use emotion to stir up the passions. It can be easy to identify this kind of expression when the writer uses phrases like *I felt* and *I sense*. However, sometimes the author will simply describe feelings without introducing them. As a reader, it is important to recognize when an author is expressing emotion, and not to become overwhelmed by sympathy or passion. A reader should maintain some detachment so that he or she can still evaluate the strength of the author's argument or the quality of the writing.

> ➢ **Review Video: Express Feelings**
> *Visit **mometrix.com/academy** and enter **Code: 759390***

In a sense, almost all writing is descriptive, insofar as it seeks to describe events, ideas, or people to the reader. Some texts, however, are primarily concerned with **description**. A descriptive text focuses on a particular subject, and attempts to depict it in a way that will be clear to the reader. Descriptive texts contain many adjectives and adverbs, words that give shades of meaning and create a more detailed mental picture for the reader. A descriptive text fails when it is unclear or vague to the reader. On the other hand, however, a descriptive text that compiles too much detail can be boring and overwhelming to the reader. A descriptive text will certainly be informative, and it may be persuasive and entertaining as well. Descriptive writing is a challenge for the author, but when it is done well, it can be fun to read.

Writing Devices

Authors will use different stylistic and writing devices to make their meaning more clearly understood. One of those devices is comparison and contrast. When an author describes the ways in which two things are alike, he or she is **comparing** them. When the author describes the ways in which two things are different, he or she is **contrasting** them. The "compare and contrast" essay is one of the most common forms in nonfiction. It is often signaled with certain words: a comparison may be indicated with such words as *both, same, like, too,* and *as well*; while a contrast may be indicated by words like *but, however, on the other hand, instead,* and *yet*. Of course, comparisons and contrasts may be implicit without using any such signaling language. A single sentence may both compare and contrast. Consider the sentence *Brian and Sheila love ice cream, but Brian prefers vanilla and Sheila prefers strawberry*. In one sentence, the author has described both a similarity (love of ice cream) and a difference (favorite flavor).

> ➢ **Review Video: Rhetorical Strategy of Comparing and Contrasting Analysis**
> *Visit **mometrix.com/academy** and enter **Code: 587299***

One of the most common text structures is **cause and effect**. A cause is an act or event that makes something happen, and an effect is the thing that happens as a result of that cause. A cause-and-effect relationship is not always explicit, but there are some words in English that signal causality, such as *since*, *because*, and *as a result*. As an example, consider the sentence *Because the sky was clear, Ron did not bring an umbrella*. The cause is the clear sky, and the effect is that Ron did not bring an umbrella. However, sometimes the cause-and-effect relationship will not be clearly noted. For instance, the sentence *He was late and missed the meeting* does not contain any signaling words, but it still contains a cause (he was late) and an effect (he missed the meeting). It is possible for a single cause to have multiple effects, or for a single effect to have multiple causes. Also, an effect can in turn be the cause of another effect, in what is known as a cause-and-effect chain.

> **Review Video: Rhetorical Strategy of Cause and Effect Analysis**
> Visit *mometrix.com/academy* and enter *Code:* **725944**

Authors often use analogies to add meaning to the text. An **analogy** is a comparison of two things. The words in the analogy are connected by a certain, often undetermined relationship. Look at this analogy: moo is to cow as quack is to duck. This analogy compares the sound that a cow makes with the sound that a duck makes. Even if the word 'quack' was not given, one could figure out it is the correct word to complete the analogy based on the relationship between the words 'moo' and 'cow'. Some common relationships for analogies include synonyms, antonyms, part to whole, definition, and actor to action.

Another element that impacts a text is the author's point of view. The **point of view** of a text is the perspective from which it is told. The author will always have a point of view about a story before he draws up a plot line. The author will know what events they want to take place, how they want the characters to interact, and how the story will resolve. An author will also have an opinion on the topic, or series of events, which is presented in the story, based on their own prior experience and beliefs.

The two main points of view that authors use are first person and third person. If the narrator of the story is also the main character, or *protagonist*, the text is written in first-person point of view. In first person, the author writes with the word *I*. Third-person point of view is probably the most common point of view that authors use. Using third person, authors refer to each character using the words *he* or *she*. In third-person omniscient, the narrator is not a character in the story and tells the story of all of the characters at the same time.

> **Review Video: Points of View**
> Visit *mometrix.com/academy* and enter *Code:* **383336**

A good writer will use **transitional words** and phrases to guide the reader through the text. You are no doubt familiar with the common transitions, though you may never have considered how they operate. Some transitional phrases (*after, before, during, in the middle of*) give information about time. Some indicate that an example is about to be given (*for example, in fact, for instance*). Writers use them to compare (*also, likewise*) and contrast (*however, but, yet*). Transitional words and phrases can suggest addition (*and, also, furthermore, moreover*) and logical relationships (*if, then, therefore, as a result, since*). Finally, transitional words and phrases can demarcate the steps in a process (*first, second, last*). You should incorporate transitional words and phrases where they will orient your reader and illuminate the structure of your composition.

> ➢ **Review Video: <u>Transitional Words and Phrases</u>**
> *Visit **mometrix.com/academy** and enter **Code: 197796***

Types of Passages

A **narrative** passage is a story. Narratives can be fiction or nonfiction. However, there are a few elements that a text must have in order to be classified as a narrative. To begin with, the text must have a plot. That is, it must describe a series of events. If it is a good narrative, these events will be interesting and emotionally engaging to the reader. A narrative also has characters. These could be people, animals, or even inanimate objects, so long as they participate in the plot. A narrative passage often contains figurative language, which is meant to stimulate the imagination of the reader by making comparisons and observations. A metaphor, which is a description of one thing in terms of another, is a common piece of figurative language. *The moon was a frosty snowball* is an example of a metaphor: it is obviously untrue in the literal sense, but it suggests a certain mood for the reader. Narratives often proceed in a clear sequence, but they do not need to do so.

An **expository** passage aims to inform and enlighten the reader. It is nonfiction and usually centers around a simple, easily defined topic. Since the goal of exposition is to teach, such a passage should be as clear as possible. It is common for an expository passage to contain helpful organizing words, like *first, next, for example*, and *therefore*. These words keep the reader oriented in the text. Although expository passages do not need to feature colorful language and artful writing, they are often more effective when they do. For a reader, the challenge of expository passages is to maintain steady attention. Expository passages are not always about subjects in which a reader will naturally be interested, and the writer is often more concerned with clarity and comprehensibility than with engaging the reader. For this reason, many expository passages are dull. Making notes is a good way to maintain focus when reading an expository passage.

> ➢ **Review Video: <u>Narratives</u>**
> *Visit **mometrix.com/academy** and enter **Code: 280100***

A **technical** passage is written to describe a complex object or process. Technical writing is common in medical and technological fields, in which complicated mathematical, scientific, and engineering ideas need to be explained simply and clearly. To ease comprehension, a technical passage usually proceeds in a very logical order. Technical passages often have clear headings and subheadings, which are used to keep the reader oriented in the text. It is also common for these passages to break sections up with numbers or letters. Many technical passages look more like an outline than a piece of prose. The amount of jargon or difficult vocabulary will vary in a technical passage depending on the intended audience. As much as possible, technical passages try to avoid language that the reader will have to research in order to understand the message. Of course, it is not always possible to avoid jargon.

> ➤ **Review Video:** <u>A Technical Passage</u>
> *Visit **mometrix.com/academy** and enter **Code: 827954***

A **persuasive** passage is meant to change the reader's mind or lead her into agreement with the author. The persuasive intent may be obvious, or it may be quite difficult to discern. In some cases, a persuasive passage will be indistinguishable from an informative passage: it will make an assertion and offer supporting details. However, a persuasive passage is more likely to make claims based on opinion and to appeal to the reader's emotions. Persuasive passages may not describe alternate positions and, when they do, they often display significant bias. It may be clear that a persuasive passage is giving the author's viewpoint, or the passage may adopt a seemingly objective tone. A persuasive passage is successful if it can make a convincing argument and win the trust of the reader.

> ➤ **Review Video:** <u>Persuasive Text and Bias</u>
> *Visit **mometrix.com/academy** and enter **Code: 479856***

A persuasive essay will likely focus on one central argument, but it may make many smaller claims along the way. These are subordinate arguments with which the reader must agree if he or she is going to agree with the central argument. The central argument will only be as strong as the subordinate claims. These claims should be rooted in fact and observation, rather than subjective judgment. The best persuasive essays provide enough supporting detail to justify claims without overwhelming the reader.

Remember that a fact must be susceptible to independent verification: that is, it must be something the reader could confirm. Also, statistics are only effective when they take into account possible objections. For instance, a statistic on the number of foreclosed houses would only be useful if it was taken over a defined interval and in a defined area. Most readers are wary of statistics, because they are so often misleading. If possible, a persuasive essay should always include references so that the reader can obtain more information. Of course, this means that the writer's accuracy and fairness may be judged by the inquiring reader.

> ➤ **Review Video:** <u>Persuasive Essay</u>
> *Visit **mometrix.com/academy** and enter **Code: 621428***

Opinions are formed by emotion as well as reason, and persuasive writers often appeal to the feelings of the reader. Although readers should always be skeptical of this technique, it is often used in a proper and ethical manner. For instance, there are many subjects that have an obvious emotional component, and therefore cannot be completely treated without an appeal to the emotions. Consider an article on drunk driving: it makes sense to include some specific examples that will alarm or sadden the reader. After all, drunk driving often has serious and tragic consequences. Emotional appeals are not appropriate, however, when they attempt to mislead the reader. For instance, in political advertisements it is common to emphasize the patriotism of the preferred candidate, because this will encourage the audience to link their own positive feelings about the country with their opinion of the candidate. However, these ads often imply that the other candidate is unpatriotic, which in most cases is far from the truth. Another common and improper emotional appeal is the use of loaded language, as for instance referring to an avidly religious person as a "fanatic" or a passionate environmentalist as a "tree hugger." These terms introduce an emotional component that detracts from the argument.

History and Culture

Historical context has a profound influence on literature: the events, knowledge base, and assumptions of an author's time color every aspect of his or her work. Sometimes, authors hold opinions and use language that would be considered inappropriate or immoral in a modern setting, but that was acceptable in the author's time. As a reader, one should consider how the historical context influenced a work and also how today's opinions and ideas shape the way modern readers read the works of the past. For instance, in most societies of the past, women were treated as second-class citizens. An author who wrote in 18th-century England might sound sexist to modern readers, even if that author was relatively feminist in his time. Readers should not have to excuse the faulty assumptions and prejudices of the past, but they should appreciate that a person's thoughts and words are, in part, a result of the time and culture in which they live or lived, and it is perhaps unfair to expect writers to avoid all of the errors of their times.

Even a brief study of world literature suggests that writers from vastly different cultures address similar themes. For instance, works like the *Odyssey* and *Hamlet* both tackle the individual's battle for self-control and independence. In every culture, authors address themes of personal growth and the struggle for maturity. Another universal theme is the conflict between the individual and society. In works as culturally disparate as *Native Son*, the *Aeneid*, and *1984*, authors dramatize how people struggle to maintain their personalities and dignity in large, sometimes oppressive groups. Finally, many cultures have versions of the hero's (or heroine's) journey, in which an adventurous person must overcome many obstacles in order to gain greater knowledge, power, and perspective. Some famous works that treat this theme are the *Epic of Gilgamesh*, Dante's *Divine Comedy*, and *Don Quixote.*

Authors from different genres (for instance poetry, drama, novel, short story) and cultures may address similar themes, but they often do so quite differently. For instance, poets are likely to address subject matter obliquely, through the use of images and allusions. In a play, on the other hand, the author is more likely to dramatize themes by using characters to express opposing viewpoints. This disparity is known as a dialectical approach. In a novel, the author does not need to express themes directly; rather, they can be illustrated through events and actions. In some regional literatures, like those of Greece or England, authors use more irony: their works have characters that express views and make decisions that are clearly disapproved of by the author. In Latin America, there is a great tradition of using supernatural events to illustrate themes about real life. In China and Japan, authors frequently use well-established regional forms (haiku, for instance) to organize their treatment of universal themes.

Responding to Literature

When reading good literature, the reader is moved to engage actively in the text. One part of being an active reader involves making predictions. A **prediction** is a guess about what will happen next. Readers are constantly making predictions based on what they have read and what they already know. Consider the following sentence: *Staring at the computer screen in shock, Kim blindly reached over for the brimming glass of water on the shelf to her side.* The sentence suggests that Kim is agitated and that she is not looking at the glass she is going to pick up, so a reader might predict that she is going to knock the glass over. Of course, not every prediction will be accurate: perhaps Kim will pick the glass up cleanly. Nevertheless, the author has certainly created the expectation that the water might be spilled. Predictions are always subject to revision as the reader acquires more information.

> ➢ **Review Video: Predictions**
> Visit ***mometrix.com/academy*** *and enter* ***Code:*** **437248**

Test-taking tip: To respond to questions requiring future predictions, the student's answers should be based on evidence of past or present behavior.

Readers are often required to understand text that claims and suggests ideas without stating them directly. An **inference** is a piece of information that is implied but not written outright by the author. For instance, consider the following sentence: *Mark made more money that week than he had in the previous year.* From this sentence, the reader can infer that Mark either has not made much money in the previous year or made a great deal of money that week. Often, a reader can use information he or she already knows to make inferences. Take as an example the sentence *When his coffee arrived, he looked around the table for the silver cup.* Many people know that cream is typically served in a silver cup, so using their own base of knowledge they can infer that the subject of this sentence takes his coffee with cream. Making inferences requires concentration, attention, and practice.

> ➢ **Review Video: Inference**
> Visit ***mometrix.com/academy*** *and enter* ***Code:*** **379203**

Test-taking tip: While being tested on his ability to make correct inferences, the student must look for contextual clues. An answer can be *right* but not *correct*. The contextual clues will help you find the answer that is the best answer out of the given choices. Understand the context in which a phrase is stated. When asked for the implied meaning of a statement made in the passage, the student should immediately locate the statement and read the context in which it was made. Also, look for an answer choice that has a similar phrase to the statement in question.

A reader must be able to identify a text's **sequence**, or the order in which things happen. Often, and especially when the sequence is very important to the author, it is indicated with signal words like *first*, *then*, *next*, and *last*. However, sometimes a sequence is merely implied and must be noted by the reader. Consider the sentence *He walked in the front door and switched on the hall lamp*. Clearly, the man did not turn the lamp on before he walked in the door, so the implied sequence is that he first walked in the door and then turned on the lamp. Texts do not always proceed in an orderly sequence from first to last: sometimes, they begin at the end and then start over at the beginning. As a reader, it can be useful to make brief notes to clarify the sequence.

> ➤ **Review Video: <u>Sequence</u>**
> *Visit **mometrix.com/academy** and enter **Code: 489027***

In addition to inferring and predicting things about the text, the reader must often **draw conclusions** about the information he has read. When asked for a *conclusion* that may be drawn, look for critical "hedge" phrases, such as *likely, may, can, will often*, among many others. When you are being tested on this knowledge, remember that question writers insert these hedge phrases to cover every possibility. Often an answer will be wrong simply because it leaves no room for exception. Extreme positive or negative answers (such as always, never, etc.) are usually not correct. The reader should not use any outside knowledge that is not gathered from the reading passage to answer the related questions. Correct answers can be derived straight from the reading passage.

Critical Thinking Skills

Opinions, Facts, & Fallacies

Critical thinking skills are mastered through understanding various types of writing and the different purposes that authors have for writing the way they do. Every author writes for a purpose. Understanding that purpose, and how they accomplish their goal, will allow you to critique the writing and determine whether or not you agree with their conclusions.

Readers must always be conscious of the distinction between fact and opinion. A **fact** can be subjected to analysis and can be either proved or disproved. An **opinion**, on the other hand, is the author's personal feeling, which may not be alterable by research, evidence, or argument. If the author writes that the distance from New York to Boston is about two hundred miles, he is stating a fact. But if he writes that New York is too crowded, then he is giving an opinion, because there is no objective standard for overpopulation. An opinion may be indicated by words like *believe*, *think*, or *feel*. Also, an opinion may be supported by facts: for instance, the author might give the population density of New York as a reason for why it is overcrowded. An opinion supported by fact tends to be more convincing. When authors support their opinions with other opinions, the reader is unlikely to be moved.

Facts should be presented to the reader from reliable sources. An opinion is what the author thinks about a given topic. An opinion is not common knowledge or proven by expert sources, but it is information that the author believes and wants the reader to consider. To distinguish between fact and opinion, a reader needs to look at the type of source that is presenting information, what information backs-up a claim, and whether or not the author may be motivated to have a certain point of view on a given topic.

For example, if a panel of scientists has conducted multiple studies on the effectiveness of taking a certain vitamin, the results are more likely to be factual than if a company selling a vitamin claims that taking the vitamin can produce positive effects. The company is motivated to sell its product, while the scientists are using the scientific method to prove a theory. If the author uses words such as "I think...", the statement is an opinion.

> **Review Video: <u>Fact or Opinion</u>**
> *Visit **mometrix.com/academy** and enter **Code: 870899***

In their attempt to persuade, writers often make mistakes in their thinking patterns and writing choices. It's important to understand these so you can make an informed decision. Every author has a point of view, but when an author ignores reasonable counterarguments or distorts opposing viewpoints, she is demonstrating a **bias**. A bias is evident whenever the author is unfair or inaccurate in his or her presentation. Bias may be intentional or unintentional, but it should always alert the reader to be skeptical of the argument being made. It should be noted that a biased author may still be correct. However, the author will be correct in spite of her bias, not because of it. A **stereotype** is like a bias, except that it is specifically applied to a group or place. Stereotyping is considered to be particularly abhorrent because it promotes negative generalizations about people. Many people are familiar with some of the hateful stereotypes of certain ethnic, religious, and cultural groups. Readers should be very wary of authors who stereotype. These faulty assumptions typically reveal the author's ignorance and lack of curiosity.

> **Review Video: <u>Bias and Stereotype</u>**
> *Visit **mometrix.com/academy** and enter **Code: 644829***

Sometimes, authors will **appeal to the reader's emotion** in an attempt to persuade or to distract the reader from the weakness of the argument. For instance, the author may try to inspire the pity of the reader by delivering a heart-rending story. An author also might use the bandwagon approach, in which he suggests that his opinion is correct because it is held by the majority. Some authors resort to name-calling, in which insults and harsh words are delivered to the opponent in an attempt to distract. In advertising, a common appeal is the testimonial, in which a famous person endorses a product. Of course, the fact that a celebrity likes something should not really mean anything to the reader. These and other emotional appeals are usually evidence of poor reasoning and a weak argument.

> **Review Video: <u>Appeal to the Reader's Emotions</u>**
> *Visit **mometrix.com/academy** and enter **Code: 163442***

Certain *logical fallacies* are frequent in writing. A logical fallacy is a failure of reasoning. As a reader, it is important to recognize logical fallacies, because they diminish the value of the author's message. The four most common logical fallacies in writing are the false analogy, circular reasoning, false dichotomy, and overgeneralization. In a **false analogy**, the author suggests that two things are similar, when in fact they are different. This fallacy is often committed when the author is attempting to convince the reader that something unknown is like something relatively familiar. The author takes advantage of the reader's ignorance to make this false comparison.

One example might be the following statement: *Failing to tip a waitress is like stealing money out of somebody's wallet*. Of course, failing to tip is very rude, especially when the service has been good, but people are not arrested for failing to tip as they would for stealing money from a wallet. To compare stingy diners with thieves is a false analogy.

> ➤ **Review Video: False Analogy**
> *Visit **mometrix.com/academy** and enter **Code: 865045***

Circular reasoning is one of the more difficult logical fallacies to identify, because it is typically hidden behind dense language and complicated sentences. Reasoning is described as circular when it offers no support for assertions other than restating them in different words. Put another way, a circular argument refers to itself as evidence of truth. A simple example of circular argument is when a person uses a word to define itself, such as saying *Niceness is the state of being nice*. If the reader does not know what *nice* means, then this definition will not be very useful. In a text, circular reasoning is usually more complex. For instance, an author might say *Poverty is a problem for society because it creates trouble for people throughout the community*. It is redundant to say that poverty is a problem because it creates trouble. When an author engages in circular reasoning, it is often because he or she has not fully thought out the argument, or cannot come up with any legitimate justifications.

> ➤ **Review Video: Circular Reasoning**
> *Visit **mometrix.com/academy** and enter **Code: 398925***

One of the most common logical fallacies is the **false dichotomy**, in which the author creates an artificial sense that there are only two possible alternatives in a situation. This fallacy is common when the author has an agenda and wants to give the impression that his view is the only sensible one. A false dichotomy has the effect of limiting the reader's options and imagination. An example of a false dichotomy is the statement *You need to go to the party with me, otherwise you'll just be bored at home*. The speaker suggests that the only other possibility besides being at the party is being bored at home. But this is not true, as it is perfectly possible to be entertained at home, or even to go somewhere other than the party. Readers should always be wary of the false dichotomy: when an author limits alternatives, it is always wise to ask whether he is being valid.

> ➤ **Review Video: False Dichotomy**
> *Visit **mometrix.com/academy** and enter **Code: 484397***

Overgeneralization is a logical fallacy in which the author makes a claim that is so broad it cannot be proved or disproved. In most cases, overgeneralization occurs when the author wants to create an illusion of authority, or when he is using sensational language to sway the opinion of the reader. For instance, in the sentence *Everybody knows that she is a terrible teacher*, the author makes an assumption that cannot really be believed.

This kind of statement is made when the author wants to create the illusion of consensus when none actually exists: it may be that most people have a negative view of the teacher, but to say that *everybody* feels that way is an exaggeration. When a reader spots overgeneralization, she should become skeptical about the argument that is being made, because an author will often try to hide a weak or unsupported assertion behind authoritative language.

> ➤ **Review Video: <u>Overgeneralization</u>**
> *Visit **mometrix.com/academy** and enter **Code: 367357***

Two other types of logical fallacies are **slippery slope** arguments and **hasty generalizations**. In a slippery slope argument, the author says that if something happens, it automatically means that something else will happen as a result, even though this may not be true. (i.e., just because you study hard does not mean you are going to ace the test). "Hasty generalization" is drawing a conclusion too early, without finishing analyzing the details of the argument. Writers of persuasive texts often use these techniques because they are very effective. In order to **identify logical fallacies**, readers need to read carefully and ask questions as they read. Thinking critically means not taking everything at face value. Readers need to critically evaluate an author's argument to make sure that the logic used is sound.

Organization of the Text

The way a text is organized can help the reader to understand more clearly the author's intent and his conclusions. There are various ways to organize a text, and each one has its own purposes and uses. Some nonfiction texts are organized to **present a problem** followed by a solution. In this type of text, it is common for the problem to be explained before the solution is offered. In some cases, as when the problem is well known, the solution may be briefly introduced at the beginning. The entire passage may focus on the solution, and the problem will be referenced only occasionally. Some texts will outline multiple solutions to a problem, leaving the reader to choose among them. If the author has an interest or an allegiance to one solution, he may fail to mention or may describe inaccurately some of the other solutions. Readers should be careful of the author's agenda when reading a problem-solution text. Only by understanding the author's point of view and interests can one develop a proper judgment of the proposed solution.

> ➤ **Review Video: <u>Present a Problem</u>**
> *Visit **mometrix.com/academy** and enter **Code: 435944***

Authors need to organize information logically so the reader can follow it and locate information within the text. Two common organizational structures are cause and effect and chronological order. When using **chronological order**, the author presents information in the order that it happened. For example, biographies are written in chronological order; the subject's birth and childhood are presented first, followed by their adult life, and lastly by the events leading up to the person's death.

In **cause and effect**, an author presents one thing that makes something else happen. For example, if one were to go to bed very late, they would be tired. The cause is going to bed late, with the effect of being tired the next day.

It can be tricky to identify the cause-and-effect relationships in a text, but there are a few ways to approach this task. To begin with, these relationships are often signaled with certain terms. When an author uses words like *because*, *since*, *in order*, and *so*, she is likely describing a cause-and-effect relationship. Consider the sentence, "He called her because he needed the homework." This is a simple causal relationship, in which the cause was his need for the homework and the effect was his phone call. Not all cause-and-effect relationships are marked in this way, however. Consider the sentences, "He called her. He needed the homework." When the cause-and-effect relationship is not indicated with a keyword, it can be discovered by asking why something happened. He called her: why? The answer is in the next sentence: He needed the homework.

Persuasive essays, in which an author tries to make a convincing argument and change the reader's mind, usually include cause-and-effect relationships. However, these relationships should not always be taken at face value. An author frequently will assume a cause or take an effect for granted. To read a persuasive essay effectively, one needs to judge the cause-and-effect relationships the author is presenting. For instance, imagine an author wrote the following: "The parking deck has been unprofitable because people would prefer to ride their bikes." The relationship is clear: the cause is that people prefer to ride their bikes, and the effect is that the parking deck has been unprofitable. However, a reader should consider whether this argument is conclusive. Perhaps there are other reasons for the failure of the parking deck: a down economy, excessive fees, etc. Too often, authors present causal relationships as if they are fact rather than opinion. Readers should be on the alert for these dubious claims.

Thinking critically about ideas and conclusions can seem like a daunting task. One way to make it easier is to understand the basic elements of ideas and writing techniques. Looking at the way different ideas relate to each other can be a good way for the reader to begin his analysis. For instance, sometimes writers will write about two different ideas that are in opposition to each other. The analysis of these opposing ideas is known as **contrast**. Contrast is often marred by the author's obvious partiality to one of the ideas. A discerning reader will be put off by an author who does not engage in a fair fight. In an analysis of opposing ideas, both ideas should be presented in their clearest and most reasonable terms. If the author does prefer a side, he should avoid indicating this preference with pejorative language. An analysis of opposing ideas should proceed through the major differences point by point, with a full explanation of each side's view. For instance, in an analysis of capitalism and communism, it would be important to outline each side's view on labor, markets, prices, personal responsibility, etc. It would be less effective to describe the theory of communism and then explain how capitalism has thrived in the West. An analysis of opposing views should present each side in the same manner.

Many texts follow the **compare-and-contrast** model, in which the similarities and differences between two ideas or things are explored. Analysis of the similarities between ideas is called comparison. In order for a comparison to work, the author must place the ideas or things in an equivalent structure. That is, the author must present the ideas in the same way. Imagine an author wanted to show the similarities between cricket and baseball. The correct way to do so would be to summarize the equipment and rules for each game. It would be incorrect to summarize the equipment of cricket and then lay out the history of baseball, since this would make it impossible for the reader to see the similarities. It is perhaps too obvious to say that an analysis of similar ideas should emphasize the similarities. Of course, the author should take care to include any differences that must be mentioned. Often, these small differences will only reinforce the more general similarity.

Drawing Conclusions

Authors should have a clear purpose in mind while writing. Especially when reading informational texts, it is important to understand the logical conclusion of the author's ideas. **Identifying this logical conclusion** can help the reader understand whether he agrees with the writer or not. Identifying a logical conclusion is much like making an inference: it requires the reader to combine the information given by the text with what he already knows to make a supportable assertion. If a passage is written well, then the conclusion should be obvious even when it is unstated. If the author intends the reader to draw a certain conclusion, then all of his argumentation and detail should be leading toward it.

One way to approach the task of drawing conclusions is to make brief notes of all the points made by the author. When these are arranged on paper, they may clarify the logical conclusion. Another way to approach conclusions is to consider whether the reasoning of the author raises any pertinent questions. Sometimes it will be possible to draw several conclusions from a passage, and on occasion these will be conclusions that were never imagined by the author. It is essential, however, that these conclusions be supported directly by the text.

> ➤ **Review Video: <u>Identifying a Logical Conclusion</u>**
> *Visit **mometrix.com/academy** and enter **Code: 281653***

The term **text evidence** refers to information that supports a main point or points in a story, and can help lead the reader to a conclusion. Information used as *text evidence* is precise, descriptive, and factual. A main point is often followed by supporting details that provide evidence to back-up a claim. For example, a story may include the claim that winter occurs during opposite months in the Northern and Southern hemispheres. *Text evidence* based on this claim may include countries where winter occurs in opposite months, along with reasons that winter occurs at different times of the year in separate hemispheres (due to the tilt of the Earth as it rotates around the sun).

Readers interpret text and respond to it in a number of ways. Using textual support helps defend your response or interpretation because it roots your thinking in the text. You are interpreting based on information in the text and not simply your own ideas. When crafting a response, look for important quotes and details from the text to help bolster your argument. If you are writing about a character's personality trait, for example, use details from the text to show that the character acted in such a way. You can also include statistics and facts from a nonfiction text to strengthen your response. For example, instead of writing, "A lot of people use cell phones," use statistics to provide the exact number. This strengthens your argument because it is more precise.

> ➤ **Review Video: <u>Text Evidence</u>**
> *Visit **mometrix.com/academy** and enter **Code: 486236***

The text used to support an argument can be the argument's downfall if it is not credible. A text is **credible**, or believable, when the author is knowledgeable and objective, or unbiased. The author's motivations for writing the text play a critical role in determining the credibility of the text and must be evaluated when assessing that credibility. The author's motives should be for the dissemination of information. The purpose of the text should be to inform or describe, not to persuade. When an author writes a persuasive text, he has the motivation that the reader will do what they want. The extent of the author's knowledge of the topic and their motivation must be evaluated when assessing the credibility of a text. Reports written about the Ozone layer by an environmental scientist and a hairdresser will have a different level of credibility.

> ➤ **Review Video: <u>Credible</u>**
> *Visit **mometrix.com/academy** and enter **Code: 827257**

After determining your own opinion and evaluating the credibility of your supporting text, it is sometimes necessary to communicate your ideas and findings to others. When **writing a response to a text**, it is important to use elements of the text to support your assertion or defend your position. Using supporting evidence from the text strengthens the argument because the reader can see how in depth the writer read the original piece and based their response on the details and facts within that text. Elements of text that can be used in a response include: facts, details, statistics, and direct quotations from the text. When writing a response, one must make sure they indicate which information comes from the original text and then base their discussion, argument, or defense around this information.

A reader should always be drawing conclusions from the text. Sometimes conclusions are implied from written information, and other times the information is **stated directly** within the passage. It is always more comfortable to draw conclusions from information stated within a passage, rather than to draw them from mere implications. At times an author may provide some information and then describe a counterargument. The reader should be alert for direct statements that are subsequently rejected or weakened by the author. The reader should always read the entire passage before drawing conclusions. Many readers are trained to expect the author's conclusions at either the beginning or the end of the passage, but many texts do not adhere to this format.

> ➤ **Review Video: <u>Writing a Response to the Text</u>**
> *Visit **mometrix.com/academy** and enter **Code: 185093**

Drawing conclusions from information implied within a passage requires confidence on the part of the reader. **Implications** are things the author does not state directly, but which can be assumed based on what the author does say. For instance, consider the following simple passage: "I stepped outside and opened my umbrella. By the time I got to work, the cuffs of my pants were soaked." The author never states that it is raining, but this fact is clearly implied. Conclusions based on implication must be well supported by the text. In order to draw a solid conclusion, a reader should have multiple pieces of evidence, or, if he only has one, must be assured that there is no other possible explanation than his conclusion. A good reader will be able to draw many conclusions from information implied by the text, which enriches the reading experience considerably.

As an aid to drawing conclusions, the reader should be adept at **outlining** the information contained in the passage; an effective outline will reveal the structure of the passage, and will lead to solid conclusions. An effective outline will have a title that refers to the basic subject of the text, though it need not recapitulate the main idea. In most outlines, the main idea will be the first major section. It will have each major idea of the passage established as the head of a category.

For instance, the most common outline format calls for the main ideas of the passage to be indicated with Roman numerals. In an effective outline of this kind, each of the main ideas will be represented by a Roman numeral and none of the Roman numerals will designate minor details or secondary ideas.

Moreover, all supporting ideas and details should be placed in the appropriate place on the outline. An outline does not need to include every detail listed in the text, but it should feature all of those that are central to the argument or message. Each of these details should be listed under the appropriate main idea.

It is also helpful to **summarize** the information you have read in a paragraph or passage format. This process is similar to creating an effective outline. To begin with, a summary should accurately define the main idea of the passage, though it does not need to explain this main idea in exhaustive detail. It should continue by laying out the most important supporting details or arguments from the passage. All of the significant supporting details should be included, and none of the details included should be irrelevant or insignificant. Also, the summary should accurately report all of these details. Too often, the desire for brevity in a summary leads to the sacrifice of clarity or veracity. Summaries are often difficult to read, because they omit all of graceful language, digressions, and asides that distinguish great writing. However, if the summary is effective, it should contain much the same message as the original text.

Paraphrasing is another method the reader can use to aid in comprehension. When paraphrasing, one puts what they have read into their own words, rephrasing what the author has written to make it their own, to "translate" all of what the author says to their own words, including as many details as they can.

Practice Test

Biological and Biochemical Foundations

Question Set 1

The sodium-potassium adenosine triphosphatase (Na+/K+ ATPase) enzyme maintains a resting potential of –70 mV across a neuronal cell membrane. A complex 3D structure, Na+/K+ ATPase is encoded by several genes. Powered by adenosine triphosphate (ATP) and consuming between 15% and 25% of a typical human cell's energy, the enzymatic pump is fundamental in maintaining the body's homeostasis. It is the pump's hyperpolarization of the neuronal membrane that results in a brief refractory period during which the cell cannot be depolarized.

Researchers have extracted a portion of the cell membrane containing the Na+/K+ ATPase and treated the tissues with an acidic solution. They measured the latency before another action potential with the following results:

Solution	Action potential latency
0.02% solution	2 msec
0.04% solution	1.88 msec
0.07% solution	0.75 msec

1. What is the approximate charge of the membrane potential during the refractory period?
    a. –65 mV
    b. 25 mV
    c. 180 mV
    d. –75 mV

2. How do the characteristics of the phospholipid bilayer of the cell impact the movement of Na+ and K+?

    a. Sodium and potassium are both highly charged cations. They cannot easily diffuse through the phospholipid bilayer, and thus they require active transport to move against a concentration gradient.

    b. Sodium and potassium are both small ions, and they can thus diffuse through the phospholipid bilayer according to the concentration gradient, but they require an ATP-powered pump to overcome the concentration gradient.

    c. The phospholipid bilayer contains phosphate molecules, which can interact with and bind to Na+ and K+.

    d. The phospholipid bilayer of a nonneuronal cell does not have Na+/K+ ATPase because nonneuronal cells do not carry an action potential.

3. What factors may change the behavior of enzymatic proteins?
    a. Temperature, diffusion, pH, and an attached molecule at the binding site
    b. Hydrogen concentration, water, and pH
    c. Temperature, hydrogen concentration, and an attached molecule at the binding site
    d. Temperature, pH, and concentration gradient

4. How does the solution applied in this experiment alter the activity of the pump?
    a. The solution deactivates some of the pumps, prolonging the refractory period.
    b. The solution deactivates some of the pumps, reducing the latency.
    c. The solution prolongs the activity of some of the pumps, prolonging the latency.
    d. The solution prolongs the activity of some of the pumps, reducing the refractory period.

5. How does the refractory period after an action potential affect a neuronal cell's ability to preserve the integrity of the action potential?
    a. The action potential cannot move in a reverse direction due to the latency produced by the refractory period.
    b. The latency protects the cell membrane from injury, which could be caused by excessive concentrations of sodium.
    c. The latency allows for a response from the target organ prior to initiation of another action potential.
    d. The latency of the action potential prevents the neuron from becoming overstimulated, and it prevents overconsumption of neurotransmitters at the synapse.

6. How could an experimental design using any of these solutions determine the relative density of Na+/K+ ATPase-activated pumps between two different types of cells?
    a. Both cell types should be treated with 0.02% and 0.04% solution. The cell type with the greatest drop in latency is the cell type with the greater density of Na+/K+ ATPase-activated proton pumps.
    b. Both cell types should be treated with 0.04% and 0.07% solution. The cell type with the smallest drop in latency is the cell type with the greater density of Na+/K+ ATPase-activated proton pumps.
    c. Both cell types should be treated with all three solutions to determine which cell types showed the biggest change in latency because that would be the cell type with the greater density of Na+/K+ ATPase-activated proton pumps.
    d. Both cell types should be treated with the 0.07% solution. The cell type showing a longer latency upon treatment with the 0.07% solution is likely the cell type with the lower density of Na+/K+ ATPase-activated proton pumps.

Question Set 2

During mitosis, deoxyribonucleic acid (DNA) replication produces a copy of the genetic information encoded in the DNA molecule. Given the specialized differentiation of eukaryotic cells, portions of the DNA molecule may be intermittently activated in some cells, but not in other cells.

A nucleotide base pair substitution mutation has been incidentally identified in a series of DNA analyses performed on a population that has a known hereditary genetic disorder that impairs T-cell function. The locus of the genetic abnormality that causes the T-cell dysfunction has not yet been established. The phenotypic effects of the incidentally located mutation have not yet been determined, if there are any.

Preliminary findings of 1000 subjects and 10,000 controls

T-cell function impairment		Presence of base pair mutation
Controls	0.001%	0%
Group 1	0.5%	2.01%
Group 2	0.67%	1.52%
Group 3	0.78%	1.67%

7. How may a substitution mutation occur and yet not produce a change in the protein that it encodes?
  a. The DNA molecule is a double helix, and therefore the complementary strand can compensate for a mutation in one strand.
  b. Due to the redundancy of the genetic code, a substitution mutation can code for the identical "correct" amino acid in a protein, and consequently it might not affect the protein structure.
  c. A eukaryotic cell is diploid, and by definition it contains two copies of every gene. The homologous copy that does not have a mutation should code for the correct protein.
  d. An abnormal protein would not be able to function, and it would most likely be destroyed by phagocytes.

8. During cell division, how could a DNA replication error resulting in a base pair substitution being repaired?
  a. During transcription, several enzymes, such as ribonucleic acid (RNA) polymerase, interact with the DNA molecule to ensure accuracy.
  b. When cell division occurs, segregation of homologous chromosomes ensures that the correct number of chromosomes ends up in each cell.
  c. It cannot be repaired. If a mutation has already occurred, every copy of the gene will be faithfully copied with the mutation through the process of semiconservative replication.
  d. DNA polymerase and the associated enzymes essentially "double-check" a replicated DNA strand to correct an error during the replication process.

9. How are the base pair mutation and the T-cell dysfunction in the above DNA analysis functionally related?
    a. It appears that the base pair mutation improves with worsened T-cell function.
    b. It appears that the base pair mutation is unrestrained, in part, by T-cell dysfunction. This is likely due to the role T-cells play in protecting the body against precancerous cells with DNA mutation.
    c. They are not directly functionally related. The increased presence of the base pair mutation in the population with T-cell dysfunction does not suggest a functional relationship.
    d. The base pair mutation may be in a locus that encodes T-cells.

10. Could the nucleotide base pair substitution and the base hereditary T-cell dysfunction share linkage?
    a. Given the marked increase in T-cell dysfunction in the population with base pair mutation, that is a likely possibility.
    b. It is unlikely given that the base pair mutation was an incidental finding.
    c. They cannot be linked on the same gene because the incidence of T-cell dysfunction is not equal to the incidence of base pair mutation.
    d. The loci of the two genes must be located near each other to establish linkage. Because T-cell function is being compared to a mutation, it cannot be established whether the conditions are located on the same gene.

11. How may RNA polymerase affect the outcome of the mutation during transcription?
    a. RNA polymerase may correct the mutation during transcription, analogously to the way that DNA polymerase may aid in repairing a mutation.
    b. RNA polymerase aids in building the mRNA molecule, which should faithfully copy the code on the DNA template, maintaining the code determined by the mutation.
    c. RNA polymerase may form transfer RNA (tRNA) molecules that match amino acids to the messenger RNA (mRNA) strand during transcription.
    d. RNA polymerase allows the rRNA molecules to join a stream of abnormal mRNA molecules to amino acids, which may exaggerate the effects of the mutation.

12. How may a DNA base pair substitution during meiosis affect the longevity of the mutation?
    a. The mutation may continue to affect the individual for the duration of his or her life, depending on its impact on the resulting protein.
    b. The mutation will only affect half of the divided cells due to the segregation of homologous chromosomes during cell division during meiosis and thus will only be partially expressed in the individual.
    c. The mutation will only affect one-fourth of the divided cells due to the segregation of homologous chromosomes during cell division during meiosis. Because the resulting cells are only haploid cells, the consequences will be less significant.
    d. The mutation will affect only germ cells, and thus it may be carried to the offspring, but it will not affect the individual in whom the mutation occurred.

Glucose 6-phosphate dehydrogenase (G6PD) deficiency is a condition in which the G6PD enzyme is deficient. This enzyme is necessary for the metabolism of certain medications such as sulfa medications and some foods such as fava beans. Symptoms include life-threatening hemolysis shortly after the ingestion of food or medication that requires G6PD for proper metabolism. Currently, there is a blood test available that can measure the presence and quantity of G6PD, but there is not a reliable genetic test for the condition. This is an X-linked recessive disorder.

A pregnant woman, Stephanie, has a family history of G6PD deficiency, but she does not have G6PD deficiency. Stephanie's father does not have the condition, and Stephanie has male cousins on her mother's side of the family who have G6PD deficiency.

13. How can one determine with certainty and without a genetic test if Stephanie is a carrier?
    a. Measure Stephanie's G6PD level.
    b. Perform a fetal ultrasound.
    c. In the absence of a genetic test, there is no way to know for certain whether Stephanie is a carrier for the condition unless she gives birth to a son who has the condition.
    d. Give her fava beans or sulfa medications and observe the reaction.

14. How would an X-linked gene be expressed as codominance in an individual's phenotype?
    a. If a female carries a nucleotide sequence on her X-chromosome that is homozygous to the nucleotide sequence on her other X-chromosome in the corresponding locus, she will express a codominant phenotype.
    b. If a female carries a heterozygous nucleotide sequence for a genome on the corresponding loci of both of her X-chromosomes, her phenotype will express characteristics encoded by both genomes if both sequences code for proteins that may exist and function in each other's presence.
    c. If a male carries a gene on his X-chromosome that is homozygous to the gene on his Y-chromosome, he will express codominance.
    d. If a male carries a heterozygous nucleotide sequence for a genome on his X-chromosome and his Y-chromosome, his phenotype will express characteristics encoded by both genomes if both sequences code for proteins that may exist and function in each other's presence.

15. If you were to learn that G6PD deficiency is more prevalent among populations that are exposed to malaria, how would you distinguish between an evolutionarily adaptive protection against malaria and a link between sickle-cell disease and G6PD deficiency?

   a. Because sickle-cell disease is also more prevalent among populations that are exposed to malaria, and because they are both X-linked conditions affecting red blood cells, they are linked by the X-chromosome.

   b. One would have to assess how frequently the two disorders occur together and separately and compare that with how frequently sickle-cell disease occurs with and separately from other disorders that occur with the same frequency as G6PD deficiency in this population.

   c. One would have to assess the frequency with which both diseases are present in the population versus the frequency with which both genetic alterations are present in the population to determine whether the genetic correspondence is equivalent to the disease correspondence.

   d. One would have to expose red blood cells of individuals with G6PD enzyme and individuals without G6PD enzyme to malaria to determine whether it is, in fact the malaria that contributed to the prevalence among the population or whether it is a genetic link.

16. How could the proteins encoded by a recessive genome differ from the proteins encoded by a dominant genome?

   a. The genome of a dominant gene codes for products that essentially cancel out the effect of the products encoded by a recessive gene on the same locus of a homologous chromosome.

   b. The proteins encoded by a recessive genome are shorter and more easily denature than proteins encoded by dominant genes on the same locus of a homologous chromosome.

   c. The proteins encoded by a recessive genome are generally not produced in the presence of a dominant gene on the same locus of a homologous chromosome.

   d. The genome of a dominant gene activates transcription and translation more effectively than the genome of a recessive gene.

17. How could the development of immunization against malaria affect the prevalence of G6PD deficiency?

   a. Because G6PD deficiency has been found to provide partial immunity against malaria, immunization against malaria would be expected to reduce the incidence of G6PD over several generations in regions with a high exposure to malaria.

   b. Because G6PD deficiency is present in the population in regions with a high exposure to malaria, the evolutionary adaptation has already occurred and is unlikely to change.

   c. Because G6PD deficiency is a hemolytic disease, an immunization against malaria would protect individuals with G6PD deficiency from the hemolytic effects of malaria and allow the disease to become more prevalent in the population.

   d. Because G6PD deficiency only provides partial protection against malaria, an immunization against malaria may or may not affect the prevalence of G6PD deficiency in the population. The prevalence would depend, most importantly, on the mortality of the G6PD itself.

18. How could administration of G6PD enzyme determine whether the triggers for the hemolytic reaction include sulfa medications and fava beans and whether there are other triggers?
    a. Administration of the enzyme could be given whenever a hemolytic reaction occurs.
    b. Administration of the enzyme could be given at random intervals to determine the intensity of hemolytic reactions to various exposures.
    c. Administration of the enzyme could be withheld in order to determine the source of the hemolytic reactions.
    d. Administration of the enzyme could be given when there is exposure to sulfa medications or fava beans, but not during other times, to evaluate whether a hemolytic reaction occurs in the absence of these exposures.

Question Set 4

Carbohydrates and proteins provide the body with four calories per gram, whereas fats provide the body with nine calories per gram.
Glucose, a simple carbohydrate molecule, enters the Krebs cycle after glycolysis yields only two ATP molecules, pyruvate and acetyl coenzyme A (acetyl-CoA). The reduced form of nicotinamide adenine dinucleotide (NADH) and flavin adenine dinucleotide (FADH2) formed in both glycolysis and the Krebs cycle subsequently enter the electron transport chain.
Complex polysaccharide carbohydrates take longer for the body to digest, absorb, and metabolize than simple monosaccharide carbohydrates.
Fatty acids are broken down to acetyl CoA, which is used in the Krebs cycle, and NADH and FADH2, which enter the electron transport chain.
Saturated fatty acids differ from unsaturated fatty acids in several ways. Saturated fatty acids are less likely to become rancid. Yet, researchers have noted an association with heart disease that makes saturated fatty acids somewhat less desirable. The causative link between saturated fatty acids and heart disease is not completely understood.

19. What chemical differences between monosaccharides and polysaccharides explains their differences in metabolism?
    a. Polysaccharides are larger molecules containing more subunits than monosaccharides, and therefore they take longer for enzymes to break down to small molecules for absorption.
    b. Polysaccharides are larger molecules containing more subunits than monosaccharides and therefore they contain more electron bonds, which produce more energy per gram.
    c. Polysaccharides are molecules with a more complex chemical configuration, and thus they enter the Krebs cycle after an initial modification, similar to the initial step of fatty acid metabolism.
    d. Polysaccharides must be broken down into small glucose subunits prior to glycolysis, and therefore it takes longer for the body to metabolize polysaccharides than monosaccharides, but they yield the same number of calories per gram.

20. How do the differences between unsaturated fatty acids and saturated fatty acids contribute to the increased tendency of unsaturated fatty acids to become rancid?
    a. Fatty acids with only single bonds are more stable and less likely to interact with other molecules in the environment, which could cause them to change their chemical structure and become rancid.
    b. Saturated fatty acids are completely saturated with electrons and therefore they are not as easily disrupted.
    c. Unsaturated fatty acids are more likely to be liquid at room temperature, so they can more quickly reach a boiling point, making them unstable molecules.
    d. Unsaturated fatty acids can have a trans configuration, and trans fats are more unstable molecules that have a higher tendency to become rancid.

21. How should unsaturated fatty acids and saturated fatty acids compare in energy yield?
    a. They should yield nine calories per kilogram. This number is primarily based on the number of bonds, which are equivalent in saturated and unsaturated fatty acids.
    b. They should yield nine calories per kilogram, which is based on the number of single bonds. There are more single bonds in saturated than in unsaturated fats, so there is a slight difference in caloric yield, with saturated fats yielding more calories than unsaturated fats.
    c. They should yield nine calories per kilogram, with some slight differences based on the relative stability. Because saturated fats are more stable molecules, they are more difficult to digest and absorb, and, because they contain some indigestible portions, they yield slightly fewer calories than unsaturated fats, which are easier to digest and absorb.
    d. It depends on the size and shape of the molecule and how many bonds are present.

22. How do the calories produced from glycolysis compare to the calories produced in the Krebs cycle and the electron transport chain?
    a. There are fewer calories produced from glycolysis than from either the Krebs cycle or from the electron transport chain.
    b. The net calories produced in glycolysis are equivalent to the net calories produced in the Krebs cycle, but fewer than those produced in the electron transport chain.
    c. The net calories produced in glycolysis are greater than the calories produced during the Krebs cycle, but fewer than those produced in the electron transport chain.
    d. The net calories produced in glycolysis are fewer than the calories produced in the Krebs cycle, but more than those produced in the electron transport chain.

23. If you were to design an experiment to better understand why there is a stronger causative relationship between saturated fatty acids and heart disease than between unsaturated fatty acids and heart disease, which of the following would you need to control?
    a. The polyunsaturated fat content versus monounsaturated fat content consumed.
    b. The number of total calories consumed by research subjects.
    c. The baseline heart condition of subjects participating in the experiment, to avoid confounding bias.
    d. The number of calories of fat consumed, to ensure that the relationship is not based on the slightly higher calorie yield of saturated fats.

24. How does oxygen affect metabolism?
    a. Oxygen is required for metabolism glucose.
    b. Oxygen can allow for the production of more ATP molecules in each step of the metabolic process, including glycolysis, the Krebs cycle, and the electron transport chain.
    c. Oxygen makes metabolism more efficient because glycolysis, which does not require oxygen, produces a low energy yield.
    d. Oxygen can accept hydrogen atoms at the end of the electron transport chain, yielding a rich supply of ATP.

Question Set 5

When blood flow to human tissue is interrupted, the lack of sufficient blood supply is called ischemia. If ischemia is not restored quickly, the affected tissue may undergo a process called infarction, which involves a series of chemical changes that damage the tissue.

The lack of blood supply results in lack of oxygen, and thus lactic acidosis. Mitochondrial dysfunction results.

Microscopic examination and chemical analysis of ischemic cells reveal membrane degeneration, excessive calcium (Ca+) inside the cell, and free radical formation, accompanied by a reactive inflammation and free fatty acid formation.

A research experiment is designed to evaluate the response of infarcted tissue to intra-arterial administration of an antioxidant. Preliminary results demonstrate that follow-up evaluation of tissue exposed to intra-arterial antioxidant injection resulted, on average, in a smaller area of infarcted tissue after seven days when compared to controls without exposure to the antioxidant. It was noted that 70% of the patients who demonstrated smaller areas of infarction also had a notable decease in edema of the ischemic tissue lasting about 6 to 10 hours after injection.

25. What is a possible explanation for the relationship among antioxidant injection, edema, and tissue damage?
    a. Antioxidants produce anti-infarction biochemical reactions that decrease the size of the infarct.
    b. Antioxidants decrease tissue damage by decreasing edema.
    c. The prevention of tissue damage may be produced by a combination of the effect of decreased edema and the injection of antioxidants.
    d. Increased blood flow causes paradoxical tissue damage due to ischemia.

26. How would mitochondrial dysfunction contribute to calcium influx?
    a. Active transport, which maintains Ca+ concentrations inside and outside the cell, requires ATP, which is produced by the mitochondria.
    b. Mitochondrial membranes contain Ca+, and thus degeneration of mitochondrial membranes leaks Ca+ into the cell's cytoplasm.
    c. The mitochondria are the site of ATP production. ATP is required to maintain Ca+ movement against the concentration gradient.
    d. The lack of oxygen results in metabolic acidosis, and the ionic shift permits Ca+ into the cell.

27. How could lactic acid production and free fatty acid formation contribute to organelle dysfunction?
　　a. The acidity of these molecular products, when uncorrected, alters the cell's pH beyond that which the cell can compensate for. Organelles, containing proteins, denature as a result.
　　b. Lactic acid production and free fatty acid formation function like free radicals, altering the structure of the molecular components of the organelles.
　　c. Lactic acids and free fatty acids crowd the organelles within the cells, preventing them from communicating with each other in the cytoplasm.
　　d. Lactic acids and free fatty acids are hydrophobic and thus can enter the membranes of the organelles, disrupting their function.

28. Why does a lack of blood supply cause lactic acidosis?
　　a. Organelle membranes are composed of hydrophilic lactic acid, which is released during organelle apoptosis.
　　b. Without inadequate oxygen, cell metabolism formation must follow an alternate pathway, which uses the pyruvate produced in glycolysis and produces lactic acid as a by-product.
　　c. Lactic acidosis provides quick bursts of energy, which the cell needs to counteract the effects of infarction.
　　d. Lactic acidosis is the result of lactic acid production because lactose is a sugar that can provide energy. It is present in dairy products.

29. Why does membrane degeneration contribute to inflammation?
　　a. The infarcted cell membrane becomes infected by microorganisms already present in the body, as evidenced by the presence of bacteria on microscopic examination of infarcted tissue.
　　b. Inflammatory cells are a component of the edematous fluid present during infarction.
　　c. The white blood cells that are present in inflammation are generally a normal component of the body and are no longer contained, due to membrane degeneration, and they are able to leak down the concentration gradient.
　　d. The cell becomes altered and the body attempts to repair itself and "clean up" debris produced by cellular degeneration.

30. What is the difference between membrane leakiness and capillary leakiness?
　　a. The leaky membrane of the capillary can allow cells to leak out, whereas the membrane of the leaky cell can allow fluid to leak out.
　　b. Membrane leakiness is a consequence of degeneration of the cell membrane and dysfunction of membrane protein channels and pumps, whereas capillary leakiness results in edema due to capillary permeability.
　　c. Membrane leakiness is the result of degeneration of the phospholipid bilayer of the cell, whereas capillary leakiness is the cause of degeneration of the phospholipid bilayer.
　　d. Membrane leakiness causes edema, whereas capillary leakiness causes inflammation.

Regulatory proteins and hormones direct embryogenesis. Germ cells originate in the embryo during the second trimester. Later, gametogenesis occurs.

The development of epithelial tissue and neuronal tissue from the common ectodermal precursor occurs in the first month after fertilization, and then cells continue to differentiate.

The mesoderm forms the heart and muscles during the first month, and the heart begins to function within the first four weeks after fertilization. Complete pulmonary function is not established until later in gestation.

31. How are genetic disorders different from developmental disorders?
    a. Genetic disorders are physical conditions, whereas developmental disorders are more complex disorders involving emotional and cognitive processing.
    b. Genetic disorders are caused by an inherited trait encoded on the DNA, whereas developmental disorders are caused by DNA damage due to environmental factors during embryogenesis.
    c. Genetic disorders are caused by alterations in the gene, whereas developmental disorders are caused by alterations in cellular differentiation.
    d. Developmental disorders may be caused by genetic alterations or by environmental causes or by unknown causes and include a diverse group of conditions characterized by physical, speech, emotional, or cognitive dysfunction.

32. How would nondisjunction affect the chromosome number of a gamete?
    a. Nondisjunction would result in a gamete that does not have exactly 23 chromosomes.
    b. Nondisjunction would result in a gamete that does not have exactly one of each chromosome.
    c. Nondisjunction causes either one more or one fewer than the correct number of chromosomes in the resulting gamete.
    d. Nondisjunction would cause nonhomologous chromosomes to be present in the gamete when there should not be.

33. If a researcher wanted to determine whether embryonic stem cells could differentiate into cells for therapeutic use, how could he or she improve the chances of success?
    a. Use cells from the ectoderm to replace ectodermal tissue, from the endoderm to replace endodermal tissue, or from the mesoderm to replace mesodermal tissue to improve the chances of proper differentiation.
    b. Use a matched-type donor to minimize the chances of transplant rejection.
    c. Use stem cells from the embryonic bone marrow.
    d. Use cells from the gamete because they have not yet differentiated.

34. How would prematurity of about six weeks affect oxygenation?
    a. Pulmonary surfactant is not well developed at this stage, and thus the baby would not have the ability to expand the lungs, leading to poor oxygenation.
    b. The skeletal muscles are not well developed at this stage, and thus inspiration would be impaired, leading to poor oxygenation.
    c. The heart is not well developed at this stage, and thus the baby would not be able to circulate oxygen to the tissue.
    d. The hemoglobin molecule is not well developed at this stage, and thus the baby would not be able to carry enough oxygen through the blood.

35. How do germ layers differ from germ cells?
    a. Germ cells are produced during gametogenesis, whereas germ layers are produced after fertilization.
    b. Germ cells are diploid cells that are precursors to gametes, whereas germ layers are composed of differentiating diploid cells.
    c. Germ layers are different parts of the germ cells.
    d. Germ cells are haploid, whereas germ layers are diploid.

36. How does the chromosome number of the germ cell chromosome produce the resulting chromosome number of a gamete?
    a. A germ cell is haploid and matures into a haploid gamete.
    b. A germ cell is diploid and divides to become two haploid gametes.
    c. A germ cell is diploid, doubles, and then divides into four haploid gametes.
    d. A germ cell is haploid, doubles, and then divides into two haploid gametes.

Question Set 7

Several organisms can invade the human body and cause what is classified as an infection. However, there are vast differences between such infective agents as bacteria, fungi, parasites, viruses, and prions.

37. Which of the following contain diploid genetic material?
    a. Parasites
    b. Bacteria
    c. Prions
    d. Viruses

38. How can a virus evade an immune response?
    a. A retrovirus can invade immune cells.
    b. It is too small to be detected.
    c. It can hide inside a cell.
    d. It can mimic a cell.

39. How does a bacterial cell reproduce?
    a. Binary fission
    b. Conjugation
    c. Sexual reproduction
    d. Insertion of genetic material into the host genome

40. How does a retrovirus differ from a virus?
    a. A retrovirus infects a host cell by inserting genetic material, whereas a virus invades the cell wall.
    b. A retrovirus causes cancer, whereas a virus causes disease.
    c. A retrovirus is an old virus.
    d. A retrovirus genome is composed of RNA, and a viral genome is composed of DNA.

41. What are the structural components of the bacterial cell?
   a. Cell wall and nucleus
   b. Cell membrane, cell wall, and nucleoid
   c. Cytoplasm, nucleus, and nucleoid
   d. Cytoplasm, cell wall, and nucleus

Question Set 8

The endocrine and nervous systems interact with each other in several ways. The hypothalamus, located in the brain, sends messages to the anterior pituitary gland via the hypothalamo-hypophyseal portal system and to the posterior pituitary gland via the hypothalamo-hypophyseal tract. Adrenocorticotropic hormone (ACTH) is released by the anterior pituitary gland and sent via the circulation to the adrenal medulla, which produces neurotransmitters that regulate the autonomic nervous system.

Myelinated axons of the somatic nervous system release acetylcholine, a neurotransmitter that binds to skeletal muscles.

42. How may demyelination of the central nervous system (CNS) affect acetylcholine release from the peripheral nerves?
   a. Demyelination of the CNS would impact the CNS response to peripheral nerve stimulation and thus would not affect acetylcholine release at the neuromuscular junction because that event occurs prior to the stimulus from the peripheral nerve entering the spinal cord.
   b. When demyelination of the CNS occurs, it can slow down the signal in the nerves, slowing down and decreasing the amount of acetylcholine released by the peripheral nerves.
   c. When demyelination of CNS tissue occurs, demyelinated neurons in the brain and/or spinal cord might not transmit an action potential, and thus they might not send messages to the peripheral nerves, which means that acetylcholine will not be released.
   d. Demyelination of the CNS does not affect acetylcholine release from the peripheral nervous system (PNS) because the CNS consists of the brain and spinal cord, whereas the PNS consists of nerves.

43. How does communication differ among the hypothalamus and the anterior and posterior pituitary glands?
   a. The posterior pituitary gland receives electrical signals from the hypothalamus, triggering the production of hormones, whereas the anterior pituitary gland receives hormones from the hypothalamus directly through the blood.
   b. Communication between the hypothalamus and the anterior pituitary gland is via the blood, whereas communication between the hypothalamus and the posterior pituitary gland is via the axons.
   c. Communication between the hypothalamus and the anterior pituitary gland is regulated by negative feedback, whereas communication between the hypothalamus and the posterior pituitary gland is regulated by negative feedback and positive feedback, due to the production of oxytocin.
   d. The hypothalamus communicates with the posterior pituitary gland by inhibiting hormone production and with the anterior pituitary gland by stimulating hormone production.

44. How may negative feedback mechanisms regulate the autonomic nervous system in the setting of a hyperactive pituitary tumor?

a. A hyperactive pituitary tumor may be expected to produce excessive adrenocorticotropic hormone (ACTH), and thus negative feedback due to overstimulation of the autonomic nervous system would reach the hypothalamus as well as the pituitary gland and the adrenal medulla, which would in turn decrease the release of ACTH from the anterior pituitary gland and epinephrine from the adrenal medulla.

b. Negative feedback mechanisms would decrease stimulation of the hypothalamus, which would produce the desired effect on the anterior pituitary gland, effectively maintaining regulation of the autonomic nervous system.

c. Negative feedback mechanisms would inhibit release of hormones that stimulate the sympathetic nervous system so that the parasympathetic nervous system can function properly.

d. A hyperactive pituitary tumor would be expected to produce and release excessive ACTH, so the negative feedback mechanisms would decrease epinephrine production by the adrenal medulla and desensitize the adrenal medulla to the excessive ACTH.

45. If researchers examined a series of CNS specimens to evaluate the rate of serotonin reuptake, how would they measure the effect of additional serotonin on the rate of serotonin reuptake?

a. Researchers would measure the difference between serotonin levels in the controls and the experimental group treated with serotonin immediately after the serotonin has had its desired effects and at several intervals after that.

b. Researchers would measure the quantity of serotonin in controls versus the experimental group treated with serotonin at intervals after the treatment to determine the rate of uptake.

c. Researchers would measure the concentration of serotonin in experimental groups treated with several different concentrations of additional serotonin.

d. Researchers would measure the concentration of serotonin in controls versus the experimental group treated with additional serotonin prior to the experiment and at several intervals after the treatment to determine the rate of reuptake.

46. How do neuroglia differ from neurons in terms of oncologic potential?

a. Neuroglia are supportive cells and thus do not have oncologic potential, whereas neurons, which are highly functioning and are more likely to be affected by toxins and free radicals, have greater oncologic potential.

b. Neuroglia are more prone to retrovirus exposure due to the selective blood-brain barrier protection of neurons, and thus they have greater oncologic potential than do neurons.

c. Neuroglial cells are better able to repair themselves, and they also have a higher oncologic potential than do neurons.

d. Neuroglia are not myelinated, whereas neurons are myelinated, and thus the exposure of neurons to carcinogens is reduced in comparison to neuroglia.

47. How would the optic nerves be impacted by a hypofunctioning adrenal medullary gland?

a. A hypofunctioning adrenal medullary gland would result in compensatory overstimulation of the hypothalamus, which would in turn overstimulate the anterior pituitary gland to release ACTH. The enlargement of the pituitary gland would produce pressure on the optic nerves.

b. A hypofunctioning adrenal medullary gland would directly stimulate activity of the pituitary gland and would result in enlargement of the pituitary gland, putting pressure on the optic nerves.

c. A hypofunctioning adrenal medullary gland would result in inconsistent overstimulation of the pituitary gland, and thus the gland would become intermittently enlarged, periodically putting pressure on the optic nerves.

d. A hypofunctioning adrenal medullary gland would result in inconsistent overstimulation of the hypothalamus and the pituitary gland, but this would not result in enlargement of the pituitary gland and thus not affect the optic nerves.

Question Set 9

Chronic anemia and acute anemia both elicit compensatory mechanisms that maintain homeostasis.

Data from a sample of patients who suffered from chronic anemia, a sample of patients who experienced acute anemia due to traumatic bleeding, and a sample of patients with a normal red blood cell (RBC) count were collected. Using a control baseline of 1 for all values, averages of the relative heart rates, erythropoietin (EPO) levels, blood pressure measurements, and respiratory rates were plotted.

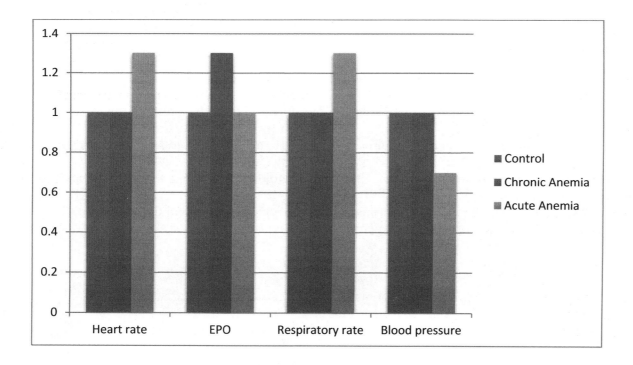

48. Why does the acute anemia in this sample cause a change in heart rate?
    a. Acute anemia results in volume deficit and O_2 deficit due to the loss of RBCs and hemoglobin.
    b. Acute anemia causes lactic acidosis due to conversion to an anaerobic metabolic pathway.
    c. Acute anemia results in CO_2 buildup, which triggers adjustment of the heart rate produced by the sinoatrial (SA) node in the heart, driven by the medulla in the brainstem.
    d. Hemoglobin breakdown, a characteristic of hemolytic anemia, results in lower oxygen-carrying capacity.

49. Which factors are most likely to control erythropoietin levels?
    a. Volume loss as blood flows through the kidneys.
    b. Oxygen concentration in the blood as it flows through the kidneys.
    c. Urine output of the kidneys.
    d. Stem cell activity in the bone marrow.

50. What factor controls blood pressure on acute anemia?
    a. Vasospasm
    b. Arterial regulation
    c. RBC concentration
    d. Venous regulation

51. How do carbon dioxide levels affect respiration?
    a. When carbon dioxide concentrations change, the adrenal medulla adjusts the respiratory rate and volume by sending hormones to adjust the width of the bronchi.
    b. When the carbon dioxide concentration changes, it acts directly on the alveoli, allowing them to expand or contract as necessary.
    c. When carbon dioxide concentrations change, the medulla in the brainstem adjusts the respiratory rate and volume.
    d. When the carbon dioxide concentration changes, receptors on the respiratory muscles adjust the rate and force of inspiration and expiration.

52. How would an agglutination reaction to a blood transfusion affect erythropoietin in the first few minutes?
    a. An agglutination reaction would stimulate erythropoietin production in the kidneys.
    b. An agglutination reaction would stimulate an attenuated response to erythropoietin in bone marrow.
    c. An agglutination reaction would inhibit the release of erythropoietin due to stimulation of the sympathetic nervous system.
    d. An agglutination reaction would maintain the level of erythropoietin within the first few minutes.

53. How would you evaluate the kidneys' response to chronic anemia?
    a. Measure the blood pressure and the erythropoietin production in comparison to controls.
    b. Measure the erythropoietin production and the urine content in comparison to controls.
    c. Measure the urine volume and the erythropoietin level in comparison to controls.
    d. Measure the blood pressure and the antidiuretic hormone in comparison to controls.

Discrete Questions

54. Fetal exposure to excessive quantities of vitamin A, a fat-soluble vitamin, such as the quantities present in some prescription-strength oral acne treatments, have been associated with neural tube defects. Folate deficiency has also been associated with neural tube defects. What would you conclude about folate in the developing fetus?

    a. An adequate supply of folate is important prior to and within the first month of gestation to decrease the risk of neural tube defects.

    b. An adequate supply of folate is necessary during the first month of gestation to prevent neural tube defects.

    c. Folate must be fat soluble, and it is necessary during the first month of gestation to prevent neural tube defects.

    d. Folate intake during pregnancy drives the development of the epidermal tissue of the fetus.

55. How does egg cell morphology differ from that of a sperm cell?

    a. An egg cell has a larger cytoplasm and more mitochondria than a sperm cell.

    b. An egg cell contains an X chromosome, and a sperm cell contains a Y chromosome.

    c. An egg cell has a nucleus, whereas a sperm cell does not.

    d. A sperm cell may be used as a donor in reproductive technology, but an egg cell cannot.

56. Antigens on the surface of pathogens provoke an immune response due to action mediated by

    a. lymphocytes

    b. leukocytes

    c. antibodies produced by B lymphocytes and other leukocytes

    d. antibodies and erythrocytes

57. How do the cell junctions between epithelial cells affect the communication between neighboring cells?

    a. Gap junctions allow a space between neighboring cells, preventing direct contact between neighboring cells, whereas tight junctions form a barrier to prevent fluid from entering between the cells.

    b. Tight junctions firmly attach neighboring cells, decreasing flexibility while increasing strength.

    c. Adhering junctions connect cells to each other to form a barrier against fluid entering between the cells.

    d. Gap junctions connect the cytoplasm between cells, allowing material to flow from one cell to another.

58. If an experiment were designed to determine the conditions that promote gluconeogenesis, which tissue would be studied?

    a. The mitochondria, because gluconeogenesis occurs in the mitochondria of a eukaryotic cell using amino acids.

    b. The slow muscle fibers, because they are rich in mitochondria and may convert to alternate energy pathways such as aerobic respiration.

    c. The liver because the liver is one of the cell types in which gluconeogenesis occurs in the mitochondria, using amino acids.

    d. Adipose tissue because fat cells undergo oxidation to enter the Krebs cycle and the electron transport chain in order to provide the body with energy in the form of ATP.

59. How does a proto-oncogene relate to an oncogene?

    a. A proto-oncogene promotes proliferation of an oncogene.

    b. A proto-oncogene is a normal gene. But if it undergoes a mutation, a proto-oncogene can become an oncogene.

    c. A proto-oncogene is a protein encoded by an oncogene.

    d. An oncogene codes for a mutation that can inhibit apoptosis, whereas a proto-oncogene codes for a mutation that affects mitosis.

Chemical and Physical Foundations

Passage 1

Read the paragraphs below and answer questions 1-5.

Analysis of a protein or food sample for amino acid composition can be critically important in evaluating its nutritive value. Amino Acid Analysis provides this information by hydrolyzing proteins into individual amino acids, separating them chromatographically, and quantitating them. Many different methods are used for these steps, and understanding the properties of proteins and individual amino acids is important in evaluating potential new methods of analysis.

Among the amino acids detected in a particular analysis are those with the properties shown in Table 1.

Table 1. Properties of selected amino acids					
Amino Acid	**Solubility in water (mol/kg at 25°C)**	**pKa$_1$**	**pKa$_2$**	**pK$_a$ R group**	**Specific Rotation $[\alpha]_D^{25}$**
L-Alanine	1.9	2.34	9.69	--	+1.8
L-Lysine	1.7	2.18	8.95	10.53	+13.5
L-Valine	0.50	2.29	9.72	--	+5.6
L-Leucine	0.17	2.36	9.60	--	-11.0
L-Tryptophan	0.065	2.38	9.39	--	-33.7
Unknown	0.060	2.19	9.67	4.25	+12.0

One of the most common ways to separate amino acids is by ion exchange chromatography. A typical amino acid analysis involves using a cation exchange resin consisting of beads of polystyrene sulfonate in a chromatographic column. In this method, the sulfonate groups on the beads are loaded with sodium ions prior to analysis. The fluid containing the amino acids passes down the column, over the beads, and exits at the bottom. Based on properties like those shown in Table 1, some of the amino acids adhere to the beads more strongly. The strongly bound amino acids travel more slowly down the column and the amino acids separate based on their relative adherence to the beads.

1. The peptide below has four labeled bonds. Which of these bonds break during hydrolysis if subjected to 6 M HCl at 110°C for 24 hours?

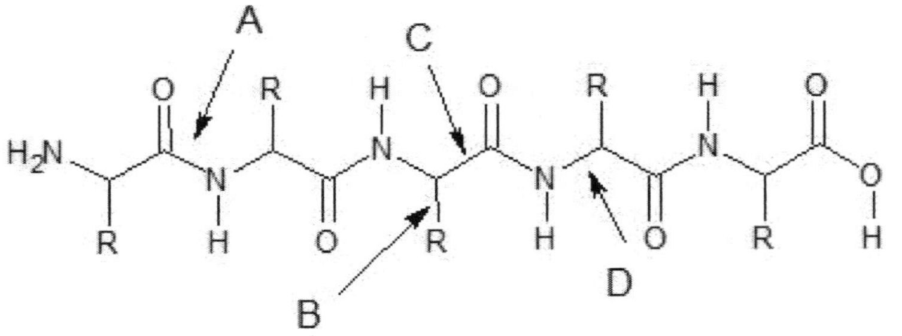

a. Bond A
b. Bond B
c. Bond C
d. Bond D

2. Based on the properties listed in Table 1, the identity of the amino acid labeled as *Unknown* is most likely to be which of the following?
a. L-Phenylalanine
b. L-Glycine
c. L-Cysteine
d. L-Glutamic Acid

3. When the amino acids listed in Table 1 separate by ion exchange chromatography using a cation exchange resin, which of the amino acids is most likely to elute last from the column?
a. L-Lysine
b. L-Valine
c. L-Tryptophan
d. The amino acid labeled *unknown*

4. Which of the following is a correct representation of the structure of L-alanine (which is also correctly known as (S)-Alanine)?

a.

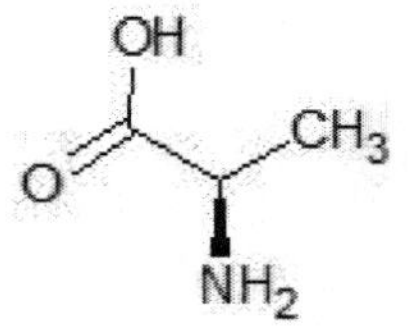

b.

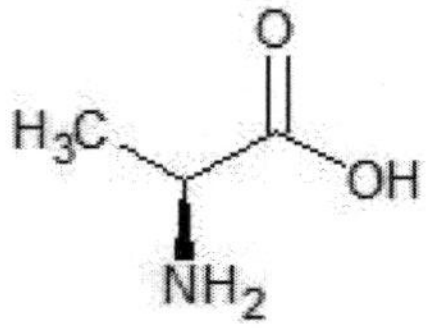

c.

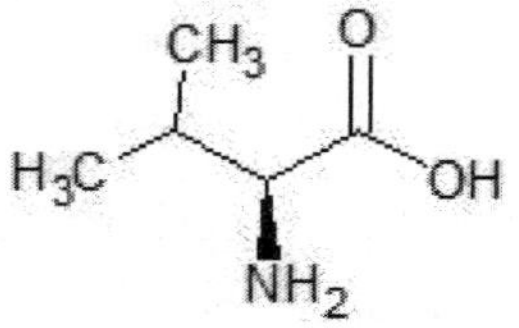

d.

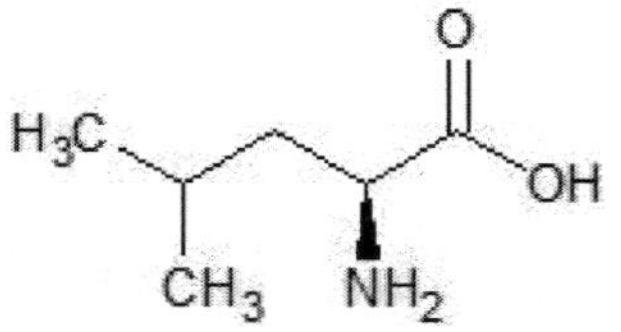

5. Assume that a fluid used in an ion exchange separation of amino acids has a pH of 5. Which of the amino acids in Table 1 provides the most buffering capacity at that pH?

a. L-Alanine
b. L-Lysine
c. L-Leucine
d. The amino acid labeled *unknown*

Passage 2

Read the paragraphs below and answer questions 6-10.

Many of the properties of molecules depend on their shapes. In some cases, such as for nitrogen-containing molecules, the oxidation states of the atoms in the molecule control the shape. Nitrogen can form stable compounds with oxidation states on nitrogen ranging from -3 to +5.

Lewis dot structures and the VSEPR (valence shell electron repulsion) theory can predict the shapes of many compounds. Shown below is the Lewis structure of ammonia, where the nitrogen atom has an oxidation state of -3.

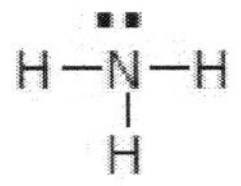

Since there are four regions of paired electrons around the nitrogen atom, we can predict those four regions will spread out as far from one another as possible, resulting in a tetrahedral shape, as shown below.

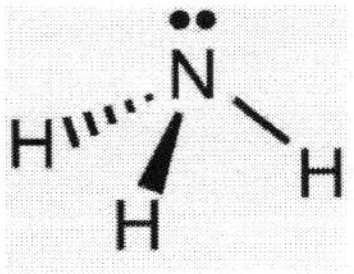

Similar analyses for other nitrogen compounds give the results shown in Table 2.

Table 2. Properties of nitrogen molecules			
Molecule	**Formula**	**Oxidation state of N**	**Shape**
Ammonia	NH_3	-3	trigonal pyramidal
Hydrazine	N_2H_4	-2	trigonal pyramidal at N
Azide ion	N_3^-	-1/3	linear
Dinitrogen	N_2	0	--
Nitrous oxide	N_2O	+1	linear
Nitric oxide	NO	+2	--
Nitrite ion	NO_2^-	+3	bent
Nitrogen dioxide	NO_2	+4	bent
Nitrate ion	NO_3^-	+5	trigonal planar

6. How many valence electrons are there in the Lewis dot structure for nitrate ion?
  a. 5
  b. 8
  c. 23
  d. 24

7. What is the formal charge on the nitrogen atom in the Lewis structure of the nitrite ion?
  a. -1
  b. 0
  c. +1
  d. +3

8. Using the information in Table 2, which of the following molecules ALL have a dipole moment?
  a. Ammonia, nitrous oxide, and nitrogen dioxide
  b. Ammonia, nitric oxide, nitrogen dioxide
  c. Nitrous oxide, nitric oxide, nitrogen dioxide
  d. Ammonia, dinitrogen, nitrous oxide

9. There are several resonance structures for the azide ion. Which is the major contributor to the actual ion structure?
  a. $N\equiv N^+ \!\!-N^{2-}$
  b. $N = N - N^-$
  c. $N^- \!\!= N^+ \!\!= N^-$
  d. $N = N = N^-$

10. One nitrite ion and one azide ion can react with each other in acid (using 2 H⁺) so that all of the nitrogen atoms change their oxidation state. The products of this reaction are one dinitrogen molecule and which other compound(s)?
  a. Nitric oxide
  b. Nitric oxide and water
  c. Nitrous oxide
  d. Nitrous oxide and water

Passage 3

Read the paragraphs below and answer questions 11-15.

^{32}P-labeled phosphate has numerous uses in both biomedical research and in clinical patient therapy. One use is as a palliative treatment for patients with painful bone metastasis. Bone takes up the phosphate and it delivers its radiation locally. The standard method of production involves bombardment of ^{32}S with neutrons. The sulfur takes on a neutron and simultaneously ejects a proton to become ^{32}P.

Direct neutron capture by ^{31}P allows a manufacturing process with improved product purity and less radioactive waste. In that process, red phosphorus was bombarded with neutrons at a rate of 8×10^{13} neutrons/(cm²·s) for 60 days. The final step involves conversion of the product into sodium phosphate and addition to sterile vials for injection. Table 3 shows the results.

Table 3. Properties of ^{32}P-phosphate made by direct neutron capture	
Property	**Result**
Radioactive half-life	14.29 days
Specific Activity	6.2±0.4 mCi/mg
Radionuclide purity	>99.9%
Radiopurity with respect to phosphate	~99%
Activity per dose	10–15 mCi
pH	7.4
Type of decay	Beta
Energy released	1.709 MeV

11. Adding phosphate to a solution containing calcium can result in a precipitate. This precipitate most likely has which stoichiometry?
   a. $CaPO_3$
   b. $CaPO_4$
   c. $Ca_2(PO_4)_3$
   d. $Ca_3(PO_4)_2$

12. An extended *in vivo* experiment involves studying the distribution and excretion of injected ^{32}P-phosphate in mice using the product manufactured by direct neutron capture with ^{31}P. The entire experiment lasts for 43 days. Compared to the radioactivity of the initial phosphate dosed to the animals, how much of the initial radioactivity remained when the experiment ends?
   1. 100%
   b. 87.6%
   c. 12.4%
   d. 1.24%

13. An extended *in vivo* experiment involves studying the distribution and excretion of injected ^{32}P-phosphate mice. Samples from each day of the 43-day experiment were stored in a -80°C freezer until analysis on day 54. Which of the following attributes of the storage conditions affects the total radioactivity of each sample?
    a. pH in the sample before freezing
    b. Temperature in the freezer
    c. Calcium concentration in the sample before freezing
    d. The storage conditions will not influence radioactivity

14. When ^{32}P decays, the product is which of the following?
    a. $^{32}_{16}S$
    b. $^{32}_{16}S^+$
    c. $^{32}_{14}Si$
    d. $^{32}_{14}Si^-$

15. Graphite is an important material in the construction of nuclear reactors. One drawback is the production of radioactive ^{14}C in the graphite by direct neutron capture, causing the material to become a long-term waste disposal problem. Which of the following materials in the graphite is the most likely atom to capture of a single neutron and become ^{14}C?
    a. $^{13}_{7}N$
    b. $^{12}_{6}C$
    c. $^{13}_{6}C$
    d. $^{14}_{5}N$

Passage 4

Read the paragraphs below and answer questions 16-20.

Bilirubin is a waste product that the body produces as it breaks down hemoglobin, and excessive bilirubin in the body can be an indicator of disease. Bilirubin is colored, and this absorption of light can be used both as a way to detect bilirubin in blood samples, and as a way to therapeutically treat excessive bilirubin in the body. Shown below is the structure of bilirubin:

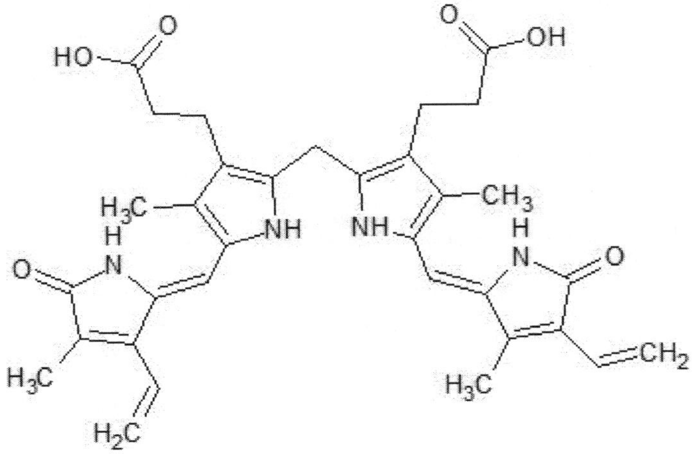

Hemoglobin O_2 can interfere with the absorbance measurements used to measure bilirubin because they both absorb light in the range from 360 to 500 nm (see Table 4). In order to subtract the contribution of hemoglobin to absorbance of bilirubin in a measurement at 457 nm, the hemoglobin concentration is first determined by measuring absorbance at 582 nm, where the bilirubin does not absorb. The expected absorbance of the hemoglobin at 457 nm is then calculated and subtracted from the actual measurement at 457 nm to get the absorbance due to bilirubin alone.

Using this method allows bilirubin in the sera of newborns with levels of 100-400 µM to be measured to within a few percent despite the potential presence of up to 25 g/L of hemoglobin O_2 (390 µM of the tetramer).

Table 4. Optical Properties of bilirubin and hemoglobin O_2		
Compound	Molar Absorption Coefficient at 457 nm ($M^{-1}cm^{-1}$)	Molar Absorption Coefficient at 457 nm ($M^{-1}cm^{-1}$)
Bilirubin	48,907	17
Hemoglobin O_2	48,496	43,304

16. The light used to detect bilirubin in the passage is which color?
    a. Red
    b. Yellow
    c. Green
    d. Blue

- 237 -

17. What is the energy of the photons used to detect bilirubin in the passage? The following constants may be useful: speed of light in vacuum = 3.00×10^8 m/s; Faraday constant = 96 485.3 C/mole; Planck's constant = 4.1×10^{-15} eV/s
    a. 0.27 eV
    b. 2.07 eV
    c. 2.7 eV
    d. 27 eV

18. The transmittance of a particular bilirubin sample is 0.85 in a cuvette with a path length of 1 cm. If analysis of the same sample takes place in a cuvette with a path length of 3 cm, what will the transmittance be?
    a. 0.39
    b. 0.55
    c. 0.61
    d. 0.85

19. What is the expected absorbance of a 1.0 μM bilirubin standard at 457 nm in a cuvette with a path length of 2 cm?
    a. 0.010
    b. 0.050
    c. 0.10
    d. 0.50

20. Which of the following structures made by modifying bilirubin would not absorb visible light?

a.

b.

c.

d.

Passage 5

Read the paragraphs below and answer questions 21-25.

One of the important impacts of the burning of fossil fuels and the elevation of the carbon dioxide concentration in the atmosphere relates to the impact of this additional carbon dioxide on the oceans. In order to study this effect, Pat begins a series of experiments to understand how carbon dioxide influences the solubility of calcium carbonate in the ocean. The shells and skeletons of many organisms, such as clams and corals, are made of calcium carbonate, and its solubility may have an impact on their ability to survive.

The solubility of calcium carbonate is governed by the solubility product constant K_{sp}
$$K_{sp} = [Ca^{2+}][CO_3^{2-}]$$

Carbon dioxide can affect this relationship by dissolving into the water as carbonic acid:
$$CO_2 + H_2O \longleftrightarrow H_2CO_3$$

The concentration of carbonate required in the K_{sp} relates to the pH through the acid/base properties of carbonic acid, bicarbonate and carbonate:
$$H_2CO_3 \leftrightarrow HCO_3^- + H^+ \quad pK_{a1}$$
$$HCO_3^- \leftrightarrow CO_3^{2-} + H^+ \quad pK_{a2}$$

where pK_{a1} and pK_{a2} are the pK_a values for carbonic acid and bicarbonate, respectively. Table 1 shows the pK_a values for these two reactions in seawater as a function of temperature:

Table 5. pK$_a$ values for carbonic acid and bicarbonate in seawater as a function of temperature		
Temperature (°C)	pK$_{a1}$	pK$_{a2}$
5	6.05	9.28
15	5.94	9.09
25	5.85	8.92
35	5.76	8.75

21. Knowing the pK_a values from Table 5 and that the pH of ordinary seawater is approximately 8.2, what form of dissolved carbon dioxide predominates in the ocean at 25°C?
    a. Carbonic Acid
    b. Bicarbonate
    c. Carbonate
    d. Not enough information is given

- 240 -

22. Starting with a mixture of solid calcium carbonate in equilibrium with seawater, Pat adds enough solid sodium carbonate to double the carbonate concentration. She then waits until a new equilibrium is established. Which of the following is the best description of the resulting mixture?
  a. Compared to the starting mixture, the dissolved calcium concentration rose
  b. Compared to the starting mixture, the dissolved calcium concentration dropped
  c. Compared to the starting mixture, the dissolved calcium concentration remained the same
  d. Some of the solid calcium carbonate dissolved

23. Starting with a mixture of solid calcium carbonate in equilibrium with seawater, Pat adds enough solid calcium carbonate to double the amount of undissolved calcium carbonate in the mixture. She then waits until a new equilibrium is established. Which of the following is the best description of the resulting solution?
  a. There is no change in the dissolved concentration of calcium or carbonate
  b. The dissolved calcium rises and the dissolved carbonate falls
  c. The dissolved calcium falls and the dissolved carbonate rises
  d. Both the dissolved calcium and the dissolved carbonate rise

24. Pat knows that adding carbon dioxide to seawater will lower the pH, and to study the system she starts by studying the addition of a strong acid, hydrochloric acid, to seawater. She starts with seawater at pH 8.2 and adds 1 M hydrochloric acid until the pH reaches 7.8. Compared to the solution she started with, which of the following statements is true for the final solution, based on the known pK_a values?
  a. The carbonate concentration rose and the carbonic acid concentration fell
  b. The carbonate concentration fell and the carbonic acid concentration rose
  c. Both the carbonate and carbonic acid concentrations fell
  d. Both the carbonate and carbonic acid concentrations rose

25. Pat is also worried about the effect of a rise in the ocean temperature on the potential solubility of calcium carbonate. She initially considers just the effect of temperature on the pK_a values in Table 1, and how those impact the concentration of carbonate in the ocean. In considering a rise in temperature from 25°C to 30°C, what happens to the concentration of carbonate in seawater?
  a. As the temperature rises, bicarbonate becomes a stronger acid, so carbonate rises
  b. As the temperature rises, bicarbonate becomes a weaker acid, so carbonate rises
  c. As the temperature rises, bicarbonate becomes a stronger acid, so carbonate falls
  d. As the temperature rises, bicarbonate becomes a weaker acid, so carbonate falls

Passage 6

Read the paragraphs below and answer questions 26-30.

The human knee joint forms a complex connection between the femur and the tibia. It is subjected to considerable forces, both when standing still and when in motion. These forces can eventually damage the knee and cause considerable pain and disability. Table 6 shows the measured forces on the knee for a variety of activities, as well as the flex angle of the knee during those activities. The forces on the knee vary with the body weight of the individual, so the forces shown in Table 6 are normalized for these differences.

Table 6. Flex angle and compressive force on the knee		
Activity	Knee Flex Angle (°)	Normalized Peak Compressive Force on Knee (times body weight)*
Cycling	60-100	1.2
Walking	15	3.0
Stairs	60	3.8
Stairs	45	4.3
Squat-rise	140	5.0
Squat-down	140	5.6
*Calculated from peak force divided by (body mass times acceleration due to gravity (9.8 m/s²))		

Since the forces acting on the knee joint are a function of body mass, a study in obese individuals demonstrated the effect of body mass reduction on these forces. Table 7 shows the changes in body mass and BMI over the course of this study.

Table 7. Weight loss during study		
Parameter	Baseline Values (kg ± SEM)	After Weight Loss (kg/m² ± SEM)
Body Mass	93.2 ± 1.3	90.8 ± 1.4
Body Mass Index	34.0 ± 0.4	33.0 ± 0.4

After adjusting each patient for baseline body mass, the reduction in peak compressive force on the knee while walking was found to be statistically significant (P = 0.002). Each 1 kg reduction in body mass was associated with a 40.6 N (1.4%) reduction in compressive force.

26. A woman with a body mass of 55 kg is standing up straight and not moving. Assuming the mass of each leg below her knee is 2.5 kg, what is the vertical force acting on each knee joint?
 a. 245 N
 b. 270 N
 c. 490 N
 d. 539 N

27. A woman with a body mass of 55 kg is walking with a knee flex angle of 15°. What is the peak compressive force on her knee?
 a. 81 N
 b. 539 N
 c. 1617 N
 d. 3593 N

28. Based on the data in the passage, a woman who loses body mass from 55 to 53 kg would have peak compressive forces on her knee while walking change in what way compared to before the weight loss?
 a. Increase by 1.4%
 b. Increase by 2.8%
 c. Decrease by 1.4%
 d. Decrease by 2.8%

29. A 65 kg woman descends twelve stairs with a total height of 3 m. She uses a 45°-knee flex angle. What is the decrease in her gravitational potential energy from descending the stairs?
 a. 195 J
 b. 819 J
 c. 1911 J
 d. 8217 J

30. At the end of a cycling test to evaluate knee joint force, the cyclists stopped rapidly. How much energy is required to stop a 70 kg man on a 5 kg bicycle, both of which are travelling 8 m/s?
 a. 280 J
 b. 560 J
 c. 2240 J
 d. 2400 J

Passage 7

Read the paragraphs below and answer questions 31-35.

The physical properties of molecules are very dependent on their molecular shapes and sizes. Alcohols, for example, form a series where the trends of physical properties with size and shape can be clearly seen (Table 8). Boiling point, heat capacity, and the enthalpy of vaporization all rise substantially as the molecular weight increases.

Likewise, these properties vary significantly for different shapes of alcohols, as seen by comparing the two isomers of propanol and the three isomers of butanol. In the case of the butanols in the table, tert-butanol has the highest heat capacity, but the lowest boiling point and enthalpy of vaporization.

Table 8. Physical properties of alcohols			
Alcohol	Boiling Point (°C)	$\Delta_{vap}H°$ (kJ/mol)	Heat Capacity (liquid; J/mol·°C; at 25 °C)
methanol	65	38	81
ethanol	78	42	112
n-propanol	97	47	144
2-propanol	82	45	89
n-butanol	118	52	177
sec-butanol	100	48	198
tert-butanol	82	46	215
n-pentanol	138	57	208
n-hexanol	158	61	240

31. The boiling point, heat of vaporization, and heat capacity of n-hexanol are all considerably higher than the same properties of methanol. The reason that best explains that result is:
   a. n-Hexanol is more effective at hydrogen bonding because it has a higher molecular weight than methanol.
   b. n-Hexanol is more effective at hydrogen bonding because of its longer alkyl chain than methanol.
   c. n-Hexanol is more effective at London dispersion interactions because it has a higher surface area than methanol.
   d. n-Hexanol is more effective at ionic interactions because it has more carbon atoms than methanol.

32. How much energy is required to raise 23 grams of liquid ethanol at 72°C to its boiling point?
   a. 138 J
   b. 336 J
   c. 672 J
   d. 1120 J

- 244 -

33. How much energy is required to convert 64 grams of liquid methanol to vapor at the same temperature?
   a. 19 J
   b. 38 J
   c. 76 J
   d. 76,000 J

34. What is the minimum increase in entropy required for the vaporization of hexanol to be spontaneous at 25°C?
   a. 178 J/(mole · K)
   b. 53.2 J/(mole · K)
   c. 24.0 J/(mole · K)
   d. 1.58 J/(mole · K)

35. Which if the following is NOT an isomer of *tert*-butanol (boiling point = 82°C)?
   a. diethyl ether (boiling point = 35°C)
   b. 2-methoxypropane (boiling point = 39°C)
   c. 2-methyl-1-propanol (boiling point = 108°C)
   d. 3-methyl-1-butanol (boiling point = 131°C)

Passage 8

Read the paragraphs below and answer questions 36-40.

The need for artificial devices for surgical replacement of damaged arteries is significant, but the demands put on the devices provide a difficult challenge for engineers. Evaluation of prototypes consisting of polymer tubing of various diameters is the first step toward developing such products.

John devised two different types of devices. One is rigid and retains its dimensions regardless of the internal pressure. The second type can expand slightly as the internal pressure increases, just as natural arteries can. For both types, testing involves a variety of different diameter tubes.

Table 9 shows some of his early testing of the flow rate of water through fixed lengths of tubing. The elastic tubing samples showed slightly higher flow rates than the rigid tubing of the same internal diameter. Using this data, John can evaluate whether the elastic tubing is expanding in a useful way compared to the rigid tubing, and whether either can do the job required.

Table 9. Evaluation of tubing as artificial arteries				
Sample	**Inner Diameter (mm)**	**Elastic**	**Rigid**	**Flow Rate (mL/min)***
A	10	No	Yes	160
B	8	No	Yes	65
C	4	No	Yes	4.1
D	1	No	Yes	0.02
E	10	Yes	No	187
F	8	Yes	No	77
G	4	Yes	No	4.8
H	1	Yes	No	0.02
*Measured with a pressure of 110 mm Hg at the proximal end and open to the air at the distal end.				

36. Which of the following represents the best ranking of the relative blood pressure in the different parts of the circulatory system?
    a. veins > venules > capillaries > arterioles > arteries
    b. arterioles > arteries > capillaries > veins > venules
    c. arteries > arterioles > capillaries > venules > veins
    d. arteries > capillaries > arterioles > venules > veins

37. Which of the following is the primary benefit provided by the elasticity of natural arteries?
    a. The minimum diastolic blood pressure is lower
    b. Blood continues to flow between beats of the heart
    c. Oxygen more readily diffuses from the arteries
    d. The walls of the arteries can be thinner than veins

38. In the initial calibration of the device to measure the flow rate through the artificial arteries, a scientist attaches a pressure gauge to the distal end of each tube. With the pressure gauge attached, the pump is turned on, but there is no flow because the gauge blocks the fluid. Which expression best describes the pressure at the end of Sample C compared the pressure at the end of Sample A?
    a. Sample C shows 25% of the pressure of Sample A
    b. Sample C shows 400% of the pressure of Sample A
    c. Sample C shows 2.6% of the pressure of Sample A
    d. Both show the same pressure

39. If the pressure of the pump used to drive the flow of the test fluid is increased from 110 mm Hg to 160 mm Hg, the flow from Sample B is most likely to be which of the following?
    a. 95 mL/min
    b. 85 mL/min
    c. 75 mL/min
    d. 65 mL/min

40. Repeating the experiments in Table 9 with whole blood instead of water gives different results. Using a whole blood sample that has viscosity four times that of water, what is the expected flow rate of whole blood through Sample G with a starting pressure of 110 mm Hg?
    a. 1.2 mL/min
    b. 1.6 mL/min
    c. 2.4 mL/min
    d. 4.8 mL/min

Passage 9

Read the paragraphs below and answer questions 41-45.

When carbon dioxide dissolves in biological solutions such as blood, it equilibrates with a number of different forms, including unhydrated carbon dioxide, carbonic acid, bicarbonate, and carbonate. The hydration of carbon dioxide and the dehydration of carbonic acid are each relatively slow, with half-lives of 18 and 0.05 seconds, respectively (Table 10).

Table 10. Reaction constants for the hydration and dehydration of carbon dioxide in water at 25°C (pH 7)

Reaction	Uncatalyzed hydration constant, k (s^{-1}) at 25°C	Uncatalyzed hydration half-life (s) at 25°C	Uncatalyzed dehydration constant k(s^{-1}) at 25°C	Uncatalyzed dehydration half-life (s) at 25°C
$CO_2 + H_2O \rightarrow H_2CO_3$	0.0375	18	--	--
$H_2CO_3 \rightarrow CO_2 + H_2O$	--	--	13.7	0.05

These conversion rates are too slow for a variety of biological processes, and many organisms employ enzymes to speed the process. Many isozymes of carbonic anhydrase catalyze both the hydration and dehydration reactions to speed processes such as excretion of carbon dioxide from the lungs.

Judy believes she has isolated a new isozyme of carbonic anhydrase from mouse tissue. She measures some of its attributes in catalyzing the hydration of carbon dioxide (Table 11). She also modifies certain amino acids in the enzyme to see how altering them affects catalysis and whether they are critical for functionality (Table 11).

Table 11. Attributes of modified versions of carbonic anhydrase to catalyze the hydration of carbon dioxide in water at 25°C (pH 7)

Enzyme Modification	Km (mM)	(Kcat; s^{-1})	Kcat/Km ($M^{-1}s^{-1}$)
Native	4.0	2×10^5	5×10^7
1	4.2	3×10^5	7×10^7
2	4.8	1.5×10^5	3×10^7
3	56.1	3×10^4	5×10^5
4	2.9	2×10^3	7×10^5
5	13.1	1×10^5	8×10^6

Judy also studies the effect of the glaucoma drug acetazolamide on the activity of these enzymes since it is known to affect the activity of other isozymes of carbonic anhydrase (Table 12).

Table 12. Attributes of modified versions of carbonic anhydrase in presence of acetazolamide (5 µM) in water at 25°C (pH 7)

Enzyme Modification	Km (mM)	(Kcat; s^{-1})	Kcat/Km ($M^{-1}s^{-1}$)
Native	26	2×10^5	8×10^6
1	40	3×10^5	8×10^6
2	4.8	1.5×10^5	3×10^7
3	160	3×10^4	2×10^5
4	12	2×10^3	2×10^5
5	56	1×10^5	2×10^6

41. A Lineweaver-Burk plot used by Judy to determine Km is a plot of which of the following parameters?
    a. $1/v_o$ vs $1/[S]$
    b. $1/Vmax$ vs $1/[S]$
    c. $1/v_o$ vs $1/Km$
    d. $1/Km$ vs $1/Vmax$

42. Which modified enzyme has the highest affinity for carbon dioxide in water at 25°C (pH 7)?
    a. Modification 1
    b. Modification 3
    c. Modification 4
    d. Modification 5

43. Which modified enzyme is able to convert carbon dioxide to carbonic acid the fastest under conditions of saturating carbon dioxide concentrations?
    a. Native Enzyme
    b. Modification 1
    c. Modification 4
    d. Modification 5

44. Based on the data in the passage, acetazolamide is which of the following?
    a. A noncompetitive inhibitor of Native Enzyme
    b. A competitive inhibitor of the Native Enzyme
    c. A mixed inhibitor of the Native Enzyme
    d. Not an inhibitor of the Native Enzyme

45. Based on the data in the passage, if Modified Enzyme 3 is tested for activity in the presence of 10 μM acetazolamide, which result is most likely?
    a. Km = 450 mM
    b. Km = 160 mM
    c. Km = 56 mM
    d. Km = 23 mM

Discrete Questions

46. The electrical energy (W) stored in the membrane potential of a living cell can be modelled as a parallel plate capacitor. If the thickness of the cell membrane doubles and the charge on each side remains the same, what is the change in the stored energy in this model?
   a. no change to W
   b. increases to $2W$
   c. decreases to $\dfrac{W}{2}$
   d. decreases to $\dfrac{W}{\sqrt{2}}$

47. Which of the following glass optics in air is a diverging lens?

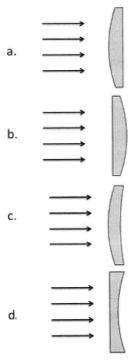

48. Which of the following chemicals is NOT produced and consumed in part of the standard tricarboxylic acid cycle?
   a. Succinate
   b. Oxalate
   c. Fumarate
   d. Malate

49. Fish living in arctic waters have a variety of adaptations to function in such a cold environment. One of these is to increase their membrane fluidity at lower temperatures, relative to temperate fish. Which of the following 22-carbon fatty acids would contribute most to increased fluidity of a cell membrane at low temperature?
   a. $CH_3(CH_2)_{20}CO_2H$
   b. all-cis-$CH_3(CH_2)_4CH=CHCH_2CH=CH(CH_2)_{11}CO_2H$
   c. all-cis-$CH_3CH_2CH=CHCH_2CH=CHCH_2CH=CHCH_2CH=CHCH_2CH=CHCH_2CH_2CO_2H$
   d. all-trans-$CH_3CH_2CH=CHCH_2CH=CHCH_2CH=CHCH_2CH=CHCH_2CH=CHCH_2CH_2CO_2H$

- 251 -

50. A protein at its isoelectric point has which of the following attributes?
   a. It moves in an electric field at a rate proportional to its molecular weight.
   b. It has no net electric charge.
   c. Its solubility is at a maximum.
   d. It contains no charged functional groups.

51. Bacteria have a cell membrane to help provide physical protection to the cell. The rigid structural framework of the cell wall is composed of which materials?
   a. polysaccharide chains covalently crosslinked with peptide chains
   b. polysaccharide chains ionically crosslinked with peptide chains
   c. proteins crosslinked with hyaluronic acid
   d. hyaluronic acid crosslinked with N-acetylneuraminic acid

52. Messenger RNA in a mammal has which of the following attributes?
   a. It is single stranded
   b. It is double stranded
   c. It is synthesized in the ribosome
   d. It contains two phosphate groups per nucleotide

53. Which of the following is the correct structure of pyrimidine?

   a.

   b.

   c.

   d.

54. Where does protein translation takes place in a eukaryote?
   a. on ribosomes in the nucleus
   b. on ribosomes in the cytoplasm
   c. on the mRNA in the nucleus
   d. on the DNA in the cytoplasm

55. Which of the following reactions shows a keto-enol tautomeric pair?

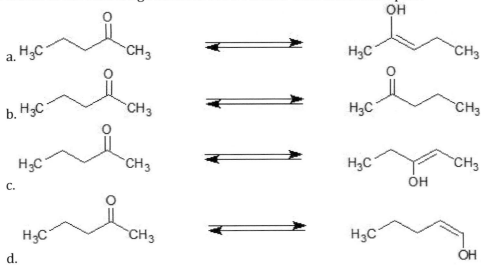

a.

b.

c.

d.

56. Which of the following structures does NOT represent a mechanistic step in the acid-catalyzed hydrolysis of methyl acetate?

a.

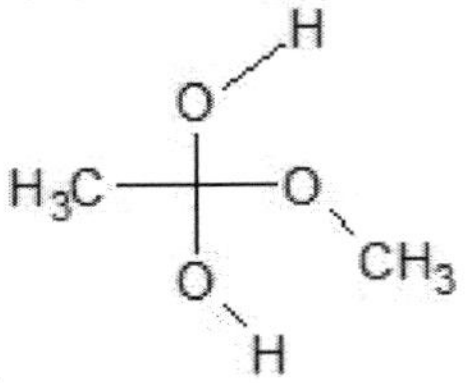

b.

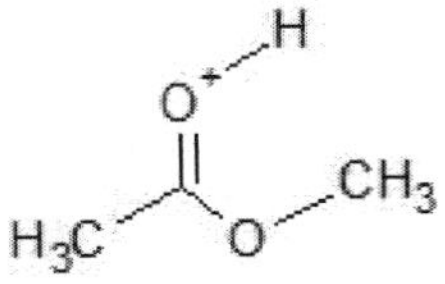

c.

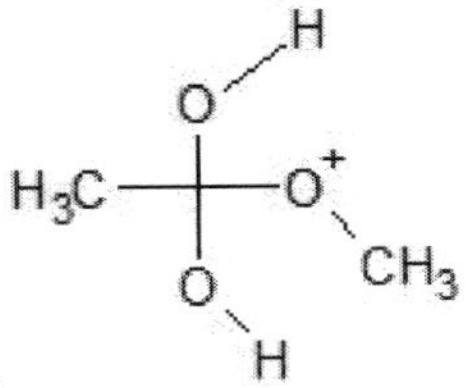

d.

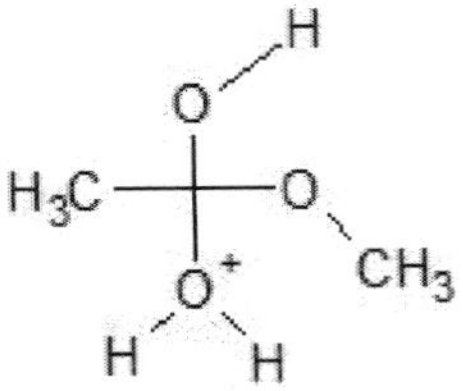

57. Isocitrate dehydrogenase catalyzes the following reaction in the tricarboxylic acid cycle:
isocitrate + NAD^+ → α-ketoglutarate + CO_2 + NADH + H^+
Which of the following half reactions correctly represent this reaction?

a. isocitrate → α-ketoglutarate + CO_2 + $2H^+$ + $2e^-$
NAD^+ + $2H^+$ + $2e^-$ → NADH

b. isocitrate → α-ketoglutarate + CO_2 + $2H^+$ + $2e^-$
NADH + H^+ + $2e^-$ → NAD^+

c. isocitrate → α-ketoglutarate + CO_2 + $2H^+$ + $2e^-$
NAD^+ + H^+ + $2e^-$ → NADH

d. isocitrate → α-ketoglutarate + CO_2 + H^+ + $2e^-$
NAD^+ + H^+ + $2e^-$ → NADH

58. Which of the following Fischer projections represents the aldohexose D-glucose?

a.

b.

c.

d.

59. Which of the following pairs of chemicals are most completely separated by simple batch distillation?

    a. $CH_3CH_2CH_3$ and $CH_3CH_2CH_2F$
    b. $CH_3CH_2CH_3$ and $CH_3CH_2CH_2Cl$
    c. $CH_3CH_2CH_3$ and $CH_3CH_2CH_2Br$
    d. $CH_3CH_2CH_3$ and $CH_3CH_2CH_2I$

Psychological, Social, and Biological Foundations

Passage 1

A retrospective research study evaluated more than 2,400 employees from three different companies to determine the risk factors for leaves of absence from work due to psychiatric ailments. Questionnaires including queries about childhood events were distributed to participants who were selected at random. Survey respondents' answers were compared to their work attendance records. Documented absences from work for psychiatric ailments were divided into the five categories listed below. Employees who had at least one documented leave of absence for a psychiatric ailment lasting for at least one day and individuals who did not have a documented leave of absence for a psychiatric ailment were included in the study. The study was designed to determine whether there was a link between childhood experiences and the development of behavioral and psychiatric disorders during adulthood. The study evaluated male and female participants aged 20–55. The data, which are reported as average days absent from work during a one-year period, are shown below.

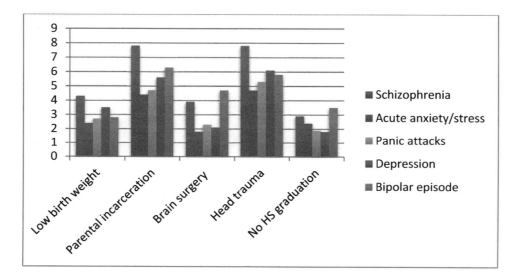

Low birth weight was considered birth weight below the 10% percentile.

Parental incarceration prior to age 18 of the study participant.

History of brain surgery prior to age 18.

History of head trauma hospitalization not requiring surgery prior to age 18.

High school graduation versus no high school graduation.

1. How could you explain the stronger relationship between head trauma and work absences than between brain surgery and work absences?

    a. Mood disorders and psychiatric disorders are often amplified by emotional events and therefore are often triggered by posttraumatic stress after head trauma, whereas surgery produces neurological changes such as weakness due to structural abnormalities.

    b. Disruptions in the central nervous system (CNS) blood-brain barrier and electrophysiological alterations in the brain that persist after head trauma cause persistent symptoms that are difficult to manage, whereas symptoms that occur after brain surgery are more often manageable with medications.

    c. Brain surgery is a therapeutic procedure that repairs disease, whereas head trauma causes disease.

    d. Brain surgery is usually asymmetric, and psychiatric ailments and mood disorders are caused by symmetric deficits.

2. Why would schizophrenia appear to be the most common cause of work absence in this study if mood disorders such as depression are more prevalent in the population?

    a. If a person has a mood disorder, the work setting is found to be therapeutic, and therefore individuals with mood disorders are less likely to take time off from work.

    b. Schizophrenia is, in fact, more common than mood disorders, but due to the social stigma, it is not as well recognized.

    c. Mood disorders are not severe enough to require affected individuals to take time off from work.

    d. Schizophrenia is the most likely of these diagnoses to precipitate exacerbations severe enough to necessitate medical treatment or hospitalization.

3. How does bipolar disorder compare to depression and schizophrenia?

    a. Bipolar disorder and depression are both mood disorders that are not associated with alterations in perception of reality, whereas schizophrenia is manifested by paranoid delusions and altered perception of reality, not mood alterations.

    b. Although bipolar disorder is manifested by extreme mood alterations, it is more likely to present with clinical characteristics that resemble schizophrenia, such as agitation and paranoia, than with predominantly depressive symptoms.

    c. Bipolar disorder produces a combination of contrasting symptoms, which requires a combination of medications that affect behavior of different neurotransmitters, whereas depression and schizophrenia often vary in symptom severity over time and require medication adjustment, but they are generally treated with medications that target a more limited group of neurotransmitters.

    d. Bipolar disorder is associated with relapses and remission, and thus individuals can take a medication "vacation," whereas depression and schizophrenia require constant therapy for symptomatic control.

4. How would you expect acute anxiety to affect attitudes toward missing work?
    a. People with acute anxiety and stress have normal brain structure and function, and thus most likely call off work only when there is a real threat in the work setting.
    b. Those with acute anxiety are most often afraid to call off work for fear of being fired, and thus they are expected to go to work even during times of illness.
    c. Acute anxiety makes the prospect of missing work and the prospect of going to work both threatening options, and thus individuals with acute anxiety view the notion of missing work as an added source of anxiety.
    d. People who are anxious are usually overachievers and transfer a sense of anxiety and drive to others around them, and thus they would be more likely to be angry with others for missing work, while forgiving themselves under the same circumstances.

5. How can social cognitive theory explain a difference in calling in sick between individuals of differing income levels?
    a. Individuals observe behavior and consequences among peers and learn through the outcomes of peers who hold an equivalent position and status whether it would be favorable or not to call in sick in that particular work environment.
    b. Those with lower income levels want to even the playing field by calling in sick, thus "compensating" for lower hourly pay by decreasing the number of hours worked.
    c. Social peer group acceptance determines whether individuals call in sick, and thus those at a lower income level strive to imitate the actions of those at the higher income level.
    d. Calling in sick at work is based on cognitive criteria that encompass the safety of coworkers, and thus social cognitive theory suggests that individuals with a greater sense of responsibility will take action to ensure that the work is done and to ensure the safety and health of the peer group.

Passage 2

Social dynamics of migrant populations may appear to be different than nonmigrant social groups at first glance. Many members of immigrant populations look to peers within their immigrant group, and particularly to influential members of the peer groups, as anchors by which they can interpret the values of the new society in light of the established values of the baseline society from which they came from and more closely identify with. The older an individual is when moving to a new setting, the more he holds the values of his original environment and the more he craves approval from peers of his native land than approval from peers of his new setting. In fact, dominant peers within an immigrant community may be so influential as to establish new social norms that they safely combine selected values of the adopted region with unalterable values of the original setting. It is through a process of subconscious and conscious exploration driven in large part by the most esteemed members of the migrant peer group that new social norms are established.

This makes the local media, which is often a binding force among inhabitants of a region, less important to immigrant communities. The media in such situations is viewed through a lens that may be different from that which is intended. However, even among indigenous social groups, local dynamics play a role in establishing social norms.

An experiment designed to evaluate conformity evaluated college students who were registered for a year-long seminar. Students' attire was noted at every class session, which met twice per week. Graduate student leaders were instructed to dress in a professional manner in order to assess whether the college students altered their attire. At the first session, 90% of the college students wore blue jeans, leggings, or shorts. Within the first month, 40% of the college students wore pants or skirts that were similar in style to the graduate students' attire, and by the last month, 70% of the college students wore pants or skirts similar in style to the graduate students' attire.

6. How does social control result in sanctions that affect college students who dress more casually than the expected standards in a seminar and sanctions that affect guests at a party attended exclusively by immigrants from the same region?

    a. Students may be excluded from opportunities to answer questions in class or lead group activities, whereas guests at a social event may be excluded from peer group conversations and further invitations if the unwritten rules of behavior are not followed.

    b. Students will receive low grades due to evaluators' perception that the students don't care about the material, whereas guests at a party will find themselves victims of peer group gossip as peers attempt to understand or explain nonconforming behaviors or styles of dress.

    c. Students will be marginalized by peers who do not want to be associated with a negative image, whereas other guests at a party would want to avoid being seen with nonconforming guests to avoid being regarded with low status.

    d. Students would work harder in the course due to a subjective personal inference that they are not ready for the level of rigor, and guests at a party would try harder to find ways to fit in with the majority of the group at the next party.

7. How would group polarization affect the actions of students who choose not to dress in more formal attire during the seminar?

    a. Students who dress in less formal attire would attempt other ways to compensate, such as showing up on time or answering questions during class.

    d. The students who dress in less formal attire would view themselves as less suited for the course and thus would study more for the seminar and achieve better test grades than those who do not.

    c. Students who dress in less formal attire for the seminar would try to undermine peers who also dress in less formal attire in order to achieve some sense of power.

    d. Students would exaggerate their casual dress style to show solidarity and rejection of the formal attire and the unwritten code associated with it.

8. Group hysteria is acceptable in one setting but not in another. What would inhibit an individual from participating in events involving group hysteria if his previous group did not accept group hysteria but his adopted group does?

    a. Social control
    b. Peer pressure
    c. Deindividuation
    d. Deviance

9. How would the prospective power of sanctions play a role in compelling dominant individuals in a small ethnic group to follow norms?

a. Dominant characters do not feel the need to follow norms because they are more likely to set the norms, and thus they can more easily choose how to blend characteristics of both cultures, often to their own preference.

b. Dominant characters do not have to follow social norms because they decide who is in the in group and who is in the out group, and thus they are not concerned about sanctions, whereas most members of the social group are concerned about sanctions.

c. Some dominant members may be acutely fearful of sanctions and thus driven to follow norms, whereas some nondominant members may be less invested in the group, and thus they are less fearful of sanctions resulting from neglecting norms.

d. Dominant characters rely on the acceptance of their lower status peers for self-esteem and social interaction, and thus they are likely to follow social norms as faithfully as less dominant individuals in the group, but with an emphasis on maintaining an appearance of less effort, and often they must be the first to "try on" social norms of the adopted culture in order to maintain unwritten status as leaders.

10. Which of the following is a method by which individuals can protect themselves against anomie?

a. Construct laws to prevent chaos.

b. Maintain a connection with a group or society to avoid the alienation that can occur from social stigma.

c. Work to ensure that expected norms are relaxed to avoid a sense of lack of acceptance from the prevailing group.

d. Uphold a strong moral compass to avoid falling into a disoriented state personally and socially.

11. Conscious awareness of and adaptations to the various standards expected in diverse settings is a personal characteristic of many individuals. How would awareness of differing agents of socialization protect an individual from the mental anguish of ostracism?

a. Awareness of the differing agents of socialization can help an individual objectively defend himself against unfair or biased reasons for ostracism so that he does not suffer from the anguish of ostracism.

b. Awareness of differing agents of socialization can build empathy, which prevents an individual from being ostracized and thus from experiencing the emotional pain of ostracism.

c. Awareness of differing agents of socialization among different populations allows an individual to combine elements of one community's social norms with that of another, essentially gaining a better rounded social ability than other members of the community.

d. Awareness of the differing agents of socialization allows an individual to understand that socialization and norms are not set as universal, which can protect an individual from the emotional turmoil of rejection.

Associative learning is generally achieved with little, if any, effort. However, our understanding of the volitional ability to harness associative learning has allowed therapists to use learning methods to help people manage acquired and inborn emotional deficits in empathy. A group of stroke survivors was assessed for their ability to identify emotions by watching videos. Two other groups, a group of age-matched individuals with Asperger's and a group of age-matched controls, were also evaluated.

The three groups participated in a yearlong longitudinal study, which involved watching five different three-minute videos. After watching one minute of each video, participants were asked to identify the emotions of the people in the video, and after watching two additional minutes of the video, participants were provided with accurate labels of the emotions represented in the videos. Tests were repeated every two months. The same video was never repeated so that participants would avoid memorizing the answers. The scores are shown below.

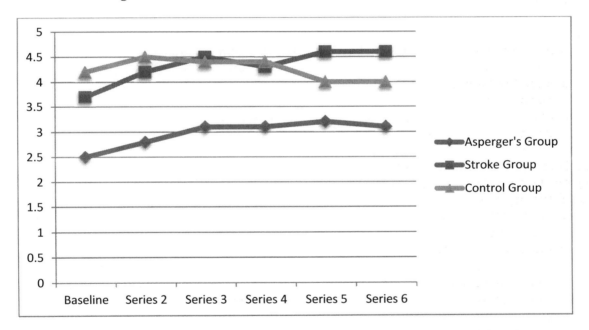

12. How would you explain the finding that the stroke group improved more than the Asperger's group?

a. The stroke group has had more real-life experiences that included positive reinforcement for correctly identifying emotions, which is a motivating factor in learning this skill, whereas the Asperger's group has not had as many real-life experiences or motivation to build on.

b. The stroke group had visual problems but not deficits in emotional perception, and thus they were more easily able to work on relearning how to recognize visual cues, whereas the Asperger's group had a more difficult task of learning how to recognize emotional cues.

c. The Asperger's group doesn't place a strong emphasis on social interaction, whereas the stroke group is invested in improving social skills to regain past abilities.

d. The Asperger's group has a deficit that is present from birth, and thus it has a severe lack of activity in certain areas of the cerebral cortex, whereas the stroke group is more disposed to the reparative effects of neuroplasticity.

13. What is the most likely explanation for the decreased score in the control group?
a. Prolonged exposure
b. Extinction
c. Habituation
d. Dishabituation

14. Using operant conditioning, which type of reinforcement schedule is most consistent with real-life application of this skill?
a. Fixed-ratio schedule
b. Fixed-interval schedule
c. Variable-interval schedule
d. Variable-ratio schedule

15. Which group would you expect to have a higher recruitment of mirror neurons in learning the correct responses?
a. The Asperger's group
b. The control group
c. The stroke group
d. All groups are expected to be equal.

16. One of the participants who had a particularly low score to begin with did not improve at all during the yearlong study. Interestingly, videos of his participation demonstrated that his own face reflected the expressions of the actors in the videos he was watching. According to classical conditioning, what does his own facial response represent?
a. The conditioned stimulus
b. The conditioned response
c. The unconditioned stimulus
d. The unconditioned response

Passage 4

The degree to which an individual believes he can control external events is determined by a combination of personal nature, environmental influences, and personal experiences that modify beliefs about the consequences of personal action. An individual's overall sense of control over his environment is generally overarching throughout most aspects of his life. Yet, an individual may have a greater or diminished sense of control over certain aspects of his life in comparison to his overall baseline sense of control.

An experiment endeavored to observe waiters' sense of control over their environment. The experiment also attempted to modify waiters' sense of control over their environment and, finally, to teach them how much control they had over their environment through the results of the experiment.

New waiters in a restaurant who were still in the training phase were divided into two groups for the experiment. One group of trainees was told that guests of the restaurant were particularly generous with tips, whereas the control group of waiter trainees was not given any verbal or nonverbal signal regarding the tipping tendencies of guests. The guests were not aware of the experiment.

At the end of the six-hour shift, the waiters were asked their subjective opinions about the tips and were asked to report the numbers. The waiters who had been previously told that guests of the restaurant were generous tippers tended to describe guests as generous, whereas the control group, who had not been provided with any persuasive messages, described the tips as average. The waiters who had been told that guests were generous received tips that were, on average, 30% higher in total than the other group.

17. What concept explains the difference in tips?
   a. Self-fulfilling prophecy
   b. Stereotyping
   c. Prestige
   d. Stigma

18. How could the owners use this experimental information to motivate staff to avoid stereotyping guests?
   a. Give the guests instruction on how to act in ways that are opposite to stereotypes.
   b. Explain the experiment to demonstrate to the staff that guests show appreciation for good treatment.
   c. Give the staff a financial incentive for treating all guests equally.
   d. Present information and examples of ways that guests behave in ways that counteract and reverse stereotypes.

19. After comparing the tips, a waiter with a strong internal locus of control would be expected to relate to a waiter who did not receive a tip in which of the following ways?
   a. With an attitude that encourages self-control in dealing with disappointment.
   b. With benevolence and charity.
   c. With concern for the victim's self-esteem more than concern for the victim's short-term finances.
   d. With blame for causing his own misfortune.

20. Which of the following would be expected to drive modifications in the control group's behavior as they serve customers throughout the six-hour shift?

a. Positive reinforcement, in which the waiters receive good tips and thus are motivated to provide high-quality service in order to continue receiving good tips.

b. Negative reinforcement, in which the waiters initially receive poor tips and are motivated to provide better service so as to receive higher tips.

c. Punishment, in which the waiters are reprimanded by their supervisor if they receive a poor tip and admonished to provide better service.

d. All three of these are expected to play a role in the modification of behavior during the shift.

21. How can instructors in the experiment use the peripheral route described in the elaboration likelihood model to persuade waiters that customers who order alcohol are more or less trustworthy than customers who do not order alcohol?

a. Instructors can stimulate the visual pathways of the waiters' peripheral nervous systems by showing them different-colored drink menus to trigger a psychological color response associated with trustworthiness.

b. Instructors can state that the non-alcohol-drinking group is trustworthy and omit mentioning the other group to raise questions about the group's trustworthiness

c. Instructors can remind a waiter of a feature present in a third group of individuals who the waiter believes to be untrustworthy, where that same feature is also present in the alcohol-drinking group.

d. Instructors can elaborate on peripheral details of the situation that are not necessarily relevant to trustworthiness to build an additive effect of peripheral details that are difficult to ignore and that outweigh the core features related to generosity.

Passage 5

Children of one or more emotionally unstable parents experience a great deal of stress, which can be expressed in a variety of ways. Multiple factors, including the condition of the parents' marriage, the degree of parental emotional instability, and parental attitudes toward and interactions with the children play roles in how the child senses and reacts to the parental emotional and behavioral turmoil.

A pediatric hospital screens for child abuse and childhood stress by asking pediatric patients to fill out nonmandatory surveys in the waiting room prior to their appointments.

Survey questions include the following:
- How good are you at taking care of yourself?
- Do you ever worry that your parent will not be able to take care of you anymore before you graduate from high school?
- Do you think that your parents are able to take care of you as well as, better than, or worse than other kids' parents?
- Do you ever have to take care of your parents?

Some open-ended questions include the following:
- What have you learned from your parents?
- What does one of your parents do that you want to learn how to do?
- What compliment does your mother give you?
- What compliment does your father give you?
- What compliment from someone who is not in your family most surprised you?
- What word best describes you?

Approximately 60% of the patients filled out the forms. Children who were younger than six years old often asked parents for help in filling out the forms. Approximately 40% of the parents refused to have their children complete the forms. It was noted that patients who had a high copay were three times more likely to refuse to fill out the forms than patients who had a low copay or no copay.

22. Which of the following factors would cause a child to avoid answers that reflect negatively on his parents?
    a. Role strain and role conflict
    b. Altruism and deindividuation
    c. Fear of role exit
    d. Obedience and role conflict

23. Why would a child try to alter a parent's back-stage self to match the parent's front-stage self?
    a. The parent's front-stage self is more desirable for the child.
    b. This is a child's attempt at impression management.
    c. In order to blend better with others.
    d. To avoid social stigma.

24. Given the disparity in compliance rates based on the level of copay, what is the most valid conclusion that can be drawn regarding the parents' response with regard to the survey?
    a. Those who had a low or no copay were more concerned with obedience toward their health-care providers.
    b. Those who had a higher copay behaved with higher sense of power and authority.
    c. Those who had a higher copay were more likely to have privacy concerns.
    d. Those who had a low or no copay were not as busy and had more time to complete the survey.

25. If a child's answer regarding a word that best describes her is based on a compliment that she receives regarding a particular trait, what influence is at play in forming her identity formation?
    a. Low self-esteem
    b. Looking-glass self
    c. Self-fulfilling prophecy
    d. Impression management

26. If a child answers that he wants to learn something from his parent, but upon learning the skill he is ridiculed by his peers, how would he most likely view his parent's lesson based on this external response?
   a. With rejection
   b. With sympathy
   c. With mistrust
   d. With craving for acceptance

Passage 6

Globalization is an inevitable result of affluence, education, and technology. Views about religion are susceptible to the influences of globalization. The way that patients view health care has historically been shaped by parochial values, but this view is becoming more influenced by attitudes and outcomes in geographically distant lands. International medicine includes international medical education, medical missions, and medical tourism. These costly enterprises are heavily swayed by the availability of and sources of funding.

An international medical care experience scholarship for medical students is funded by an organization dedicated to promoting young women's education (YWE) for the longitudinal purpose of reducing infant mortality and domestic abuse. Scholarship recipients will see patients in a local clinic. Recipients will also maintain contact with young female patients by sending them reminders to enroll in school, encouragement to study for exams, and requests to report whether they have passed each year of school

Electronic medical records (EMRs) are also being implemented in the region, and although they are being funded and set up by a different organization, the YWE program has made plans to allow scholarship benefactors to use the EMR system for input and gathering patient information during medical visits in the local clinic.

Medical student scholarship applicants are asked several questions during the interview including the following questions: "How important is it to respect the religion of tribes and regions?" and "What do you define as a cult versus a religion?"

27. How could a hidden curriculum influence which applicants are granted the scholarships?
   a. The scholarship benefactors may want students to teach religion classes to villagers, despite the fact that it is not stated as one of the responsibilities in the program description.
   b. The scholarship benefactors may want to select students who are of the same religion as members of the YWE program to make working together easier.
   c. The scholarship benefactors may be irreligious and believe that all religions are cults and thus select applicants who feel the same way.
   d. The scholarship benefactors may have a biased opinion of religion and use the program to indoctrinate students in their viewpoint on religion, even though it is not the stated objective.

28. How would the medicalization of domestic abuse affect treatment of domestic abuse survivors in the region where this medical project is taking place?
    a. It would cause the burden of care to fall solely on physicians.
    b. It would eliminate the gender stigma of men who are victims of domestic abuse.
    c. It would result in increased funding and attention being devoted to addressing the issue.
    d. It would become tolerated as a medical condition rather than viewed as the fault of the perpetrator, and thus it may become socially acceptable.

29. According to the concept of symbolic interactionism, how would you expect a medical student's interaction with a patient in another culture to proceed if the patient reminds the student of a friend who betrayed her trust?
    a. She would be expected to try to ignore the reminder of the betrayal by adopting an intentionally cheerful attitude around the patient.
    b. She would be expected to subconsciously attempt to repair her feelings regarding the broken relationship through her interactions with the patient.
    c. She would be expected treat the patient with mistrust based on the patient's similarities with the betraying friend.
    d. She would not be expected to have any response because symbolic interactionism describes a strictly voluntary response.

30. When electronic medical records (EMRs) are implemented in the region described in this example, there will be a lag in the seamless adoption of the EMR system. How does culture lag explain the relative similarities in adoption rates of EMRs among developing and developed nations despite the profound material differences?
    a. Developed nations lag behind in EMR technology because they do not have a large enough workforce to construct the technology, so it is easier for developing nations to catch up with EMR despite material disadvantages.
    b. Both developing and developed nations take time to adopt newly available technology, so a nation that lacks the material resources can implement EMR almost as quickly a nation with material resources because the people in both cultures spend time learning how to use the technology before it becomes widely available and practical for use.
    c. The technology lags behind the culture in developed nations due to resistance because of the innate efficiency of the health-care workforce in developed countries, so the end result is that a system such as EMR is adopted at the same rate in developed and developing nations.
    d. The technology pulls the developing nations forward so that people can learn how to use technology as well as the people in developed countries.

31. How would a woman who was chronically deprived of power and independence in the population being served by the YWE program view a meritocratic environment, as compared to another woman who was unable to attain recognition in such an environment due to lack of effort?
    a. The woman without power and the woman who failed despite having had opportunities would each disapprove of a meritocracy because neither was able to achieve recognition.
    b. The woman without power positively views a system of meritocracy because she believes it would have allowed her to achieve recognition, whereas the woman who failed craves a different system in which she would be shielded from failure.
    c. The woman without power appreciates the meritocracy because she can enjoy experiences through mirror neurons, whereas the woman who failed cannot do so.
    d. It depends on each person's individual experiences and alliances and well as his or her social position and empathy.

Passage 7

The prison population is largely supported by public funds. Health care is provided to prisoners through public funds, and therefore reduction of disease-related complications is expected to reduce the cost of maintaining the health of prisoners. This population has unique demographic characteristics and a different distribution of health conditions than the general population.

Persistent pain, refractory to pain medication, was noted in a cost-control analysis of prisoner health costs. Attempts to decrease costs by using generic medications were found to be ineffective after a six-month trial. A different approach was then adopted. This approach was to determine the etiology of pain and treat the underlying cause.

A preliminary subset of prison patients with refractory neuropathic pain was selected. A retrospective chart review conducted using the medical records of a prisoner population and the medical records of controls sought to evaluate the etiology of neuropathic pain, a condition associated with a variety of etiologies.

The results are found in the chart below.

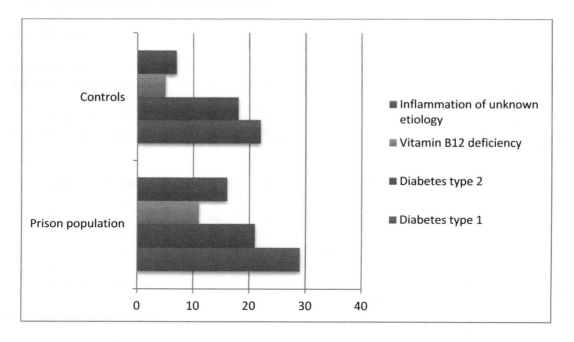

32. What could explain the relatively higher incidence of inflammation of unknown etiology in the prison population compared to the other diagnoses?

    a. Inflammation of unknown etiology noted at higher rates in the charts of the prison population is indicative of diminished access to care, which results in reduced accuracy of diagnoses of etiology and reduced treatment of inflammatory conditions.

    b. Inflammation is a finding in the central nervous system tissue of individuals with drug abuse and with psychiatric diagnosis, both of which increase the risk of criminal behavior.

    c. The prison setting exposes people to infections that trigger difficult-to-diagnose inflammatory conditions.

    d. People with inflammation are excluded from the general population and therefore have to turn to criminal behavior.

33. Why would type 1 diabetes be so much more common in the prison population?

    a. People with type 1 diabetes are marginalized in society and thus more likely to unfairly end up in prison.

    b. Prisoners can't get the necessary insulin, and therefore they are more likely to have persistent type 1 diabetes.

    c. It is not likely more common, but rather it is a more common cause of neuropathy due to lack of access to health care and lack of compliance.

    d. Poor parenting started in utero causing low birth weight, and also the same poor parenting led to criminal behavior.

34. Would treatment with vitamin B_{12} pills or vitamin B_{12} injections for remission of neuropathic pain simultaneously be effective in preventing dementia in the prison population?

    a. Both treatments would only be effective in preventing dementia among individuals who have a vitamin B_{12} level in the low range, but not among individuals who have adequate levels of vitamin B_{12}.

    b. Vitamin B_{12} pills would not be effective in prevention of dementia due to ineffective absorption through the stomach, but vitamin B_{12} injections would be effective in preventing dementia.

    c. Neither treatment would help in preventing dementia because individuals who suffer from vitamin B_{12} deficiency-related neuropathy are not necessarily susceptible to vitamin B_{12} deficiency-related neuropathy.

    d. Either treatment would be effective in preventing the development of dementia caused by vitamin B_{12} deficiency.

35. Why would an individual in this study population fear effective treatment of neuropathy?

    a. Once treatment is achieved, medical attention will decrease in frequency, and thus attention and interaction with supportive health-care staff will diminish.

    b. Pain medications for neuropathic pain offer pleasant side effects, and thus they are desirable.

    c. If the neuropathy is effectively treated, health reimbursements would decrease, making it difficult to obtain supplemental income and health coverage.

    d. Effective treatment of neuropathy requires diagnosis using small needles and electrical shocks.

Passage 8

Balance impairment results from several neurological conditions. Balance relies on integration among the senses, including vision, hearing, and proprioceptive touch.

Consciousness-altering drugs disrupt balance through several different mechanisms that can last while a drug is in its active chemical form and even after the body metabolizes and eliminates the drug from its system through the residual physiologic action of metabolites or prolonged receptor activity. The mechanisms by which a psychoactive compound can cause addiction are distinct from the mechanisms by which a psychoactive compound diminishes balance. A study using blood analysis to measure the concentration of metabolic by-products of a psychoactive drug as well as physiological parameters such as pulse and blood pressure was performed on volunteers who were given the drug in a low-dose oral form for the study. Measurements were taken 30 minutes after drug use. Approximately half of the participants were users of the drug, whereas half had not previously used the drug. Users varied in their frequency and amounts of drug use. Results of the measured parameters are below.

Objective measures of balance:
- Romberg rated 1–10 (where 10 is perfect)
- Toes walking rated 1–10 (where 10 is perfect)
- Standing on one foot rated 1–10 (where 10 is perfect)

	Blood Pressure	Pulse	Metabolite 1	Metabolite 2	Romberg	Toe Walking	Balance on One Foot
Drug Users	129/89	102	0.67%	0.89%	6.1	5.9	6.23
Non-Drug Users	137/92	116	0.42%	0.92%	6.4	5.78	6.56

36. Why did the drug user group have a lower blood pressure and pulse than the nonuser group and a higher concentration of metabolite 1?
    a. The drug users had a higher level of metabolite 1 because they already had some metabolites in their bodies prior to the experiment. This made additional drug intake inconsequential.
    b. The drug users experienced altered metabolism of the compound due to repeated exposure to the drug. The drug users also experienced a diminished physiological response to the drug compared to the non-drug users.
    c. The drug users became addicted to the drug because they needed it to manage blood pressure. Thus, the drug users were primed to have lower blood pressure and pulse rate in response to the drug.
    d. The drug users' ability to properly metabolize the chemical is enhanced by frequent use. The drug users had better baseline health to begin with, and thus they have lower blood pressure and pulse than the non-drug users.

37. How can a psychogenic drug affect immediate responses to visual and auditory threats if it doesn't cause objective vision or hearing deficits?
  a. The response time to visual and auditory threats is slowed because psychoactive drugs affect the processing and integration of sensory information as well as the speed of the responses.
  b. Psychoactive drugs make threats appear to be nonthreatening, and thus they slow the individual's perception that a response is needed.
  c. The person's vision and hearing slowly deteriorate with the use of psychoactive drugs over the long term, but the effect is subclinical, and therefore it is not diagnosed.
  d. Addiction is a by-product of the use of psychoactive drugs, and addiction alters conscientiousness.

38. Why would some individuals view perceived socially threatening situations as less threatening with the use of consciousness-altering drugs than without the use of consciousness altering drugs?
  a. Sensory adaptation
  b. Diminished self-awareness
  c. Overconfidence
  d. Memory decay

39. How does emory affect an individual's physiological response to a consciousness-altering drug?
  a. Memory of impaired consciousness helps an individual consciously resist the effects of a consciousness-altering drug in order to adapt behavior to stay safe and avoid an excessive physiological response to the drug.
  b. Memory of the previous experience with the drug elicits a degree of neurotransmitter release ahead of time.
  c. Memory does not affect a person's physiologic response.
  d. Sensory memory allows an individual to recall previous experiences and restimulate sensory receptors.

Passage 9

The circadian rhythm is driven by the pineal gland in the brain. Some individuals are more sensitive to disruptions in their circadian rhythm than are others.

A study of shift workers attempted to determine whether their disrupted circadian rhythms could be adjusted with meditation. Participants were selected from a company that operates on a 24-hour basis. There was a reported high turnover, reported as a four-year average span on the job. However, some employees were working at the company on a shift basis for up to 25 years. Newer workers may have been new to shift work, or they may have had jobs entailing shift work prior to this employment. Participants were selected at random among this company's employee population who performed shift work.

Workers were asked to participate in meditation sessions two times per week. Twelve hours after work shifts were completed, phone text questions were sent out, asking participants to rate their levels of fatigue and stress on a scale of 1–10. Objective weights were measured and reported at weekly intervals.

The nonintervention shift workers, on average, rated their stress at the following levels:
- levels of 6.2 after 3 weeks
- levels of 5.9 after 6 weeks
- levels of 6.7 after 9 weeks
- levels of 6.6 after 12 weeks

The intervention shift workers, on average, rated their stress at the following levels:
- levels of 6.3 after 3 weeks
- levels of 4.7 after 6 weeks
- levels of 3.3 after 9 weeks
- levels of 3.4 after 12 weeks

The weight-gain chart is below.

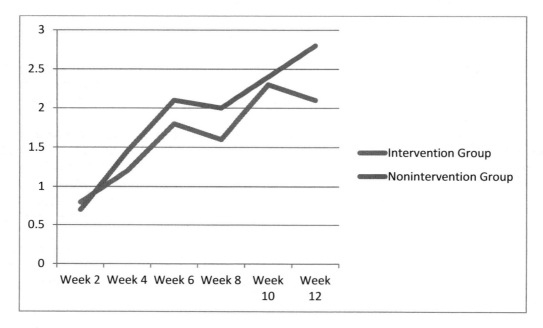

40. How did disruption of the circadian rhythm affect weight gain?
    a. As a result of being awake during the night on some days and during the day on other days, participants were not able to maintain a steady diet.
    b. When the circadian rhythm is interrupted, there is usually a lack of exercise combined with increased sleep, so individuals don't have the opportunity to burn calories.
    c. Study participants' meal cycles were disrupted, causing fluctuations in metabolism as well as hunger and overeating.
    d. Seasonal affective disorder (SAD) resulted from lack of regular exposure to sunlight. SAD causes depressive symptoms associated with overeating.

41. How did participants' reports of their fatigue and stress levels reflect their sleep–wake cycle adjustments with meditation?
    a. Individuals learned to become more alert through meditation.
    b. Meditation helped participants undergo adjustments of the sleep–wake cycle, including a shorter lag prior to the first rapid eye movement (REM) period.
    c. Long-term potentiation elicited with the aid of meditation helped in learning adaptations after long-term sleep variations.
    d. Neural plasticity is encouraged by meditation, and this mobilized neurons to readjust the sleep–wake cycle.

42. How would study participants' problem-solving responses be affected by lack of sleep?
    a. Selective attention is more pronounced because of a decreased ability to focus.
    b. Problem solving depends on intelligence, so it is not impaired.
    c. Selective attention and divided attention are impaired by lack of sleep.
    d. Brainstem-controlled reflexes are severely impaired by lack of sleep.

43. If a participant experienced a catastrophic event during the later weeks of the study, how would her stress self-rating compare to an individual who had an anxiety disorder?
    a. The participant who experienced situational stress would rate her stress level as low because she understands that her experience is the result of a situation, whereas the participant with an anxiety disorder would rate her stress level as high because she experiences physiologic anxiety.
    b. The participant who has experienced a catastrophic event would rate her stress level as especially high during the period in which she is experiencing the effects of stress, whereas the participant with an anxiety disorder would rate her stress as high due to the stress of participating in the study itself.
    c. The participant who has an anxiety disorder would rate her stress as high throughout the study, whereas the participant with acute stress would experience a protective effect against stress as a result of the study.
    d. The participant with a catastrophic event would rate her stress level with a number that deviated from her usual stress rating during the weeks in which she is experiencing the effects of the situational stress, whereas the participant with an anxiety disorder would have a relatively consistent self-rated stress level.

44. Which of the following is the LEAST valid conclusion that could be drawn from the apparent stabilization of average stress levels in week nine and beyond in the intervention group and the nonintervention group?
    a. The intervention achieved its maximum effectiveness after only nine weeks and should not be expected to further positively impact the stress of participants.
    b. The apparent stabilization observed in the responses of the nonintervention group is the result of simple random variation.
    c. Members of the nonintervention group observed the lower stress levels in members of the intervention group, and their stress levels increased to a steady higher level as a result of envy.
    d. After several surveys, members of both groups developed a learned response to the questions and consistently reported the same responses.

Discrete Questions

45. Population-based studies demonstrate an increased predisposition for schizophrenia in individuals who have Parkinson's disease and in their family members. How can you explain these findings?
    a. Dopamine is the common factor in these disorders, and thus medications for one disorder may trigger the other disorder.
    b. Genetic loci for both disorders are proximate to each other, and thus, unaffected family members of Parkinson's patients may experience schizophrenia.
    c. Environmental factors predispose to both disorders, and families often share environmental situations.
    d. The average age of onset of schizophrenia is in the early twenties, whereas the average age of onset of Parkinson's disease is later, so it is difficult to do an accurate study on siblings.

46. If an individual is requested to fill out a brief anonymous survey sent by mass email, what social factor is most likely to prevent the individual from responding?
    a. Peer pressure
    b. Positive reinforcement
    c. Bystander effect
    d. Social norms

47. Why would a person revert to a habit of blaming others for his unhappiness after having discontinued that habit for several years?
    a. Instinctive drift
    b. Because new issues causing unhappiness arise
    c. Because his original theory that others are responsible is proven correct
    d. Extinction

48. How does the limbic system control an individual's response to human faces?
    a. The occipital lobe allows detailed perception of faces.
    b. The amygdala is a portion of the limbic system that assesses faces for traits such as trustworthiness.
    c. The hippocampus is a portion of the limbic system that aids in remembering names based on facial recognition.
    d. The temporal lobe is activated in the process of recognizing faces.

49. How does Korsakoff's syndrome affect an individual's ability to function independently?
    a. It causes emotional lability manifest by unexplained crying episodes.
    b. It causes vision loss.
    c. It causes amnesia.
    d. It causes thiamine deficiency.

50. How does emotional stress impact the endocrine system and the autonomic nervous system?
    a. Serotonin is increased, whereas epinephrine is decreased in response to emotional stress.
    b. Cortisol is decreased, and epinephrine and norepinephrine are increased as a result of emotional stress.
    c. Acetylcholine and cortisol are increased, whereas epinephrine and norepinephrine are decreased in response to emotional stress.
    d. Epinephrine, norepinephrine, and cortisol are increased as a result of emotional stress.

51. How can the genetic versus environmental etiology of behavioral traits be differentiated based on metabolic brain imaging studies?

a. Metabolic brain imaging studies cannot differentiate between genetic and environmental etiologies because if a metabolic variation is noted, it is a phenotypic trait not a genotypic trait.

b. Environmental factors should not alter the physiological function of the brain, and thus, metabolic brain imaging studies are an effective means of identifying genetic behavioral traits.

c. Metabolic brain imaging studies determine the functional activity of different regions of the brain and thus can help in identifying subclinical pathology in unaffected relatives of affected individuals, potentially establishing a genetic etiology.

d. If metabolic changes can be triggered by environmental stimuli, then it is more likely that the trait is environmental in etiology rather than genetic.

52. How may ascribed status in a primary group affect a person's dedication to the secondary group?

a. The person who has low ascribed status in the primary group rejects the primary group in favor of the secondary group.

b. The person who has a higher ascribed status in the primary group is dedicated to promoting the primary group's status within the secondary group.

c. It is difficult to counteract or change ascribed status, which can motivate an individual to be more devoted to the secondary group and to work harder on earning achieved status in the secondary group.

d. The person who has a higher ascribed status in the primary group rejects the secondary group for fear of not attaining the same status.

53. How does attribution error explain a professor's attitude toward a student arriving late to class versus the professor's attitude when she, herself, arrives late to class?

a. The professor gives herself permission to start class upon her own arrival, whereas she is disappointed that the student did not try hard enough to please her.

b. The professor acknowledges that she may arrive late to class due to external factors such as traffic but attributes the student's tardiness as the result of a personal deficit or negligence.

c. The professor would be upset when she arrives late to class because this compromises class time, whereas she views the student's late arrival as an issue that only penalizes the student.

d. The professor would view the student's tardiness as disruptive to the whole class, whereas she views her own tardiness as inconsequential because she does not produce an interruption when she arrives late, but rather, a delay.

54. How could a teenager's primary group function to lower her self-esteem while the secondary group raises her self-esteem?

a. The primary group assigns ascribed status, whereas the secondary group assigns achieved status, which is more important to a teenager and thus raises her self-esteem.

b. The secondary group's opinion is more important to the teenager because the secondary group is composed of peers, whereas the primary group is her family. Thus, the secondary group has the power to raise the teenager's self-esteem even if the primary group lowers it.

c. The primary group provides direct feedback, whereas the secondary group provides indirect feedback. Thus, because indirect feedback is not as insulting, the primary group lowers the self-esteem and the secondary group raises it.

d. Whether the status is achieved or ascribed, in this example, the status given to the teenager is self-confidence building in the secondary group and devaluing in the primary group.

55. How does perception of an acceptable family structure change within a culture?
   a. Diffusion is the passive sharing and transfer of cultural norms and values, and thus perception is affected by watching surroundings.
   b. Transmission is the method by which a culture alters its routines.
   c. Assimilation describes blending into a new culture, and thus those who assimilate must accept different family structures within the new community.
   d. Multiculturalism describes the integration of different cultures within a geographic region, including what each culture considers an acceptable or normal family structure.

56. How would racialization affect attitudes toward the evaluation and treatment of infertility in a patient who is part of a population typically associated with high birth rates?
   a. The patient and the doctor are more likely to see the problem as a serious problem due to the deviance from the typical rates of fertility associated with the patient's race.
   b. The doctor is more objective, whereas the patient is more concerned about social exclusion.
   c. The patient would consider the problem within the context of being a medical issue, whereas the doctor's attitude is colored by prejudice.
   d. The patient and the doctor would make inaccurate judgments based on ethnic and racial stereotypes.

57. In light of the fertility problem noted in the previous question, how would the theory of intersectionality influence the doctor-patient relationship and the patient's marriage?
   a. The patient thinks the doctor and the spouse can't understand the experience.
   b. The intersection of cultures between the couple's experience is more helpful for the doctor than that of the patient alone.
   c. The intersection of cultures allows the doctor to work with the patient to create a better therapeutic plan that the patient will comply with.
   d. The intersection of male and female experiences causes conflict in the context of infertility.

58. Pheromones are chemicals that can be detected by other organisms of the same species. Most scientific knowledge about pheromones comes from studies of animal species, not humans. However, evidence suggests that humans also release and respond to pheromones. Why are pheromones associated with both sexual attraction and aggression?
   a. The physiological response varies depending on the gender of the person releasing the pheromones and the gender of the recipient.
   b. The physiological response varies depending on the intention of the person releasing the pheromone.
   c. Pheromones encompass a variety of chemicals, and not all recipients have active pheromone receptors at a given time.
   d. The physiological response depends on how many people are present because the concentration gradient of the chemical pheromone disseminates among many individuals, altering the type of group response.

59. A physician has a high population of teenage patients who come to him for medical care. He notes that some teens drive themselves to clinic appointments, whereas others come in with their parents. The physician reports that the teen patients who drive themselves tend to have better recoveries. However, a chart review reveals that the recoveries are equivalent between both groups, with equal incidence of complications. Furthermore, the chart review also reveals that the majority of the teenagers who are driven by their parents come from a neighborhood of a different socioeconomic level than the majority of the teenagers who drive themselves. How would you explain the doctor's faulty conclusion?

    a. Belief perseverance

    b. Poor recall

    c. Self-fulfilling prophecy

    d. Labeling theory

Critical Analysis and Reasoning Skills

Passage 1

It is mathematics, not art, which clearly drives trends in fashion, design, and music. The true mathematical genius can calculate what the populace is prepared to accept as the color, material, or style that represents modernity. The mastermind of quantitative statistical analysis can then sell his manufactured productions to the masses, masking his algorithmic talents as an intangible artistic gift.

Artists, by nature, are inspired to creativity through emotion. These sensitive passions may deliver original art, but the depth of artistry will not produce that which the general public is prepared to accept or to incorporate into daily life.

The evolution of trends in color, melodies, and material follows principles based on what the eye and the mind interpret as new. Yet, there is more than originality that drives public approval of fashion. While the new may appear to be new, it must never be too different from the old, or else the populace will reject it as too strange.

Thus any successful designer must be, above all else, a brilliant mathematician. He must consciously compute patterns in shades of color and material that others can only appreciate on a subliminal level. The changes brought about by fashion must convince the consumer that he is forward thinking, while subconsciously comforting him at the same time. The designer must be intentionally aware of the consumer's boredom with available products around him, while allowing the consumer to cling to the features that he needs on a deep emotional level.

It is the fashion critic who exists in the middle of this relationship between the designer and the consumer. The critic, who lives a dedicated, reflective love of design, is more prone to boredom by what is currently available than the consumer. Thus he is likely to reject the creation of the highly mathematical designer, and instead be drawn to the creations of the true artist. The consumer, only frivolously interested in fashion as an amusement rather than as a deeply meaningful symbol of himself, often rejects the opinions of the critic as eccentric, impractical, and outlandish.

Thus, there is a wide disconnect between the critic and the consumer. In the meantime, the mathematical, systematic designer continues to please the wide audience, to the dismay of the critic and the artist. The true artist, however, may enjoy lavish praise from the critic. However, if he remains true to himself, he cannot overcome his lack of appeal to the consumer who is not obsessed with art and fashion.

A true artist has a signature that is independent of current fashion. The mathematician knows that too much change can be unsettling for the consumer and takes caution to avoid disturbing the peace of the consumer's existence, convincing him that his taste is a sign of his extraordinariness, when in reality, that which he believes to be his own individual preference is so predictable that it can be charted on a graph.

What, then, is the true artist to do? Should he learn the methodical rules as a student of the designer? Or should he continue to attempt to astonish the audience with his own brand of magic, hoping that when he finally reaches the pinnacle of popular recognition, his works will crush the limited scope of math and science?

1. According to the passage, what is the central difference between a designer and an artist?
  a. The designer intends for mass production, while the artist does not intend to mass-produce his creations.
  b. The designer bases his work on his assessment of what will be accepted, while the artist creates through emotion.
  c. The designer has had a high level of formal education, while the artist is self-taught.
  d. The designer is wealthier than the artist.

2. Suppose that an artist were to receive a negative review from a respected art critic. According to the passage, how would the artist react?
  a. The artist would publicly condemn the critic as unsophisticated.
  b. The artist would try to improve his work to please the critic.
  c. The artist would stay true to his signature style, choosing to retain his creativity despite lack of praise.
  d. The artist would become a student of the designer.

3. According to the passage, a successful designer must be a "brilliant mathematician." What does the author mean by the phrase "brilliant mathematician"?
  a. Someone who is so advanced in mathematical skills that he can deceive others.
  b. A person who has reached a very advanced level in sophisticated models of math and who is able to do calculations without the aid of a calculator.
  c. A person who is brilliant in all areas of academics, as math is an inclusive indicator of academic abilities.
  d. A person who is able to take mathematical principles and apply them to design.

4. Based on the premise of the passage, how would a commercially successful musician react to a negative review from a respected music critic?
  a. He would not be very concerned because his goal is to achieve popularity and recognition among the populace, not music critics.
  b. He would reformulate his approach to better tailor to the tastes of the music critic who can sway the public.
  c. He would shower the music critic with gifts to win his approval.
  d. He would attempt to gain favor with different music critics so they can give him valuable insight into the tastes of the public.

5. According to the passage, what is one choice the artist has in overcoming his inability to achieve popular acceptance?
  a. He can learn to be more like the commercially successful designer.
  b. He can accept his station in life as a starving artist.
  c. He can try to gain acceptance and praise from art critics.
  d. He can try to become better at mathematics than anyone else, in order to squash his competition.

6. Suppose the author is a buyer for a large commercial fashion retailer. Based on the premise of the passage, how would you describe the likely relationship between the author and the commercial designer?

    a. They are generally loyal business partners who share the same objective of reaching a wide popular consumer base.

    b. They are competitors, each trying to outdo the other.

    c. They are generally business partners, but the commercial designer attempts to appeal to many buyers, while the buyer shops around among many commercial artists.

    d. The author wants to entice artists to leave their trade and become commercial designers.

Passage 2

The Meeting of St. Anthony and St. Paul, a painting by Sassetta, lies in the National Gallery of Art in Washington D.C.

Like many of his contemporaries, Sassetta often used religious events and symbolism in his work. The image, which was painted on wood, relays a sense of warmth and comfort provided by the use of easy, rounded brush strokes; soft colors; and a soothing backdrop. The scene depicts several characters, including a busy gardener. The two men for whom the painting is named stand at the opening of a wide and welcoming cave. As St. Anthony and St. Paul greet each other, they bend towards each other ever so slightly, appearing to be shorter than the mouth of the cave. The cave itself is presented as a spacious underground tunnel, arcing from below, as a miniature hill above it forms a softly curved walkway for casual passersby. The sand, the trees, and the grass surrounding the cave from all directions are lush, soft, and full of life. The area bordering the cave appears to be a hilly community, populated with villagers.

The painting surely would inspire a visitor to seek solace and peace in the area around the famed cave, located in the depths of Egypt's hot and mountainous desert.

However, the entry of the cave itself is not nearly as generous, nor is the immediate environment bursting with greenery, as it appears to be in the painting. In fact, in reality, one cannot help but wonder how St. Anthony managed to discover the short, narrow opening of the cave that blends inconspicuously with the mountain in which it is nestled. Deeply embedded in dense rock, there is almost no loose sand to be found. Above the cave there is no walkway—only the hard, jagged, steep mountain that would be challenging, if not dangerous, to climb for anyone but a seasoned mountain climber. Even more bewildering, the walk up to the cave, which is located about a quarter of the way up the mountain, is only made possible because of the man-made, irregularly-shaped steps extending from the bottom of the mountain up to the cave, which must have been painstakingly paved.

Surely the Italian artist must not have travelled to Egypt to visit the mountain itself. Yet he knew of the mountain and the cave. He must have learned the details of the setting through stories that passed through many fervent storytellers before finally reaching his ears.

The cave itself can only be accessed through a short opening, followed by a constricted, elongated entrance that unexpectedly widens after at least 40 steps, at which point a soft, illuminating sunlight fills the sizeable cave that is large enough to hold at least 10 adults comfortably. The coolness inside the cave is mild, unlike the blistering heat immediately outside. However, because the atrium is so narrow as to

- 280 -

be deceiving, one wonders why someone unfamiliar with the inside would venture past the tight entryway.

Perhaps Sassetta did know such details about the inside of the cave. Could it be that his warm portrayal was an attempt to represent the inside of the cave, rather than revealing the misleading exterior?

7. According to the passage, how does the painting of the mountain's landscape diverge from the landscape of the mountain itself?
    a. The colors are soft in the painting, but the colors of the mountain are harsh in reality.
    b. The painting conveys a sense of warmth, while the mountain is cold.
    c. The painting presents the mountain as green and full of life, while in reality it is rocky and jagged.
    d. The painting suggests that the mountain is small, while in reality it is quite large.

8. Suppose the author of this passage encountered a wild animal inside the cave. What would the author conclude about Sassetta's knowledge of the cave?
    a. Sassetta had never personally visited the mountain or the cave, and thus had an inaccurate idea about the setting, which was reflected in his painting.
    b. Sassetta was aware of the wild animal, but was hiding the truth about the harsh reality of the cave because he wanted his painting to be calm and serene.
    c. Sassetta had lived in the cave and had been able to survive despite the brutal environment.
    d. Sassetta visited the cave, but did not encounter a wild animal, and thus did not portray an animal in the painting.

9. How does the author explain a discrepancy between the artistic representation of a setting and the setting itself?
    a. The alterations in climate modify the topography of the land over time.
    b. Sassetta's research into the details of the environment was flawed due to political partiality.
    c. The artist was commissioned to produce a painting of historical and religious relevance, so he used names of well-known Christian saints to elevate the status of his painting.
    d. The artist's purpose was to portray the feelings evoked by the site, rather than the physical features.

10. Based on the passage, why did the author venture past the atrium of the cave if it was so unwelcoming?
    a. He was adventurous and he went to the locale to challenge himself.
    b. He was convinced that there must be a tunnel leading to the exit from the cave.
    c. He wanted to create a painting of the inside of the cave.
    d. He was, in some way, familiar with the inside of the cave.

11. If the artist had not used religious representation in this painting, instead painting anonymous people and naming the painting *Peace*, how would this have affected the identification of the cave?
    a. The cave would have seemed less peaceful without the religious representation and fewer people would be interested in locating it.
    b. Without some historic context or narrative provided by the artist, there would have been no reason to believe the actual location existed.
    c. Geographic characteristics and clues found in the painting would have been used to guide a seeker to the mountain and the cave.
    d. The author would have had to research the artist's life to determine where the mountain and cave were to be found.

12. Was the author alone on the journey to St. Anthony's cave?
    a. Yes, the author was alone, searching for the mountain he saw in a painting and found it in Egypt.
    b. No, the author was likely with at least one guide, given the difficulty in climbing the mountain and finding the location of the cave.
    c. No, the author was accompanied by at least 10 adults.
    d. Yes, the author was probably alone because he did not mention other travelers.

Passage 3

In 1926, esteemed Spanish architect Antonio Gaudi was struck by a moving tram. Seriously injured, he was transported to a hospital. He had no identifying information and was thus given the medical treatment considered appropriate for a pauper. His condition deteriorated. After some time, a chaplain recognized him as the famous, highly respected Antonio Gaudi. Despite the hospital's fervent efforts it was too late for the prominent architect to benefit from the best medical treatment available, and he died shortly afterwards.

This true story seems almost as it were made up to prove a point about healthcare policy. Fairness, mercy and justice are all central tenets in the formulation of healthcare policy in developed countries.

Whether a physician delivers care to a pauper or to an esteemed pillar of the nation itself, healthcare decisions are based on a number of complex factors. The most obvious element of medical care is determining the best treatment option. Yet, even this choice is not always a simple or straightforward judgment that can be boiled down to a basic checklist. Minimally divergent scientific studies and discrepancies in clinical research data that differ by only a few percentage points can arbitrarily alter the favored options made available for millions of patients.

The tale of Antonio Gaudi seems to indicate that the better medical options for his injuries were clear. The ability of the patient to pay for the care appears to be a central component of the outcome in this situation. However, there are always other, more subtle factors at play when it comes to choosing among the available alternatives in medical treatment.

For instance, the value of a person to the people around him and to society may play a role in the quality of healthcare delivered. How many people are expected to mourn the loss of an unknown pauper? This is an ethical question that may seem disgusting to many of us.

Another important factor at play in healthcare delivery is whether the patient will put in the effort to maintain his health after the professional care is delivered. For example, will he keep his surgical wounds clean? Will he take his medication? Will he follow dietary instructions? Imagine the heartbreak of the medical team who worked for hours to save the life of a patient only to learn that he indulged himself in harmful recreational drugs before his wounds had healed.

Yet current healthcare policy is in a tug of war between the rights of the Antonio Gaudis of the world and the rights of the pauper. For society to pay for the pauper who cannot pay for himself, society must have either an abundance of extra resources or a sense of responsibility towards the anonymous pauper. The monetary value of a person who cannot pay for his own healthcare is an issue that cannot be resolved in any dignified way. A true case of mistaken identity illustrates the grey area of healthcare rights and responsibilities like no fact-filled political debate or rambling health policy book can. What if the mistaken identity were reversed? What if the pauper was the doppelganger of a famous person?

13. Suppose healthcare policies were debated between two political opponents, how would a political candidate appeal to the broadest voter base?
    a. The candidate would discuss a detailed policy proposal to be transparent to voters.
    b. The candidate would discuss generalities that favor the majority of the voters based on their socioeconomic status, salaries, and benefits.
    c. The candidate would display a sense of fairness to the most disadvantaged members of society.
    d. The candidate would remind voters that their situation is better than that of citizens in most other countries.

14. Based on the passage, how is "best medical care" defined?
    a. Best medical care is determined by scientific studies and clinical research data.
    b. Best medical care is arbitrarily determined based on the study authors who push their data as superior to other data.
    c. Best medical care is defined based on widely divergent results which produce data that clearly demarcate the ideal treatment options for all patients.
    d. There is no accurate definition of best medical care, as it is assigned completely arbitrarily.

15. The passage asks, "How many people are expected to mourn the loss of an unknown pauper?" Why is this question described as disgusting?
    a. The question is described as disgusting because it suggests the presence of a degenerative, unsightly disease.
    b. The question is described as disgusting because it raises the point that few people will mourn the loss of a pauper.
    c. The question is described as disgusting because it suggests that if few people would mourn the loss of a paper, the hospital might not exert great effort in saving his life.
    d. The question is described as disgusting because it suggests that there is a grey area in health policy.

16. When the passage brings up the point that some patients may not put in the effort to maintain health after professional care is delivered, who is the author concerned about?
    a. The author seems concerned that some patients might not receive proper instruction in self-care after release from the hospital.
    b. The author is concerned that the public is forced to pay for the healthcare of a person who might not follow through with necessary self-care.
    c. The author is concerned about the few loved ones who will mourn the loss of the pauper.
    d. The author is concerned about the medical staff who will exert a great amount of effort, only to have it go to waste when some patients do not put in the effort to care for themselves.

17. Suppose the story at the beginning of the passage described an infamous, unrecognized escaped convict. Based on the premise of this passage, how would the monetary value of the person's life be determined?

    a. The monetary value of an escaped convict's life would be less than that of a pauper or of a famous architect who could pay for his own care.

    b. The monetary value of a criminal is equal to that of a pauper or a famous architect.

    c. It depends on whether society has an abundance of resources.

    d. The monetary value of a person's life cannot be resolved in any dignified way.

18. What does the author imply about fact-filled political debates and rambling books?

    a. They may or may not be accurate, but they do not get at the crux of the dilemmas in health policy the way this true story does.

    b. They are valuable, but they are biased due to partisanship and political motives.

    c. They may be inaccurate because of statistical error and inconsistency in healthcare costs.

    d. They are unfair to people who cannot pay for their own healthcare.

Passage 4

A number of well-conducted surveys suggest that ageism is emerging as a legitimate obstacle in the workplace. Mature workers increasingly report an alarming lack of job security as well as age-related barriers to finding jobs once the need arises. Despondent and anxious, the outcry has become impossible to ignore for many growing companies that flourish on competitiveness, but do not want to stand accused of discrimination. Yet, at the same time, an abundance of salary data reports point to a trend of superior compensation associated with seniority, even among experienced workers who change jobs. There must be an explanation for this disparity.

The answer could lie in a tendency of the work environment to operate in a "survival of the fittest" mode. Seasoned workers who have proven themselves valuable in the workplace may indeed enjoy generous promotions in position and salary. Yet, given the job insecurity reported by older workers, it appears that age alone does not guarantee promotions, salary advances, or even basic contract renewal.

Perhaps older workers who are frustrated in their job searches are being unrealistic, expecting offers of leadership positions better suited to their high-performing peers. A more practical option could involve pursuing jobs that demand fewer responsibilities, offer less prestige, and provide lower rates of reimbursement. On the other hand, such entry-level positions may not be open to experienced workers who are humble enough or desperate enough to seek them.

Perhaps the older workers who feel a sense of job insecurity are not actually inferior workers, but might, in fact, be honest citizens who found themselves victims of bullying, bias, or dishonesty at the hands of their former peers and supervisors. Perhaps older workers who consider themselves at a disadvantage in the professional world display a poor work ethic, behave with entitlement, or rest on their laurels.

The professional world is not solely based on performance. Some may suffer due to poor social skills, unattractive appearance, or naïveté. Jobs that provide generous compensation packages are generally few and far between, as the workplace hierarchy is pyramidal. Fewer administrators are needed to manage and direct many mid-level employees. Is it realistic, then, to assume that all workers who started in the same position with the same qualifications will go on to enjoy a slice of the best piece of pie? Yet, is it fair for older workers to be discarded as outdated and unskilled simply because they are average? Those who want to continue to do the same tasks for many years, resisting new technology, may eventually find themselves vulnerable to a bitter reality.

So whose responsibility is it to keep stale workers up to date? Should workplace leaders employ paternalistic attitudes, holding their unmotivated workers' hands in the scary waters of newness? Or should the workplace employ only the fittest, regardless of the cost? Both approaches are susceptible to inducing a degree of bitterness—either on the part of the below-average worker who is shed by his innovative employer or on the part of his coworkers who must pick up the slack while he passively and peacefully grows deep roots in the company.

19. The passage asks, "Should the workplace employ only the fittest, regardless of the cost?" What is the meaning of "cost" in this phrase?
    a. "Cost" taken here means the overall cost to the company in productivity, as better workers may cost more and thus may decrease the company's profit.
    b. "Cost" is taken to mean the cost of producing bitterness among aging employees who are shed because they are not the fittest.
    c. "Cost" taken here means that, when the workplace is hierarchical, those at the bottom may suffer from a sense of discouragement as a consequence of remaining at a deferential role.
    d. "Cost" taken here means that, when a company employs only the fittest, it may stand accused of discrimination.

20. The author wavers in attempting to explain why a senior worker may be at a disadvantage in the workplace. Why do you think the author is so ambiguous?
    a. The author has been accused of discrimination and would like to avoid another such incident.
    b. The author wishes to fire one or more underperforming senior employees, but is unsure whether the employees have a poor work ethic, or suffer from setbacks to good job performance due to issues such as workplace bullying.
    c. The author is upset that aging workers suffer from job insecurity, but wants to present a balanced point of view.
    d. The author is an indecisive individual, which is precisely the problem with average workers.

21. Suppose young workers were complaining of discrimination in the workplace. How would that change the premise of the passage?
    a. The author would definitely feel that young workers have no right to complain because they have many years ahead of them to earn and save money.
    b. There would not be such a concern about a responsibility towards young workers because they have not invested years learning the skills needed for the company and the industry as a whole.
    c. The author may feel a responsibility towards helping young workers develop to their potential.
    d. The passage would likely have a tone of urgency regarding possible accusations of discrimination, as younger people are more vocal regarding their rights.

22. What does the passage suggest about older workers who are leaders and presumably receive high levels of monetary compensation?

a. They are high performers who achieve recognition either through hard work or through intimidation and bullying.

b. They made it to the top of the workplace pyramid, but no one can really pinpoint why.

c. They are completely secure in their jobs and they do not fear unemployment.

d. They have chosen to give entry-level positions to young people, rather than to senior workers, in an attempt to mentor new leaders.

23. If you were to learn that the vast majority of older workers who have been laid off were mothers who requested part-time work hours after having received excellent company-created performance reviews, how would that affect the author's concern about discrimination?

a. The author would be rightly concerned about discrimination charges, given that good performance reviews bolster a laid off worker's sense of unfairness.

b. The author would be able to resist discrimination charges because part-time work hours are inherently less valuable to a company.

c. The author would be able to support the layoffs because of issues related to tardiness and lack of technology know-how.

d. The author would have to redefine the qualities of a valuable worker to avoid discrimination charges.

24. Suppose that computers and robots took over most laborious workplace tasks. Would jobs that provide generous compensation packages remain few and far between?

a. No, because everyone would become a supervisor to the computers and robots.

b. There would be many jobs that provide generous compensation, but they would be available at outside companies.

c. Yes, these jobs would remain scarce because few leaders are needed to supervise computers and robots, which do not take responsibility for high-level decisions.

d. Few people would need to work, so they would have more time to become entrepreneurs.

Passage 5

Objective testing of children's academic and reasoning abilities has become highly valued in public schools. Students' performance benchmarks are used in combination with each individual student's year-to-year improvement to provide objective criteria with which to evaluate school and teacher effectiveness, which is then used as a financial incentive.

Yet, all educators and parents know that standardized measures obtained through multiple choice examinations provide only a limited view of educational gains.

The problem lies in the excessive classroom time devoted to standardized testing. This time does not serve in any way to provide students with educational enhancement, but rather steals from learning opportunities. Even more than divesting valuable time, the ensuing exhaustion that results from sitting for lengthy examinations leaves students less equipped to benefit from any remaining constructive instruction during the remainder of the school day.

On the other hand, non-curriculum based activities such as recess, field trips, and school assemblies enhance students' abilities to absorb concepts and to exercise creativity.

The rigid requirements imposed by hours and hours of in-school testing create a tenuous situation in which emergency school cancellation becomes particularly damaging to students because, while a number of school days are forsaken, the total number of hours devoted to standardized testing remains inflexible, disproportionally affecting instructional classroom time in school.

Some schools' academic functioning is undoubtedly poor. Students in a percentage of school districts lag behind in basic skills such as reading, math, writing, and reasoning. The harmful long-term effects of such deficiencies cannot be understated. Yet, implementing required testing in all school districts to identify the few that underperform seems a monumentally wasteful way of identifying and managing educational shortcomings.

Perhaps a better method would include devoting time and energy to providing additional instruction in the schools that repeatedly underperform on widely-used exams such as the SAT and ACT. Or perhaps, online courses designed to reteach lagging skills can make the time spent on this matter more productive than consuming classroom time with testing that does not serve to educate the majority of the students. Surely, with today's technology, computer programs can be used to identify benchmark skills and, subsequently, to teach students at a gradual and personalized pace.

In fact, if testing must remain a part of schooling, then computerized tests coupled with supplementary activities should be required of all students. Those who lag behind would be directed to math and reading problems that help them learn the skills necessary to reach appropriate targets, while those who test ahead of grade level can be given the opportunity to practice with problems that challenge them and make them even better academically.

Most importantly, the classroom itself is a valuable place for all students. Do the high academic achievers have nothing to learn from those who perform at lower levels in math? Could not the lower scholastic achievers be gifted socially? Standardized testing misses the societal value of schools completely. School children benefit from being with their peers in the school setting more than they benefit from the academic instruction provided by the schools.

25. The passage states that "all parents and educators know that objective measures provide a limited view of educational gains." What data is used to support this statement?
   a. It is obvious that this statement is true, so no data is needed.
   b. Parents and educators have reported these facts through personal narratives to the author.
   c. No data is provided to support this statement. It is the author's opinion.
   d. No data is provided to support this statement, thus it is false.

26. Suppose the author is a teacher at a school in which students generally perform in the 60th percentile on standardized tests and her students performed in the 88th percentile, well above the school's average. How would that inform your interpretation of the author's purpose?
   a. The teacher is showing off her superior teaching skills, and is thus drawing attention to testing results.
   b. This teacher feels competent in teaching the basics and wants to have more freedom in teaching.
   c. The teacher wants to show other teachers how to improve their students' objective scores.
   d. The teacher would like to defend her school from being penalized for low test scores.

27. According to the passage, what is the biggest problem with testing?
   a. It consumes time and energy from learning in the classroom.
   b. It does not provide accurate insight into children's educational ability.
   c. It does not examine social skills.
   d. It does not inherently provide a means to repair lagging skills.

28. The passage says that "perhaps online courses to reteach lagging skills can make the time spent on this matter more productive..." What do the words "this matter" refer to?
   a. Over-testing of school children, which results in wasted time and exhaustion.
   b. The problem of underperforming schools and students who lag behind their peers in some academic skills.
   c. The inability to teach students that lag behind.
   d. The fact that students who have to do homework on worksheets do not get immediate feedback on their answers.

29. Suppose the author were asked about the value of student diversity. What do you think the answer would be?
   a. The author most likely values student diversity because it allows students to learn more about culture and art, reinforcing the material learned in the classroom.
   b. The author most likely does not value student diversity because it can be overwhelming, possibly preventing teachers from being able to teach academics at a uniform level.
   c. The author likely does not think that student diversity is necessarily good or bad for students.
   d. The author likely values student diversity because interaction with students who are different teaches school children social skills.

30. The author states that, "school children benefit from being with their peers..." Which of the following statements is most likely to accurately represent the author's view about teachers' interactions with school children?
   a. Schoolteachers should spend more time focusing on group activities instead of the curriculum.
   b. Schoolteachers should have students share their test scores with each other as a way to promote healthy competition.
   c. Schoolteachers come from varied backgrounds and thus can teach children about different cultures using maps and projects.
   d. Schoolteachers have different personalities, and exposure to these different personalities allows students to learn how to navigate the social world.

Passage 6

It is only now with the minimally requisite impartiality that economists and historians can begin to piece together the meaning behind the economic disaster that grew, in part, out of the proliferation of subprime mortgage rates in the 1990s. Articles and books already abound on the subject, but most are colored by too much self-interest, political partisanship, special interests, and even emotions stemming from personal consequences of the events.

The economic atmosphere of the 1990s appeared to be unparalleled to many of those living it. Low interest rates coupled with the promise of economic growth, property appreciation, and unquestioned rising incomes set the stage for speculation in the housing market and the business world alike. Globalization also provided a seemingly sage explanation for the acceptance of unprecedented expansion, even for those who were skeptical of the ability of domestic economic growth to provide enough support to justify the disproportionate optimism characteristic of those years.

However, it seems that the notions of creative destruction and capitalism as a perfect self-regulating system may have delivered the ultimate weakness in preventing the corruption that was part of the eventual collapse of economic growth.

It was an environment that seemed one in which everyone could profit, leaving behind any traditional sense that for one to win, someone else must lose. The principle of unrestricted inflation itself suggests a profit for all, as inflation promised, sometimes with validity and sometimes erroneously, to feed the income of many. Yet, reality proves that the price paid by the consumer must be finally acknowledged as a net loss for the consumer. The denial that insists that the consumer benefits to such a degree from inflation—either directly in wages or through investments that seamlessly filter to everyone—asserts that the consumer can forever remain unscathed by increasing costs of goods and services.

The irony of this flawed supposition is that, while it rewards innovation in a classically capitalist system, it craves rewards for those who took no part in innovation at all. Congratulating itself, this high-flying yet benevolent economy fails to see itself as the untruthful Ponzi scheme that it really is.

The supposition that, even if profits are temporarily exaggerated, they will buffer any future plateau, was, unfortunately, also flawed. And those who suffered from great losses were not necessarily responsible for the faulty reasoning that led to an inescapable trap, as they simply accepted employment and bought shelter as is necessary to live.

It may have been a strange sense of responsibility carried by some at the top of the economic ladder that necessitated a degree of belief that wealth was being shared. Yet many who found themselves in the same position chose instead to abuse the freedom that leadership provided them, surreptitiously deceiving those who trusted them without any regard for the future.

How then, can elected officials prevent themselves from being blinded to corruption when they are able to relish and take responsibility for the achievement of the good outcomes they so fervently work towards? Are not economic prosperity and creativity the goal of a society? How can lawmakers prevent themselves from savoring noble outcomes, instead persistently probing for hidden problems?

31. What role did globalization play in the economic disaster described in the passage?
    a. It provided a backdrop for economic growth that would not have been sustained domestically.
    b. It provided a rational explanation for skeptics of unprecedented expansion.
    c. It created a situation in which global growth could allow everyone to be a winner.
    d. It created an environment of extremes, allowing some nations to experience generous growth, while others quietly suffered.

32. How could a belief in capitalism as a perfect self-regulating system fail to prevent corruption?
    a. It allowed for unchecked dishonesty to occur because of the unwarranted dependence on capitalism as a self-regulating system.
    b. It causes dishonesty because it rewards inequalities in income, as opposed to a socialist system, which does not incentivize disparities in output.
    c. It allows oppression of those who are not financially creative.
    d. It does not provide a setting that allows for laws that limit the effects of subprime mortgages.

33. Who does the author believe to be most responsible for the economic disaster of the 1990s?
    a. The lawmakers because they did not notice deceptive practices.
    b. The unreasonably optimistic business leaders.
    c. Those who unwisely invested their assets in speculative ventures.
    d. Those who corrupted the economy by deceitful practices.

34. Suppose that lawmakers who had noticed the corruption and wanted to prevent economic disaster had been forcibly prevented from doing so by lawmakers who were financially influenced by corrupt businesspeople. How would the author most likely describe lawmakers?
    a. The author would describe lawmakers as a group without enough background in economics.
    b. The author would describe lawmakers as put into office by equally corrupt voters.
    c. The author would describe them as a heterogeneous group of varied interests and ethics.
    d. The author would describe the lawmakers as cynical and always looking for problems.

35. How does guilt play a role in the economic disaster described in the passage?
    a. Guilt prevents some business leaders from acting in a corrupt manner.
    b. Guilt forces some business leaders to share wealth.
    c. Guilt forces lawmakers to look the other way, not wanting to believe that anyone could be culpable of corruption.
    d. Guilt allows some business leaders to pat themselves on the back for creating a system that they believe is beneficial for everyone.

Passage 7

Thomas Mann's 1929 novella, *Mario and the Magician*, skillfully uses familiar elements of the human psyche to establish for the reader the manner and techniques that a government has at its disposal to manipulate its population. Yet, while some believe the ending of the story to be an exhibition of liberty, it is not reassuring that one of the victims of the brutal magician ends his torment by killing the tyrant.

The story most certainly had the impact on the audience that was originally intended by the author at the time it was written, and it is because of this that he was relegated to exile. But after the fascist era ended, the anecdote depicts a disturbing tale because the use of human interaction as a tool for symbolism underscores one of the many weaknesses of human character.

Indeed, political submission is often acknowledged as inescapable, even today. However, the toleration of personal indignities is more alarming in today's world, reflecting feebleness in self-determination that is viewed as more dishonorable and less understandable that it was at the time of the novella.

The advances in the science of psychology have made a weak sense of dignity something to be ashamed of. In fact, those who suffer from biologically based

- 290 -

debilitating psychiatric illness may suffer less reproach than those who simply display an ineffectuality of disposition, passivity, or a subordinate personality.

Fiction of the past may be grounded on an acceptance as normal of personality traits that are seen as reprehensible in a western view of the world that rewards self-assurance above all other elements of one's personality. Indeed, a lack of self-confidence is often seen as a product of bad mothering in the same way that biochemical psychiatric disorders were seen as a consequence of bad mothering in years past, prior to modern scientific discoveries.

Timeless fiction speaks to a deep place in human consciousness that transcends culture and time. The manner in which we appreciate most fiction is based largely on cultural norms, which differ among societies and generations, deeming most fiction only transiently relevant.

For Mario to resort to destroying the cruel villain assumes that he does not have the power to resist the villain, to coexist with the villain, or to dominate him. It clearly communicates that the only way Mario and his fellow victims can escape the treacherous magician is to eliminate him from the world completely. A more sophisticated approach would be more useful to the modern reader. The simplistic murder by any of one of the magician's victims, or even by the hero of the story himself, just emphasizes how the magician is so easily able to hypnotize all of his victims, to their dismay.

The political analogy aside, the conviction in the innate human ability to overcome tyrannical domination or any form of hypnosis is noteworthy in the sense that it is not a timeless principle. Thus, politically symbolic fiction, in general, is not as likely to enjoy timeless appeal as other types of fiction because it relies on basic creeds of society to illustrate its point, tenets that may be so outdated at a later era as to alter the message as it was originally intended.

36. According to the premise of this passage, can a fictional story be timeless in appeal?
    a. It cannot, because the basic societal values change so much over time as to make central points not relatable.
    b. Only if the author of the fictional story has better insight into the deep-seated and unchangeable traits of human nature than the author discussed in this passage.
    c. A fictional story can have timeless appeal if it does not rely on tenets that become so outdated as to lose resonance with the reader.
    d. A fictional story can have timeless appeal, but not necessarily across all cultures.

37. Did the story of *Mario and the Magician* achieve the objectives of its author?
    a. Yes, he made his message clear to the audience as evidenced by his exile.
    b. He had many messages and it is unclear whether they were well received.
    c. He was not viewed as a political leader or a revolutionary, but rather was exiled. This indicates that he failed in his objective.
    d. Given that Thomas Mann is a well-known author, it appears that he achieved recognition, which is likely his most important objective.

38. Suppose Thomas Mann's father was a high-ranking official in the rising fascist government. How would this affect the psychological interpretation of the story?

a. The story would have been less dangerous for Thomas Mann because his father would have pardoned him.

b. The hero's actions would have to be interpreted in light of a son's rebellion against his father.

c. The story would be viewed as Thomas Mann's complaint that his father did not appoint him to a high rank in the government.

d. The story would have to be reinterpreted as a support for fascism, given a son's loyalty to his father.

39. How has the science of psychology affected those with a weakness of character?

a. It has made them stronger and better able to overcome their character weaknesses.

b. It has provided a biological explanation for weakness of character.

c. It has freed them from the oppression of bad mothering.

d. It has made weakness of character something to be ashamed of.

40. How is political submission viewed in the world today, as suggested by the passage?

a. It is a product of weak self-determination.

b. It may be inescapable at times.

c. It is prevalent when there is an absence of political fiction and symbolism in political fiction.

d. It is inevitable.

41. How might the author have preferred the story of *Mario and the Magician* to end?

a. The author would have liked to see a less extreme solution, possibly to help him model a solution to a problem that he is dealing with.

b. The author would have preferred to see the group of victims joining together to destroy the oppressor, for a more unified solution.

c. The author would have liked to see the magician submitting to the victims and apologizing.

d. The author would have preferred a different ending because the murder in this story was too violent.

Passage 8

Sustainable energy is innately equipped with ample features that make it attractive to consumers. The public, generally conscientious, but with understandably limited power over energy sourcing and pricing, favors the idea of clean energy. A sustainable stock of energy allows for thoughtful preservation, rather than consumption of the environment due to the renewability of natural and non-consumable resources. A minimal need for the use of contamination-prone production techniques that have a tendency to produce damaging effects such as air and water pollution makes sustainable energy desirable.

However, many who are responsible for providing energy comprehend the inherent difficulty that is one of the realities of harnessing and preserving some forms of the abundant and readily available springs of sustainable energy, such as solar power and wind energy, obtained, for instance, through the use of innocuous windmills. They argue that barring powerful incentives (or disincentives) and revolutionary methods of stabilizing energy in a reservoir-like form, the current mechanisms of producing and consuming sustainable energy have already neared their peak capacity for applied use.

However, the problems with the dominant energy sources and our dependence on heavy energy consumption are not going to go away, but instead are likely to worsen if left unchecked. Efforts to curb worldwide energy use have not been a priority for any reputable faction. Thus, sustainable energy offers a reasonable path to forge as we look for solutions.

Investment in sustainable energy is one mechanism that consumers have the power to use to encourage the research and development of sustainable energy by putting actual dollars and self-interest into the process.

Legislation and advocacy are other steps that the consumer can use to encourage the development of sustainable energy, but these steps require a reasonable amount of time, energy, money, and research into the substance of the science as well as the sociological repercussions.

Investments in sustainable energy sources can serve to provide a solid and reliable approach for consumers to benefit from the inevitable future developments in engineering. Surely, a broad-based investment methodology can help secure a buffer against policy, business, and technological variants in this area. Given the budding potential, coupled with the demand for sustainable energy, it is unlikely to be a risky investment or a short-term trend in emerging technology.

Different types of renewable energy include wind energy, solar energy, wave-generated energy, plant produced energy, and others. Some of these technologies are likely to be developed further by existing energy suppliers while emerging energy suppliers may also enter the industry. When research is the primary goal, it is likely that competing companies will have similar interests in terms of political lobby. It is only after the profitability of sustainable energy becomes undeniable that competing profit centers will battle, limiting profit margin and essentially creating an environment in which the science can progress, but the business becomes complex. Such a scenario is unlikely to disrupt an investor's plans in the near future, or even in the next 20-30 years. However, before this danger materializes, forewarnings will abound, easily providing notice to consumer-investors to safely divest.

42. How would the author explain a significant investment loss to a client who invested in sustainable energy years ago?

a. The author would likely explain the loss as a consequence of a lack of financial responsibility among energy producing companies.

b. The author would likely explain the loss by stating that sustainable energy was not financially profitable in the past, but that it will be in the future.

c. The author believes that risky investments are unwise, and would advise the client to steer clear of making the same mistake again.

d. The author believes that investments must have inherent value beyond simple numbers, and thus would say that the investment was beneficial to the community as a whole, even if it was not beneficial to the individual.

43. Based on the passage, why is sustainable energy attractive to consumers?

a. Sustainable energy is more efficient than other forms of energy.

b. Sustainable energy is naturally produced and thus less costly.

c. Sustainable energy is a product of nature, and thus does not involve the same amounts of chemicals that may harm the environment.

d. Sustainable energy does not get old or expire, thus requiring disposal, which can harm the environment.

44. How may legislation alter the use of sustainable energy?
    a. Legislation can disincentivize energy sources that produce pollution to the environment.
    b. Legislation can require companies to consume less energy in their operations.
    c. Legislation can protect the consumer from the effects of pollution by providing individual consumers with more choices regarding their energy suppliers.
    d. Legislation can provide consumers with more transparent information regarding sustainable energy and other energy sources so that consumers can make informed choices.

45. Why is the author interested in telling the reader about sustainable energy?
    a. The author is a proponent of clean energy due to concerns about the environment.
    b. The author is starting a new company and wants to raise funds for his company.
    c. The author is appealing to investors to convince them to invest in diversified sustainable energy funds.
    d. The author has a strong interest in educating the reader about the benefits of sustainable energy.

46. How may existing energy suppliers interact with emerging energy suppliers in the field of sustainable energy?
    a. They may partner with each other in the areas of research and development, at least early in the process.
    b. They may not compete with each other in the areas of research and development.
    c. They may join forces to overcome legislative barriers to distribution.
    d. They may leave each other alone while they focus on gaining footing in the areas of research and development.

47. What is the scientific barrier to the proliferation of the use of sustainable energy?
    a. It is difficult to extract energy from sustainable sources.
    b. It is difficult to preserve extracted energy from sustainable sources.
    c. It is not practical to use energy obtained from sustainable sources.
    d. Sustainable sources are already at their peak because nature cannot make more sustainable material.

Passage 9

The interaction between humans and animals encompasses a range of vital relationships. Animals may assist as part of a laboring workforce, as beloved human companions and as food sources. A respect for the gentle creatures as well as the wild beasts of nature is an essential part of preserving these varied bonds, which often depend on one another. Even when animals are raised for the ultimate purpose of the sustenance of humans or other living creatures, the maintenance of animals' dignity during their lives plays a large role in a farmer's awareness. Yet, the unique connection between man and animal in situations when animals pose a threat to man must incorporate a special reverence for life itself.

The fascinating and true account of Jim Corbett's commissions to exterminate threatening man-eating tigers identified in human inhabited communities in the early 1900s illuminates the balance between human safety and a guarded admiration for the animal kingdom.

Man-Eaters of Kumaon, authored by Jim Corbett, is widely recognized as historically accurate in its details. A conservationist and a military officer, he was called upon at times by the British government to hunt rare man-eating tigers that were jeopardizing the lives of clans in Indian villages.

One of the most fascinating ventures in the book is the precarious story of a Bengal tiger given the name Thak. She was a tiger who had previously survived an unexplained gunshot wound. By the time she was recognized by the British government, she was notorious as a man eating tigress who terrorized villages while she dwelled in a region populated with Indians and where the British government had plans to dispatch hundreds of workers for a construction project. Interestingly, Jim Corbett, having already succeeded at hunting assignments directed at several other man-eating tigers, grew to understand the habits of tigers. He explained Thak's unusual man-eating practice, not characteristic of most tigers, to her desperation during a period of possible incapacity for a time after having been shot and badly wounded. It is unclear when or why she had been targeted and by whom, but this explanation postulated by an experienced tiger expert suggests a rapidly evolving impact of the human population on the survival behaviors of animals. While man-eating may have been a survival skill that served to save her at a desperate time, it has certainly served its short-lived value, and later operated to resolve her unavoidable fate.

The interaction between the tiger and her hunter was complex. She became suspicious, growing cautious and deliberately eluding usual tiger hunting techniques, perhaps because she had been shot before, and thus was already schooled in the possibility that sudden, unexpected threats unfamiliar to the wild could overwhelm her at any time. Yet, despite her intelligence, she still succumbed to her instinctive needs for nourishment and breeding. Boisterously calling for a mate, she was caught by the hunter who was able to draw her closer with a loud response, finally killing her and leaving the village safe again. Planned construction began, without the threat of tigers.

This was Jim Corbett's last tiger hunt. After this experience, he became a photographer of tigers, with the objective of capturing their majesty in their natural habitat.

48. How does the passage depict the astuteness of the tiger?
   a. It was typical of a tiger in survival mode.
   b. Unusually sharp, and able to detect and elude human hunters.
   c. She was primitive, because she succumbed to innate needs that resulted in her discovery and death.
   d. Her intelligence was inferior to that of the hunter, who was able to shoot her.

49. Why does respect for the tiger play a role in the hunt?
   a. The method of hunting the tiger should be humane, as an injury can result in more pain and agony for the tiger than killing it.
   b. Respect is not relevant because the tiger is not being raised as a pet.
   c. The best means of showing respect would be to capture the tiger and place her elsewhere.
   d. Respect for the tiger in this instance prevents the further killing of tigers.

50. How does evolution, as discussed in the case of Thak, play a role in producing man-eating tigers?
    a. The principle of survival of the fittest can make a trait such as man-eating more prevalent.
    b. Over time, the abundance or lack of prey can cause an ecosystem to favor man-eating behavior among predators.
    c. Mutations in the genes of tigers can create a man-eating tendency.
    d. Impactful events can cause a behavioral change in predators due to adaptation.

51. How would the intimate knowledge of tiger habits that made Corbett an expert tiger hunter translate into his new profession of photographing tigers?
    a. It would help him locate tigers while they are mating.
    b. It would help him recognize when a tiger is hungry so it can be fed, posing less danger to the photographer.
    c. It would help him interpret a tiger's movements, sounds, and smell to know whether it is safe to photograph.
    d. It would help him to capture close-up still photos after befriending the tiger.

52. Suppose that Thak had given birth to a baby tiger one week before her death at the hands of the hunter, and this tiger later grew up to be a man-eating tiger like its mother. What impact would this have on Corbett's theory of why Thak was a man-eating tiger?
    a. It would indicate that the man-eating trait was probably environmental rather than learned.
    b. It would support the possibility that Thak was genetically predisposed to eating humans.
    c. It would have little impact on the theory about Thak, since her offspring's behavior can be explained by having learned the behavior from its mother.
    d. It would imply that Thak's memories of being hunted by humans were passed down to her offspring.

53. Suppose the man-eating tiger, Thak, had killed the hunter rather than being killed by him. How would the author likely describe the hunter's techniques?
    a. The techniques were suitable for hunting tigers in the past, but species evolve to counter hunters' techniques over time.
    b. The techniques were too reliant on the hunter's personal experiences, rather than on scientifically proven methods.
    c. The techniques were effective for many tigers, but were not sophisticated enough for a tiger that had been previously survived being shot.
    d. The techniques could not have been improved upon, given that this hunter was the preeminent tiger hunter of the time.

Answer Key and Explanations

Biological and Biochemical Foundations

Question Set 1

1. D: *Hyperpolarization* means a more extreme difference in electrical charge than the –70-millivolt (mV) baseline. A charge of –75 mV is more negative than a charge of –70 mV, and thus a membrane with –75 mV is hyperpolarized.
A charge of –65 mV is closer to zero than –70 mV, and thus it would not be hyperpolarized. A charge of 25 mV is also closer to zero than a charge of –70 mV, and thus it would also not be hyperpolarized. A charge of 180 mV is farther away from zero than –70 mV, and it could be defined as hyperpolarized. However, given that the refractory period produced by the pump's hyperpolarization is brief, the charge of the membrane could not be so far from the resting potential of –70 mV. Given that the hyperpolarization is an overcorrection of the action potential, it could not result in a positive charge, but it would be expected to result in a more negative charge than the –70 mV resting potential of the cell membrane.

2. A: Sodium and potassium are highly charged positive ions and are not lipid soluble. Therefore, they need a protein channel or an enzymatic protein to move across the hydrophobic portion of the plasma membrane.
Sodium and potassium are both small ions that can diffuse across some membranes, but because they are hydrophilic, they cannot diffuse across the fatty cell membrane. The phosphate present in the phospholipid bilayer is tightly bound to fatty acids and therefore cannot interact with Na+ and K+. A neuronal cell contains more Na+/K+ ATPase in its cell membrane than other cells of the body. But most cells contain Na+/K+ ATPase embedded in their cell membranes because it is used as a means to drive active transport.

3. C: The temperature can alter the 3D shape and, thus, the behavior of an enzymatic protein by altering the covalent bonds due to changes in electron movement. The hydrogen concentration, often fluctuating with pH, but also fluctuating in the presence of water molecules, can also alter the 3D shape of a protein because hydrogen is a very reactive atom due to its single electron in the outer shell. A molecule that attaches to the binding site of an enzymatic protein can alter the protein's structure and function.
Diffusion is not a factor in altering enzymatic protein shape or behavior. Water and pH both determine the hydrogen concentration, so answer B is redundant and does not include temperature, a very important determinant of the behavior of enzymatic proteins. Answer D is not correct because the concentration gradient can change the availability of a substrate, but it does not change the behavior of a protein.

4. B: Under normal circumstances, one of the effects of the pumps is to produce latency while returning the membrane to its resting potential. The more concentrated solution in this experiment made the latency shorter, and thus it must have deactivated some of the pumps, producing a reduced latency time period.
The solution did not prolong the refractory period. The length of the refractory period is directly correlated with the latency because it is the refractory period that makes it impossible for the NA+/K+ ATPase to resume activity. If the solution worked to prolong the activity of some pumps,

then the latency would have been longer with the more concentrated solutions, particularly with the 0.07% solution.

5. A: Because of the refractory period, an action potential cannot stimulate a membrane that has already been stimulated within the refractory period, and thus an action potential cannot move in the reverse direction,
Excessive concentrations of sodium could potentially damage the cell, but the latency period does not remove sodium from the cell; instead, it is the result of a slight change in the membrane's charge due to the movement of sodium. The refractory period is often believed to have some relationship with the target organ or with the synapse, but it does not. A different pathway could potentially stimulate the target organ again. Similarly, the synapse may receive a signal from a different source, and thus it is not mandatorily protected by the refractory period, which takes place at some distance.

6. D: The 0.07% solution had the most dramatic effect on the cells in this experiment. It would be expected that the cell with a lower Na+/K+ ATPase-activated proton pumps at baseline would have a more dramatically reduced action produced by deactivation of the pumps and, consequently, a shorter latency.
The greatest drop in latency between the two less-concentrated solutions would not necessarily clarify which cell has a higher density of pumps. The difference in latency between the two higher concentrations of solution, while more effective in deactivating the pumps than the lower concentration, would not necessarily deactivate the pumps of greater density more or less than the pumps of lower density, and it would be unreliable to interpret the data that way. Similarly, the relative change in latency upon exposure to all three solutions would not reveal which cell has a higher or lower density of Na+/K+ ATPase-activated proton pump.

Question Set 2

7. B: The genetic code is redundant. There are 64 codons and only 20 amino acids used in protein formation. Because of this redundancy, often a substitution mutation has no effect on the protein product.
The complementary strand in a DNA molecule must follow the base pairing rules. If a mutation of any sort affects one strand, it automatically must affect the other. The homologous copy of a DNA molecule may or may not be able to compensate or correct for a mutation — depending on whether the homologous, nonmutated DNA molecule codes for a dominant or nondominant gene. An abnormal protein product encoded by a faulty DNA molecule might be destroyed by the body's immune system, but, depending on its ultimate function, it may wreak havoc on the body, causing mild to serious problems.

8. D: Enzymes such as DNA polymerase can work to correct an error during DNA replication, which is an important part of cell division.
Cell division does not involve transcription. Transcription is the process by which a single-stranded mRNA molecule is produced based on a DNA template. DNA replication is the process by which a double-stranded DNA molecule is produced based on a DNA template. Segregation of homologous chromosomes occurs during cell division in meiosis to ensure one copy of each gene, rather than during the replication process, which is part of mitosis. A substitution mutation can be repaired when it occurs, and this is the role of some of the enzymes that are involved in the DNA replication process.

9. C: There is a weak association between the two conditions. However, it does not appear to be a functional relationship, because there is not a direct increase in T-cell impairment with base pair mutation.

The base pair mutation does not improve with worsened T-cell function because there is only one data point of improvement between group 1 and group 2. But there is an increase in base pair mutation between the control group and group 1 as with between group 2 and group 3. T-cell function plays a role in protecting the body against precancerous cells, but in this situation it does not appear that T-cell dysfunction is the reason for the mutation because of the fact the controls had some T-cell dysfunction without base pair mutation. More importantly, there was also a decrease in base pair mutation between groups 1 and 2 despite the increase in T-cell dysfunction. The fact that the base pair mutation is more prevalent than the T-cell dysfunction does not support the answer that the base pair mutation causes the T-cell function impairment.

10. A: The dramatic increase in the presence of base pair mutation in the experimental group suggests an association between the two conditions. However, there does not appear to be a causative effect or a functional relationship, based on the pattern of the results. Genetic linkage would be the most likely explanation for the difference between the control group and the experimental group.

The fact that the base pair mutation was an incidental finding speaks to whether the genotypic mutation results in a phenotypic change, which it might not, as discussed in question (1). Linkage between two genes does not necessarily have to result in a 1:1 correlation or a direct, linear relationship. The loci of the two genes must, indeed, be located near each other to establish linkage. However, comparing function to genetics in this instance does not preclude a nearby location. In fact, in many instances, an observation such as this is the hint or clue in locating a genetic abnormality on a gene.

11. B: During transcription, enzymes involved in producing a messenger RNA (mRNA) molecule work to make a faithful copy of the nucleotides encoded on the DNA molecule, even if it is faulty. RNA polymerase will not correct a substitution mutation or any mutation during transcription, because a mutation is part of the DNA molecule. When transfer RNA (tRNA) molecules match amino acids to mRNA molecules, this puts the abnormal code into "action." But this step is a part of translation, not transcription. The rRNA does play a role in joining tRNA and amino acids with mRNA molecules during translation, not transcription. But the consequences of this step will maintain the effects of the mutation, not decrease or increase it.

12. D: Meiosis results in the production of germ cells. A mutation during meiosis affects the offspring, but not the individual in whom the mutation occurred.

The mutation will not affect the individual at all, regardless of whether the impact on the protein encoded for is negligible, mild, or serious. The mutation will affect all of the haploid daughter cells produced during meiosis, because it would occur during DNA replication and prior to segregation and reductional division.

Question Set 3

13. C: Given that her father is not affected by this X-linked recessive disorder, her carrier status can only be determined retrospectively if she has a son who has G6PD deficiency.

Stephanie's G6PD levels are expected to be normal or near normal even if she is a carrier. This disorder is a metabolic disorder and does not manifest anatomically; thus, it would not be detectable by ultrasound. Exposing her to the offending agents may or may not produce a hemolytic reaction in the fetus – but such a trigger could be dangerous and is thus neither a safe nor a reliable way to check for her carrier status.

14. B: An X-linked gene can be expressed as codominance if the heterozygous homologous X-chromosomes both have genomic sequences encoding proteins that can be expressed simultaneously, essentially producing a blend of characteristics.
If the homologous genes on the X-chromosomes are homozygous, then the phenotype expressed will be either homozygous dominant or homozygous recessive, but not codominant. The genes on the Y-chromosome do not correspond to the genes on the X-chromosome, and thus there is no opportunity for codominance.

15. B: To determine linkage, one would have to evaluate whether the two disorders occur together at a rate higher than expected based on their individual rate in the population. Similarly, the reverse statistical analysis would yield similarly useful information: assessing how frequently G6PD deficiency occurs with and separately from other disorders that occur with the same frequency as sickle-cell disease in this population.
The fact that both genomes are located on the X-chromosome does not imply linkage. Linkage occurs when genes on the same chromosome are located at nearby loci, decreasing the chances of crossing over. The genetic prevalence versus the phenotypic occurrence would not help in determining whether malaria resistance was an evolutionary advantage for individuals with G6PD unless this data were compared with data from generations ago. Whether the RBCs have a hemolytic response to malaria exposure can help in assessing how malaria affects RBCs with and without G6PD enzyme, but not whether there could have been any linkage with sickle-cell disease or whether the response of the RBCs was, in fact, an evolutionary advantage.

16. A: The genomes of a dominant and recessive gene both work independently of one another to produce products. This explains the phenomenon of codominance. However, the products of a dominant gene are expressed, whereas the products of a recessive gene are not, mainly because the products of a dominant gene cancel out the expression or behavior of the products of a recessive gene.
The proteins encoded by either recessive or dominant genes may be long or short, small or large. Products of recessive genes are not expressed less due to denaturing of proteins, but rather because of some type of interaction with or effect of products produced by dominant genes. A dominant gene's products may "turn off" the genetic transcription of a recessive gene, but the presence of the dominant gene itself would not turn off transcription. RNA assembly of nucleotides encoded by a dominant genome is not more effective or more powerful for dominant genes than for recessive genes.

17. D: G6PD deficiency provides partial protection against malaria, and therefore a vaccine that protects against malaria may affect the incidence of G6PD deficiency in the population after some generations, but it might not if the mortality of the enzyme deficiency itself is high.
Answer A is too simplistic for a real population. Although adaptation most likely has already occurred to a degree, that does not preclude further adaptation within the population if the circumstances change due to a vaccination. An immunization would protect individuals from the hemolytic effects of malaria, but there are other triggers for hemolysis in G6PD-deficiency-affected individuals than malaria. Additionally, malaria produces hemolysis among those without G6PD deficiency, so an immunization would not preferentially aid those with the deficiency.

18. C: If the enzyme replacement were completely withheld, this would be the most effective way to determine the triggers of hemolysis. Of course, it would be unethical to willingly expose patients to potential triggers of hemolysis and withhold the enzyme.

The enzyme itself could not correct a hemolytic reaction in progress, but rather the absence of the enzyme causes a hemolytic reaction in response to certain triggers. Administration at random intervals would not differentiate between various triggers. Answer D would not establish whether sulfa medications and fava beans trigger hemolytic reactions because the enzyme would potentially prevent the hemolytic reaction. But this method could identify other triggers.

Question Set 4

19. D: Polysaccharides are metabolized in the same manner as monosaccharides, but they must first be digested and absorbed, as well as broken down into smaller subunits prior to entry into glycolysis, prolonging the metabolic process, but yielding the same energy per gram.

Polysaccharides are indeed larger and take longer to digest and absorb. But it is important to understand that there is a difference between digestion, which is breaking down the bolus into small molecules for absorption, and metabolism, which involves energy production.

Polysaccharides are, indeed, larger than monosaccharides, and they do contain more calories than monosaccharides, but they contain the same number of calories per gram. Polysaccharides are directly broken down into simple glucose molecules and enter glycolysis, unlike fatty acids, which undergo a different initial step of oxidation prior to entering glycolysis.

20. A: Saturated fatty acids only have single bonds, and this molecular configuration is more stable than unsaturated fatty acids, which have double bonds and may be destabilized by molecules in the environment.

Saturated fatty acids are completely saturated with hydrogen atoms, not with electrons, which are subatomic structures of hydrogen atoms. Unsaturated fatty acids are more likely to be liquid at room temperature and to reach a boiling point faster than saturated fatty acids, but it is not this feature that makes them more likely to become rancid. Unsaturated fatty acids can have a trans configuration, but a trans configuration is not associated with greater molecular instability. Unsaturated fatty acids with a cis or with a trans configuration have a greater tendency to become rancid than saturated fatty acids.

21. B: It is the number of single bonds in a molecule that yields energy. Saturated fatty acids have more single bonds than unsaturated fatty acids and thus contain slightly more calories per gram. The number of calories is based on the number of single bonds and double bonds. But two single bonds yield more calories than one double bond, which means that despite the equivalent number of bonds, the caloric count per gram is slightly higher in saturated fats. Some molecules are more difficult to absorb. Starches, for example, which are complex carbohydrates, may contain indigestible portions that are not absorbed and thus do not yield calories. This feature does not analogously apply to fatty acids. Unsaturated fats contain fewer calories per gram than saturated fats due to the lack of double bonds within saturated fat molecules, regardless of the size or total number of bonds per molecule. The size of the molecule and the number of bonds affects the mass and thus the weight. Calories are considered per gram, which takes into account the size and number of bonds.

22. B: Glycolysis consumes 2 ATP molecules and produces a gross yield of 4, which is a net yield of 2 ATP molecules. The Krebs cycle yields 2 ATP molecules, whereas the electron transport chain yields 32 ATP molecules.

23. D: Because saturated fats contain slightly more calories than unsaturated fats, such an experiment would require control of caloric intake to differentiate the effects of saturated fat versus unsaturated fat, independent of calories.

If the experiment were designed to determine the difference between saturated versus unsaturated fatty acids in the context of heart disease, adding another variable, which is the measure of polyunsaturated fat, would not directly help answer the question. The numbers of total calories consumed by research subjects can affect the development of heart disease, but this would not help to differentiate the effects of saturated versus unsaturated fats. Preexisting heart disease can certainly alter the results, but it wouldn't alter the difference between saturated fat versus unsaturated fat.

24. C: Oxygen allows metabolism to produce more ATP per glucose molecule than the ATP produced in glycolysis alone, which does not require oxygen. Because the Krebs cycle and electron transport chain together produce 34 ATP molecules, oxygen makes metabolism more efficient. Oxygen is not required for the metabolism of glucose, although the metabolism is less efficient in the absence of oxygen. Oxygen is not required for glycolysis, and thus it is not part of every step in the metabolic process. It is the electrons in the electron transport chain that result in the rich supply of ATP, not hydrogen.

Question Set 5

25. C: The experimental results do not demonstrate or prove that the antioxidant is responsible for the decrease in edema or that edema is the cause of tissue damage. However, because patients exposed to the antioxidant had a smaller area of infarcted tissue, it appears that the antioxidant has a beneficial effect. Most, but not all, of the patients with smaller areas of infarct also had decreased edema, suggesting that edema may also play a role. This suggests that some type of combination of the presence of edema and antioxidants was at play when decreased tissue damage was observed. There was no measured relationship to blood flow. It is unclear exactly why the antioxidant-injected samples showed deceased damage, and it is a leap to suggest that the antioxidants themselves produce chemicals or biochemical reactions that decreased the size of the infarct or the edema.

26. C: Most of the cell's ATP production occurs in the mitochondria. The Ca+ concentration is maintained by active transport, which requires ATP. Ca+ leaks into the ischemic cell due to passive transport when ATP is inadequate to overcome the concentration gradient.

Active transport does maintain the Ca+ concentration, but ATP is produced in the mitochondria, not by the mitochondria, which is an important distinction. Mitochondrial membranes contain Ca+, but mitochondrial dysfunction occurs prior to mitochondrial degeneration, and the calcium influx is largely a consequence of mitochondrial dysfunction. The lack of adequate oxygen forces the cell to rely in lactic acidosis, which can cause ionic shifts. But this is not the driving force behind the calcium influx.

27. A: In small quantities, lactic acids and free fatty acids are tolerable due to the cell's ability to buffer mild pH changes. However, in an ischemic setting, the cell cannot correct the pH changes, and thus the proteins that form the structural and functional components of the organelles begin to denature.

Lactic acids and free fatty acids are acidic, meaning that they contribute hydrogen atoms to the environment, whereas free radicals are deficient in electrons. Although the volume of acidic molecules within the cell is not beneficial for the organelles, their pH is their most harmful characteristic and thus the most immediately damaging consequence. Free fatty acids are hydrophobic and thus may be able to pass through organelle membranes, but they cause organelle dysfunction from outside the organelle in the cytoplasm as well.

28. B: A cell relies on anaerobic respiration when aerobic respiration, which depends on oxygen, cannot provide the necessary substrates for the Krebs cycle and the electron transport chain. The by-product of anaerobic respiration is lactic acid.

Lactic acidosis is the product of lactic acid production during infarction, not the consequence of a molecule already present in the cell, the organelles, or the membranes. Lactic acid is a by-product of anaerobic respiration, which provides energy, but the lactic acid itself does not provide energy. Lactate is a sugar present in dairy products, whereas lactose is an enzyme that breaks down lactate. Lactic acid is a by-product of anaerobic metabolism. Although the three molecules have similarities in structure and name, and they can be easily confused, they are not the same.

29. D: As the tissue becomes damaged and the cells become altered, inflammatory white blood cells arrive to remove debris and to repair damaged tissue.

There have been microorganisms noted in and around infarcted tissue, and the presence of subclinical infection has been imputed as a possible contributor to ischemia, but not directly to the fast damage of infarction that occurs as a result of ischemia. The inflammatory cells are a component of edematous fluid that is present during infarct, but this does not explain how membrane degeneration contributes to inflammation because the inflammation is more likely a response to the membrane degeneration. The white blood cells that arrive so quickly during the inflammatory response to ischemia are likely already present in the body moments prior to the ischemic event; however, they arrive to the site of damage as a result of cytokines and other modulators, rather than due to passive transport driven by the concentration gradient.

30. B: The physical degeneration of the phospholipid bilayer of the membrane, as well as the dysfunction of protein channels and pumps, allows ions and other molecules to leak into or out of the cell, driven by the concentration gradient. Capillary leakiness is the result of separation of the endothelial cells that line the capillaries, which can allow fluid and cells, including inflammatory cells, to leak into or out of the capillary.

The membrane of the capillary, if it becomes pathologically permeable, would allow fluid and cells to leak in or out. The membrane of the cell would allow fluid and ions into or out of the cell if it becomes leaky. Membrane leakiness both contributes to and results from degeneration of the phospholipid bilayer, whereas capillary leakiness results from separation of the endothelial cells that line the capillaries. Membrane leakiness and capillary leakiness both contribute to edema and inflammation by allowing fluid, white blood cells, and other molecules to flood the site.

Question Set 6

31. D: Developmental disorders may have a number of possible etiologies, including alterations of the genome or environmental causes. Developmental disorders may begin prior to fertilization, due to alterations in the gamete, during embryogenesis, or even after birth.

Genetic disorders as well as developmental disorders may both include physical conditions, defects in emotional processing, or cognitive disorders. Genetic disorders involve alterations in the DNA nucleotide sequence and can be produced before, during, or after embryogenesis as a result of inherited DNA alterations, environmentally triggered DNA alterations, or spontaneously occurring DNA alterations.

32. B: Nondisjunction is the imperfect separation of homologous chromosomes during meiosis and results in a gamete that does not have one of each chromosome from a homologous pair. Nondisjunction may result in a chromosome number other than 23, but nondisjunction may result in a chromosome number of 23 if a different nonhomologous chromosome replaces one chromosome. Most of the time, nondisjunction results in 22 or 24 chromosomes in a haploid gamete, but this is not necessarily the case because nondisjunction might result in replacement of one chromosome with a nonhomologous chromosome or it may result in more than one missing or more than one extra chromosome.

33. A: Using one of these germ layers to replace the type of cell that originates from the corresponding type of germ layer maximizes the potential for proper differentiation. A matched-type donor may minimize rejection, but this would not improve the chances for proper differentiation. Bone marrow stem cells would have already progressed beyond the embryonic stage of ectoderm, mesoderm, and endoderm, making them less likely to differentiate into the target cell type. Gametes are unfertilized and are therefore haploid, so they are not able to replace diploid cells.

34. A: Pulmonary surfactant develops late in gestation, and therefore prematurity can result in respiratory distress syndrome, which occurs because the alveoli may collapse when pulmonary surfactant is deficient, leading to poor oxygenation.
The skeletal muscles are not the factor limiting oxygenation when premature birth occurs at this stage of fetal development. The heart function and hemoglobin are both adequate because respiratory support for premature babies born at this stage of fetal development provides adequate oxygen to the body.

35. B: Germ cells are diploid cells that will later undergo meiosis to produce haploid gametes, whereas germ layers are composed of diploid cells. The ectoderm, mesoderm, and endoderm are the differentiating germ layers of the embryo.
Germ cells are not produced during gametogenesis. Gametes are produced during gametogenesis. Germ layers are produced after fertilization. Germ layers are not parts of germ cells. Germ cells are diploid, as are the cells of germ layers. These terms sound similar, and thus they can be confusing.

36. C: A germ cell is a diploid cell produced during embryogenesis. After birth, during puberty or adulthood, oogenesis and spermatogenesis produces gametes, which are haploid cells. A germ cell replicates its chromosomes and produces four daughter gametes, each with a haploid chromosome number.
A germ cell does not mature into a gamete, but, rather, it undergoes a more complex process of gametogenesis. A germ cell does not simply divide to produce two gametes. A germ cell is diploid.

Question Set 7

37. A: A parasite can be haploid or diploid and may go through phases of diploid or haploid genomic number.
Bacteria and viruses are haploid, whereas prions do not contain genetic material.

38. C: A virus may invade a cell and evade an immune response by essential hiding inside the cell so that leucocytes may not identify the virus. Sometimes the virus alters the host cell so that the cellular immune system is activated.

A retrovirus can invade immune cells, as is the case with the human immunodeficiency virus (HIV), but other viruses that selectively invade cells that are not part of the immune system may evade an immunologic response as well. So deactivating the immune system is not the only mechanism a virus uses to avoid identification and destruction by immune cells. And not all viruses infect immune cells. A virus is small, and this aids in its evasion of the immune system by allowing it to enter inside a cell, but it is not too small to be detected by the immune system. A virus does not typically mimic a cell, but instead it enters the cell and uses the cell's genetic tools to make new copies of itself.

39. A: Binary fission is the process by which bacteria grow and replicate their DNA and then divide. Conjugation is a method of transferring genetic material between bacteria, and it may be a part of the bacterial reproduction process. Bacteria do not reproduce by sexual reproduction. A virus inserts its genetic material into the host's genome, whereas bacteria do not.

40. D: A retrovirus genome is composed of RNA nucleotide, whereas a viral genome is composed of DNA. Both insert into the host cell and use its reproductive tools to make new viruses.
Both a retrovirus and a virus may insert genetic material into a host cell's DNA, and they can both enter the cell membrane of the host. The cell wall is present in bacterial cells but not in human cells. A retrovirus or a virus can alter a cell's DNA to cause a precancerous transformation of the host cell. A retrovirus is not an old cell, despite the sound of the name.

41. B The bacterial cell has a cell wall; a cell membrane and cytoplasm; and a nucleoid, which holds the DNA. But a bacterial cell does not have a nucleus.

Question Set 8

42. C: Nerves that are part of the CNS often send messages to the peripheral nervous system (PNS). The somatic nerves in the PNS may then send nerve signals that ultimately release acetylcholine at the neuromuscular junction. Because an action potential is an all-or-none event, demyelination in the CNS may prevent any signal from reaching the peripheral nerve.
It is true that afferent peripheral nerves send electrical signals to the CNS, but acetylcholine, associated with nerves that stimulate skeletal muscle, is a neurotransmitter associated with efferent nerve stimulation that originates in the CNS. An action potential is an all-or-none event, and thus demyelination does not result in slowing or a diminished signal, but it results in either no effect or in a complete loss of the action potential. The CNS interacts with the PNS, and thus, depending on the exact location of demyelination, CNS problems can affect the PNS.

43. B: The hypothalamus communicates with the anterior pituitary gland through the vascular system and with the posterior pituitary gland through axon extensions. Additionally, the posterior pituitary is composed of neuronal tissue, whereas the anterior pituitary, despite its location in the brain, is not neuronal tissue.
The hypothalamus produces hormones that are sent to the posterior pituitary gland through the axons, are stored in the posterior pituitary gland, and then are released. The anterior pituitary gland makes hormones in response to chemical stimulation from the hypothalamus.
Communication between the hypothalamus and both the anterior pituitary gland and posterior pituitary gland is regulated by positive and negative feedback. Negative feedback is the predominant mechanism. Oxytocin, released by the posterior pituitary gland, is associated with elements of positive feedback, but the anterior pituitary gland responds to positive feedback as

well. The hypothalamus primarily stimulates hormone release or hormone production and release in both the anterior and posterior pituitary.

44. A: A hyperactive pituitary tumor may overstimulate the adrenal medulla, and thus produce negative feedback reaching several levels, including the hypothalamus and the pituitary gland, and the adrenal medulla would regulate the hormones that regulate the autonomic nervous system. The negative feedback regulating the hypothalamus would not be the only negative feedback in place, and, alone, it would not effectively control the hyperactivity of the anterior pituitary gland. Although negative feedback would help regulate hormonal production, it is unlikely to effectively balance the activity of the sympathetic and parasympathetic divisions of the autonomic nervous system. Additionally, negative feedback generally works to decrease stimulation of hormones rather than to directly inhibit them. It is not characteristic that overproduction of ACTH would desensitize the adrenal medulla to overstimulation. Hormone regulation is most commonly controlled by negative-feedback mechanisms.

45. D: The change in concentration over time would be partially controlled by the rate of reuptake, but it would also be controlled by other mechanisms of serotonin decomposition. Taking initial measurements of concentration and following the change at several intervals would help determine the effect of additional serotonin on the rate of reuptake.
The reuptake function does not rely on a neurotransmitter having a desired effect on an end organ. Reuptake or any type of neurotransmitter deactivation is based on concentration, not quantity. The results of the experiment comparing different concentrations of serotonin treatment would not provide as much value as comparing a treated group to a control group because a baseline value is necessary to establish the normal rate of reuptake.

46. C: Neuroglial cells are better able to repair themselves than are neurons, and possibly because of their increased capacity for cell division over a person's lifespan, they may undergo alterations that could lead to cancer.
Neuroglia are indeed supportive cells, but this characteristic does not preclude cancer potential. Neurons are not more likely to experience toxin, free-radical, or retrovirus exposure than do neuroglia due to their functional status. The blood-brain barrier protects the CNS, including the neurons and the neuroglial cells, and thus retroviruses, which can cause oncologic changes, are not preferential to neuroglia or neurons. Both neuroglia and neurons are myelinated, but some neuroglial cells provide myelin for the neurons. Myelin is not protective against cancer-causing materials. Myelin insulates neuronal tissue to maintain the action potential.

47. D: A hypofunctioning adrenal medulla would result in inconsistent compensatory stimulation of the hypothalamus and pituitary gland rather than a steady overstimulation. But the compensatory response of the pituitary would not cause a benign or malignant enlargement of the pituitary gland, and thus it would not affect the optic nerves.
Pituitary enlargement would produce pressure on the optic nerves, but overstimulation by negative feedback mechanisms should not cause enlargement of the pituitary gland. The thyroid gland is the gland typically associated with enlargement in response to hypofunction, hyperfunction, hypothyroidism, or hyperthyroidism.

Question Set 9

48. A: The oxygen deficit that results from blood loss as well as the volume deficit stimulates a compensatory response of the heart rate.

Although a lack of oxygen may force the body to use an alternate metabolic pathway that results in lactic acidosis, this is not the driving force behind the resulting tachycardia. CO_2 buildup does provide feedback to the brainstem medulla that adjusts the heart rate, but in the setting of acute anemia, it is the volume loss and oxygen deficit that elicit the heart rate adjustment. Hemolytic anemia is a type of acute anemia, but it is caused by the breakdown of red blood cells within the body, not by the volume loss experienced during traumatic bleeding.

49. B: The kidneys detect the oxygen concentration in the blood and produce erythropoietin to stimulate the bone marrow to produce erythrocytes, which are red blood cells.
The volume of fluid that passes through the kidneys is a factor in determining the urine output from the kidneys, but it does not stimulate erythropoietin production. The stem cells in the bone marrow respond to erythropoietin to increase the production of red blood cells.

50. B: Blood pressure is a measurement of arterial pressure. In the setting of acute anemia, arterial regulation adjusts in response to fluid levels, tissue needs, and oxygen concentration.
Vasospasm may occur in the setting of acute bleeding that causes tissue irritation or in the setting of acute hypertension. Red blood cell concentration is not a factor in acute anemia, but it is a factor in chronic anemia. Venous regulation is the regulation of veins, which are blood vessels. However, blood pressure is measured in arteries, not in veins.

51. C: The brainstem medulla detects carbon dioxide levels and sends hormones to adjust the size of the alveoli, the width of the bronchi, and the rate and force of inspiration by control of the respiratory muscles.
The medulla in the brainstem is different from the adrenal medulla, which is part of the adrenal gland, a gland that sits above the kidney. The kidney also has a renal medulla. Although the name "medulla" repeats in anatomy, these are distinct locations that can be easily confused.

52. D: Within the first few minutes of an agglutination reaction, the acute hemolysis would stimulate the sympathetic nervous system, but this would not have an effect on erythropoietin to correct the hemolytic anemia yet.
Eventually, if the patient survives a hemolytic reaction, the kidneys would produce erythropoietin to increase red blood cell production in the bone marrow. The response to erythropoietin would not increase or decrease due to anemia or hemolysis, and the sympathetic nervous system would not inhibit the release of erythropoietin.

53. A: The kidneys control and adjust blood pressure in response to several factors, including fluid content and fluid volume. The kidneys produce erythropoietin in response to oxygen concentration and oxygen partial pressure.
The urine content is a function of the kidneys, but the kidneys' response to blood pressure determines the fluid content in the body. The urine content depends on a number of factors, and thus it would not be a reliable measurement of the kidneys' response to chronic anemia. The urine content and volume are dependent on fluid and electrolytes. Antidiuretic hormone is produced in the anterior pituitary and acts on the kidneys, so it would not be a good indicator of the kidneys' response to chronic anemia.

Discrete Questions

54. A: The neural tube begins to develop within the first month of gestation, so a folate deficiency resulting in neural tube defects would be expected to begin having deleterious effects within or even prior to the first month of gestation.

If a vitamin deficiency increases the risk of any type of birth defect, an adequate supply of the vitamin does not necessarily prevent all of the defects from occurring because developmental problems generally have more than just one etiology. Thus, eliminating one of the causes does not necessarily eliminate all of other causes of the defect. Although vitamin A is fat soluble, one cannot infer that all vitamins impacting gestation are fat soluble because there are several routes by which nutrients can reach the fetus. Although epidermal tissue and nerve tissue are derived from a common germ layer, they diverge and thus do not necessarily rely on the same nutrients for proper differentiation.

55. A: An egg cell is larger than a sperm cell, containing a larger cytoplasm with more adenosine triphosphate (ATP)-producing mitochondria.

An egg cell is haploid, as is a sperm cell. A sperm cell may contain a Y or an X chromosome, whereas an egg cell must contain an X chromosome and cannot have a Y chromosome. Both egg cells and sperm cells have nuclei. In reproductive technology, a sperm cell or both an egg cell and a sperm cell can be isolated and used in an in vitro procedure.

56. B: Leukocytes are white blood cells. Antigens on pathogens elicit a leukocyte response. Lymphocytes are a subset of leukocytes.

B-lymphocytes make and release antibodies in response to antigens on the surface of pathogens. Other leukocytes, T-cells, do not produce or release antibodies, instead carrying out the cell-mediated immune response, which is not antibody mediated. Erythrocytes are red blood cells and do not have a major role in the body's immune response, nor do they produce antibodies.

57. D: The names of junctions between cells are often counterintuitive. Gap junctions form a channel between the cytoplasm of neighboring cells, allowing material to flow from one cell to another.

Gap junctions do not allow a space between neighboring cells, despite the name's implication. Tight junctions form a barrier to prevent fluid from passing between neighboring cells, whereas adhering junctions cement neighboring cells together. It is not adhering junctions that form a barrier to block fluid, it is tight junctions.

58. C: The liver, the kidney, and the small intestine cells can use amino acids in the process of gluconeogenesis in the mitochondria. The mitochondrion is the site for gluconeogenesis, but not all cells are capable of gluconeogenesis. The muscle fibers, particularly the slow muscle fibers, are rich in mitochondria, but muscle cells are not a site for gluconeogenesis, even when an alternate energy-producing pathway is needed. Adipose tissue stores fat molecules. The energy-producing process that uses fat molecules is not gluconeogenesis, but rather oxidation and then entry into the Krebs cycle and the electron transport chain. Gluconeogenesis uses amino acids to build carbohydrate molecules for energy.

59. B: A proto-oncogene is a normal gene that may undergo an alteration and become an oncogene. An oncogene is an abnormal gene that may cause cancer. Proto-oncogenes generally encode for cell activity related to cell death or cell division. Thus, when proto-oncogenes are altered in certain ways, cells may become cancerous.

A proto-oncogene does not promote an oncogene, although the name would make it sound so. A proto-oncogene is not a protein, although the name could be mistaken for a protein. A proto-oncogene encodes functions related to cell apoptosis and mitosis, as does an oncogene, because they are both forms of the same gene. But a proto-oncogene is normal, whereas an oncogene is abnormal.

Chemical and Physical Foundations

Passage 1

1. **A**: Bond A is the amide bond linking the amino acids together to form a peptide. For amino acid analysis, hydrolysis of peptide bonds with hydrochloric acid is preferred over hydrolysis with strong base because hydrochloric acid is much less likely to break any other bonds in a protein, leaving the individual amino acids largely intact.

2. **D**: (L-Glutamic Acid). The easiest way to recognize the correct answer is by the pK_a of the R group of this amino acid. Since it has a pK_a of 4.25, it must be a carboxylic acid. Of the choices given, only glutamic acid has a carboxylic acid on the R group.

3. **B**: (L-Lysine). This question requires understanding of how cation exchange chromatography separates amino acids based on charge, as well as recognizing the charge on amino acids based on memorization of the structures or the pK_a data presented in the passage.

The protonated amine groups on the amino acids carry a positive charge. These positive charges interact most strongly with the negatively charged sulfonate groups on the ion exchange beads. If you did not know that sulfonate is negatively charged, you can deduce this fact by recognizing either that it is a cation exchange resin, or that it is preloaded with positively charged sodium ions. When the positively charged amine groups interact with the negatively charge beads, the beads slow the movement of those binding amino acids down the column.

In this example, L-Lysine, with the positively charged R group (seen from the pK_a of the R group in Table 1) and the positively charged α-amino group consequently carries two positive charges, while all of the other choices only carry one positive charge (from the α-amino group). Hence, L-Lysine interacts more strongly with the negatively charged beads and is the slowest of the amino acids listed to elute from a cation exchange chromatography column.

4. **B**: ( ). Choice (b) is the stereochemical representation of L-alanine. Incorrect answers are: (a) D-alanine, (c) L-valine, and (d) L-leucine. This question requires understanding of the structure of amino acids (by memorization), as well as stereochemistry, either by memorization, or by determination using the rules of organic chemistry for R and S enantiomers. The specific rotation values given in the passage are not, by themselves, useful in figuring out structure.

5. **D**: (The amino acid labeled *unknown*). Examination of the pK_a values in Table 1 provides this answer. Buffering by an acid/base pair is strongest near the pK_a of the acid. Of the amino acids available as choices, only *unknown*, with an R group pK_a of 4.25 has a pK_a near 5, so only it buffers at that pH. This fact is why most amino acids (except histidine) do not generally provide significant buffering in the physiologic range of pH 6-8.

Passage 2

6. D: (24). Each of the three oxygen atoms contributes six, nitrogen contributes five, and the negative charge contributes one additional electron.

7. B: (0). The formal charge is the difference between the charge on the valance electrons in an individual atom (such as the nitrogen atom), and the charge on the electrons assigned to it in the Lewis dot structure. Nitrogen has five valence electrons when it is an individual atom, and the Lewis dot structure of nitrite has five assigned to it (one for the single bond to oxygen, two for the double bond to the other oxygen atom, and two nonbonding electrons). Since there are five valance electrons in the individual atom and five electrons assigned to it in the nitrite ion, the formal charge is zero.

8. B: (Ammonia, nitric oxide, nitrogen dioxide). Ammonia is trigonal pyramidal with nitrogen at the vertex, so the polar bonds from the nitrogen to each of the hydrogen atoms add together to form a molecular dipole pointing up through the nitrogen atom. Nitric oxide consists of only two atoms with different electronegativity, so it has a molecular dipole pointing from the nitrogen to the oxygen atom. Nitrogen dioxide is a bent molecule, so the two polar bonds from the central nitrogen atom to the two oxygen atoms add together to give a molecular dipole pointing through the oxygen atom and away from the nitrogen atoms. Nitrous oxide is incorrect because it is a linear molecule and the contributions to the molecular dipole from each of the polar nitrogen to oxygen bonds cancel each other out. Dinitrogen is incorrect because it is a molecule consisting of two identical atoms, and so there are no polar bonds.

9. C: ($\overset{-}{N}=\overset{+}{N}=\overset{-}{N}$). Of the possible resonance structures, (c) has the fewest formal charges and hence is the dominant form. The answer (a) is a possible resonance structure for azide ion, but since it has more formal charges than (c), it is not the dominant contribution. The answers b and d are not dominant resonance structures of azide ion since they do not satisfy the octet rule around each of the nitrogen atoms.

10. D: (Nitrous oxide and water). The easiest way to solve this problem is to balance the redox reaction, starting with:

$$N_3^- + NO_2^- + 2H^+ \rightarrow N_2 + ???$$

Balancing the nitrogen atoms means the right hand side must contain an additional two nitrogen atoms. Given the answer choices, that means either one N_2O or two NO molecules.

$$N_3^- + NO_2^- + 2H^+ \rightarrow N_2 + N_2O + ???$$

or

$$N_3^- + NO_2^- + 2H^+ \rightarrow N_2 + 2NO + ???$$

Balancing oxygen atoms (two on the left implies two on the right) by adding water to the right gives a balanced reaction for the first equation (and is the correct answer):

$$N_3^- + NO_2^- + 2H^+ \rightarrow N_2 + N_2O + H_2O$$

However, the second reaction is already balanced with respect to oxygen, so must not have any water as a product:

$$N_3^- + NO_2^- + 2H^+ \rightarrow N_2 + 2NO + ???$$

Since this reaction producing nitric oxide cannot balance with respect to H and O, either with or without water added to the right hand side, it cannot be the correct choice.

Passage 3

11. D: ($Ca_3(PO_4)_2$). Calcium is an alkaline earth metal that, as an ion, always carries a +2 charge. Phosphate (PO_4^{3-}) carries a -3 charge. In order to achieve charge balance, there must be equal positive and negative total charges in the crystal, so there must be three calcium ions for every two phosphate ions.

12. C: (12.4%). While an exact equation can determine how much radioactivity remains as a function of time, it is easiest to estimate in this case. Forty three days is about three half-lives (3 × 14.29 = 42.87 days). Each half-life drops the radioactivity by half. At day 0 the activity is 100%, after 1 half-life it is 50%, at 2 half-lives it is half again, or 25%, and after three half-lives it is half again, or 12.5%. The answer is 12.4% because 43 days is just a little longer than three half-lives.

13. D: (The storage conditions will not influence radioactivity). Radioactive decay rates are not dependent on temperature or the chemistry around the atom, which is why radioactive decay rates are so useful for dating old objects or tracking the movement of atoms.

14. B: ($^{32}_{16}S^+$). According to Table 3, ^{32}P undergoes beta decay. Beta decay involves a neutron turning into a proton with the loss of an electron. Consequently, the nuclear charge increases by +1. When starting with phosphorus that has 15 protons, an increase of one proton turns the atom into a sulfur atom with 16 protons. Since the phosphorus atom started with no charge, and lost an electron with a negative charge, the final atom must have a positive charge.

15. C: ($^{13}_6C$). Capture of a neutron adds a neutron to the nucleus, and leaves the electrons and protons unchanged. Consequently, to get to $^{14}_6C$ by neutron capture, one has to start with a carbon atom with one less neutron.

Passage 4

16. D: (Blue). The wavelength used to detect bilirubin in the passage is 457 nm. Blue light has wavelengths between about 450 nm and 495 nm.

17. C: (2.7 eV). The equation used to calculate the energy of a photon from the wavelength is E = hc/λ, where h is Planck's constant, c is the speed of light in a vacuum, and λ is the wavelength. In this case, E = (4.1 ×10^{-15} eV/s)(3.00 × 10^8 m/s)/(457 nm) = (1.2 × 10^{-6} eVm/s)/457 nm. In order to divide the values, first convert nm into meters. 1 nm = 1 × 10^{-9} m, so 457 nm = 4.57 × 10^{-7} m. Substituting 4.57 × 10-7 m for 457 nm in the earlier equation gives E = (1.2 × 10^{-6} eVm/s)/(= 4.57 × 10^{-7} m), which equals 2.7 eV. The Faraday constant is not required to answer this question.

18. C: (0.61). Transmittance is the fraction of light passing through the sample , T = P/P_0, where T is transmittance, P_0 is the incident light, and P is the light passing through the sample. The easiest way to determine this answer is to recognize that for each 1-cm that the light penetrates through the solution, 0.85 (85%) of the initial light passes through. Since the same fractional decrease is true for each of the 1-cm lengths, the transmittance is 0.85 × 0.85 × 0.85 = 0.61.

This answer can be also calculated from the Beer-Lambert Law, $T = 10^{-\varepsilon lc}$, where ε is the molar absorptivity, l is path length in cm, and c is the concentration. The only variable in this equation that changes is l. For the 1 cm path length, $T = 10^{-\varepsilon lc} = 10^{-\varepsilon c} = 0.85$. For a 3 cm path length, $T = 10^{-\varepsilon lc} = 10^{-3\varepsilon c}$. Separating the exponent into two parts, we get $T = (10^{-\varepsilon c})^3$ and substituting in 0.85 for $10^{-\varepsilon c}$ we get $T = (0.85)^3 = 0.61$.

19. C: (0.10). Absorbance is defined by Beer's Law, $A = \varepsilon lc$, where A is absorbance, ε is the molar absorptivity, l is path length, and c is the concentration. In this case, $\varepsilon = 48{,}907$ M^{-1}cm^{-1}, l is 2 cm, and $c = 1$ μM $= 1 \times 10^{-6}$ M. Consequently, $A = (48{,}907$ M^{-1}cm$^{-1})(2$ cm$)(1 \times 10^{-6}$ M$) = 0.098$ which rounds to 0.10.

20 C:

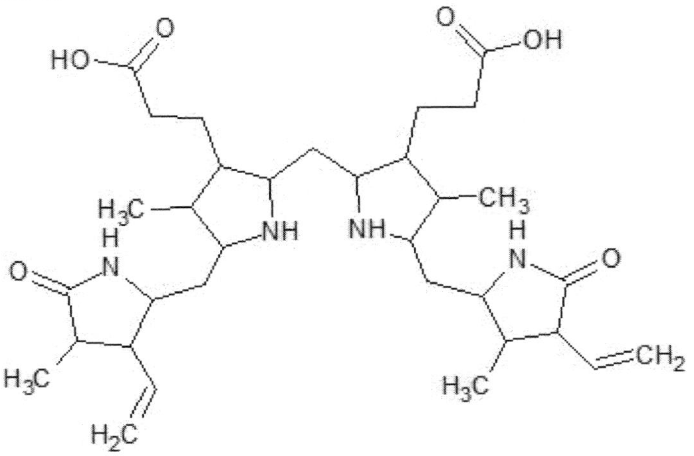

Conjugated carbon-carbon double bonds in organic compounds such as bilirubin absorb visible light. There are no conjugated double bonds remaining in structure (c), so it would not absorb visible light. Structure (a) has the two carboxyethyl moieties removed, and these structures would not eliminate the absorption of visible light by the conjugated double bonds. Structure (b) has methyl esters on the carboxylic acids, which would not significantly alter the absorption of light. Structure (d) has added two hydrocarbon moieties to the structure, which would not preclude the absorption of light by the conjugated double bonds.

Passage 5

21. B: (Bicarbonate). This question focuses on understanding the meaning of acid/base chemistry, buffers, and pK$_a$ values. From the pK$_a$ value of the carbonic acid/bicarbonate buffer system
$H_2CO_3 \leftrightarrow HCO_3^- + H^+$ pK$_{a1}$ = 5.85
we can see that pH 8.2 is well above the pK$_a$ (5.85), so there must be substantially more of the conjugate base, bicarbonate, than carbonic acid.

From the pK$_a$ value of the bicarbonate/carbonate buffer system
$HCO_3^- \leftrightarrow CO_3^{2-} + H^+$ pK$_{a2}$ = 8.92
we can see that pH 8.2 is well below the pK$_a$ (8.92), so there must be substantially more of the conjugate acid, bicarbonate, than carbonate. Hence, the answer must be B.

22. B: (Compared to the starting mixture, the dissolved calcium concentration dropped). This question focuses on the use and meaning of a solubility product.
$K_{sp} = [Ca^{2+}][CO_3^{2-}]$

Since there is solid calcium carbonate and a solution at equilibrium, the K_{sp} must be equal to the solubility product constant, and any additional calcium or carbonate added to the system pushes the K_{sp} higher than the constant, and precipitation results. Only carbonate was added and calcium carbonate precipitated, so calcium must have declined. The sodium is unimportant to the question except as a way of delivering the carbonate.

23. A: (There is no change in the dissolved concentration of calcium or carbonate). This question focuses on the nature of a solubility product and the fact that solid materials do not enter such a calculation as they do not change their concentration.
$K_{sp} = [Ca^{2+}][CO_3^{2-}]$

The fact that there is no term for the solid material in the K_{sp} demonstrates that the amount of solid material present is not important to the solubility. As long as there is some solid material in contact with the solution at equilibrium, the solution is saturated (that is, all that can dissolve has dissolved). Having more or less solid material present does not change the amount that can dissolve at equilibrium, as long as there is some undissolved solid calcium carbonate.

24. B: (the carbonate concentration fell and the carbonic acid concentration rose). This question focuses on acid/base chemistry, and Le Chatelier's principle.
$H_2CO_3 \leftrightarrow HCO_3^- + H^+$ $\quad$ pK$_{a1}$ = 5.85
$HCO_3^- \leftrightarrow CO_3^{2-} + H^+$ $\quad$ pK$_{a2}$ = 8.92

At pH 8.2, we are below pK$_{a2}$ and above pK$_{a1}$. Consequently, there is both carbonate and bicarbonate (and a small amount of carbonic acid) present. On addition of a strong acid, H$^+$, the pH drops. As that happens, Le Chatelier's principle tells us that both of the reactions shown above will push to the left: carbonate converts into bicarbonate and bicarbonate converts into carbonic acid. Consequently, carbonate declines and carbonic acid increases.

25. A: (As the temperature rises, bicarbonate becomes a stronger acid, so carbonate rises). This question involves knowing that a lower pK$_a$ implies a stronger acid, as well as the fact that a stronger acid will dissociate into H+ and it conjugate base more than a weaker acid. As the temperature rises from 25°C to 30°C, the pK$_a$ of bicarbonate drops from 8.92 to 8.75. The drop in pK$_a$ shows that it is becoming a stronger acid. As the bicarbonate becomes a stronger acid, the reaction below shifts more to the right:
$HCO_3^- \leftrightarrow CO_3^{2-} + H^+$ $\quad$ pK$_{a2}$

Consequently, it dissociates more into H+ and carbonate, and carbonate rises.

Passage 6

26. A: (245 N). If each leg below her knees has a mass of 2.5 kg, then her total mass above her knees is 55 kg – 2 × (2.5 kg) = 50 kg. The force of gravity is 9.8 m/s^2, so the gravitational force pulling down on her body from $F = ma$ is F = 50 kg × 9.8 m/s^2 = 490 kg m/s^2. 1 N (Newton) = 1 kg m/s^2, so the total force is 490 N. Since only half of that force is on each knee, the answer is 490/2 N = 245 N.

27. C: (1617 N). According to Table 1, a woman walking with a knee flex angle of 15° experiences a peak compressive load on her knees of three times her body weight. The force can then be calculated as 3×55 kg $\times 9.8$ m/s^2 = 1617 kg m/s^2 = 1617 N.

28. D: (Decrease by 2.8%). According to the passage, each 1 kg loss in body weight resulted in a 1.4% decline in the peak compressive load while walking. So a 2 kg loss in body weight is associated with a $2 \times 1.4\%$ = 2.8% decline in peak compressive load.

29. C: (1911 J). Gravitational potential energy is weight times height, or mass times acceleration due to gravity times height. In this case, mass is 65 kg, acceleration due to gravity is 9.8 m/s^2, and the height is 3 m. PE = 65 kg $\times 9.8$ m/s$^2 \times 3$ m = 1911 kg m^2/s^2. Since 1 kg m^2/s^2 = 1 J (joule), the answer is 1911 J. The facts of the knee flex angle used and the number of stairs are unimportant to the question.

30. D: (2400 J). The energy required to stop the man and bicycle is the same as the kinetic energy of motion. The kinetic energy of linear motion is calculated from KE = ½ mv^2. We use m = 75 kg to account for both the bicycle and the man, and m = 8 m/s. KE = ½ $\times 75$ kg $\times 8$ m/s $\times 8$ m/s = 2400 kg m^2/s^2. Since 1 kg m^2/s^2 = 1 J (joule), the energy required = 2400 J.

Passage 7

31. C: (n-Hexanol is more effective at London dispersion interactions because it has a higher surface area than methanol). The positive interactions between methanol molecules and between n-hexanol molecules consists primarily of hydrogen bonding and London dispersion forces. Methanol has a higher proportion of hydrogen bonding moieties (the -OH groups) than does n-hexanol (because the hexyl chain is large and has no role in hydrogen bonding except potentially getting in the way), so methanol is more effective at hydrogen bonding (ruling out answer choices a and b). There are no ionic interactions between these uncharged molecules, so choice d is incorrect. London dispersion forces take place between molecules, including nonpolar molecules, though the interaction of instantaneous multipoles. The strength of these forces depends on the number of electrons involved and the surface area of interaction, so larger molecules tend to interact more.

32. B: (336 J). Ethanol has a molecular weight of 46 g/mole, so 23 grams is 0.5 moles. To determine the energy required to warm the ethanol to its boiling point, we use the heat capacity of 112 J/mol·°C. The rise in temperature is 72°C to 78°C, or an increase of 6°C. The energy of warming is 0.5 mol $\times 6$°C $\times 112$ J/mole·°C = 336 J.

33. D: Methanol has a molecular weight of 32 g/mole, so 64 grams is 2.0 moles. To determine the energy required to vaporize the methanol, we use the heat of vaporization of 38 kJ/mol. The energy required is 2 moles $\times 38$ kJ/mol = 76 kJ, or 76,000 J.

34. A: To determine spontaneity of a phase transition, we use the free energy, ΔG. To be spontaneous, ΔG must be negative. Knowing $\Delta G = \Delta H - T\Delta S$, we can state that $\Delta H - T\Delta S < 0$. We can use ΔH from the table (53.2 kJ/mol) and T = 25°C = 298 K. Putting those values into the equation, we get 53.2 kJ/mol $-298K \times (\Delta S) < 0$. Subtracting 53.2 kJ/mol from both sides we get $-298K \times (\Delta S) < -53.2$ kJ/mole. Dividing by $-298K$ we arrive at $\Delta S > 0.178$ kJ/(mole · K) (note that when dividing both sides of an inequality by a negative number, the inequality switches: < becomes >), or 178 J/(mole · K) is the minimum increase in entropy.

35. D: (3-methyl-1-butanol). Isomers are compounds with the same molecular formula and different structural organization. In this case, some isomers of *tert*-butanol are alcohols, but others are not. The chemical formulas for a, b, and c are all the same as *tert*-butanol: $C_4H_{10}O$. The formula for choice d is $C_5H_{12}O$, so it is not isomeric with *tert*-butanol. The boiling points are not useful in answering this question.

Passage 8

36. C: (arteries > arterioles > capillaries > venules > veins). Blood pressure drops continuously as one proceeds through the circulatory system, out of the heart and back again. The order of progression through the system is consequently the answer.

37. B: (Blood continues to flow between beats of the heart). With each beat of the heart, the pressure in nearby arteries rises. The increased pressure expands these arteries. When the pressure from the heart declines, the arteries relax to their original size, squeezing out blood that continues to push through the system until the heart beats again. Choice a is wrong because the diastolic pressure rises because of arterial expansion and contraction, and would be very low without it. Choice c is wrong because oxygen does not generally leave the arteries in significant quantities. Choice d is wrong because the walls of arteries are thicker than the walls of veins.

38. D: (Both show the same pressure). The fact that there is no flow means that this is a question relating to static pressure. According to Pascal's Law, static pressure applied to any part of a fluid transmits equally to all other parts of the fluid. In this case, it transmits unchanged through the tubing regardless of diameter.

39. A: (95 mL/min). According to Poiseuille's Law, flow through a pipe is directly related to the pressure across the pipe. In this case, the pressure increases from 110 mm Hg to 160 mm Hg, which is a factor of 160/110 = 1.45. Since the flow at 110 mm Hg for Sample B was 65 mL/min, the new flow rate is 1.45 × 65 mL/min = 95 mL/min.

40. A: (1.2 mL/min). According to Poiseuille's Law, flow through a pipe is inversely related to the viscosity of the fluid. In this case, the viscosity increases by a factor of four. Since the flow at 110 mm Hg for Sample G was 4.8 mL/min, the new flow rate is 1/4 × 4.8 mL/min = 1.2 mL/min. The fact that the tubing is slightly elastic will have no significant effect on the change in the flow rate with viscosity.

Passage 9

41. A: (a. $1/v_o$ vs $1/[S]$). A Lineweaver-Burk plot is a graph of $1/v_o$ vs $1/[S]$, where the x-intercept is $-1/Km$ and the slope is Km/Vmax.

42. C: (Modification 4). The Michaelis Constant, Km, is the substrate concentration at which the substrate occupies half of the active sites on the enzyme. A lower value of Km means higher binding strength since it takes less substrate in solution to occupy the active site. From Table 11, Modification 4 has the lowest Km (2.9 mM) and so has the highest binding strength.

43. B: (Modification 1). Kcat is a measure of the turnover rate of substrate in the active site of the enzyme under optimal (substrate saturation) conditions. The time required to process a single substrate is 1/Kcat. Faster conversions mean a higher Kcat, or a lower 1/Kcat. From Table 11, Modification 1 has the higher Kcat (3×10^5 s^{-1}) and hence the fastest conversion time (1/Kcat) of $1/(3 \times 10^5$ s$^{-1}) = 3.3 \times 10^{-6}$ s.

44. B: (A competitive inhibitor of the Native Enzyme). A competitive inhibitor increases the Km and leaves Kcat unchanged. A competitive inhibitor is competing with carbon dioxide for the binding site. When the inhibitor gets into the binding site, it effectively makes the carbon dioxide unable to bind and reduces the apparent binding (increasing Km). Kcat is unchanged because, by definition, Kcat is determined in a condition where there is a great surplus of the substrate (carbon dioxide) and the reaction is not substrate limited. With unlimited substrate, the active site is always occupied by substrate, regardless of whether there is an inhibitor present in solution or not. Answer (a) is wrong because for noncompetitive inhibition, Km is unchanged and Kcat is reduced. Answer (c) is wrong because for mixed inhibition, Km is increased and Kcat is reduced. Answer (d) is wrong because the Km rose, so acetazolamide is an inhibitor.

45. A: (Km = 450 mM). The easiest way to answer this question is to look at the trend between the Km of Modified Enzyme 3 in the absence of inhibitor (56.1 mM; Table 11) and the Km in the presence of 5 μM of acetazolamide (160 mM). This inhibitor at 5 μM increased the Km by a factor of two. Additional inhibitor added to reach 10 μM will further increase the Km, and the only choice higher than 160 mM is choice a (450 mM).

Discrete Questions

46. C: (decreased to $W/2$). Electrical energy (W) in a parallel plate capacitor is defined as W = $CV^2/2$, where C is the capacitance and V is the voltage. Capacitance (C) of a parallel plate capacitor is defined by C= εA/d, where ε is the permeability, A is the cross-sectional area of the plates, and d is the distance separating the plates. Combining equations we have W = εA $V^2/2d$. Consequently, when d doubles (to 2d), the energy (W) decreases to W/2.

47. D: A diverging lens is thinner in the middle than at the edges. Only choice d is thinner in the middle. Choices a, b, and c are all thicker in the middle than at the edges and are converging lenses.

48. B: (oxalate). In part of the tricarboxylic acid cycle, succinyl-CoA → succinate → fumarate → malate → oxaloacetate, so choices a, c, and d are wrong. Oxalate is the correct choice because it is not consumed in the standard tricarboxylic acid cycle. The similarly named but different molecule, oxaloacetate, is part of the cycle but oxalate is not.

49. C: Unsaturated fatty acids (choices b, c, and d) have lower melting points and lead to more membrane fluidity than saturated fatty acids (choice a) of a similar length because the double bonds break up the packing of the chains. The more unsaturation sites (that is, the more double bonds) the lower is the melting point and the higher the membrane fluidity. In addition, cis double bonds have a larger effect on melting point and fluidity than trans double bonds because the cis bonds disrupt packing to a greater degree. Choice c is the correct answer because it has the most unsaturation and has all cis bonds.

50. B: (It has no net electric charge). The definition of the isoelectric point is the pH where the protein has no NET electric charge, but it can contain equal numbers of positive and negative

charges (indicating answer d is wrong). Since the protein has no net negative charge, it does not move in an electric field (indicating a is wrong). When proteins have no net negative charge, they no longer repel each other electrically and tend to precipitate, reducing the solubility (indicating answer c is wrong).

51. A: (polysaccharide chains covalently crosslinked with peptide chains). The rigid structural framework of the cell wall is a peptidoglycan, and is composed of parallel polysaccharide chains (largely a repeating disaccharide of N-acetyl glucosamine and N-acetylmuramic acid. It is covalently crosslinked via the carboxylic acid group on the N-acetylmuramic acid. The composition of the peptide varies with the species of bacteria.

52. A: (It is single stranded). Messenger RNA is single stranded and made in the nucleus or the mitochondria in a process called transcription. RNA contains one phosphate per nucleotide.

53. C: ( ). Pyrimidine is an aromatic six-membered ring with nitrogen groups at the 1 and 3 positions. Structure a is imidazole. Structure b is pyrrole. Structure d is pyridine.

54. B: (on ribosomes in the cytoplasm). In eukaryotes, ribosomes are located in the cytoplasm, and that is where protein translation (synthesis) takes place. Prokaryotes are different, and translation can take place on ribosomes in their nuclei.

55. A: ( ). Although flipped in orientation from each other, choice a shows keto-enol tautomers. In such a pair, the double bonded oxygen becomes a hydroxyl group attached to the same carbon, and a double bond forms between the carbon of the previous carbonyl and an adjacent carbon atom. Incorrect choices c and d show the oxygen migrating to a different carbon atom, and incorrect choice b shows the same form in two different orientations with no enol form.

56. C: ( ). The mechanistic steps in the acid-catalyzed hydrolysis of methyl acetate are methyl acetate → answer b → answer d → answer a → → products. Answer c shows a positive charge on an oxygen atom that has just two bonds. The only other mechanistic step in this reaction that has a positive charge on this oxygen atom also has a hydrogen atom attached to it:

- 318 -

57. C: When added together, the half reactions in choice c correctly give the full reaction. The NAD$^+$/NADH half reaction of choice a has too many protons, and too much positive charge, on the left hand side, and consequently is not a balanced half reaction. Choice b has NAD$^+$ and NADH on the wrong sides of its redox half reaction to add up to the full reaction. The NAD$^+$/NADH half reaction of choice b is also not electrically balanced. Choice d has too few protons in the isocitrate/ α-ketoglutarate half reaction, and is not electrically balanced.

58. D: The question reminds one that glucose is an aldohexose , which is an aldehyde-terminated six-carbon sugar. Choice d correctly shows glucose as a six-carbon sugar with a terminal aldehyde group. Choices a (D-ribose) and c (D-xylose) show five-carbon sugars and are clearly incorrect. Choice b (D-fructose) shows a six-carbon sugar with a ketone group at the second carbon rather than an aldehyde at the terminal carbon (hence it is a ketohexose rather than the required aldohexose), and is incorrect.

59. D: ($CH_3CH_2CH_3$ and $CH_3CH_2CH_2I$). Answering this question requires knowing two things. First, that separations by simple batch distillation are most complete with two compounds that differ the most in boiling point. Second, that the boiling point of homologous alkyl halides (and most other organic compounds) rises as the molecular weight rises. In this case, the boiling points are propane (–42°C), n-propyl fluoride (–3°C), n-propylchloride (47°C), n-propylbromide (71°C), and n-propyl iodide (102°C). So the combination of propane and n-propyl iodide has the largest boiling point difference.

Psychological, Social, and Biological Foundations

Passage 1

1. B: Severe head trauma, particularly that prompting hospitalization, produces defects in the function of the brain and spine blood-brain barrier, mild electroencephalogram (EEG) changes, and neurotransmitter dysfunction. Physiological changes induced by head trauma can produce and exacerbate mood disorders as well as psychiatric conditions. These symptoms are particularly challenging to manage, and many head trauma patients are living with refractory symptoms. The mood disorder symptoms that occur after brain surgery may be debilitating, but the treatment protocols are more effective and well established at this time than are the treatment protocols for severe head trauma. The psychiatric sequelae of head trauma are notably increased even when posttraumatic stress is controlled for as a factor. Brain surgery is a therapeutic procedure, but brain surgery survivors experience a higher incidence of mood disorders and psychiatric ailments than the general population. Although brain surgery is typically asymmetric, electrophysiological findings demonstrate that individuals with schizophrenia exhibit deficits in cerebral lateralization as well.

2. D: Schizophrenia is less prevalent than are mood disorders such as depression, but symptomatic episodes of schizophrenia are more likely to require intensive medical attention. Individuals with diagnosed mood disorders experience fluctuations in symptoms more often due to lack of proper medication than to social factors such as work. The work setting may alleviate some symptoms of mood disorders for some individuals but may exacerbate symptoms of mood disorders as well. Schizophrenia occurs at rates between 1% and 2% of the population, which makes it common, but not as common as mood disorders. Symptoms of mood disorders can be severe enough to prevent people from functioning and also may require intense medical treatment and/or hospitalization.

3. B: Bipolar disorder often presents with symptoms of agitation and paranoia that appear similar to symptoms of schizophrenia. In fact, the two conditions may be confused or misdiagnosed in the initial stages. Bipolar disorder is a mood disorder characterized by episodes of depression and episodes of mania. The episodes of mania are, more often than not, unsettling for the individual who has bipolar disorder. Depression is a mood disorder predominantly characterized by feelings of sadness, despair, and loss of hope. Schizophrenia is characterized by paranoid auditory delusions as well as agitation and a number of other symptoms. However, individuals with diagnoses of bipolar disorder or with diagnoses of depression may experience severely altered perceptions of reality, albeit not as frequently as individuals who suffer from schizophrenia. Individuals with schizophrenia also experience dramatic mood shifts in addition to the delusions and hallucinations that are a hallmark of schizophrenia. Bipolar disorder is, indeed, characterized by opposing symptoms, and the symptoms of schizophrenia and depression are often more homogeneous. However, surprisingly, the combination of medications required and the neurotransmitters targeted are not more complicated in the treatment of bipolar disorder than in the treatment of depression or schizophrenia. The treatments and combinations of medications required to control symptoms of depression and symptoms of schizophrenia are surprisingly complex. Depression, schizophrenia, and bipolar disorder are all disorders with a degree of symptom variation. Individuals with any of the three disorders may be able to take a medication "vacation," but overall, patients more often than not need to take medication in order to manage symptoms.

4. C: Acute anxiety can be so acute that anxiety may build over hours, days, or weeks and cause episodes when affected individuals are unable to function in the work setting due to real or perceived threats so severe that it may result in the inability to function in the work setting. However, missing work itself causes anxiety that may be out of proportion to the real repercussions of missing work. Acute anxiety can cause an individual to feel threatened when there is a minimal or even nonexistent threat. Symptoms of acute anxiety can be more severe than the fear of being reprimanded for missing work. Anxiety is not the same as determination or conscientiousness, and thus it does not necessarily have an impact on an individual's attitude toward coworkers' work attendance.

5. A: Social cognitive theory explains behavior when individuals observe others' actions and the consequences of those actions in order to determine the effects of social and interpersonal interactions. Thus, individuals observe the outcome when peers call in sick in order to determine whether it would be beneficial or detrimental. When individuals observe others calling in sick, they take into account whether there was a benefit or penalty for that action and also whether those observed are subjected to similar work conditions and policies. Social cognitive theory is about learning by observing and modeling, rather than offsetting perceived unfairness. The incentive theory of motivation explains that individuals act in certain ways to gain rewards. Although rewards such as free time or rest may be a motive for calling in sick, social cognitive theory is about absorbing information about actions, including whether those actions bring about positive rewards. Responsibility toward others is a motivating factor in behavior, but it is not typically learned through social cognitive observations, but through reasoning.

Passage 2

6. A: Sanctions are methods by which unwritten rules of social control are enforced by excluding those who do not follow norms. Sanctions in the social setting are not associated with concrete penalties such as low grades. Sanctions are mechanisms of exclusion rather than social tactics such as gossip or overt shunning. Peers may try to avoid those who do not conform for fear of being similarly excluded. This action itself is not a form of sanctions, but it is rather an action taken by those who are not in a dominant position in order to avoid the consequence of sanctions. The long-term consequences of sanctions on those who are excluded may be actions such as leaving the situation or adjustment of behaviors to fit social norms, but that is not a description of how social controls operate to produce sanctions.

7. D: Group polarization is the inclination of individuals within a group to deliberately become more like each other while they amplify the contrast in their behavior or beliefs from those of another, usually opposing, group. In this example, group polarization would likely result in a group of students who insist on a more casual style of clothes than they would have worn otherwise, in order to bond with each other while rejecting the unwritten, more formal, dress code. Group polarization would result in less formally dressed students believing that they are correct in their style of clothes, and thus they would not feel the need to "compensate" for shortcomings. The tendency of students to study more or less based on factors such as attire is more in line with the idea of a self-fulfilling prophecy than with group polarization. The undermining of fellow students who are also dressed less formally is the opposite of the solidarity expected as a result of group polarization. Students might, however, respond by undermining the more formally dressed students who belong to the other group.

8. A: Social control is a method by which individuals avoid actions that might result in some type of rejection. In this example, the rejection is unlikely to actually take place because the peer group is not present currently, only in the individual's memory. The previous peer group in this example has functioned to place strong social control even in its absence. Peer pressure may influence an individual to participate in activities he may have not otherwise joined. Deindividuation occurs when an individual becomes less self-aware within a group and takes actions he might not have done on his own. Deindividuation encourages, rather than discourages, group hysteria. Deviance is the nonconformity to social norms; it is not a driving force in avoiding group action. Deviance would describe behavior of an individual who would risk rejection by acting in a way that is likely to be rejected by the peer group.

9. C: Whether a character is dominant or not within a social group is often determined more by a person's individual temperament combined with his investment and devotion to the group than by his concern about sanctions. Dominant members of a social group may or may not be more or less affected by the prospect of social sanctions than less dominant members of the group. Dominant characters are not necessarily as independent of the need for social acceptance as the group may believe. Dominant characters do have a great deal more influence than other members of the group, but they often look to other, less influential members for subtle cues. A portion of dominant personalities is very dependent on their status and prestige, but not all of these individuals have a strong need for their established social position or place an extremely intense effort on maintaining the social hierarchy.

10. B: Anomie is the circumstance in which society lacks moral guidance. Individuals may experience a sense of alienation in this context. Therefore, an individual can shield himself from this type of isolation by maintaining an association with a group that holds a set of principles with which the individual, for the most part, agrees. Creating laws does not necessarily preserve moral standards, but rather it establishes the appearance of selected moral standards. Promoting more lenient principles or ethics may create a new sense of inclusion for some individuals, but this can easily exclude a different set of individuals at the same time, and thus it does not necessarily foster a sense of inclusive acceptance nor protect against a sense of isolation. Maintaining personal principles can help prevent a sense of ethical disorientation, but this does not prevent a feeling of isolation from a principled and ethical community.

11. D: When a person is aware of the various agents involved in socialization, he is more resistant to the negative psychological effects of social exclusion. However, even those who are knowledgeable regarding the range of social and psychological elements of behavior can be susceptible to the emotional effects of social inclusion and exclusion. An understanding of the differing agents of socialization can aid an individual in adapting to expectations and avoiding social errors that can lead to exclusion, such as deviating from norms. This understanding can help a person defend himself against formal methods of exclusion resulting from bias or unfairness. Defending oneself aids in financial or legal issues, but it does not aid in gaining social inclusion. Empathy is a beneficial trait that can prevent social ostracism in most circumstances, but it is not a result of the understanding and awareness of agents of socialization. Blending the norms of different social groups is not an effective way to gain social acceptance because some peer groups may have completely opposing ideas of standards and acceptable behavior, and they may reject the social norms of another society.

12. A: Learning is an ongoing process facilitated by lessons such as this experience, but it also involves improving with practice within the context of real life. The stroke group had a baseline deficit in their ability to accurately identify emotions, compared to controls, but also had a history of intact emotional recognition prior to the stroke. This aided in supplementing the ability to learn the lessons taught through the experiment. Stroke survivors experience deficits in emotional recognition independent of acquired visual deficits. The majority of individuals with Asperger's disorder would prefer to have satisfying social interactions. Neuroplasticity is a characteristic of neuronal tissue, and individuals who have Asperger's as well as stroke survivors have a degree of neuroplasticity. Neuroplasticity refers to the ability of neurons to be redirected or reprogrammed. Both groups are teachable, a trait which depends on the ability to learn, not on neuroplasticity.

13. C: Habituation is decreased response to an input. The control group initially improved in performance and then declined, likely due to diminished response or interest to the stimulus. Prolonged exposure is a type of therapy intended to diminish a negative response. Extinction occurs when a conditioned response no longer produces a positive reward and therefore diminishes. This is not the case in this experiment. Dishabituation is the renewed response to an input that ceases and then restarts again.

14. D: A variable-ratio schedule is a pattern in which reinforcement is given after a variable number of correct responses. In real-life situations, positive feedback linked to accurately identifying emotions does not occur with each success or after a set ratio of success, but, instead, at random. A fixed-ratio schedule is a pattern or reinforcement that is given after every successful task or every other successful task or another fixed ratio. This is not consistent with real life because human responses are not so predictable. A fixed-interval schedule suggests that the positive reinforcement occurs at exactly the same interval after successful completion of the task. As with a fixed-ratio schedule, this is not consistent with real life. A variable-interval schedule is a pattern of reinforcement that is given at different intervals after successfully doing the task. In this instance, positive reinforcement may occur immediately or it may occur after a prolonged period of time after correctly reading a person's emotions. Generally, accurately reading emotions, if rewarded, occurs within a reasonably consistent time frame. Thus, the variable-interval schedule is less similar to real life than the variable-ratio schedule.

15. B: The control group has the least innate deficit in neuropsychological function and is better able to learn social skills through voluntarily imitating other people.

16. D: In classical conditioning, the unconditioned response is the natural response that occurs in response to a stimulus. In this instance, the study participant imitates or reflects the emotions that he is viewing, even without being able to accurately identify the emotion itself. The conditioned response is a learned response to a stimulus, which would be a conditioned ability to correctly identify emotions. The unconditioned stimulus is the event that triggers a response, which in this instance would be the emotions viewed in the videos. The conditioned stimulus is an additional stimulus that is often associated with the unconditioned stimulus and thus evokes the same response as the unconditioned stimulus. There is no conditioned stimulus in this experiment. The names of these stimuli and responses may seem confusing.

Passage 4

17. A: A self-fulfilling prophecy describes an outcome that occurs because a prediction influences behavior that makes the outcome more likely. In this instance, the waiters who believed that guests were generous were more likely to provide service that encouraged guests to give them larger tips. Stereotyping is the use of an oversimplified belief about a subgroup of individuals. Although the waiters were told that the guests were generous tippers, there was no implication or belief that a certain subtype of guests had particular traits. Prestige describes the esteem given to an individual or group. Some of the waiters in the experimental group might have attributed prestige to the guests, but it was the behavior of the waiters and the promise of a material reward that drove the difference in tips. Stigma describes a negative attitude toward an individual, a group, or a characteristic. Stigma is associated with discrimination, not with positive behavioral modification.

18. B: After an experiment such as this one, individuals are able to effectively alter their behavior if they understand the factors that contributed to the positive outcome. Instructing guests to defy stereotypes might change the preconceived stereotypes of the waiters, but the brief interactions and possibly inconsistent "acting" of guests may shape a different set of stereotypes, even if false. Giving financial incentives can alter behavior, but may not alter beliefs. Presenting objective information that counteracts stereotypes is not as effective as real-life experiences in overcoming stereotypes.

19. D: A man with a strong internal locus of control believes that he has a great deal of influence and control over events in his life. Thus, he would have a tendency to have less compassion and to blame others for their misfortune, believing that they bear a degree of responsibility for their own bad outcomes. A strong internal locus of control is a principle held by an individual who believes that he has a significant effect on events, which is not the same as self-control. Self-control is the ability to restrain one's own behavior or emotions. Although a strong internal locus of control shifts the responsibility for external events toward the individual, it does not necessarily foster or preclude or a sense of altruism, which is a separate matter. A person with a strong locus of control may or may not value self-esteem more or less than material possessions.

20. A: This experiment initiates a virtuous cycle of positive behavior by seeding the participants with the expectation of rewards and reinforcing that behavior when they respond appropriately. Positive reinforcement adds a reward when good behavior takes place, whereas negative reinforcement removes a negative consequence when a desirable action is taken, and punishment adds a negative consequence when an undesirable action is taken. Negative reinforcement is not the absence of a reward; it is the absence of an undesirable outcome.

21. C: According to the elaboration likelihood model, the peripheral route is a weak method of persuasion that is effective when the recipient of the message has little ability, background, or interest in the subject. Thus, if the feature present in an untrustworthy person is emphasized to a waiter, he might also view the customer as untrustworthy because the customer has the same feature, even if it is irrelevant. Visual pathways are not part of the elaboration likelihood model. Omission is not a method used through the peripheral route in the elaboration likelihood model; peripherally associating two concepts is the method used. Using irrelevant or peripheral details is not a component of the elaboration likelihood model; associating these details is the main component.

Passage 5

22. D: The child is dependent on the parent, and thus she is likely to obey instructions. Additionally, the child is in a role that entails allegiance toward the parents. The opposing demands of honesty in the survey and loyalty toward her parents presents an example of role conflict because honest answers may reflect poorly on the parents or might make them unhappy. Role strain is the description of a stress and pressure induced by a role, but not necessarily a conflict. Role strain is a component of some children's roles, but it is not a factor that would cause the child to avoid certain answers on the survey. Altruism is behaving in a kind and unselfish way for the benefit of others. A child might avoid answering questions that could hurt his parents out of altruism, but deindividuation, which is a loss of self-awareness in the group setting, is not a factor. Role exit is a voluntary process in which an individual leaves an undesirable role or identity. Although the child may wish for role exit and fear it at the same time, answers on the questionnaire do not have an impact on the process of role exit.

23. A: The child may see a front-stage self that the parent puts on for others and wish that the more private and authentic behavior, described as the back-stage self, was as pleasant, confident, or kind as the front-stage self. The parent's front-stage self is an attempt at impression management, whereas the back-stage self is largely unseen by everyone except those who are closest to them. An improvement of the back-stage self is not witnessed by others and thus would not help with blending in. However, children tend to believe that others' front-stage selves match their back-stage selves, while they fret and agonize over their own families' inadequate back-stage selves. Social stigma occurs when a person, group, or object is rejected. This requires recognition of undesirable qualities, which would not happen if the front-stage self were acceptable.

24. B: Those who had a higher copay felt more authority and power over the details regarding their health-care visit and thus were three times more likely to refuse to have their children fill out the survey than their counterparts who had a low copay or no copay. Parents who had a low copay did not demonstrate obedience by participating because the survey was nonmandatory. Individuals who pay a higher or lower copay do not have differences in the amount of private information shared with the health-care system. Similarly, there is no consistent relationship between how busy an individual is and how high his copay is.

25. B: The looking-glass self describes the tendency of a person's sense of self to be heavily influenced by others' perceptions and feedback. Thus, an individual who repeatedly receives a particular compliment, even if it is inconsistent with his self-view, will begin to believe that he possesses the attributes credited to him. Compliments, particularly when echoed by several individuals, raise the recipient's self-esteem. Compliments are also more likely to be accepted by an individual who already has a healthy self-esteem. A self-fulfilling prophecy is an alteration of behavior based on beliefs, rather than an alteration of the beliefs themselves. Impression management in psychology is a description of a person's conscious or subconscious control of others' perception of himself. This example is the reverse of impression management because it is an example of altered perception of self in response to others' impressions.

26. A: The child is likely to reject his parent as a role model based on the ineffectiveness of the lessons learned and the spurn of the target audience. The child is naturally more inclined toward self-preservation, and thus sympathy toward the parent is a low priority compared to the psychological wounds incurred by rejection of the parent's lesson. Although the child will reject the parent, it is not necessarily due to a feeling of mistrust because the parent may be incompetent, but

this may not be due to overt disingenuousness. The child looks to the parent for modeling and for acceptance, but, upon rejection from peers, the child does not turn to the parent as a substitute for peer acceptance.

Passage 6

27. D: The benefactors of the scholarship may have biases that impact the selection of students, even unintentionally. These biases may also continue to play a role in shaping the students' experiences throughout the trip. Hidden curriculum is less directed than the example in choice A, which would be a deliberate, not a hidden, means of approaching the goal. The selection process might be biased toward students who practice or believe in the same religion as members of the scholarship organization, but this does not reflect a hidden curriculum because it would not constitute *teaching* the recipients of the scholarship, but rather selecting students who already have the same religion as the benefactors. The exact attitude toward religion of the interviewers or the benefactors is not entirely clear based on the questions asked during the interview.

28. C: Medicalization of a social problem can result in increased health-care funds, training, time, and attention allotted for the care and toward the prevention of the condition. Health-care funds are allotted to medical care delivered by physicians as well as to care that is delivered by other health-care providers. Medicalization of domestic violence could result in treatment of victims or perpetrators as patients with medical conditions. Medicalization of a social problem can help reduce stigma over the long run, but such a consequence requires a great deal of planning and public awareness. Medicalization of a condition is not, in itself, capable of reducing stigma. However, medicalization would not result in tolerance of violence, even if the behavior were considered to be caused by a psychological ailment of the perpetrator.

29. B: According to the concept of symbolic interactionism, individuals view others as representatives of previous experiences. This means that the student would be expected to subconsciously view the patient as a meaningful symbol of the broken friendship and thus might attempt to repair the broken relationship through her interaction with the patient. The theory of functionalism would suggest that the student view the patient through a more pragmatic lens and would approach the interaction with the goal of learning about the patient's medical condition or the goal of improving the patient's medical condition. The expectations of a student health-care provider to be completely objective is unrealistic because previous interactions, particularly emotionally consequential interactions, more often than not play a role in how we view others. Given that her experiences cause her to subconsciously link the patient with her former friendship, she might not directly understand her strong feelings of mistrust that are provoked by the patient. The concept of association is about learning, not about misplaced interpersonal judgments.

30. B: Culture lag describes the delay in practical adoption of scientific advances such as technology. The electronic medical record (EMR) is an example of a technology that has theoretical benefits as well as practical disadvantages in real-world application. Thus, while the workforce adapts, it is not relevant whether the material acquisition of resources is present or not, because seamless application of EMR tools is not instantaneous and does not coincide with the availability of the material equipment. The size of the workforce is not a limiting factor that contributes to culture lag, but rather, the learning curve is the major factor. It is true that attitudes and preexisting efficiency can limit or promote adoption of new technology, but that is not the factor in cultural lag. In some instances, technology can aid developing nations and diminish material disadvantages, but adopting new technology depends on whether people can learn the necessary skills.

31. D: A meritocracy is a system in which recognition is based on earned status, rather than ascribed status. Although either woman in this example would have reason to resent the recognition awarded to high achievers in a meritocracy, acceptance or rejection of the system itself is a product of multiple factors, including the individual's social position and empathy toward others. The woman who did not have power or independence may believe that she could have achieved recognition had she been given the opportunity, but her lack of freedom might have led her to believe that she is incapable. The woman who failed might prefer a system that doesn't bare her failures, but she might also have hope that she could have a second chance, which is a more common opportunity for people who exist in a system of meritocracy. Mirror neurons are physiological occurrences that aid people in modeling behavior, not in imaging behavior that is unlikely ever to occur.

Passage 7

32. A: Inflammation is a nonspecific finding that may be particularly difficult to diagnose. Therefore, it may be detected on diagnostic tests, but in a population with a lack of follow-up care and access to care, it is likely that the etiology may not be determined and that the treatment may not be initiated. This population is also less likely to seek out care, particularly for subtle findings such as nonspecific inflammation. Inflammatory findings are noted in central nervous system (CNS) tissue of patients with psychiatric illness and patients with drug abuse, but CNS inflammation is not of high enough quantity to increase inflammatory cells in the blood. A condition such as inflammation of unknown etiology refers to inflammation determined by blood tests or peripheral nerve/muscle biopsy, rather than inflammation noted on CNS specimens. The prison population is at a higher risk of certain infections, but fevers and other signs of infection, rather than neuropathic symptoms, would accompany the inflammation noted during infections. People with inflammatory conditions often suffer from pain, tiredness, weakness, and other symptoms, but they are not generally excluded from the general population and would not be expected to turn to crime as a result of their symptoms or disease.

33. C: Type 1 diabetes would not increase the chances of an individual going to prison due to either criminal behavior or bias in the legal/judicial system. However, this population is more likely to have neuropathy due to periods of untreated type 1 diabetes, and the results of the chart review, which assessed patients with neuropathy, show higher rates of neuropathy than in the general population, regardless of the etiology. People with medical disease are, indeed, marginalized in society. However, type 1 diabetes is not expected to increase the rates of incarceration among those who have the condition. The lack of proper diabetes treatment, which would cause an increased rate of neuropathy, most likely occurred during times when the patients were not in prison because access to a necessary medication such as insulin, as well as compliance with medications, would be better in this population when health care is provided and monitored, than when individuals at high risk of noncompliance with medical instructions are on their own. Low birth weight has been associated with later development of type 1 diabetes in the child as well as with psychiatric illness later in the life of the child. Psychiatric illness itself is correlated with incarceration, but it is unclear how much parenting quality is a factor. Low birth weight, although associated with later development of type 1 diabetes in the child, is not associated with poor parenting because there are a number of medical causes of low birth weight. Additionally, high maternal weight gain is also associated with the development of diabetes later in the life of the child.

34. C: There are several medical conditions rooted in vitamin B_{12} deficiency including neuropathy, dementia, spine dysfunction, and anemia. Yet, despite the common etiology, the manifestation of one disorder caused by vitamin B_{12} deficiency does not necessarily mean that another manifestation will develop. Dementia in this population would be expected to have a wide variety of etiologies, with vitamin B_{12} being only one of many. Thus, vitamin B_{12} pills or shots would not be expected to decrease the presence of dementia. Although vitamin B_{12} deficiency contributes to dementia, many individuals with dementia do not have low levels of vitamin B_{12} and many individuals with dementia have other etiologies. It would be more effective to treat patients based on their individual risk factors. Most of the time, vitamin B_{12} pills are not absorbed, and people who are vitamin B_{12} deficient require injections for effective treatment.

35. A: Although the prison population is often labeled with many negative attributes, the vast majority of prisoners respond well to and seek positive support such as health-care interactions. The medications that are useful for neuropathic pain management do not have pleasant or addictive side effects. Treatment for medical conditions does not provide prisoners with additional funds or health-care benefits. Often, diagnosis of neuropathy involves electromyography (EMG) and nerve conduction studies, which use needles and electric shocks. Although some patients are apprehensive, the vast majority of patients of all demographics are easily able to understand the procedure and undergo testing without fear or hesitancy.

Passage 8

36. B: The body has many responses to a psychoactive drug, including metabolism of the substance and systemic effects. According to the data, the drug users in this instance had a quicker conversion to metabolite 1 than non-drug users. Because of the body's repeated exposure to the drug, the systemic effects are less pronounced in drug users than in individuals who were not previously exposed to the drug. Metabolic by-products of a compound are unlikely to last long enough in the blood to alter measurements in the study. Addictive drugs are typically addictive because they have an impact on the reward pathway in the brain by directly acting on the central nervous system or by changing a person's physical appearance, not as a result of health effects such as hypertension control. Frequent use may stimulate the body to make metabolite 1 faster or may cause metabolite 1 to last longer. However, the metabolic alterations induced by frequent use do not necessarily mean that the body is metabolizing the drug in a way that is superior. The metabolic changes induced by frequent use could have negative effects.

37. A: Psychoactive drugs, even those that are stimulants, can affect central processing and integration of sensations and can slow the production of a response. Although some drugs that affect the central nervous system (CNS) are abused because users crave a pleasant experience attributed to the drug, there is no uniformity of pleasant responses and psychoactive drugs do not convert unpleasant threats to pleasant experiences, but instead, they diminish sensory integration and may make a person unaware of threats. Psychoactive drugs do not usually harm sensory functions. Neurons involved in memory, mood, and decision making are more often targeted by long-term damage induced by psychoactive drugs. Conscientiousness is not the same as consciousness. Although most psychoactive compounds have an effect on the level of alertness (consciousness), some drug-addicted individuals also experience changes in conscientiousness (reliability and responsibility). However, consciousness does not impact a response to sensory threats, but rather the behaviors that impact daily life.

38. B: Often, consciousness-altering substances make a person less aware of and less able to integrate sensory input such as vision and proprioception. They can also make a person less aware of subtle social cues that may seem threatening. Individuals who view social interactions as particularly threatening may be more prone to use substances that can make them less aware of their social surroundings. Sensory adaptation is the body's normal adaptation to continuous sensory input, and it does result in a person ceasing to notice a sensation, but it is not relevant to social interactions, and it is a normal neurophysiological response even in the absence of psychogenic drug use. Overconfidence results when a person miscalculates his or her own abilities. This can cause a person to miscalculate his abilities when using psychoactive drugs; however, overconfidence is an evaluation of oneself, not of the outside circumstances, and it does not necessarily require the use of drugs. Memory decay is the loss of memory over time and typically refers to factual memory, whereas social apprehension is a much more complex response that is not based on the recall of factual information.

39. B: The brain can encode the memory of previous experiences, triggering the release of some neurotransmitters in anticipation of a chemical effect. However, this response is limited. Although it is very common for individuals to believe that they can "overcome" effects of a drug due to experience, memory itself does not make a person better able to willingly resist the physiological effects of a chemical substance. Memory can have a real effect on physiologic behavior by eliciting neurologic, metabolic, or endocrine responses. This effect can be pronounced or mild. Sensory memory describes the body's ability to maintain memory of a feeling elicited by a sensory stimulus. This allows a person to remember the sensations of pain, temperature, position, etc. for a brief time even after the stimulus is removed. Repeated consciousness-altering drug use would not elicit responses based on short-term sensory memory, but rather those based on longer term, more complex memory systems.

Passage 9

40. C: The circadian rhythm is most associated with sleep, but the 24-hour cycle in response to light and dark stimuli also affects the times when we anticipate food and our bodies prepare to digest and metabolize nutrients. Additionally, disruption in eating habits contributes to weight gain or malnutrition in people who have chronic disruption of the sleep–wake cycle unless deliberate efforts are made to regulate caloric and nutritional intake. Of note, some individuals are more prone to lose weight when the sleep–wake cycle is disrupted. Wakefulness during the day after disruption of circadian rhythm is not necessarily associated with weight gain. Although individuals with a disruption in their circadian rhythm might eat if they can't fall asleep during the day, they are also prone to overeat at night. But the metabolic alterations and fatigue are more significant in causing the weight gain. Usually, individuals with circadian-rhythm disruptions do not sleep a total number of hours more than usual, although fatigue can contribute to a lack of exercise. However, depending on the type of work, a high total number of calories might be used. Seasonal affective disorder (SAD) is the name for mood dysfunction, typically depression, which results from lack of daytime sunlight. Some individuals who suffer from SAD may gain weight, but this is caused by depression or by medications used to treat depression, not by circadian-rhythm disturbance.

41. B: Individuals may have adjusted to irregular sleep patterns by involuntarily developing shorter sleep latency periods and arriving at deep stages of sleep more quickly. However, meditation only minimally affected their overall stress and fatigue levels, even after adjustment of the sleep–wake cycle. Alertness is not expected to readjust or accommodate to chronic sleep disruption, even if individuals participate in meditation. In fact, individuals may operate at a lower level of alertness

with slowed responses or less sophisticated responses. Long-term potentiation describes a neural process that plays a role in memory formation, but it is not strengthened by sleep disruption. Neural plasticity describes the process by which neurons are recruited to take over functions of other neurons, or relearn functions. This occurs in situations involving compensation for brain damage, but it is not involved with restructuring the circadian rhythm. Mediation would not activate neural plasticity to overcome disruptions in the sleep–wake cycle.

42. C: Selective attention describes the ability to voluntarily focus on specific tasks or problems while ignoring distractions. Divided attention describes the ability to multitask. Both of these are impaired by sleep deprivation. Selective attention is dependent on alertness and is not an involuntary response to fatigue, and thus, choice A is incorrect. Problem solving relies partially on intelligence, but intelligence is a product of the ability to pay attention and focus, both of which are impaired with lack of sleep. Although an individual may retain the ability to problem solve even in the face of sleep deprivation, subclinical impairment is expected. Brainstem reflexes rely on synapses in the motor neurons and therefore are unlikely to be impaired by sleep deprivation.

43. D: The participant who experienced a catastrophic event during the study would experience high levels of stress that may be exacerbated by her sleep patterns. The participant who has an anxiety disorder should rate her stress consistently throughout the study. The individual who suffers from anxiety may give herself a rating that could be high or low, depending on her perception of the stress scale. However, it should be consistent. Whether either participant has any insight into the cause of her stress does not diminish the experience or the physiologic response to stress. The study itself could increase stress for a person who suffers from anxiety, but often, participating in a study provides a sense of comfort for people with anxiety due to either a placebo effect or to the idea that they are receiving attention from a health-care provider. Similarly, being part of a research study can alleviate or exacerbate the stress experienced during a situational difficulty.

44. C: There is no indication that the participants are in a position to observe any participants outside their group, and indeed it would be poor study design to allow for such. A lack of further lowering of reported stress levels may indicate that the intervention has achieved all it can in terms of reducing stress. Obviously, you would want more than a single pair of data points to confirm, but this is a distinct likelihood. The nonintervention group is not expected to have any variation at all beyond random variation, so it is perfectly valid to expect an apparent stabilization there to be random. It is also to be expected that participants will eventually tire of producing new responses and begin repeating old responses.

Discrete Questions

45. B: Although not all individuals affected by these conditions have an identified genetic trait, the genetic anomalies associated with schizophrenia and Parkinson's disease have been found near each other. Dopamine activity and dopaminergic receptors are, in fact, common factors in these disorders. Although medication for one disorder may produce symptomatic side effects of the other, these symptoms are almost always reversible with medication adjustment. Environmental factors are only minor elements for the development and risk of schizophrenia and Parkinson's disease. The average age of onset of schizophrenia is during the early twenties, and the average age of onset of Parkinson's disease is during one's sixties, but this does not preclude sibling studies.

46. C: The bystander effect is when an individual is less likely to take part in an action when he assumes that someone else in the group will take action, essentially making his action unnecessary or even redundant. Thus, if a mass email is received, an individual may consider his response inconsequential. Peer pressure is unlikely to have an effect on his decision to respond to or ignore the anonymous survey request. Positive reinforcement could motivate him to respond to the survey if he has received a beneficial result of filling out a survey in the past. Social norms do not generally come into play in the context of anonymous acts.

47. A: Instinctive drift is the tendency for animals or humans to return to natural tendencies. Once the person stops putting in effort or becomes stressed, he will have a tendency to revert back to behavior that takes less effort. New issues may arise, but if he continues with his efforts, he does not have to succumb to former habits. A habit of blaming others for misfortune or in taking responsibility for one's own difficulties is based on attitude, rather than evidence. Extinction refers to conditioned behavior that ceases after the feedback ceases. In this example, the habit is a negative habit rather than a conditioned response.

48. B: The amygdala is responsible for recognition of traits such as honesty in other people's faces. The occipital lobe is the visual center, which forms the brain's perception of vision received through the optic nerve. However, neither the optic nerve nor the occipital lobe is part of the limbic system. The hippocampus aids in recollection of emotions, not in associating facial recognition with names. The temporal lobe is essential for recognizing faces, but it is not part of the limbic system.

49. C: Korsakoff's syndrome, also referred to as Korsakoff's psychosis, manifests with antegrade and retrograde amnesia and problems with spatial planning of movements. Pseudobulbar palsy is another disorder of movement that is often associated with dementia and causes unexplained crying episodes. Vision loss is not a feature of Korsakoff's syndrome, although eye movement impairment is a feature of Wernicke's encephalopathy, which usually accompanies Korsakoff's syndrome. Korsakoff's syndrome is a result of thiamine deficiency, often seen in late-stage alcoholics. It does not cause thiamine deficiency.

50. D: The autonomic nervous system is stimulated by epinephrine and norepinephrine in response to emotional stress, whereas cortisol, which increases blood glucose levels, also increases in response to emotional stress. Stress does not have a dramatic effect on serotonin, but serotonin is typically decreased in response to stress. Acetylcholine is a neurotransmitter that controls skeletal muscles and is not dramatically altered by stress.

51. C: Metabolic imaging studies can detect subclinical symptoms, and thus, they may be useful in detecting preclinical abnormalities or similarities in brain dysfunction in relatives of individuals with psychiatric symptoms. Individuals with genotypic traits may have subclinical physiological changes that can only be detected by metabolic brain imaging studies. Environmental factors can produce alterations in the physiology and metabolism of brain activity. Both genetic and environmentally induced behavioral traits are susceptible to environmental factors, and thus, alterations in metabolism as a response to an environmental stimulus would not distinguish between environmental or genetic etiology.

52. C: Ascribed status is often more difficult to escape from, and thus, a person who feels defined by his ascribed status within his primary group might focus more of his energy and time on achieving status within the secondary group. Of importance in such instances, the primary group is more firmly established, often comprised of lifelong connections, whereas it is easier to find new secondary groups throughout life. The person with low ascribed status in the primary group might

or might not reject the primary group and might or might not turn to the secondary group as a substitute for approval. Some members of a primary group seek to advocate for the whole group within the secondary group. This is often a person who has high status within the primary group, particularly if it is ascribed. But promoting the primary group is not a presumed consequence of higher ascribed status within the primary group. Some individuals who are granted ascribed elevated social status choose to isolate themselves from the secondary group in order to relish in the benefits and self-confidence provided by the primary group. But many such individuals do not reject the secondary group, instead gaining confidence in their ability to thrive within the secondary group because of the approval provided by the primary group.

53. B: Attribution error describes the professor's recognition that she arrived late as being due to external factors, contrasting with her explanation of the student's late arrival as a fault of the student. The attribution error is not the same as attribution of power, which credits outcome to a person's actions. The professor may, indeed, experience stress due to her lateness that affects class time. She may also view a student's late arrival as a disruption. However, these are not examples of attribution error.

54. D: The primary group is the close group who may have known the teenager for a longer period of time and has closer interpersonal interactions with the teenager. Usually, the teenager is more dependent on the primary group. The secondary group is a wider group of acquaintances and possibly teachers. Achieved status is earned based on the teenager's social skills, athletic abilities, or other personal talents that are appreciated and valued. Ascribed status is independent of the teenager's individual personality and is based on factors such as family position or birth order. If the secondary group views the teenager with more esteem and treats the teenager better than the primary group does, the secondary group may raise the teenager's self-esteem while the primary group simultaneously lowers the teenager's self-esteem. The primary and secondary groups might have little, if any, interaction, and they may see the teenager through completely different lenses and value systems. The primary or secondary group can assign either ascribed or achieved status to any member of the group. Depending on the situation, sometimes the primary group is more important to a teenager and sometimes the secondary group is more important. Either group can provide positive or negative feedback, either directly or indirectly, depending on established patterns of communication.

55. A: Diffusion occurs when a culture adopts norms and values of other cultures, and thus, different family structures can become accepted within a culture through the effects of diffusion from other cultures. Transmission is the passing of values within a culture through generations, and thus, it is associated with preservation of values and systems, not with change. Assimilation is the blending or adapting to a new culture by migrant individuals, and therefore, it primarily describes the process of change in behavior of the migrant individual, rather than a change in perception by either of his cultures. Multiculturalism describes acceptance of diverse cultural traditions within a nation. It is primarily associated with acceptance of distinctive cultural identities rather than with changing ideas of what is acceptable.

56. D: Racialization occurs when a particular race or ethnic community (particularly a minority group) is associated with a particular trait. When racialization occurs, the ethnic community can begin to identify itself by the stereotypes ascribed to it by the majority. In this example, the patient and the doctor are both subject to racial stereotypes regarding the emblematic fertility of the patient's community. The attitudes of the patient and of the doctor can result in viewing infertility as more serious due to the atypical occurrence within the patient's population or as less serious because it is uncommon in the patient's community. Racialization can result in the physician

approaching the problem with a less objective viewpoint because the physician is human and is not immune from stereotyping patients. The patient is not invulnerable from stereotyping herself based on beliefs about her community, race, or ethnicity.

57. A: The theory of intersectionality explains that discrimination can be a product of several different layers and types of oppression combined. In this example, the patient who experiences infertility may feel that the physician cannot understand her experience, even if the physician is a female, because of the different types of discrimination that result from being a female, from being infertile, and from being of this patient's particular cultural background. Similarly, the patient would also feel that her husband couldn't have the same experience that she, as a female, has, and thus cannot understand her feelings about the medical and social situation. The theory of intersectionality is not about combining different individual's experiences, but rather about the levels of one person's unique experiences based on his or her combined sources of discrimination. The combination of cultures does not help the outcome based on the theory of intersectionality. Taking into account the combined viewpoints of men and women in the context of infertility does not exacerbate the conflict.

58. C: There are a variety of pheromones, all chemicals released by individuals and detected by other individuals through chemical receptors present in the recipient. Situations and settings provoking the release of the different pheromones vary. Responses depend on the recipient's chemical receptors, which may undergo modulation in different situations and settings. It is likely that individuals of different genders release dissimilar pheromones and possess dissimilar pheromone receptors. However, not all females in the same location are expected to respond to pheromones in the environment in exactly the same way. Similarly, not all males in the same location are expected to respond to pheromones in the environment in exactly the same way. Pheromones are released involuntarily, not voluntarily or based on intention. The concentration gradient is not dependent on the number of people because the pheromones are not likely to be "consumed" by some individuals, leaving fewer chemicals available for other individuals' pheromone receptors to bind to.

59. A: The physician has a belief that teenagers with certain characteristics are more likely to have a better recovery. The demographic and personal differences misled the physician based on his preexisting belief, and his belief still persisted despite the fact that the objective facts are not as he imagines. Poor recall should affect the physician's opinions about both sets of patients. Labeling theory occurs when individuals behave in a way that is consistent with the way society describes them. This is not an example of a self-fulfilling prophecy because the outcome was not dependent on any preexisting bias. Given the similar outcomes of both sets of patients, labeling theory is not a factor here.

Critical Analysis and Reasoning Skills

Passage 1

1. B: The designer in this passage is one who creates based on his objective assessment of what will become popular, while the artist creates based on inspiration and emotion.

The passage implies that the designer intends for his creations to be mass-produced, but it does not state that the artist does not intend for his work to be mass-produced. The passage does not indicate whether the designer or the artist has received formal education. The passage implies that the designer has more commercial success than the artist, but does not state that wealth is a central difference between the two.

2. C: According to the passage, the artist may enjoy lavish praise from the critic, but the passage does not state that the artist always enjoys such praise, or that such praise supersedes his creativity or his signature style.

The passage does not present the typical artist as publicly denouncing those who do not appreciate his work. The passage implies that the artist does not consider it an improvement to change his style to suit the tastes of others, even critics. And the passage suggests that if the artist were to consider becoming a student of the designer, he would do so to please the masses, not the critic.

3. D: According to the passage, the "brilliant mathematician" can take an idea that is not typically presented in a mathematical way, such as design, and convert it to a mathematical formula to predict what the public will accept and embrace.

The passage implies that the designer can mask his concrete, mathematical talents as an artistic gift, but not that he specifically deceives others. The passage does not imply that the "brilliant mathematician" as described here can do calculations in his head or that he is a high achiever academically.

4. A: According to the premise of this passage, the commercially successful musician works to try to tailor to the tastes of the masses, not to music critics.

He would be unlikely to change his work to please a music critic, as his goal is to please the public. According to the premise of this article, the opinion of the critic does not influence the public nor does the critic know how to or care to provide insight into popular tastes.

5. A: According to the passage, the artist has the choice of learning the methodical approach from the successful designer or continuing to work hard on his brand of magic.

Accepting his station in life is not consistent with overcoming his inability to achieve popular acceptance. Also, the passage does not imply that the artist is starving, but simply that he may not have achieved widespread commercial success. The passage does not suggest that the artist could attempt to gain acceptance and praise from art critics in order to overcome his ability to gain popular acceptance, as the critic and the masses have differing opinions. The passage does not imply that if the artist learns mathematics, his work will become more popular. Instead, the passage suggests that it is the designer's application of mathematical principles to art that makes him successful, not his knowledge of mathematics.

6. C: Based on the premise of the passage, a buyer for a retailer would choose among designs of commercial designers while commercial designers would try to sell their work to retailers.

The passage does not suggest that commercial designers are secure in their work with retailers, but rather implies that they must keep working to try to appeal to consumers. The passage does not suggest that commercial designers compete with retailers. More importantly, the passage does not suggest that anyone wants to entice artists to enter the commercial world, or that there is a shortage of designers or artists.

Passage 2

7. C: The painting portrays a mountain with grass, trees, and a gardener, implying that the florae need tending. The author says that the mountain is densely rocky and jagged.
The passage did not mention whether the colors of the mountain were similar or different than the colors in the painting. The passage also did not state that the mountain was cold, but rather that there was a blistering heat outside the coolness of the cave. The passage does not imply that the painting represents the mountain as a small mountain.

8. A: The author expects the painting to reflect an accurate portrayal of the artist's knowledge of the cave. The author expects the painting to reflect an accurate portrayal of the cave and seems surprised that the mountain is unlike the mountain in the painting. The author's initial explanation of the discrepancy is that the painter did not personally know about the reality, but instead was relying on hearsay. Thus, if the author encountered a wild animal, he would conclude that the painter was unaware of animals in the cave.
The author does not suggest that the painter was hiding the truth, but rather that he was attempting to accurately portray the feelings associated with the cave and the mountain. The author does not seem to think that the painter could have survived among wild animals, nor does the author seem to understand that the setting may have changed since the painting was created.

9. D: The author infers that the painting is the artist's best attempt to represent the mountain and the cave, but that while the feelings evoked by the cave are different from its appearance, they more accurately represent the whole experience than the mountain does.
The author does not entertain the idea that climate change could have played a role in changing the topography of the land at the site. The author does not seem to believe that the artist did research on the subject, but rather that he "learned the details through stories passed by fervent storytellers," implying a passive knowledge rather than active research. The author does not entertain the idea that the painting was commissioned or that there was a motive in adding religious symbols.

10. D: The author states that "one wonders why someone unfamiliar with the inside of the cave would venture past the entryway," implying that he must have had some familiarity with what to expect inside in order to have ventured past the entryway.
The author does not reveal a sense of adventure, nor does he seem to believe there is a passageway to the exit of the cave. The author does not suggest that he has any plans to create paintings of the area, but instead seems to have gone to the location seeking tranquility as proposed by the painting.

11. B: It would have been extremely difficult to determine whether the mountain and cave even existed without some clues about the story or the location from the artist.
The painting might have a greater impact on someone who can associate it with and cares about the events depicted in the painting, but the author describes the colors, the style of painting, and the scene as peaceful, seemingly independent of historical context. The geographic details found in the painting would be unlikely to help locate the area in the painting because the actual site was

- 335 -

different in many key features than the site represented in the painting. Because it is unclear whether Sassetta ever personally visited the location, research on the artist's life probably would not have been useful in determining the location.

12. B: Given the author's description, it is highly unlikely that he was able to find this location alone, and likely had a guide who was familiar with the location and knew the author's mission in finding the mountain and the cave.

The author was probably not alone, and there is no reason to believe that there were 10 adults present. The author estimates that at least 10 adults could fit inside the cave, but this is presented as an estimate. The author did not mention other travelers, but this does not mean that there were no travelers. The passage gives the impression that the author was not knowledgeable enough about the climb to make it alone, but does not give enough detail to ascertain who was with the author.

Passage 3

13. B: The candidate would appeal to the majority of voters by describing a healthcare environment that improves and compliments their socioeconomic situation.

The candidate would be at a disadvantage by spelling out too many details that could potentially be criticized. Favoring the most disadvantaged may paint the candidate as kind and caring, but would not appeal to voters who want better healthcare policy for themselves. Scolding voters or pointing out that they have it better than others is likely to make a candidate appear self-righteous and unconcerned about constituents.

14. A: According the passage, best medical care is determined based on clinical studies that show only a few percentage points of advantage, but that determine the fate of millions of patients. While the passage implies that the difference between the results of scientific studies are exaggerated, the passage does not argue that best medical care is completely arbitrary, and acknowledges that it relies on scientific data.

The passage does not imply that study authors push their data as superior, or that any such action has any impact. The passage states that scientific data used to determine best medical care is minimally divergent, rather than widely divergent. The study does not imply that there is no definition of best care at all, but instead that the definition may be too standardized based on scientific results that do not support widespread standardization.

15. C: The passage asks a question and describes it as disgusting because the question implies that the hospital might not put in exceptional effort to keep someone alive if it seems that no one will notice whether he lives or dies.

The passage does not suggest that the disease itself or the appearance of the pauper is disgusting. The question does not suggest that few people will mourn the loss of a pauper, but rather supposes it as the premise in suggesting that some may not consider his life worth saving for that reason. The question does not specify that there is a grey area in health policy, but rather poses an ethical element as one of the reasons that health policy is so complicated.

16. D: The passage is sympathetic to the feelings of the medical team who may experience "heartbreak" after exerting effort on a patient who does not then take care of his health.

The author does not show any concern for the patient who might not receive proper instruction on self-care, instead implying that the patient may not follow instructions. The author seems concerned with the public's ability to pay for healthcare of those who cannot pay, but not in the context of follow up self-care. And the author does not express concern about the family of the pauper at all.

17. D: While the passage brings up the dilemma, it does not attempt to resolve the issue of how a person's value to society can be calculated.
The passage does not make a strong stand that one person's life is more valuable than another's life, nor does the passage say that they are equivalent in value. The passage says that society might pay for the healthcare of the poor if there are abundant resources, but it does not draw a link between the availability of resources and the value of a person's life.

18. A: The author is clearly impressed by the story and its ability to illustrate a central dilemma in healthcare policy in a manner superior to prepared debates and lengthy books.
The passage does not address the idea of partisanship or political motives in the healthcare policy debates, nor does it indicate that data may be inaccurate. The passage does not indicate that political debates lean towards either fairness or unfairness for people who can or who cannot pay for their own healthcare.

Passage 4

19. D: The premise of the passage is that companies cannot ignore the outcry of older workers because they may stand accused of discrimination by the discarded older workers.
The cost here does not focus on economic cost incurred by wasted wages. While bitterness among workers is mentioned as a byproduct of shedding ineffective employees, it is not mentioned in the context of direct cost to the company. Instead, the accusation of discrimination is noted as a concerning outcome. Discouragement due to remaining in a lower position is not mentioned as a negative cost to the company. Instead, it is the outcry of older workers due to job insecurity and trouble finding a job that may reflect poorly on the company.

20. B: The author conveys a sense of responsibility towards both the older workers and towards the company. The author attempts to show compassion towards the average worker, but carries some frustration regarding the worker's performance.
It does not appear that the author has been accused of discrimination, but that he sees the very real possibility of that outcome if he does not approach the problem carefully. The author does not seem to primarily come from the perspective of sympathizing with the aging workers, despite a few attempts to explain that they may be victims of unfair circumstances. A conclusion about whether the author is indecisive in general cannot be drawn from the brief passage, which has a tone of hesitancy, but can also be seen as a sense of careful thoughtfulness. There is no evidence that the author is indecisive as a general rule.

21. C: The author conveys a sense of responsibility, but doesn't know exactly how to direct it. This suggests that if it were younger workers voicing an outcry about discrimination, the author may defend himself and his company, but would also consider some attempts at remedying the situation.
The passage does not give any indication that the author would feel that any workers have "no right to complain," or that the number of remaining years of earning potential plays a role in their rights. The passage does not state that it is because of older worker's years invested in the company that he might have to keep them on as employees. The passage does not touch on inherent differences in attitude between older and younger workers or whether one population is more vocal, and thus potentially damaging, regarding workplace discrimination.

22. A: The passage provides a few explanations for why lower-ranked senior employees may have not reached high status, including bullying, bias, and dishonestly. The passage also describes "high performing" leaders, thus implying the contrasting models for how leaders may have attained their professional status.

The passage does not suggest that no one can understand or point to why individual high earning leaders reached their position; indeed, several possible models are provided. The passage also does not jump to the conclusion that high earning older workers are secure in their jobs. Early in the passage, it is mentioned that senior-level workers earn high incomes even when they change jobs, thus opening the door to the idea that job transitions occur even among those who are paid well. The passage does not state for sure that entry level positions are not open to older workers, but instead questions whether they are available to older workers. Furthermore, the passage does not attempt to explain why the entry-level position might not be open to older workers or who could be making the decisions.

23. A: The author is very concerned about charges of unfair discrimination, and if the insecure or laid off workers had received excellent reviews, this would not bode well for the company.

The author would have a hard time defending the premise that part-time workers who received excellent performance reviews were less valuable to the company. Tardiness was not mentioned as a basis for worker insecurity, while part-time work does not necessarily go hand-in-hand with a lack of technology know-how. Redefining the qualities of a valuable worker after the fact would be problematic if performance reviews were built on criteria set by the company in the first place.

24. C: There would be only a few people needed to oversee the work of many computers and robots, which can execute workplace tasks, but cannot make decisions.

There is no reason to believe that everyone would become a supervisor or an entrepreneur. Based on the premise of the passage, many mid-level workers are not high achievers, and thus, by inference, are unlikely to be effective supervisors or entrepreneurs. The overall premise of the article is that there are few jobs, both within and outside the company, that provide generous compensation and that some of the insecure workers may not qualify for these positions, even if they change jobs.

Passage 5

25. C: The author does not support this statement with any facts, and thus it must be viewed as an opinion in the context of the passage.

The statement is not necessarily obvious, particularly because the standardized tests that the author so strongly disapproves of are so prevalent, suggesting that some qualified educators believe they have value. Of course, the prevalence of the standardized examinations neither proves nor disproves their value either. However, even if a statement appears to be obvious, it cannot be accepted as true without some evidence. There is no account in the passage that parents or teachers have reported any facts or narratives to the author that support this statement. However, even if there is no data provided to support the statement, the statement is not automatically deemed false.

26. B: The teacher most likely feels that she has achieved adequate test scores in her classroom, and wants to spend more time on enriching activities for her students.

It is highly unlikely that the teacher is trying to show off, as she carries an attitude throughout the passage that inferior test scores should be addressed, but that trying to achieve higher test scores is not as valuable as other things learned in the classroom, such as social skills. It does not seem that a score of 60th percentile, the average in her school, would be a cause for penalty that she needs to defend. The author does not seem focused on raising children's scores and seems more concerned with offering enriching activities to adequately performing students than tutoring students or other teachers in how to raise test scores.

27. A: The author states that "the problem lies in excessive time devoted to testing" and goes on to say "even more than divesting valuable time, the ensuing exhaustion... leaves students less prepared for any remaining constructive instruction."
The author does not say that testing provides inaccurate insight, but rather that it is limited in value. The author does not suggest that standardized testing of social skills would be valuable. The author suggests a means for repairing lagging skills, but does not state that this absence is the problem with standardized testing. Instead, it is proposed as a compromise if testing must remain part of schooling.

28. B: The passage acknowledges that schools that have a disproportionate number of students who lag behind in academic skills must be identified and that the problem must be managed. The passage acknowledges that lagging behind academically is harmful for students.
The passage does not suggest that online courses to reteach lagging skills would save time or free children from exhaustion due to testing, but instead proposes this idea as a way to address the academic shortcomings that may be identified by testing. The passage also does not imply that there is an inability to teach students that lag behind and it does not criticize worksheets and homework as flawed.

29. D: The author values social skills more than academic skills. The passage already states that kids who are gifted socially can be of great benefit to their peers, implying that kids learn social skills from each other. Student diversity would certainly be expected to enhance those benefits, based on the tone and attitude of the article.
The author does not seem to have an attitude that the benefits of social skills lie in enhancing academic skills. The author does not seem to believe that academic uniformity would be beneficial to students, teachers, or schools. Also, the author's attitude does not seem to be one of a person who would not have an opinion about diversity one way or the other.

30. D: Based on the ideas presented, if the author were to focus on schoolteachers' interaction with students, it would likely be in the context of students' exposure to varied schoolteachers' personalities as beneficial.
While the author values extra activities, it does not seem that the author would prefer for teachers to cut back on curriculum-based activities. The biggest complaint the author has is with excessive testing. The author values student interactions, but does not seem to think that sharing scores among students would be a beneficial student interaction, as the author does not highly value ranking by tests scores, particularly so openly. The author seems to value subjective social interactions among students, and thus, carrying over that attitude towards teachers, would be more likely to view teachers' personalities as beneficial for students rather than formal education about teachers' cultural backgrounds.

Passage 6

31. B: Globalization provided a seemingly sage explanation for economic expansion. The passage says that skeptics of unprecedented economic growth embraced globalization as a reasonable explanation for a change in traditional rules of economics.

The passage does not actually state that globalization fulfilled a role in economic growth, but rather that it was attributed the role. It is implied that the credit given to globalization may have been overstated. The passage does not address any inequities that may have been avoided or that may have resulted from globalization. In fact, the passage does not address any actual economic or social consequences of globalization, only presumed effects.

32. A: Capitalism is not described as negative in this article, but instead is described as having inherent features that do not necessarily discourage or encourage corruption when left unchecked. Capitalism is not presented as a system that encourages dishonesty or that particularly allows oppression. Capitalism is not blamed for the absence of laws that limit the effects of subprime mortgages. Instead, it is stated that the belief in capitalism as a perfect self-regulating system contributed to the problem, suggesting that some level of regulation may have been lacking.

33. D: While the passage puts blame on all of the above-mentioned entities, the root of the blame is cast on corrupt individuals.
The passage implies that lawmakers, optimistic leaders, and unwise investors all played a role in the economic crisis, primarily due to inability to act on underlying problems or inability to see underlying problems, but does not cast the lion's share of the blame on any of these individual entities.

34. C: The author has a tendency of describing consumers and businesspeople as varied in personal characteristics and knowledge, and thus would likely describe lawmakers the same way.
The author would be unlikely to make a sweeping statement that lawmakers were unprepared with an adequate financial background if the lawmakers did not all avoid addressing the problem issues. Similarly, the author would be unlikely to blame any problems caused by lawmakers on the public or the voters because the passage implies a sense of limited power in terms of the public's control over the actions of elected lawmakers. The author would not suggest that those who wanted to stop corruption were looking for trouble, because the author seems to view lawmakers as responsible for the well-being of constituents.

35. D: Guilt was noted as one if the driving forces that seems to have led some business leaders to believe that their actions were beneficial for everyone.
The passage does not imply that guilt prevented business leaders from behaving with corruption, but seems to imply that business leaders were either inherently benevolent or inherently corrupt. It is not suggested that guilt caused lawmakers to fail to detect corruption, but that satisfaction in seeing prosperity among the people played a larger role. It is not suggested that leaders truly shared wealth, but rather that they convinced themselves that they were sharing wealth.

Passage 7

36. C: A fictional story can have timeless appeal if readers can still find a way to connect to it. This is more likely if the central basis of the story is not so completely outdated that the reader cannot find enjoyment in the story.
The idea that changes in societal values inescapably deem a fictional story unrelatable is untrue, as the core of the story may still appeal to audiences of a different era, even if some societal values have changed. The passage does not imply that the author of the story did not have insight, but rather that his goals were immediate. The passage does not address the fact that people of different cultures may have different values and thus divergent appreciation for fictional stories.

37. A: Thomas Mann, the author of the story, was exiled. This indicated that, at the very least, the government understood his message.

A playwright with a political message is not necessarily looking to be well received, as a playwright of an entertaining play would be. Similarly, a playwright is not a political leader and thus it is unlikely that he viewed political leadership as an objective. He received recognition due to the fact that his message was recognized and rejected by the government system that he was writing against.

38. B: The story would have to be interpreted in light of a personal relationship between father and son in addition to the political message.

The novella may be more or less dangerous for the author as well as the father, depending on the intensity of political persecution. The idea that the story's author was bitter and expressing frustration at not having a high position does not fit well with his objection and with the cruelty with which he drew the magician. The story would not work in terms of being reinterpreted in support of fascism because the magician who hypnotizes his victims was killed at the end. It would be difficult to reinterpret that aspect of the story.

39. D: Modern psychology is attributed as responsible for defining weakness of character and limited self-confidence to be viewed as reprehensible products of bad mothering.

The science of psychology does not seem to have provided a method for helping people with low self-confidence become stronger or defining a biochemical basis as an explanation for a subordinate personality. According to the passage, modern psychology has blamed bad mothering for producing weakened character without providing a solution for either the mother or the offspring.

40. B: The passage acknowledges that, while the era of fascism has ended, there are situations in which political submission is inescapable.

The passage does not imply that the subjects of political tyranny have any character traits that predispose them to that situation. The passage also does not suggest that political fiction or symbolism can serve to help free people from political submission. Similarly, while the passage acknowledges the existence of inescapable political submission, it does not go as far to say that it is inevitable.

41. A: It appears that the author is looking for a way to manage a seemingly inescapable problem, and is looking to the story as a potential model, but finding only an unreasonable solution.

The author does not express a desire to see a group action and he does not seem to imagine that the magician could be believably likely to apologize. The author is not pleased with the ending, but expresses displeasure at elements of the ending besides violence. The passage does not express a sense of disapproval of the violent act itself, just at the fact that the violent act is not practical to most situations.

Passage 8

42. B: The author would likely explain that sustainable energy had not been well developed enough to yield a profit in the past.

The author would not suggest that the companies were irresponsible, because it is these same companies that he is presumably trying to promote to the reader. The author would be unlikely to tell a client to avoid further investments in sustainable energy, and would promote the idea that they may have been risky investments in the past, but are no longer risky. The author is not suggesting that the reader put money into investments purely for social responsibility, incurring an individual financial loss for the good of the whole.

43. C: The passage says that sustainable energy has many attractive features, including less harm to the environment during production.
The passage does not suggest that sustainable energy is more efficient or less costly to society or to individuals and the passage does not address any issues regarding the life cycle or the disposal of energy.

44. A: Legislation can incentivize or disincentivize the use of different types of energy.
The tone of the passage does not support the idea that decreasing energy consumption is realistic or desirable. The pollution effects mentioned in the passage include air and water pollution, which would not differ from consumer to consumer based on individual choices in energy sources. The premise of the passage is that consumers cannot individually change their own energy source, but that an overall overhaul of the production and maintenance of sustainable energy is needed, which requires more than simple transparency allowing individual consumers to make informed choices. In fact, the passage seems to discourage consumer education into the matter, emphasizing the limited benefits.

45. C: The author mentions diversification of investments as well as safe investments and a long-term outlook. He appears to be selling an investment in a sustainable energy fund that incorporates investments in a variety of emerging and existing energy suppliers.
The author mentions the benefits of clean energy, but only briefly and without mentioning any particulars about science, health, or the environment. The author does not seem to be attracting investors into his own company, as he is not selling a specific plan, but instead remaining broad and non-specific with regard to pros and cons of the various types of sustainable energy. The author's primary goal is not in providing education to the reader regarding details about sustainable energy.

46. D: They might have similar lobbying interests during the research and development phase, and thus might not disrupt each others' lobbying progress.
However, because they are competing companies, they are unlikely to help each other in areas of research and development or in business aspects related to barriers to distribution. They would likely compete with each other in areas of research and development, as the company who can develop a patent sooner is likely to benefit financially.

47. B: It is difficult to preserve sustainable energy in a holding form for later use. This is the challenge presented in the passage.
The passage does not state or imply that it is difficult to extract sustainable energy or that sustainable energy is not practical for application. Similarly, the passage does not allude to any limitations in nature restricting the availability of adequate amounts or quantities of sustainable energy.

Passage 9

48. B: The passage states that the tiger was able to elude the hunter until she finally called out for a mate, allowing the hunter to locate her, lure her in, and finally kill her.
The passage states that the tiger was deliberately eluding usual tiger hunting techniques, suggesting that she was more intelligent than a typical tiger living through a hunt. The passage does not imply that her instincts made her less astute, simply that they sabotaged her. The passage does

not say that the tiger was less intelligent than the hunter because he was able to shoot her. The hunter had a weapon, an advantage that the tiger did not have.

49. A: The method of hunting must be humane in order to prevent wounding the tiger, which can prolong the animal's suffering.
Respect is relevant in every situation between man and animal, as suggested in the first paragraph of the passage. The tiger in this story is a man-eating tiger, and thus safe capture and feeding are likely to put her human caregivers in great and possibly unpredictable danger. There is no implied link between respect for the tiger in the hunt and safety of other tigers in this community or outside it.

50. D: In the case of Thak, the evolved trait of man-eating is explained as an immediate adaptation following her injury due to her inability to hunt her usual prey.
Survival of the fittest relates to the suitability of an animal to reproduce and pass on its genes. The passage does not imply that the trait of man-eating was carried from parent to offspring or that any genetic alteration or mutation occurred. The passage does not suggest that man-eating developed as a response to environmental changes or scarcity of prey, or that it develops over a long period of time.

51. C: A knowledgeable photographer will understand from various clues whether or not it is safe to photograph a tiger.
Locating a tiger while it is mating or feeding is not necessarily the reason for a photographer to understanding a tiger's habits. It is unlikely for a photographer to befriend a tiger. While rare instances may have occurred, most photographers of wild animals do not befriend their subjects, but rather maintain caution and safety.

52. B: The tiger hunter's theory as introduced in the passage was that Thak's inability to hunt her usual prey during her injury caused her to change her habits as a means of survival. However, if it were later discovered that she gave birth to a man-eating tiger, this theory of adaptation and survival would have to be reconsidered in light of the possibility that there may have been some type of genetic predisposition.
It would not indicate an environmental cause because no other tigers in the area were reported to have adopted similar habits. The idea that Thak could have already taught her tiger to hunt humans at only one week of age is unlikely. There is no evidence to support the idea that memories can be passed down to offspring.

53. C: Even if the techniques failed to eliminate Thak, and even if the hunter was killed by the tiger, it does not change the fact that the techniques were effective in killing other tigers before Thak. According to the passage, this tiger was more challenging and sophisticated than previous tigers. The passage does not suggest that tigers in general had evolved to be able to counter hunting techniques, but rather that this individual tiger was different. Additionally, it is suggested in the passage that this type of hunt was relatively rare. Due to the infrequency of this type of task, science related to hunting a man-eating tiger was likely non-existent, and this hunter had more knowledge and experience than anything that could have been found elsewhere. The techniques, while likely the best available, could undoubtedly have been improved upon, as such a subjective task can always improve with experience, even among the most skilled hunters.

Secret Key #1 – Time is Your Greatest Enemy

To succeed on the MCAT, you must use your time wisely. Many students do not complete at least one section. The Writing Sample requires two essays with only thirty minutes for each. The other sections require you to answer questions give you an average of at most ninety seconds to complete each question. As you can see, the time constraints are brutal. To succeed, you must ration your time properly.

Many test sections are separated into passages. The reason that time is so critical is that 1) every question counts the same toward your final score, and 2) the passages are not in order of difficulty. If you have to rush during the last passage, then you will miss out on answering easier questions correctly. It is natural to want to pause and figure out the hardest questions, but you must resist the temptation and move quickly.

Success Strategy #1

Pace Yourself

Wear a watch to the MCAT Test. At the beginning of the test, check the time (or start a chronometer on your watch to count the minutes), and check the time after each passage or every few questions to make sure you are "on schedule." Remember that you have around 1.3 minutes per question. Since that may not be easy for most people to pace against, remember that you can spend 13 minutes every ten questions, which makes it easier to keep track of your time.

If you find that you are falling behind time during the test, you must speed up. Even though a rushed answer is more likely to be incorrect, it is better to miss a couple of questions by being rushed, than to completely miss later questions by not having enough time. It is better to end with more time than you need than to run out of time. Once you catch back up, you can continue working each problem at your normal pace. If you have time at the end, go back then and finish the questions that you left behind.

If you are forced to speed up, do it efficiently. Usually one or more answer choices can be eliminated without too much difficulty. Above all, don't panic. Don't speed up and just begin guessing at random choices. By pacing yourself, and continually monitoring your progress against your watch, you will always know exactly how far ahead or behind you are with your available time. If you find that you are one minute behind on a multiple-choice section, don't skip one question without spending any time on it, just to catch back up. Spend perhaps 45 seconds on the next four questions and you will have caught back up more gradually. Then you can continue working each problem at your normal pace.

Furthermore, don't dwell on the problems that you were rushed on. If a problem was taking up too much time and you made a hurried guess, it must be difficult. The difficult questions are the ones you are most likely to miss anyway, so it isn't a big loss. It is better to end with more time than you need than to run out of time.

Lastly, sometimes it is beneficial to slow down if you are constantly getting ahead of time. You are always more likely to catch a careless mistake by working more slowly than quickly, and among very high-scoring students (those who are likely to have lots of time left over), careless errors affect the score more than mastery of the material.

Estimation

For some math questions, estimate. Calculation takes time, and you should avoid it whenever possible. You can usually eliminate three obviously wrong choices quite easily. For example, suppose 48 mL of solution have been poured into a beaker in 11 seconds, and you are asked to find the rate of pour. You are given these choices:

A. 250 mL/s
B. 42 mL/s
C. 4.4 mL/s
D. 1.2 mL/s

You know that 48 divided by 11 will be a little over 4, so you can pick out C as the answer without ever doing the calculation.

Scanning

For passages, don't waste time reading, enjoying, and completely understanding the passage. Simply scan the passage to get a rough idea of what it is about. You will return to the passage for each question, so there is no need to memorize it. Only spend as much time scanning as is necessary to get a vague impression of its overall subject content.

Secret Key #2 – Guessing is Not Guesswork

You probably know that guessing is a good idea on the MCAT- unlike other standardized tests, there is no penalty for getting a wrong answer. Even if you have no idea about a question, you still have a 25% chance of getting it right.

Most students do not understand the impact that proper guessing can have on their score. Unless you score extremely high, guessing will significantly contribute to your final score.

Monkeys Take the MCAT

What most students don't realize is that to insure that 25% chance, you have to guess randomly. If you put 20 monkeys in a room to take the MCAT, assuming they answered once per question and behaved themselves, on average they would get 25% of the questions correct. Put 20 college students in the room, and the average will be much lower among guessed questions. Why?

1. MCAT intentionally writes deceptive answer choices that "look" right. A student has no idea about a question, so picks the "best looking" answer, which is often wrong. The monkey has no idea what looks good and what doesn't, so will consistently be lucky about 25% of the time.
2. Students will eliminate answer choices from the guessing pool based on a hunch or intuition. Simple but correct answers often get excluded, leaving a 0% chance of being correct. The monkey has no clue, and often gets lucky with the best choice.

This is why the process of elimination endorsed by most test courses is flawed and detrimental to your performance- students don't guess, they make an ignorant stab in the dark that is usually worse than random.

Success Strategy #2

Let me introduce one of the most valuable ideas of this course- the $5 challenge:

You only mark your "best guess" if you are willing to bet $5 on it.
You only eliminate choices from guessing if you are willing to bet $5 on it.

Why $5? Five dollars is an amount of money that is small yet not insignificant, and can really add up fast (20 questions could cost you $100). Likewise, each answer choice on one question of the MCAT will have a small impact on your overall score, but it can really add up to a lot of points in the end.

The process of elimination IS valuable. The following shows your chance of guessing it right:

If you eliminate this many choices:	0	1	2	3
Chance of getting it correct	25%	33%	50%	100%

However, if you accidentally eliminate the right answer or go on a hunch for an incorrect answer, your chances drop dramatically: to 0%. By guessing among all the answer choices, you are GUARANTEED to have a shot at the right answer.

That's why the $5 test is so valuable- if you give up the advantage and safety of a pure guess, it had better be worth the risk.

What we still haven't covered is how to be sure that whatever guess you make is truly random. Here's the easiest way:

Always pick the first answer choice among those remaining.

Such a technique means that you have decided, **before you see a single test question**, exactly how you are going to guess- and since the order of choices tells you nothing about which one is correct, this guessing technique is perfectly random.

Let's try an example-

A student encounters the following problem on the Biological Sciences test:

In Experiment 3, the amine will be?
  A. neutralized
  B. protonated
  C. deprotonated
  D. eliminated

The student has a small idea about this question- he is pretty sure that the amine will be deprotonated, but he wouldn't bet $5 on it. He knows that the amine is either protonated or deprotoned, so he is willing to bet $5 on both choices A and D not being correct. Now he is down to B and C. At this point, he guesses B, since B is the first choice remaining.

The student is correct by choosing B, since the amine will be protonated. He only eliminated those choices he was willing to bet money on, AND he did not let his stale memories (often things not known definitely will get mixed up in the exact opposite arrangement in one's head) about protonation and deprotonation influence his guess. He blindly chose the first remaining choice, and was rewarded with the fruits of a random guess.

This section is not meant to scare you away from making educated guesses or eliminating choices- you just need to define when a choice is worth eliminating. The $5 test, along with a pre-defined random guessing strategy, is the best way to make sure you reap all of the benefits of guessing.

Specific Guessing Techniques

Slang

Scientific sounding answers are better than slang ones. In the answer choices below, choice B is much less scientific and is incorrect, while choice A is a scientific analytical choice and is correct. Example:

A. To compare the outcomes of the two different kinds of treatment.
B. Because some subjects insisted on getting one or the other of the treatments.

Extreme Statements

Avoid wild answers that throw out highly controversial ideas that are proclaimed as established fact. Choice A is a radical idea and is incorrect. Choice B is a calm rational statement. Notice that Choice B does not make a definitive, uncompromising stance, using a hedge word "if" to provide wiggle room.
Example:
A. Bypass surgery should be discontinued completely.
B. Medication should be used instead of surgery for patients who have not had a heart attack if they suffer from mild chest pain and mild coronary artery blockage.

Similar Answer Choices

When you have two answer choices that are direct opposites, one of them is usually the correct answer.
Example:
A. Paragraph 1 described the author's reasoning about the influence of his childhood on his adult life.
B. Paragraph 2 described the author's reasoning about the influence of his childhood on his adult life.

These two answer choices are very similar and fall into the same family of answer choices. A family of answer choices is when two or three answer choices are very similar. Often two will be opposites and one may show an equality.
Example:
A. Operation I or Operation II can be conducted at equal cost
B. Operation I would be less expensive than Operation II
C. Operation II would be less expensive than Operation I
D. Neither Operation I nor Operation II would be effective at preventing the spread of cancer.

Note how the first three choices are all related. They all ask about a cost comparison. Beware of immediately recognizing choices B and C as opposites and choosing one of those two. Choice A is in the same family of questions and should be considered as well. However, choice D is not in the same family of questions. It has nothing to do with cost and can be discounted in most cases.

Hedging

When asked for a conclusion that may be drawn, look for critical "hedge" phrases, such as likely, may, can, will often, sometimes, etc, often, almost, mostly, usually, generally, rarely, sometimes. Question writers insert these hedge phrases to cover every possibility. Often an answer will be wrong simply because it leaves no room for exception. Avoid answer choices that have definitive words like "exactly," and "always".

Summary of Guessing Techniques

1. Eliminate as many choices as you can by using the $5 test. Use the common guessing strategies to help in the elimination process, but only eliminate choices that pass the $5 test.
2. Among the remaining choices, only pick your "best guess" if it passes the $5 test.
3. Otherwise, guess randomly by picking the first remaining choice that was not eliminated.

Secret Key #3 – Practice Smarter, Not Harder

Many students delay the test preparation process because they dread the awful amounts of practice time they think necessary to succeed on the test. We have refined an effective method that will take you only a fraction of the time.

There are a number of "obstacles" in your way on the MCAT. Among these are answering questions, finishing in time, and mastering test-taking strategies. All must be executed on the day of the test at peak performance, or your score will suffer. The MCAT is a mental marathon that has a large impact on your future.

Just like a marathon runner, it is important to work your way up to the full challenge. So first you just worry about questions, and then time, and finally strategy:

Success Strategy #3

1. Find a good source for MCAT practice tests.
2. If you are willing to make a larger time investment, consider using more than one study guide- often the different approaches of multiple authors will help you "get" difficult concepts.
3. Take a practice test with no time constraints, with all study helps "open book." Take your time with questions and focus on applying the strategies.
4. Take another test, this time with time constraints, with all study helps "open book."
5. Take a final practice test with no open material and time limits.

If you have time to take more practice tests, just repeat step 5. By gradually exposing yourself to the full rigors of the test environment, you will condition your mind to the stress of test day and maximize your success.

Secret Key #4 – Prepare, Don't Procrastinate

Let me state an obvious fact: if you take the MCAT three times, you will get three different scores. This is due to the way you feel on test day, the level of preparedness you have, and, despite MCAT's claims to the contrary, some tests WILL be easier for you than others.

Since your acceptance and qualification for scholarships will largely depend on your score, you should maximize your chances of success.

You know your abilities and can probably base a good guess as to what you might expect based on other standardized tests and percentile rankings that you have scored in the past.

By checking with your university of choice, you can determine what score you will need to be accepted or to receive a scholarship. This will give you an idea of how difficult it will be for you to meet your targeted goal. Use this to determine how much you should study beforehand. There is no need to waste hours of precious time studying if you can easily make the score that you need, and likewise if you are going to need to do a lot of studying, it is better to go ahead and find out just how much will be required.

Don't take the MCAT as a "practice" test. Feel free to take sample tests on your own, but when you go to take the MCAT, be prepared, be focused, and do your best the first time!

Secret Key #5 - Test Yourself

Everyone knows that time is money. There is no need to spend too much of your time or too little of your time preparing for the test. You should only spend as much of your precious time preparing as is necessary for you to get the score you need.

Once you have taken a practice test under real conditions of time constraints, then you will know if you are ready for the test or not.

If you have scored extremely high the first time that you take the practice test, then there is not much point in spending countless hours studying. You are already there.

Benchmark your abilities by retaking practice tests and seeing how much you have improved. Once you score high enough to guarantee success, then you are ready.

If you have scored well below where you need, then knuckle down and begin studying in earnest. Check your improvement regularly through the use of practice tests under real conditions. Above all, don't worry, panic, or give up. The key is perseverance!

Then, when you go to take the test, remain confident and remember how well you did on the practice tests. If you can score high enough on a practice test, then you can do the same on the real thing.

General Strategies

The most important thing you can do is to ignore your fears and jump into the test immediately- do not be overwhelmed by any strange-sounding terms. You have to jump into the test like jumping into a pool- all at once is the easiest way.

Make Predictions

As you read and understand the question, try to guess what the answer will be. Remember that several of the answer choices are wrong, and once you begin reading them, your mind will immediately become cluttered with answer choices designed to throw you off. Your mind is typically the most focused immediately after you have read the question and digested its contents. If you can, try to predict what the correct answer will be. You may be surprised at what you can predict.

Quickly scan the choices and see if your prediction is in the listed answer choices. If it is, then you can be quite confident that you have the right answer. It still won't hurt to check the other answer choices, but most of the time, you've got it!

Answer the Question

It may seem obvious to only pick answer choices that answer the question, but the test writers can create some excellent answer choices that are wrong. Don't pick an answer just because it sounds right, or you believe it to be true. It MUST answer the question. Once you've made your selection, always go back and check it against the question and make sure that you didn't misread the question, and the answer choice does answer the question posed.

Benchmark

After you read the first answer choice, decide if you think it sounds correct or not. If it doesn't, move on to the next answer choice. If it does, mentally mark that answer choice. This doesn't mean that you've definitely selected it as your answer choice, it just means that it's the best you've seen thus far. Go ahead and read the next choice. If the next choice is worse than the one you've already selected, keep going to the next answer choice. If the next choice is better than the choice you've already selected, mentally mark the new answer choice as your best guess.

The first answer choice that you select becomes your standard. Every other answer choice must be benchmarked against that standard. That choice is correct until proven otherwise by another answer choice beating it out. Once you've decided that no other answer choice seems as good, do one final check to ensure that your answer choice answers the question posed.

Valid Information

Don't discount any of the information provided in the question. Every piece of information may be necessary to determine the correct answer. None of the information in the question is there to throw you off (while the answer choices will certainly have information to throw you off). If two seemingly unrelated topics are discussed, don't ignore either. You can be confident there is a relationship, or it wouldn't be included in the question, and you are probably going to have to determine what is that relationship to find the answer.

Avoid "Fact Traps"

Don't get distracted by a choice that is factually true. Your search is for the answer that answers the question. Stay focused and don't fall for an answer that is true but incorrect. Always go back to the question and make sure you're choosing an answer that actually answers the question and is not just a true statement. An answer can be factually correct, but it MUST answer the question asked. Additionally, two answers can both be seemingly correct, so be sure to read all of the answer choices, and make sure that you get the one that BEST answers the question.

Milk the Question

Some of the questions may throw you completely off. They might deal with a subject you have not been exposed to, or one that you haven't reviewed in years. While your lack of knowledge about the subject will be a hindrance, the question itself can give you many clues that will help you find the correct answer. Read the question carefully and look for clues. Watch particularly for adjectives and nouns describing difficult terms or words that you don't recognize. Regardless of if you completely understand a word or not, replacing it with a synonym either provided or one you more familiar with may help you to understand what the questions are asking. Rather than wracking your mind about specific detailed information concerning a difficult term or word, try to use mental substitutes that are easier to understand.

The Trap of Familiarity

Don't just choose a word because you recognize it. On difficult questions, you may not recognize a number of words in the answer choices. The test writers don't put "make-believe" words on the test; so don't think that just because you only recognize all the words in one answer choice means that answer choice must be correct. If you only recognize words in one answer choice, then focus on that one. Is it correct? Try your best to determine if it is correct. If it is, that is great, but if it doesn't, eliminate it. Each word and answer choice you eliminate increases your chances of getting the question correct, even if you then have to guess among the unfamiliar choices.

Eliminate Answers

Eliminate choices as soon as you realize they are wrong. But be careful! Make sure you consider all of the possible answer choices. Just because one appears right, doesn't mean that the next one won't be even better! The test writers will usually put more than one good answer choice for every question, so read all of them. Don't worry if you are stuck between two that seem right. By getting down to just two remaining possible choices, your odds are now 50/50. Rather than wasting too much time, play the odds. You are guessing, but guessing wisely, because you've been able to knock out some of the answer choices that you know are wrong. If you are eliminating choices and realize that the last answer choice you are left with is also obviously wrong, don't panic. Start over and consider each choice again. There may easily be something that you missed the first time and will realize on the second pass.

Tough Questions

If you are stumped on a problem or it appears too hard or too difficult, don't waste time. Move on! Remember though, if you can quickly check for obviously incorrect answer choices, your chances of guessing correctly are greatly improved. Before you completely give up, at least try to knock out a couple of possible answers. Eliminate what you can and then guess at the remaining answer choices before moving on.

Brainstorm

If you get stuck on a difficult question, spend a few seconds quickly brainstorming. Run through the complete list of possible answer choices. Look at each choice and ask yourself, "Could this answer the question satisfactorily?" Go through each answer choice and consider it independently of the other. By systematically going through all possibilities, you may find something that you would otherwise overlook. Remember that when you get stuck, it's important to try to keep moving.

Read Carefully

Understand the problem. Read the question and answer choices carefully. Don't miss the question because you misread the terms. You have plenty of time to read each question thoroughly and make sure you understand what is being asked. Yet a happy medium must be attained, so don't waste too much time. You must read carefully, but efficiently.

Face Value

When in doubt, use common sense. Always accept the situation in the problem at face value. Don't read too much into it. These problems will not require you to make huge leaps of logic. The test writers aren't trying to throw you off with a cheap trick. If you have to go beyond creativity and make a leap of logic in order to have an answer choice answer the question, then you should look at the other answer choices. Don't overcomplicate the problem by creating theoretical relationships or explanations that will warp time or space. These are normal problems rooted in reality. It's just that the applicable relationship or explanation may not be readily apparent and you have to figure things out. Use your common sense to interpret anything that isn't clear.

Prefixes

If you're having trouble with a word in the question or answer choices, try dissecting it. Take advantage of every clue that the word might include. Prefixes and suffixes can be a huge help. Usually they allow you to determine a basic meaning. Pre- means before, post- means after, pro - is positive, de- is negative. From these prefixes and suffixes, you can get an idea of the general meaning of the word and try to put it into context. Beware though of any traps. Just because con is the opposite of pro, doesn't necessarily mean congress is the opposite of progress!

Hedge Phrases

Watch out for critical "hedge" phrases, such as likely, may, can, will often, sometimes, often, almost, mostly, usually, generally, rarely, sometimes. Question writers insert these hedge phrases to cover every possibility. Often an answer choice will be wrong simply because it leaves no room for exception. Avoid answer choices that have definitive words like "exactly," and "always".

Switchback Words

Stay alert for "switchbacks". These are the words and phrases frequently used to alert you to shifts in thought. The most common switchback word is "but". Others include although, however, nevertheless, on the other hand, even though, while, in spite of, despite, regardless of.

New Information

Correct answer choices will rarely have completely new information included. Answer choices typically are straightforward reflections of the material asked about and will directly relate to the question. If a new piece of information is included in an answer choice that doesn't even seem to relate to the topic being asked about, then that answer choice is likely incorrect. All of the information needed to answer the question is usually provided for you, and so you should not have to make guesses that are unsupported or choose answer choices that require unknown information that cannot be reasoned on its own.

Time Management

On technical questions, don't get lost on the technical terms. Don't spend too much time on any one question. If you don't know what a term means, then since you don't have a dictionary, odds are you aren't going to get much further. You should immediately recognize terms as whether or not you know them. If you don't, work with the other clues that you have, the other answer choices and terms provided, but don't waste too much time trying to figure out a difficult term.

Contextual Clues

Look for contextual clues. An answer can be right but not correct. The contextual clues will help you find the answer that is most right and is correct. Understand the context in which a phrase or statement is made. This will help you make important distinctions.

Don't Panic

Panicking will not answer any questions for you. Therefore, it isn't helpful. When you first see the question, if your mind goes blank, take a deep breath. Force yourself to mechanically go through the steps of solving the problem and using the strategies you've learned.

Pace Yourself

Don't get clock fever. It's easy to be overwhelmed when you're looking at a page full of questions, your mind is full of random thoughts and feeling confused, and the clock is ticking down faster than you would like. Calm down and maintain the pace that you have set for yourself. As long as you are on track by monitoring your pace, you are guaranteed to have enough time for yourself. When you get to the last few minutes of the test, it may seem like you won't have enough time left, but if you only have as many questions as you should have left at that point, then you're right on track!

Answer Selection

The best way to pick an answer choice is to eliminate all of those that are wrong, until only one is left and confirm that is the correct answer. Sometimes though, an answer choice may immediately look right. Be careful! Take a second to make sure that the other choices are not equally obvious.

Don't make a hasty mistake. There are only two times that you should stop before checking other answers. First is when you are positive that the answer choice you have selected is correct. Second is when time is almost out and you have to make a quick guess!

Check Your Work

Since you will probably not know every term listed and the answer to every question, it is important that you get credit for the ones that you do know. Don't miss any questions through careless mistakes. If at all possible, try to take a second to look back over your answer selection and make sure you've selected the correct answer choice and haven't made a costly careless mistake (such as marking an answer choice that you didn't mean to mark). This quick double check should more than pay for itself in caught mistakes for the time it costs.

Beware of Directly Quoted Answers

Sometimes an answer choice will repeat word for word a portion of the question or reference section. However, beware of such exact duplication – it may be a trap! More than likely, the correct choice will paraphrase or summarize a point, rather than being exactly the same wording.

Slang

Scientific sounding answers are better than slang ones. An answer choice that begins "To compare the outcomes..." is much more likely to be correct than one that begins "Because some people insisted..."

Extreme Statements

Avoid wild answers that throw out highly controversial ideas that are proclaimed as established fact. An answer choice that states the "process should used in certain situations, if..." is much more likely to be correct than one that states the "process should be discontinued completely." The first is a calm rational statement and doesn't even make a definitive, uncompromising stance, using a hedge word "if" to provide wiggle room, whereas the second choice is a radical idea and far more extreme.

Answer Choice Families

When you have two or more answer choices that are direct opposites or parallels, one of them is usually the correct answer. For instance, if one answer choice states "x increases" and another answer choice states "x decreases" or "y increases," then those two or three answer choices are very similar in construction and fall into the same family of answer choices. A family of answer choices is when two or three answer choices are very similar in construction, and yet often have a directly opposite meaning. Usually the correct answer choice will be in that family of answer choices. The "odd man out" or answer choice that doesn't seem to fit the parallel construction of the other answer choices is more likely to be incorrect.

Additional Bonus Material

Due to our efforts to try to keep this book to a manageable length, we've created a link that will give you access to all of your additional bonus material.

Please visit http://www.mometrix.com/bonus948/mcat to access the information.